BEN JONSON

VERA EFFIGIES DOCTISSIMI POETARVM ANGLORVM BEN: IOHNSONII.

Ro: Vaughan fecit.

Johnſoni typus, ecce! qui furoris.
Antiſtes ſacer, Enthei, Camenis,
Vindex Ingenij recens Sepulti,
Antiquæ reparator vnus artis,

Defuncta Pater Eruditionis,
Et Scenæ veteris novator audax.
Nec fœlix minus, aut minus politus
Cui solus similis, Figura, vivet.

O could there be an art found out that might
Produce his ſhape ſoe lively as to write. Ab: Holl:
Are to be Sould by William Peake.

Frontispiece Engraving of Jonson by Robert Vaughan which accompanied the First Folio of his *Works* in 1616, when Jonson was 44, showing him crowned with bays as a mark of his status (*British Library*)

BEN JONSON

HIS LIFE AND WORK

ROSALIND MILES

ROUTLEDGE & KEGAN PAUL
LONDON AND NEW YORK

First published in 1986 by
Routledge & Kegan Paul Ltd
11 New Fetter Lane, London EC4P 4EE

Published in the USA by
Routledge & Kegan Paul Inc.
in association with Methuen Inc.
29 West 35th Street, New York, NY 10001

Set in 10 on 11 pt Baskerville
by Inforum Ltd, Portsmouth
and printed in Great Britain
by Billings and Sons Ltd, Worcester

Library of Congress Cataloging in Publication Data

Miles, Rosalind.
Ben Jonson, his life and work.

Bibliography: p.
Includes index.
1. Jonson, Ben, 1573?–1673.   2. Authors, English—
Early modern, 1500–1700—Biography.   I. Title.
PR2631.M54   1986   822'.3 [B]   86–2283

British Library CIP Data also available

ISBN 0–7102–0838–3

IN MEMORY OF

KATE FLINT

MAGISTER OLIM, AETERNUM AMICUS
TO WHOM I OWE
ALL THAT I AM IN ARTS, ALL THAT I KNOW

CONTENTS

PREFACE

A GOOD life is as difficult to write as it is to live, and the difficulties are compounded when the subject led as many lives as Jonson did. This book is intended to supply the need for a modern scholarly biography of this great writer whose varied and important career has still not aroused the interest or affection accorded to his much quieter contemporary, Shakespeare. In an age which has seen the rediscovery of many obscure Elizabethan and Jacobean works, Jonson remains generally neglected and undervalued. Most people know him only as the author of three or four plays. Yet equally important, in his eyes at least, are his poetry, his contribution to critical thought, and his role in literary history. Additionally Jonson cries out to be better known not simply because of his greatness as a writer but because of his fascination as a brilliant, original and exciting man.

The need for an up-to-date and accurate biography of Jonson has been particularly pressing because he incorporated so much of his own life in his work. Where Shakespeare effaced himself to the point of anonymity, Jonson always conveys the power of his own personality. Explicitly and implicitly he is an intense presence in everything he wrote. The raw materials of his life were astonishingly varied: classical scholar and bricklayer, courtier and convicted murderer, moralist and libertine. In his work he adopted a wide assortment of roles: stern classicist, man about town, snarling satirist, urbane Horatian, starveling poet, glutton and sensualist. What is the reader to make of these often contradictory *personae* without some objective account to help in assessing the degree of truthful reporting, ironic invention, or heroic self-mythologising involved?

To give as full a picture as possible I have used a variety of sources. In the main I have tried to let Jonson speak for himself: no previous 'life' has made such detailed use of the many and candid personal allusions which lie scattered throughout his work. Another principal source has been the eleven-volume edition of Jonson's works by C.H. Herford and Percy and Evelyn Simpson (Oxford, 1925–52). I have also been able to take advantage of the more recent discoveries about Jonson's life, and modern scholarly evaluations of the range and variety of his output. Finally I have acted upon Jonson's own precept and practice in following the principle of classical historians that the gossip, rumour and anecdote surrounding a great one's life are as informative as the facts about him; but I hope I have not blurred the distinction.

My aim has been to produce a reliable and accessible account to serve both those who wish to know Jonson in full and those who need simply to dip into some phase of his career. For ease of reading I have normalised in all quotations contemporary forms like the long s, the i/j and u/v, and scribal conventions like contractions and superscript letters. I have also modified punctuation throughout in order to simplify the often elaborate contemporary conventions, especially Jonson's own.

In one respect however Jonson's practice is sacrosanct, the spelling of his own name. He sought to be known as 'Jonson' and signed himself so in every one of his surviving autographs. His contemporaries generally ignored or resisted his wishes and called him by the much more common name of 'Johnson'. This has resulted in great confusion; he appears as 'Jonson', 'Johnson', 'Ionson' and 'Iohnson', occasionally all together within the pages of one book such as his second Folio *Works* of 1640. Only the emergence of the equally individualistic Samuel of that ilk in the next century crystallised Ben's preference as a handy means of distinguishing between the two great bears of English literature.

In the ten years' work which this study has entailed I have incurred debts of gratitude to numerous scholars and institutions. I would particularly like to thank Dr Tom Matheson, Professor Peter Davison, Professor Arthur Scouten, Professor Gordon Donaldson, Professor Jan McDonald, Professor Derick Marsh, A.G. Lee MA, Librarian of St John's College, Cambridge, Robert A. Shannon FSA Scot., and John Field, Archivist of Westminster School. The librarians of the Bodleian, the British Museum, the National Library of Scotland and the reference libraries of Birmingham, Coventry, Dumfries and Carlisle have offered ready and invaluable help. Above all my friends Professor Alexander Leggatt and Mark Lucas have stood good angels to this project and it is my pleasure to record my deep appreciation here.

My highest wish now is none other than Jonson's own, 'to make readers understanders'; I have above all wanted him to be better

PREFACE

known and loved. My one regret is that expressed by Fulke Greville in his *Life of Sidney* (1652): 'I find myself still short of that honour he deserved, and I desired to do him'. But like Greville I have done all I can to direct the reader finally to my subject's own work, 'whereof (you see) death hath no power'.

Rosalind Miles
Corley Hall
Corley

LIST OF DATES

1572 11 June: Jonson born
1594 14 November: marries Anne Lewis
1596 His first son born and named Benjamin
1597 August: Jonson imprisoned for his part in the scandalous play, *The Isle of Dogs.* Released 3 October
1598 Jonson's first surviving full-length play, *The Case is Altered*, well known by the Easter of this year
Every Man In His Humour
22 September: arrested for killing a fellow-actor, Gabriel Spencer. 6 October: pleaded self-defence, granted benefit of clergy and released after branding on the thumb and the confiscation of all his goods
1599 *Every Man Out Of His Humour*
December – a second son born and named Joseph
1600 The 'War of the Theatres' began, and continued into the next year
Cynthia's Revels
1601 *Poetaster*
1602 Took up residence with Sir Robert Townsend, and subsequently with Esme Stuart, Seigneur D'Aubigny, separating from his wife for five years
1603 24 March: accession of James I
May: death of Jonson's eldest son, aged seven
June: Jonson's first contact with the royal family when *The Satyr* was written and performed for Queen Anne and Prince Henry at Althorp in Northamptonshire·
Sejanus staged: Jonson called before the Privy Council to answer for it
1604 *The King's Entertainment in Passing to his Coronation*

1605 6 January: *The Masque of Blackness,* Jonson's first masque
Imprisoned with Chapman for offending libels in *Eastward Ho!*
5 November: Gunpowder Plot, Jonson involved
1606 *Hymenaei*
Jonson 'presented for correction' with his wife at the Consistory
Court for recusancy: full hearing 26 April
Volpone
1607 *Entertainment for the King at Theobalds*
Entertainment for the King by the Merchant Taylors' Company
1608 January: *The Masque of Beauty*
The Hue and Cry After Cupid
February: second son named Benjamin born
1609 February: *The Masque of Queens*
Epicœne
1610 25 March: Jonson's daughter Elisabeth born
6 April: his third son born and named Benjamin
The Alchemist
Jonson acted as witness in the Roe litigation
1611 *The Masque of Oberon*
Love Freed From Ignorance and Folly
Catiline
18 November: Jonson's second son Benjamin buried
1612 *Love Restored*
Jonson travelled to France and Belgium as tutor to the young
Walter Raleigh
1613 Early summer: Jonson returned to London
29 December: *The Irish Masque at Court*
1614 1 January: *A Challenge At Tilt*
31 October: *Bartholomew Fair*
1615 6 January: *The Golden Age Restored*
1616 1 January: *Mercury Vindicated From The Alchemists At Court*
1 February: Jonson granted a pension by James I and recognition as 'the royal poet', the first Poet Laureate in the history of
the British monarchy
The Devil Is An Ass
Publication of the Folio of Jonson's *Works*
Christmas His Masque
1617 6 January: *The Vision of Delight*
22 February: *Lovers Made Men*
1618 6 January: *Pleasure Reconciled to Virtue*
Jonson's journey to Scotland
1619 Returns home
19 July: granted honorary degree from Oxford University

1620 17 January: *News From The New World Discovered In The Moon*
Summer: *Paris Anniversary*
1621 3 August: *The Masque of the Gypsies Metamorphosed*
1622 6 January: *The Masque of Augurs*
1623 19 January: *Time Vindicated to Himself and to his Honours*
November: fire destroyed Jonson's library, books and papers
1624 August: *The Masque of Owls*
1625 9 January: *The Fortunate Isles and Their Union*
27 March: death of James I
1626 *The Staple of News* broke Jonson's ten-year absence from the public theatre
1628 2 September: Jonson made City Chronologer in succession to Thomas Middleton
26 October: called before the Attorney-General for examination in connection with the assassination of the Duke of Buckingham
Jonson suffered paralytic stroke from which he never fully recovered
1629 *The New Inn*
1630 Charles I ordered the increase of Jonson's pension from 100 marks to £100, with a tierce of sack annually in addition
1631 9 January: *Love's Triumph Through Callipolis*
22 February: *Chloridia*, Jonson's last masque at court
1632 *The Magnetic Lady*
1633 *The Tale Of A Tub*
The King's Entertainment at Welbeck
1634 30 July: *Love's Welcome At Bolsover*, Jonson's last masque
1637 6 August: Jonson died in his sixty-fifth year and was buried in Westminster Abbey on 9 August

CHAPTER 1

BOYHOOD

BEN Jonson was born on 11 June 1572. Apart from the date nothing else is known of his birth. No documentary evidence has been found, and the date itself has to be deduced from scraps of information about his later life (see Appendix for the full details). Jonson was destined to become not only one of England's greatest dramatists but an enthusiastic performer in the public arena of his day. He had a talent for self-assertion which at its height was the joyous expansion of an outstanding personality, at its worst an unattractive self-publication and jealous quest for attention at all costs. It is one of the ironies of his richly varied life that Jonson should have made so characteristically modest an entry onto 'this great stage of fools'.

The absence of documentation may result from his having been born in or around London – country parishes or small towns more readily preserved the records of a Shakespeare or Marlowe. Whatever the place he was fortunate in the date of his birth. An Elizabethan baby stood a better chance of survival through its tender early months in the summer. The 11 June is also, as Jonson himself noted of his birth date, the feast day of St Barnabas, familiarly known as Barnaby the Bright, and in 1572 under the old calendar it was the longest day of the year.

Jonson left no written comment on his early days. He always assumed that posterity would be more interested in the man he became than the infant he was. He was more forthcoming about the family from which he sprang, telling the poet Drummond of Hawthornden that 'his grandfather came from Carlisle, and he thought from Annandale to it' (HS I, 139).[1] The Annan where Jonson believed his grandfather originated is a small town outside Dumfries, just over the border in Scotland. Jonson critics have been quick to seize upon this connection of the Westminster writer with the lurid annals of the blood-soaked Borders. For the lowland Scots clan of the Johnstones,[2] from whom Ben Jonson certainly thought that he took his origins, were sufficiently bold and brilliant to be plausible ancestors even of a poet, fighter, scholar, and trouble-maker of Jonson's genius.

For Johnstones were prominent over a wide area of human affairs. The earliest members of this great family make their appearance in charters and documents as far back as 1170. The Laird of the Johnstones held the rough land round the head of Moffat Water, Annandale, and Johnstones throve and flourished in a wild country where 'no merely mortal horse could keep its feet, nor merely mortal rider the saddle' in the words of Sir Walter Scott. They were a true warrior clan, a bloody breed in a pitiless time and place. The climax of *Macbeth* for instance comes to life in the action of the Johnstone who slaughtered Douglas Earl of Moray, at the battle of Arkinholm on 1 May 1455, hacked off his head, and sent it in triumph and tribute to his sovereign, James II.

Yet these were not simply a band of butchers and cut-throats. In the years before Jonson's birth they showed their Renaissance spirit in their fondness for litigation, equally ready for a fight through the courts as for a skirmish over the hills. Down the centuries Johnstones enthusiastically engaged in the acrimonious legal wrangling that unsettled their region in action and counter-action over land, tenancies, cattle, holdings, and all the pettifogging paraphernalia of ownership. Johnstones revitalised in every age the force of the dry mediaeval saying, 'Take, have, and keep, are pleasant words.'

By the sixteenth century the rise and progress of this clan had been remarkable. Yet for all their strength and skill they could not stave off the might and malice of their old enemy England. The history of this period abounds in episodes which provided the circumstances for a grandfather of Jonson to have migrated across the Border, changing his allegiance and his nationality as he did so. The aftermath of the Battle of Solway Moss on 24 November 1542 is one such example, when Henry VIII attacked Scotland with the dual aim of exerting his sovereignty over the country and securing himself against a stab in the back when he made war across the Channel on France.

Solway proved by universal consent to be the most shameful engagement in the history of Scots arms. The hosts of Scotland, hopelessly riven by a factious leadership, threw away a sure victory over a much smaller army on their own territory. A contemporary speaks bleakly of the appalling rout that ensued: 'the soldiers cast from them their pikes, culverins, and other weapons fensible; the horsemen left their spears; and so without judgment, all men fled'.[3] About one thousand Scots were taken prisoner by the English – earls, lairds, barons, gentlemen and commoners.

In the normal course of war these Scots could expect to be ransomed or simply returned, according to their rank. Overtly at least there was no confusion as to where their loyalty lay. Relations of any sort with the English were treason; up to 1600 even marriage over the border was not permitted. Nobility and gentry were expected to honour their oath of allegiance and turn out for their king in time of war. In return feudal custom dictated that the captured prisoner could rely on his lord to strive for his ransom or release. Deeds and charters still in existence testify to the efforts of Johnstones among others to bring home the unfortunates taken at Solway Moss. Several men undertook an obligation to John Johnstone of that Ilk on 4 January 1543 on behalf of 'ane honorabill man and our cousinge Henry Stewart', so that Johnstone should 'do his exact diligence' to redeem Stewart.[4]

But this deed has an interesting clause suggesting that the matter was not as straightforward as it seems. Johnstone was only to arrange Stewart's ransom with the prisoner's 'own express consent and assent'. It was not taken for granted that 'the said Henry' would wish to be returned to his people. Despite the bitter and ancestral enmity between the two races, despite laws and prohibitions to the contrary, there were few Scots in the Border territories who did not somehow enter into dealings with the English. It was always possible that after defeat and capture a Scot could decide to throw in his lot with the victorious side.

This course of action was much in evidence during the events both before and after the Battle of Solway Moss. Whether activated by political foresight or personal greed some of the Scots nobility had so far lost sight of their ancient allegiance as to be in the pay of the English and even to aid the enemy invasions. On the battlefield itself certain earls and lairds were not unwilling to be made prisoner rather than fight on under their despised King, James V. James, the youthful nephew of Henry VIII, outplayed both in the chambers of diplomacy and on the field of war by his uncle, had forfeited their respect and with it his right to their loyalty and service. A migrant Scot could honourably resume his arms in service under a new stronger king over the border.

Such were the circumstances in which Jonson's grandfather could have made his removal from Scotland to England. Annan itself did not escape the terror of war. In 1546 the English invaded the region and razed Annan to the ground. The neighbourhood chiefs and residents were forced to offer their submission and swear fealty to the English king. English State Papers describe the surrender of the Johnstones and the taking of the heir of the clan to England as a hostage. And there is from other sources substantial evidence of Scots emigrating to England and settling there in the sixteenth century.

It is then among these migrants from the embattled Borders that Jonson imagined his grandfather. Whoever he was he must have been a daring, strong and flexible man. To submit to the events of fate is one thing; to make a fresh career in the service of a new country and its king is quite another. Jonson was unequivocal about this, insisting to Drummond that his grandfather 'served King Henry VIII and was a gentleman' (HS I, 139). Henry VIII died in 1547, so the great step which Englished the fortunes of Johnstone's descendants was taken before then.

Jonson himself displayed great pride in his assumed origins. He took up the arms of the Johnstone family, as Drummond noted: 'his arms were three spindles or rhombi, his own word [around] them, *Percunctator* or *Perscrutator*' (HS I, 148). These Latin words derive from the actions of questioning, and of seeing through, respectively. They are both remarkably appropriate to Jonson's later intellectual activities. So too is the patriarchal heritage and dignity to which he laid claim, as one of the founding elements of his sense of destiny and conviction of his own uniqueness.

Jonson's father is a figure of more substance than the shadowy Scots grandfather. As Jonson told Drummond, 'his father lost all his estate under Queen Mary, having been cast into prison and forfeited, at last turned minister' (HS I, 139). This knotty communication can be unravelled to yield up a little more than it offers on the surface. The gentleman adventurer in his voyage from Annan to England via Carlisle had clearly managed to amass some 'estate' and the complaint for its loss suggests that it was quite considerable.

Next, if Jonson's father suffered under Mary Tudor during her brief reign from 1553–1558, it could only have been for remaining staunch to the doctrine of Protestantism in the face of the Queen's attempts to lead her people back from the Reformation to the Old Faith. This Tudor monarch was the least ruthless, self-seeking or acquisitive of all her ego-dynamic family. She never cast envious eyes upon the land, monies, holdings or monopolies of her subjects as even the best of her kin did. If Jonson's father 'lost all his estate' under Queen Mary, it cannot have been his money that brought about his fall.

The Queen herself constantly made plain that her primary concern was with religion. This emerges with a touching clarity from one of her first proclamations, issued from Richmond Palace on 18 August 1553, only two days after the funeral of Edward VI: 'Her Majesty . . . cannot forsake that faith which the whole world knows her to have followed and practised since her birth. . . . She desires greatly that her subjects may come to embrace the same faith quietly and with charity, whereby she shall receive great happiness'.[5] For Mary, her

Roman Catholicism had been the one consolation of a desperately deprived childhood, and the strongest emotional link with the only human being who had ever truly loved her, her mother Catherine of Aragon. The comfort and relief that it had brought to her beleaguered soul she was determined not to deny to the least of her subjects. In her subsequent illness and progressive emotional derangement she was never able to grasp the cruelty of this kindness.

The tribulations of Jonson's father probably occurred after November of 1554. At this point after the early flurries and disorders of her reign Mary was ready to let the mismanaged nation feel the spur of her new government. In this month she summoned her third Parliament and the work of conversion began in earnest. This Parliament was employed to define Catholic orthodoxy and to require it by law. Despite the well-founded caution of her Spanish husband Philip II who urged slowness and moderation, Mary was not to be turned from her narrow path of the reclamation of souls.

Jonson senior was more fortunate than many to escape with his life. As the fires of Smithfield burned down the years some three hundred Protestants died for their beliefs. Mary's five-year reign proved the undaunted mettle of the English people and earned her the perpetual damnation of the nickname 'Bloody Mary'. The fires of torment also illuminate her victims for posterity to pity and to wonder at; their memorial is Foxe's *Book of Martyrs* (1563), the harrowing but inspirational account of their boundless courage and enormous suffering. The fact that Jonson's father attracted attention suggests that he was in or around London, for it was there that the persecutions centred.

Yet Jonson's father could have turned back. Part of the torture of Mary's processes was the opportunity provided for recantation and conformism. The rescue of souls was Mary's aim after all, and not senseless terrorism. Bishop Hooper died in a slow fire at Gloucester with his pardon before his eyes to the last. Jonson's father must have 'lost all' through the kind of determination that his son later raised to the level of bull-necked intransigence. It is fascinating irony of Jonson's life that like his father he ran into trouble with the authorities over his religion; and even more ironic that Ben himself nearly 'lost all' through his passionate adherence to that very Roman Catholic faith which his father as strenuously had abjured.

Jonson's father risked all his worldly goods through his defence of the Reformed doctrines. Whatever his distresses his belief was not overturned, since he 'at last turned minister' and took holy orders before the birth of his son. Mary Tudor died in 1558. Since it is inconceivable that the baleful attentions of her agents would have settled upon a minor, Jonson's father must have been in his twenties at this time. Consequently the man who awaited the birth of his first

5

child some sixteen years later in the summer of 1572, would have been around forty. This accords well with the tradition of him recorded by the Oxford historian Anthony Wood that he was ' a grave minister of the gospel.'

But just before his child was born, the minister died. So Jonson described himself to Drummond: 'a minister's son . . . born a month after his father's decease' (HS I, 139). Perhaps the 'grave minister's' first and last gift to his son was the highly distinctive Hebrew Christian name. Benjamin was an uncommon name at this time, unlike the thousands of Johns, Thomases and Williams. Had Jonson had, like Shakespeare, an unusual surname rather than forename, his origins would have been considerably easier to unravel.

A 'Benjamin' is traditionally the child of his father's old age, the last and most dearly loved boy. A minister of the gospel would hardly have been ignorant of the Biblical foundation of the tradition, where in Genesis 42 Benjamin is the child of Jacob's declining years. But the name could equally well have been his mother's choice. Any woman newly widowed and about to undergo an Elizabethan childbirth would find an echo of her feelings about her baby in the outburst: 'If ye take this also from me . . . ye shall bring down my grey hairs in sorrow to the grave' (Genesis 44: 29).

Jonson himself was attached to his unusual name. Although he always shortened it to 'Ben' he gave it later to three of his own sons in turn. And in his mature life if not as a young boy he possessed the linguistic skills to yield up to him the name's Hebrew meaning of 'fortunate'. Its secondary meaning is 'dextrous', both deriving from a root-meaning of 'right-handed'. Jonson plays with the intensity of deep feeling on all these meanings in the epitaph (Epigram 45) which he wrote on the death of his little son at seven years old:

Farewell, thou child of my right hand, and joy . . .

He also showed the value that he placed on a distinctive name by altering his commonplace surname, Johnson, to the unique form that he has made his own forever, 'Jonson'.

But this was yet to come. At the time the prime duty of Mistress Johnson to herself and the son she had borne was to survive. It was a troubled time. Sir Francis Drake in 1572 sailed to the Indies, but while some were opening up the new world others were struggling to preserve the peace of the old. The Ridolfi Plot of 1571 had shown that the North of England had not awoken from its dreams of a Catholic revival. The following year saw the execution of the northern Earl of Northumberland, and on the continent the hideous shock of the massacre of Protestants on St Bartholomew's Day for which Queen Elizabeth and all the court wore mourning. Contemporaries noted that Master Secretary Walsingham, the Queen's spymaster-spider at the centre of his web of intelligence, kept his lamp burning late at night as he worked tirelessly against the enemies of Protestantism. Parallel with these events was the steady growth of Puritanism, significant in Jonson's later career. Although he never failed to mock it relentlessly, in his lifetime it grew too strong to be put down by humour and came to threaten more than the enjoyment of cakes and ale.

Survival then was the order of the day. Jonson later spoke of his mother in a way that makes it clear that she was a woman of great courage. Her resourcefulness in coping with her widowhood and childbed were equalled by her hardiness, since she was still alive and active as late as 1605. Jonson's own unusual strength, stamina and longevity fully indicate that his parental endowment had provided him with a stout constitution. But the bravest of women may not wish to struggle on alone. Not long after the death of her husband, Mistress Johnson married again.

This was an event of great significance in Jonson's life. His mother's choice of a new husband was to prove an undying mortification for her son. For Jonson's stepfather was a bricklayer and the ignominy of this trade hung about the poet all his days. Anyone offended by Jonson thereafter fell at once to reminding him of this connection; he was called a 'mortar-treader', a 'whoreson lime-and-hair rascal', and 'the wittiest fellow of a bricklayer in all England'.[6]

But with the despised bricklayer emerge the first faint markings in the trackless wastes of Jonson's early years. It does not seem as if this marriage succeeded in relieving the Johnsons mother and son from poverty. Jonson told Drummond that he was 'brought up poorly' (HS I, 139), and Gerard Langbaine was to write in 1691 that Jonson 'sprang from mean parents'. But it succeeded in binding Jonson to the city of Westminster with which he is always associated for the rest of his long life.

For it is with the bricklayer that the Westminster connection first clearly comes into being. Early historians state with no authority that Jonson was born in Westminster. So says Thomas Fuller, who included Jonson in his *Worthies of Westminster* (1662), in a statement which demonstrates that the only person who can be truly linked with the city is Mistress Johnson's second husband:

> Ben Jonson was born in this city. Though I cannot, with all my industrious inquiry, find him in his cradle, I can fetch him in his long coats. When a little child, he lived in Harts-horn-lane near Charing Cross, where his mother married a bricklayer for her second husband.

7

As a matter of fact wherever Jonson was born it was not Westminster. Neither of the two parishes which composed it at the time has any record of his baptism. But as an Elizabethan child went into 'long coats' as soon as it was toddling, he moved there when he was still very young. William Winstanley, writing in 1587, repeats Fuller in his declaration that Hartshorn Lane was the site of the bricklayer's residence. This lane in which Jonson found his earliest home was also known as Hartshorn Alley, or Christopher Alley. It was pulled down about 1761 and Northumberland Street, Strand, erected in its place.

For centuries nothing at all was known about the man Jonson's mother married. But recently a bricklayer who lived in Hartshorn Lane has been discovered and there is a very strong likelihood that this was Jonson's stepfather. A lease of property in Hartshorn Lane granted in 1586 refers to 'the little garden lately made over the sewer of ditch by Robert Brett', and references to him and to his family are fairly frequent in the parish records of St Martin's-in-the-Fields from 1580 onwards. Although he is referred to as 'the bricklayer', he eventually became a man of some substance, and at the time of his death in 1609 he was a Master of the Tilers' and Bricklayers' Company, a master-builder, and no mere artisan.[7]

Westminster in the last quarter of the sixteenth century was a particularly stirring environment for an impressionable boy. The city combined the dignified with the disgusting in true Renaissance style. The seat of government and the abode of power, boasting the Royal Palace, the Law Courts, and the Mother of Parliaments herself, it was yet a particularly poor and undeveloped example of a medieval city. The great Abbey of St Peter, spiritual core of Westminster, was responsible for this. The huddle of mean and squalid tenements that snuggled incongruously around the skirts of the Abbey was a legacy of the medieval abbots and of the church's immemorial custom of sanctuary.

This 'mischievous right', in the phrase of the Westminster historian John Sargeaunt, was one by which a sharp-witted malefactor could escape the consequences of his wrong-doing by claiming the protection of the church. It continued in Westminster when it had fallen out of use elsewhere and drew under the shadow of the great walls a floating population of villains and vagabonds. Westminster's reputation for debauchery was drily summed up in 1592 by the Elizabethan poet and pamphleteer, later a colleague of Jonson's, Thomas Nashe:

> Westminster, Westminster, much maidenhead hast thou to answer for at the Day of Judgment; thou hadst a sanctuary in thee once, but hast few saints left in thee now![8]

Other factors too contributed to Westminster's unique character. The church would never sell land nor grant long lease. No residents therefore would build for the future, but threw up cheap temporary constructions. Rapid expansion under the Tudors had created a ribbon development of streets and passages, with alleys running off. In Jonson's childhood there was a complete string of jerrybuilt houses, both large and small, on both sides of Fleet Street and around the Abbey itself. This was a continual reproach to a concerned but hamstrung executive. Westminster was a royal city, but the Queen could not get to her Palace or Parliament except by water.

Westminster held then in its Abbey one of the most ancient and sacred places of the English race, yet it was encompassed with the foulest haunts of vice and idleness. The labyrinth of narrow twisting lanes became year by year more thronged and noisome. Badly paved and worse lighted, the streets were covered with every kind of ordure and filth. Butchers slaughtered their cattle in these foetid alleys, while live animals wandered the lanes and yards at will. These surroundings seem to have been almost calculated to produce the unique vision of the mature Jonson, the transmutation of things low and base into art. In the words of Robert Adams, this was 'not only his trade, but his special gift' – 'making gold out of human garbage'.[9]

Yet for all this it must not be forgotten that Westminster was at this time really in the country. The human flotsam and jetsam of the population was compressed in a very narrow area. A walk of a few yards in any direction except towards London would quickly carry a boy beyond the reach of the houses. Hartshorn Lane led directly to the Embankment. To the north two minutes' walk would bring Jonson into St James's Park and leaving the Cockpit and Spring Gardens on his right he could walk through the fields to Hampstead and Highgate. To the west was the road to Chelsea and on the south lay the marshes of Tuttle Fields. As references in his later plays show Jonson knew these areas and their inhabitants well.

Yet for the young Jonson the real interest must have lain within the city rather than outside it. For it was here that Jonson went to school, gaining that education which was the foundation of his life and thought, and which he never ceased to prize even in old age. Fuller states that Jonson was 'first bred at a private school in St Martin's Church', the parish of Robert Brett the bricklayer. St Martin's remained Jonson's parish throughout his boyhood and youth. Now on the east side of Trafalgar Square it was formerly, as its modern name 'in-the-fields' shows, in open country. From this obscure dame school beginning Jonson was rescued by a stroke of good luck at a critical moment of his life.

For someone took an interest in the little boy and sent him to the great Westminster School. The identity of this benefactor is not clear; Drummond's terse note records that he was 'put to school by a friend (his master Camden)'.[10] William Camden was Jonson's first teacher and later much more: mentor, model and dear friend. This remarkable man was Westminster School's second master for almost eighteen years until he acceded to the headship in 1593. Born in 1551 he was a man of nearly thirty when Jonson came to the school and as second master had charge of the lower forms in which Jonson spent his early years. This was no easy task. The entire teaching strength of Westminster School at this time consisted of the headmaster and his deputy. The work of teaching and policing one hundred and twenty boys must have sat heavily on two pairs of shoulders, aided though they were by a system of monitors.

But Camden was a man of patience and industry. In addition to the burden of daily instruction he found time to rewrite one of the school's text books, and his new Greek grammar remained in use for many generations. In his private life he was a gifted scholar whose work earned the respectful attention of the whole of the civilised world. His Latin treatise *Britannia*, a pioneer work of antiquarian research, was published in 1586 while Jonson was still at Westminster School. It was an immediate success, establishing Camden as a leading figure in European scholarship. He followed it with *Remains of a Greater Work Concerning Britain* in 1605. Yet busy as he was he always showed a concern for his pupil's welfare and there are many stories of his personal kindness. It was to this gentle and dedicated man that Jonson came as a pupil.

Any boy at school in the sixteenth century could have done with such a sympathetic teacher. Tudor schools were harsh, monuments to pedantry and rigidity, with discipline maintained at a level indistinguishable from cruelty. The pupils spent their years in a constant struggle with the classics, in practice, Latin, since the authors of ancient Greece were usually read in Latin translation. For most boys the work consisted of the painful production of bad to mediocre Latin exercises and the heroic effort of reproducing the much-admired convolutions of Ciceronian prose.

What this meant for a boy who was not good at Latin emerges feelingly from one contemporary account. This was a pupil's reproach to the famous Nicholas Udall, dramatist and essayist, headmaster of Eton and subsequently of Westminster School before his death in about 1556:

> To Paul's I went, to Eton sent,
> To learn straightway the Latin phrase,
> Where fifty-three stripes given to me
> At once I had:

> For fault but small or none at all
> It came to pass that beat I was.
> See, Udall, see, the mercy of thee
> To me, poor lad![11]

Udall was certainly a leading figure among those described as 'the wisest of your great beaters' by another educationalist, the tutor to Edward VI and Queen Elizabeth, Roger Ascham, in *The Schole-Master*. But he was by no means exceptional. Jonson himself spoke scornfully to Drummond of a poor teacher as one who spent his days 'sweeping his living from the posteriors of little children' (HS I, 138). In the nature of things no scholar at Westminster could totally escape the rod. But with a gifted and caring teacher Jonson is likely to have been spared the worst rigours of the contemporary school system. This inference is supported by Jonson's own later declaration in favour of a humane regime for schoolboys: 'from the rod or ferrule I would have them free, as from the menace of them, for it is both [degraded] and servile' (HS VIII, 615).

In all its aspects the entry to Westminster was the major formative experience of Jonson's life and art. St Peter's College Westminster, to give it its formal title (originally the name of the entire Abbey and only much later of its educational arm), was already in the 1580s a school of great antiquity, having originally grown up within the cloisters of the Benedictine monastery there. When in 1540 the monastery was dissolved the school was re-founded by Henry VIII himself. This was the beginning of the institution of the 'King's Scholars'. Henry VIII's foundation was for a time reversed when the Benedictines were briefly restored under Mary Tudor. But the school was decisively re-established by Elizabeth I in 1560.

Although not its founder, Queen Elizabeth proved to be the real mother of the school. Henry VIII's statutes had provided for forty scholars and no more. Elizabeth's enjoined that the Queen's Scholars were to be drawn from the ranks of boys who had already been one year in the school. It was the admission of these 'Town Boys', in addition to the forty who were to be chosen for scholarships at the end of the first year, that gave Jonson the chance of the education that meant so much to him. In 1572, the year of Jonson's birth, Edward Grant was appointed as headmaster. An old Westminster himself, Grant was a prominent Greek scholar and widely respected for his erudition. Under him the school settled down to a period of quiet and steady growth.

The Queen took a lively interest in her new foundation. She attended the Latin play on more than one occasion and visited the school to see the boys at work. In addition to this invaluable royal

11

patronage the school derived much from its geographical position. It was located only a few hundred yards away from the Palace of Westminster, until Henry VIII's reign a royal residence and still the seat of government and justice. The historic building of Westminster Hall had for centuries been the scene of legal activity at every level from the pettiest to the highest. As an elderly man, in one of the last plays he ever wrote, Jonson recalled the legal cant of 'all the languages of Westminster Hall', and parodied the conduct of the law and its antiquated jargon and terminology:

> Pleas, Bench or Chancery; fee-farm, fee-tail,
> Tenant in dower, at will, for term of life,
> By copy of court roll, knights' service, homage,
> Fealty, escuage, soccage or frank almoigne,
> Grand sergeanty or burgage.
>
> (*The Staple of News*, IV.iv.103–7)

Two great state trials took place in this hall during Jonson's boyhood, that of Anthony Babington on 13 April 1586, and the Earl of Arundel on 18 April 1589. The 1601 trial of Essex took place there too, and five years later it was the site of the trial of Guy Fawkes and his co-conspirators in the Gunpowder Plot, with which Jonson was personally involved. And Jonson himself as an adult answered at the Bar here for defaulting on a debt in 1599 (HS XI, 572–3). This jumbling of matters high and low was an everyday feature of the place.

Westminster schoolboys took a keen interest in the law cases conducted in Westminster Hall although their presence was not always welcome or pleasing to the barristers. An anecdote of the reign of Charles I tells of one who objected to the presence of a Westminster pupil in these terms: 'Boy, get you gone, this is no school'. 'No,' the boy replied, 'For if it were, all you gowned men would go up for false Latin!'[12] Another potent source of instruction was the nearby House of Commons. The pupils of Westminster School have always held the privilege of attending the debates and Jonson put his early experiences of these two theatres of life to good use. Magistrates, clerks, lawyers, politicians, public proceedings and performances of all kinds crowd the Jonsonian stage from the outset of his career and form the staple of his tragedies as well as of his comedies.

The organisation of Westminster School was carefully regulated. At the top of the tree were the forty Scholars. These were the only boys who were full members of the foundation. They were resident boarders – a dubious distinction when it is recalled that they had to live, to study, and to sleep two to a bed, crowded into the monks' former granary, which used to stand in the middle of Dean's Yard behind the

Abbey. Next in status were the Pensioners; these too were boarders, and held an intermediate rank between the Scholars and the other boys who were not on the foundation at all. Non-foundation boys were divided into Peregrines, who were boys from the country living with kinsmen or friends, and Oppidans, who, as the sons of Westminster residents, did not need to board at all. For Jonson this was his first introduction to the intricate and often apparently meaningless divisions of the Elizabethan hierarchy.

All boys, nominally at least, entered the school on equal terms. No boy could be admitted to a scholarship before the age of eight, when he had to have been in the school for a year. The youngest admission being therefore at seven years of age, Jonson could not have begun at the school before 1579. Much turned on winning a scholarship at the end of the first year. The qualifications required were not stringent – what gained a boy the prize was an acquaintance with the eight parts of speech and the ability to write moderately, and these easy terms were those required for admission to the school in the first place.

But the winning of a scholarship meant not only financial help and a membership of the school's elite. It opened a path either to Christ Church, Oxford, or to Trinity College, Cambridge. Statutes provided that three Westminsters were to go annually to each of these colleges. But the boys had to be Queen's Scholars. A scholarship therefore offered the only route whereby entry to Oxford or Cambridge became possible for a boy from a family which would not normally send its son there – a bricklayer's, for instance.

The election to these scholarships on which so much depended was laid down by Elizabeth's statutes of 1560. Special regard was to be paid to a boy's intellect, learning, character, and want of means. Those responsible for making the choice had to take an oath of impartiality. But in practice their selection of candidates was marked by a quite undisguised favouritism. The electors made no pretence of fulfilling the requirements. Each in fact claimed the right to nominate a boy of his own personal choice as scholar.

No-one in 1580 exerted that right on behalf of Ben Jonson. It is ludicrous that this prodigiously talented and hard-working individual was passed over in favour of lesser lights. Most probably he failed the election which could have made such a difference to his future simply for want of influential friends. Jonson's own later actions and remarks testify to his own acute sense of what might have been. He took a particular pride in his honorary degree from Oxford in 1619, and feelingly lamented to Drummond among a jumble of other regrets that he 'might have been a rich lawyer, physician or merchant' (HS I, 149).

Still, Jonson had the immeasurable benefit of the Westminster

13

education itself, and in the day-to-day conduct of the school the difference between the Scholars and others would not have been so marked. The whole school was taught under one roof, since it was among the school's ideals to promote the common life. The Queen's Scholars rose at 5 a.m. to the thundering Latin cry of 'Surgite!' (rise up) from the monitors of the dormitory, while the Town Boys made their way through Westminster's notorious streets for the real start of the day at 6 a.m. But once foregathered with the second master (in Jonson's time his beloved Camden) for prayers which always included Psalm 47 and the Lord's Prayer, all the boys of the school were subjected to the same minutely detailed routine.

After morning prayers the second master taught in turn the lowest two forms. Meanwhile one monitor took the names of late-comers and absentees while another, dignified with the title of *monitor immundorum et sordidorum puerorum* (the monitor of dirty and filthy boys), scrutinised hands and faces throughout the school – a dirty face brought down punishment upon its owner. At 7 a.m. the Headmaster came, and the boys 'said repetition' of their lessons. All the boys in the form spoke together, led by one known as the *custos*, who held this office as a punishment. A boy who made three spelling mistakes in an exercise, 'said more than three words wrong in a rule', or spoke English (the official language for all school transactions was Latin) became *custos* till another culprit was detected. No hour was allotted for breakfast, but in actuality the hour between eight and nine was not spent in school.

It is worth stressing the frequency and importance of religious observation in the school life of Tudor times, preserving as it did so many features of the monastic establishment from which it had sprung. After breakfast more lessons were followed by more prayers, including Psalm 122, and thanksgiving for the Queen and other school benefactors. After prayers came dinner, preceded by a long grace, accompanied by a reading aloud from the Old Testament, and followed by grace again. On the return into school, monitors took charge until the second master returned at 1 p.m. An hour later the Headmaster appeared again and lessons went on until 6 p.m. An hour's break was allowed mid-afternoon and twice a week an hour was given to music with the choir-master. Finally the pupils were dismissed with an evening prayer. For the rest of his life Jonson was to maintain these habits of prayer and worship.

Westminster differed from other schools of its time in one important respect, the emphasis placed on the study of Greek. At Eton a boy did not begin Greek until the sixth form and even then he concentrated upon grammar, and read no Greek authors. The great Greek poets and dramatists were known to the average Tudor schoolboy in

Latin if at all. At Westminster the boys began Greek in the fourth
form where the inevitable study of grammar was always enlivened by
readings from the *Dialogues* of Lucian (later to re-surface in Jonson's
work as one of the elements that went into the creation of *Volpone*). By
the sixth form a young Westminster was familiar with Isocrates,
Plutarch, Demosthenes and Homer in the original, all of whom would
have been quite beyond the ken of his Etonian contemporary.

At the top of the school Greek studies were supplemented by
Hebrew; afternoon lessons included Greek grammar for the sixth
form and Hebrew grammar for the seventh, with lessons from the
Psalter for both forms in both tongues. Other work consisted of
translation, and conversion of prose pieces into verse and verse into
prose. Topics were set for written exercises in these ancient languages
which had to be brought to the teacher the next day. The work load
was so heavy that the boys had to sit up, or get up, at all hours of the
night to finish these exercises for which no time was allowed in a
packed school day lasting for twelve hours and continuing with
regular impositions and religious observations until bedtime. Boys
often gave in to fatigue and a humane custom permitted a flagger to
drop his head on his desk and catch up on his sleep, once he had
obtained permission to '*dor*' – the Latin word for sleep dating from the
days when Latin was the common language of the school. Under this
exhausting regime Jonson developed the stamina which was so
conspicuous a feature of his personality later in life.

Certain aspects of Westminster's life and practice remained with
Jonson ever after. One of these was the heavy stress on memory
training. Boys had to learn by heart speeches of Virgil, Euripides,
and others and even whole orations of Cicero and Demosthenes,
sometimes as a punishment but also as a normal part of school work.
The less the pen is used, the more active is the memory. In his
adulthood Jonson prided himself on having a good natural endowment in this respect but also on having made the effort to cultivate it.
And much of what Jonson's memory later returned to him 'readily,
and without stops', as he liked to boast, was drawn from the boyhood
storehouse which had been patiently crammed during the long hours
of the Westminster day.

So much for Ben Jonson, scholar. Westminster School also fed the
emerging playwright in him. This school had from its re-founding in
1560 a particularly strong dramatic tradition. A performance of a
Latin play was required by the Queen's statutes every Christmas
during what is still called Play Term. Three plays in all were
performed annually, a Latin play, an English play, and a play put on
in English by the choirboys. Acting in the Elizabethan period was
regarded as a necessary limb of education, and there was no school of

15

note which did not from time to time stage the plays of Terence and Plautus, and other Latin pieces.

The purpose of this was not only to develop the boys' confidence, but to strengthen their Latin. Latin was the chief instrument of education and the medium through which almost all knowledge had to be acquired at that time, so it had to be known thoroughly, confidently, colloquially. Acting or simply watching familiarised the boys with the highest thoughts in the highest style of the old masters. And with its forms of greeting, expressions of gratitude or regret, enquiries after individuals and outbursts of pain or joy, it also made them experience it as a living language, not a dead one. This was the attitude to Latin that Jonson always held.

Westminster school built upon this Tudor tradition to achieve a distinction of its own. In Elizabeth's reign the school even formed a company of child actors and young Westminsters made up an 'aery of children' to tread the boards of the Blackfriars Theatre like the 'little eyases' condemned in *Hamlet* (II.ii.338–9). A good deal was expected from the young performers on the occasion of the school play, when the Queen herself might be present. She had after all first instituted the Latin play so that the scholars might 'the better be accustomed to proper action and pronunciation'. Good elocution and a graceful carriage were required. Jonson was later to satirise the ignorance of those who could not grasp the value of this acting experience for the boys:

> They make all their scholars play-boys. Is't not a fine sight to see all our children made interluders? Do we pay our money for this? We send them to learn their grammar and their Terence, and they learn their playbooks. (*The Staple of News*, III Intermean, 46–50)

Jonson shared with his fellows the training and preparation for the school plays. This gave him all that he ever had in the way of a grounding in drama and performance. But later he was able to earn his living as a professional actor, and his skill in reading aloud and recitation made the Duke of Newcastle say that he had never heard any man read as well as Jonson. This strongly suggests that he had had a valuable training in gesture, diction and expression. And the ingenious use of characters and situations from Roman comedy in his first stage success, *Every Man In His Humour* (1598), shows the work of an imagination fed on Plautus and Terence, besides the plays of native dramatists such as the writer-headmaster Udall.

This love of the classics was to prove Westminster's greatest single legacy to Jonson. His own pride in his classical knowledge is clear from his often-quoted pronouncement that Shakespeare had 'small Latin and less Greek', and he was certainly more advanced in his studies than most educated people of his time. It was from the classical grounding received at Westminster that Jonson drew not only his major inspiration but the pattern of his habits of work and even the structure of his thought. Even in his middle age he still continued with the methods of classical composition inculcated at school; discussing his poetry with Drummond Jonson stated that 'he wrote all his [verses] first in prose, for so his master Camden had learned him' (HS I, 143).

In both verse and prose Jonson modelled all his efforts upon the writers of Greece and Rome. For him the work of the ancients remained the only true originals – 'they opened the gates, and made the way that went before us', he declared simply (HS VIII, 567). His dependence upon classical authors for plots, characters, ideas, and innumerable expressions is legendary. Dryden's brilliant phrase to describe the extent of Jonson's reliance upon the ancient writers is justly famed: 'you track him everywhere in their snow'.

Another important and lasting influence in Jonson's life was that of the friendship made there with Camden. After Jonson left school the pupil-teacher relationship matured into a warm respect and affection. Jonson later described Camden as 'magister olim, aeternum amicus' – 'a teacher once but now for ever a friend'. In the acquaintance with Camden he demonstrated for the first time what was to prove one of his major characteristics, the ability to form bonds of regard which leaped over conventional barriers of age, rank or social station. Jonson's love and gratitude to this man in particular who was the first to recognise and to nourish his special gifts shines through the tortuous syntax of a verse tribute composed later:

> Camden, most reverend head, to whom I owe
>   All that I am in arts, all that I know . . .
> What name, what skill, what faith hast thou in things!
>   What sight in searching the most antique springs!
> What weight, and what authority in thy speech!
> Man scarce can make that doubt, but thou canst teach . . .
>   (Epigram 14)[13]

In addition to friendship Camden gave Jonson his abiding notion of the dignity of literary work. Camden's training, his faith in the Renaissance concept of the poet as teacher instructing by delight, formed Jonson's thinking and his idea of himself in a way that he was never to abandon.

Attending Westminster School was the first great step in Jonson's life, and one of whose advantages he was fully aware. Writing later of the value of a school education as against a private tutor, he wrote, 'to breed [children] at home is to breed them in a shade, where in a school they have the light and heat of the sun' (HS VIII, 614). He further condemns from his own experience the mechanical contemporary practices in education when rote-learning and intellectual force-feeding crammed the young mind: 'a youth should not be made to hate study, before he know the causes to love it, or taste the bitterness before the sweet; but be called on and allured, intreated and praised, yea, when he deserves it not' (HS VIII, 614).

In time however Jonson had to leave school. According to the account of Izaak Walton in 1680, Jonson remained until 'the 6 degree, that is, the uppermost form in Westminster School'. Walton's version is weakened by his distance in time from the events he is describing, not to mention 'his being then eighty-seven years of age'. But it came to Walton from George Morley, Bishop of Winchester, who knew Jonson well, and it is not inherently improbable. Jonson's knowledge of Greek, though not as good as his Latin, strongly suggests that he proceeded beyond the fourth form, at which stage the study of Greek was introduced.[14] By the statutes of Westminster School he could not have remained there after his eighteenth birthday. By the end of 1590, at the latest, he was out in the world.

Without a scholarship Jonson had no hope of attending Oxford or Cambridge. But later critics insisted on favouring him with a university education which he never had. Fuller confidently reported that Jonson was 'statutably admitted into St John's College in Cambridge . . . where he continued but a few weeks for want of further maintenance'.[15] Anthony Wood took Jonson's apocryphal university career a stage further, stating that he studied at Cambridge till he was 'of ripe years' at which point he 'came of his own account to Oxon, and there entered himself in Christ Church' (the college with which Westminster School had special ties through its three closed scholarships there). Wood goes on to relate that Jonson 'took his Master's degree in Oxon (or conferred upon him) *anno* 1619'. There is not a shred of evidence to support this version of events and Jonson's own word against it. He said to Drummond that 'he was Master of Arts in both the universities, but by their favour, not his study' (HS I, 139).

For Jonson's reality was painfully different from the groves of academe. All that life offered to the stepson of a bricklayer was a future in the same trade. Jonson was 'taken from school' (the phrase implies against his will) and 'put to another craft', as Drummond noted, adding 'I think it was to be a wright or bricklayer' (HS I, 139). Drummond's second guess was the correct one; Fuller reports that Jonson 'was fain to return to the trade of his father-in-law [stepfather]', again in terms suggesting Jonson's reluctance.

For there is no doubt about Jonson's reaction. The work was quite repugnant to him, something he told Drummond that he 'could not endure'. All the early accounts hang together in stressing his unwillingness to enter this trade, the element of compulsion involved, and the shortness of his service in it. John Aubrey noted that 'he wrought some time with his father-in-law', while Walton's version is that Jonson's stepfather 'made him (much against his will) to help him in his trade' (HS I, 178 and 181). Jonson must have felt as much desire to be a bricklayer as Shakespeare did to run an ailing agricultural business in Stratford-upon-Avon.

Clearly Jonson's lack of higher education coupled with his formidable scholarship formed a paradox that later commentators felt bound to account for. His own unusual personality also lent itself to mythologising. Aubrey is specific in his declaration that Jonson was employed as a bricklayer in the building of a garden wall of Lincoln's Inn next to Chancery Lane. Coincidentally 'a knight, a bencher, walking though and hearing him repeat some Greek verses out of Homer, discoursing with him and finding him to have a wit extraordinary, gave him some exhibition to maintain him at Trinity College in Cambridge' (HS I, 5).

Despite the reappearance of the myth of the university education there is much here that is plausible. Robert Brett was employed on work in Lincoln's Inn in 1590 and 1591, when Jonson would have left school, and was also responsible for the New Buildings erected in Lincoln's Inn between 1600 and 1609. Fuller has another version of the same story; 'he helped in the building of the new structure of Lincoln's Inn, when, having a trowel in his hand, he had a book in his pocket'. Jonson reciting aloud, Jonson with a book always about him, Jonson who never lost the power to impress even the highly educated with the range and tenacity of his scholarship – this is the Jonson who appears again and again whenever he was talked of, for the rest of his life.

But even with his books and his Greek Jonson could not bear the life of a bricklayer's apprentice. When he broke away he did so with a vengeance; he left England, and travelled to the Netherlands to join up with the English army, then on active service there. This could well have been in 1591, when a special effort was being made to reinforce the English expeditionary forces.

The war in the Low Countries was an epic struggle which was to drag on for another half century after Jonson's intervention. Elizabeth's aim was to try to maintain the precarious balance of power between rival Catholic and Protestant interests. To do this she had to establish a military presence there strong enough to stiffen the Dutch resistance to their Spanish overlords without seeming to interfere too obviously in the affairs of another sovereign nation. By the early 1590s with the defeat of the Armada in 1588 the danger of provoking the might of Spain had receded to some extent. Nevertheless Spain remained a lion, if one whose beard had been singed, and Elizabeth would not abandon the gallant little Netherlands to the lion's paw.

For Jonson the Flemish foray promised an escape into adventure and held out the prospect of noble and heroic action. Going to war was a conventional gesture of gallantry at the time and there was no sense of its being inappropriate to a poet. Apart from 'England's darling' Sir Philip Sidney, the poets Gascoigne and Lodge both made the same choice. But the reality of the experience bore little relation to the romantic preconception. To enlist in the English army at that time, and in that war, a man would have to be not only brave and hardy but desperate as well. Ill-organised from home, badly led in the field, the soldiers endured the ravages of warfare inadequately armed, poorly clothed, and worse fed. It comes as no surprise that Jonson did not serve for long, 'returning soon' to London, in Drummond's phrase.

But before his return Jonson performed one act which he recalled with pride even in his age. The war in the Netherlands was at the beginning of the 1590s passing through one of its more languid phases. Since the famous battle of Zutphen in 1586 at which Sidney made his legendary death, there had been no considerable encounter. In the absence of any real action Jonson made his own. Amidst failure and despair Jonson managed to turn the situation into one of those outstanding displays of his individualistic personality for which he was and remains truly remarkable.

In this war the Westminster schoolboy became a man, in the oldest and most primitive way – by killing another man. This was not part of the normal chance of war. Jonson recounted to Drummond how 'he had, in the face of both the camps, killed an enemy, and taken *opima spolia* [rich spoils] from him'.[16] Jonson had challenged one of the invading Spanish forces to single combat in the no-man's land between the two opposing armies and they had fought it out to the death. When he had killed his adversary Jonson stripped the body of its valuable weapons and armour. As the Latin quotation indicates, Jonson was fulfilling in life a story common in classical literature. The refugee bricklayer had taken on a role straight out of Homer and Virgil. It is striking how completely this story in its blend of ruthless aggression with the extravagant expression of the romance of the classical ideal exemplifies so much of what was to come in his later life.

Bloodied and triumphant the hero had no appetite for sitting out a dreary and uneventful war. Jonson returned to London, with two indelible new attributes. First he had learned to fight well enough not only to kill this unnamed soldier but later on an opponent younger than he was and armed with a superior weapon. Further he had learned a respect for true soldiers and a contempt for cowards and braggarts that stayed with him all his life and coloured many aspects of his work.

In two poems thought to have been written in 1601 Jonson reflected on his war episode (Epigrams 107 and 108). The second is addressed to 'true soldiers', and links his own military service with his work as a writer:

> I swear by your true friend, my muse, I love
> Your great profession, which I once did prove,
> And did not shame it with my actions then,
> No more than I dare now do with my pen.[17]

To the end of his days Jonson was impressed by courage in arms, devoting Epigram 66 for instance to the heroic stand of four brave Englishmen against an army of four hundred, when all the rest of their force had fled the field.

Jonson returned to England to embark on the career by which we now know him and to address himself to the serious business of adult life. His youth and adolescence had been passed in stirring times; he was four when James Burbage built the very first English theatre, and eight when Drake returned from successfully circumnavigating the globe in the *Golden Hind*. These had too been times of intense anxiety for English people of either the Catholic or the Protestant persuasion; Jonson was fifteen when Mary Queen of Scots was executed, and sixteen when little England stood alone against the tyrant Spain and achieved the unhoped-for victory over the Armada in 1588.

But these events seem to have left no mark on him. In his life Jonson expressed only the most fleeting awareness of international affairs and his interest in politics was strictly limited. In addition Jonson's career conveys the impression that he had very little youth; no salad days, no chance to fleet the time carelessly before adult responsibilities set in. Jonson springs forth fully made up, studying, quarrelling, writing and acting, from the first recorded mention. When we next hear of him it is in connection with the stage which was to be his passion and his bane for the rest of his days, often loathed but never finally abandoned. Here in the 1590s Jonson emerges as an actor and writer. These were the first steps towards the most coveted title of all, 'Ben Jonson, poet'.

CHAPTER 2

PLAYER

WHEN Jonson returned from the war in the Netherlands his compelling need was to find some means of survival. The military foray had proved a short-term adventure and 'returning soon' to London left him without any financial support or occupation. Some years were to pass before he can be positively connected with the professional theatre in 1597. How did he live in this time?

The likelihood is that Jonson returned to the detested craft of his stepfather for a while. Later evidence that Jonson became a freeman of the bricklayers' company to which his stepfather belonged proves that he must have been bound apprentice and served out his seven-year term. This may have been before, after, or interrupted by the Flemish adventure. But anything less will hardly account for the persistence of his later association with the trade. One brief episode of bricklaying after leaving school and never repeated could not provide material enough for the repeated insults of Jonson as a bricklayer, nor account for the virulence and persistence of these jibes. However reluctantly, Jonson worked at this trade for long enough to become 'the wittiest fellow of a bricklayer in all England'.

He did not, however, give up his intellectual ambitions. Back in England, as he told Drummond, he 'betook himself to his wonted studies'. Whatever his way of life Jonson made a point of carrying on what 'his master Camden had learned him', both in the habit of study and in the classical substance. This cannot have been easy for a bricklayer. But it was to set something of a pattern. The tension between the academic and the artisan was to remain with Ben Jonson all his life. In the theatre of his day he found a métier that would allow him to explore both these aspects of his unique and complex personality.

Jonson could hardly have entered it at a more auspicious time. The

survival of the theatre in those early days was very much dependent
upon its attracting such able young men who were hindered only by
personal circumstances from more conventional means of advance-
ment. For English drama stood upon no very sure foundation. It is
true that the defeat of the Armada in 1588 had given the theatre a
joyous uplift as it had to so much else in the life of the nation, and the
succeeding years saw a flood of nationalist and historical drama. The
upsurge of confidence created an optimistic climate for development
and investment.

The year 1592 for instance saw the refurbishment of the Rose Theatre.
Originally built in 1587 it was now thoroughly overhauled to receive
the Lord Strange's Company of players under the management of
Philip Henslowe, who with the famous Edward Alleyn as their chief
actor had every expectation of success. Two years later in 1594
Francis Langley, goldsmith and citizen of London, was licensed to
erect the Swan Theatre in Paris Gardens – his poetical name for it
drawn from the flocks of swans in which the Thames then abounded,
these graceful creatures being one of the famous sights of old London.
The theatre which went up in 1595 was erected upon an old-
established area for playing – a performance was taking place on that
site while the priests of St Saviour's church sang the *Dirige* for the soul
of Henry VIII in 1547 – but it was a new playhouse, and new
playhouses need new actors and writers.

But this thrusting theatrical growth was not of any great age or
strength. The theatre was in fact fighting for its young life against
discouragement and misfortune. On 23 June 1592 a serious riot in
Southwark led the Privy Council to order all playhouses in and
around London to be closed until Michaelmas (29 September). This
blow was followed by a severe outbreak of the plague in August, more
serious than any since the visitation that had devastated London in
1563. The playhouses were forbidden to operate for fear that their
audiences would spread the disease. Not until 29 December were the
Lord Strange's Men able to resume playing at the Rose. This respite
was short-lived. One month later, in 1593, the plague once more
broke out with unusual ferocity. On 1 February 1593 playing was
again inhibited by proclamation, with the consequent total loss to the
players of their means of livelihood.

1593 has come down to later days as one of the worst plague years in
history, one continuous terror. Between ten and seventeen thousand
people died and most of the acting companies were forced to embark
upon protracted tours of the provinces since they had no hope of being
allowed to act in London. 1594 too was ruined for the players by long
enforced closures of their theatres. The plague was never very far
away and when it came it struck with hideous suddenness. People

were forbidden to congregate together in crowded places in the hope of minimising its grip upon the population.

Another threat lay in the attitude of the authorities, both local and national, to the theatres. They were regarded as hot-beds of personal immorality and political subversion, attended by light women and dangerously idle men. These large groups of pleasure-seekers could it was feared be a threat to the security of Church and state; equally, the plays themselves were potential instruments for the propagation of radical dissent, by spreading ideas hostile to the established government and its relations with foreign powers. The setbacks which the central and civic bodies inflicted upon the theatre companies seem to have been received as occupational hazards, and they became easier to avoid or to tolerate as the players established themselves. But even the most successful of the acting companies remained vulnerable both to natural disaster and to the virulent Puritan disapproval which was eventually to pull them down altogether. In 1596 the satirist Nashe sounded a common complaint when he lamented that 'the players are piteously persecuted by the Lord Mayor and the Aldermen'.

The young Ben Jonson, then, could hardly have entered the theatre with any hopes of security, financial or otherwise. Another related disadvantage of the thespian life was its lowly status. Dramatists and actors alike were subject to the centuries-old prejudice against their 'whoorish art'; their work taught and fostered vice, preached sedition, undermined the Scriptures, as well as feeding the plague by gathering people together. At best the players could hope only to be treated like upper servants. All this could not have weighed too heavily on the impecunious youngster of the 1590s – it was, after all, a major advance on bricklaying. Later, though, he came to regret that he had ever associated himself with the public stage, a form of entertainment accorded by its detractors little more prestige than bear-baiting, with which it shared both premises and audience.

But young men must live. And Jonson's own needs were brought into sharper focus by his assumption of the traditional masculine responsibility for another. At the end of 1594, at the age of twenty-two, Jonson took a wife. The parish register of St Magnus the Martyr by London Bridge contains the following entry for November 14 of that year: 'Beniamine Johnson and Anne Lewis married'. Since she was a parishioner of St Magnus Jonson's bride may well have lived on London Bridge itself – the greater part of that parish consisted of the large and beautiful houses for which the venerable bridge was famous throughout Europe. These opulent dwellings were inhabited by the wealthier citizens, mainly merchants, and it has been suggested that Anne Lewis could have been employed in one of them as a maid.[1]

Jonson certainly knew London Bridge well and refers to it far more frequently than do any of his fellow-dramatists. In his *Epicœne* it is jokingly described as a good place for a suicide attempt, while in *The Staple of News* he comments on how frequently the ancient arches needed repairing. Jonson's marrying a woman from this parish supports the proposition that he had already become an actor, either living in Bankside or accustomed to the daily crossing of the Bridge on the way to the Rose, Paris Gardens, or Newington Butts – indeed, Morose in *Epicœne* links London Bridge with Paris Gardens as places where 'the noises are at their height and loudest'.

Of Jonson's wife almost nothing is known except her name. His one recorded comment on her comes from the winter of 1618–19 when he told Drummond that 'he married a wife who was a shrew yet honest' (HS I, 139). This tribute to her 'honesty' implies a high valuation of her worth since it was 'of all styles' the one which he loved best himself. If Jonson was noting here his wife's fidelity to her marriage vows ('honest' could mean 'chaste' when applied to a woman in seventeenth-century usage), then this is the more impressive since he often made a grass widow of her, and for long periods too: he told Drummond that 'five years he had not bedded with her, but remained with my lord D'Aubigny'. It is also quite clear that on his side Jonson did not feel himself bound to marital chastity; he owned to Drummond that he was 'in his youth given to venery' (sexual indulgence), and elaborated this with anecdotes vaunting a variety of lubricious interludes (HS I, 139).

Anne Lewis would have needed all the power of address and personality to hold her own with her robust and wayward spouse. But the course of such a married life would sharpen even a blunt tongue, and provide plenty of exercise for a shrewish one. Jonson was not an ideal husband. He was unsuited to the condition, both temperamentally and through his acquired habits of life. As a married man Jonson, like most writers, made a very good bachelor.

And Jonson's vagaries as a partner were echoed by his insufficiency as a provider. There was never enough money; he told Drummond that he had not made as much as two hundred pounds from *all* his plays; 'poetry had beggared him' (HS I, 149). Nor was there, for Mistress Jonson, a fine large family house like that which must have made it easier for Anne Shakespeare to bear her husband's absences and the peripatetic life of an actor. Jonson had nothing to offer his wife except himself and his talent, both of which he withdrew from her at his pleasure.

But there were greater afflictions in store than this. The inexpressible desolation of the loss of children might well sour the sweetest disposition; and here alone Jonson's wife had full cause of that grief which consolation can only insult, and time can never assuage. Of the babies born to Anne and Ben Jonson, none survived childhood. Jonson has left his own account of his feelings for two of them. The early years of the marriage saw the birth of a little girl, who was christened Mary.[2] This child lived for only six months, and her passing was the subject of a delicate epitaph from her father:

> Here lies, to each her parents' ruth,
> Mary, the daughter of their youth;
> Yet all heaven's gifts being heaven's due,
> It makes the father less to rue.
> At six months' end she parted hence
> With safety of her innocence;
> Whose soul heaven's Queen (whose name she bears)
> In comfort of her mother's tears,
> Hath placed among her virgin train;
> Where, while that served doth remain,
> This grave partakes the fleshly birth,
> Which cover lightly, gentle earth.
>
> (Epigram 22)

This tribute to his daughter is the more remarkable when we consider that Jonson left no written record of any sort about either his mother or his wife. The tone of the poem, although tender, is not grieving. Unless the reference to 'her mother's tears' is purely conventional the suggestion is that Jonson's wife found the loss harder to bear than he did.

These early years also produced a son, named Benjamin for his father. Born some time in 1596 he too was cut down in childhood. But unlike Mary he had lived long enough to wind himself about his father's heart. His death was therefore a far more keenly felt grief as Jonson was later to demonstrate (Epigram 45). Mary and Benjamin were not the only children born to Jonson and his wife; this is made clear by the titles which Jonson gave to their epitaphs, 'On my *first* daughter', 'On my *first* son'. The uncertain state of Elizabethan parish records has confused the search, while the commonness of the patronymic has thrown up a variety of claimants to Ben Jonson as their sire – these will be considered in their place. But these two children are two whom we can be sure of since he himself acknowledged them. But with the death of Benjamin he seemed, in his own words, to 'lose all father', and from 1603 he is silent on the subject.

The year 1594 was remarkable for two events other than Jonson's marriage both of which had significant personal implications for the new bridegroom. In February amid relief and rejoicing King James of Scotland's queen gave birth to her first child at Stirling. The longed-for prince was baptised Henry in deference to his father's hopes of one day ascending the throne of the Tudors. However unlikely it would have seemed at this time, Jonson's entire professional future was to be bound up with James, Anne and their children, and the little prince was to grow up into one of Jonson's most discerning patrons.

A birth, and a death. On 15 August 1594 the funeral took place of Thomas Kyd. Born only a few days before Elizabeth I came to the throne in 1558, Kyd had been one of those who helped to make her reign glorious in perpetuity for its literary achievement. He had found his own voice as the author of the most popular play of the age, *The Spanish Tragedy*. But then he had had the misfortune to become entangled with his fellow-dramatist, Marlowe, in matters deep and dangerous. Arrested in May 1593 on charges of libel against the state and atheism, he was imprisoned and subjected to what he described as 'pains and undeserved tortures'. This treatment appears to have hastened his death. He passed the remnant of his life enduring 'bitter times and privy broken passions', poverty, misery and rejection. Ignorance, innocence even, was no defence for a suspected playwright against the might of a suspicious state.

At the onset of Jonson's working life in the theatre his career both as actor and writer was bound up with the work of Kyd. Quite how Jonson contrived to change the trowel for the quill is not known, but he certainly made his way into the drama as an actor first. John Aubrey recorded that 'he acted and wrote at the Green Curtain (but both ill [badly]), a kind of nursery or obscure playhouse, I think towards Shoreditch or Clerkenwell' (HS I, 179). There is some confusion here. The only theatre adjacent to Clerkenwell was the Red Bull, famous for its horrible 'tear-throat' style of acting, while the Curtain is in Shoreditch.[3] But Jonson's theatre *début* as an actor is beyond question.[4] Years later a current enemy was to taunt him with this, jeering 'I have seen thy shoulders lapped in an old player's cast cloak'.[5] And the part with which Jonson is inextricably associated is that of Hieronimo, the leading role in Kyd's *The Spanish Tragedy*.

It is characteristic of Jonson that he should have dived into the theatre at the deep end. For the part of Hieronimo, an old man driven mad with grief, calls for enormous emotional power and exceptional histrionic technique. It is hardly the role for a young and inexperienced actor. Yet his detractor, fellow-playwright Thomas Dekker, insisted that Jonson 'took mad Hieronimo's part, to get service among the mimics [actors]', and reminded him of 'when thou ran'st mad for the death of Horatio' (Hieronimo's son in the play). It is clear, too, that this was in a touring company; Jonson's apprenticeship in the theatre included the dismal experience of being a strolling player in the provinces. Dekker's jibes include this dig: 'Thou hast forgot how

27

thou amblest in leather pilch [cloak] by a play-wagon, in the high-way'. Jonson himself in *Poetaster* makes rueful reference to the necessity which compels the players to tour – 'to travel, with pumps full of gravel . . . after a blind jade [horse] and a hamper' (III.iv.168–70). He knew, too, the inadequate fit-up conditions under which itinerant actors were expected to perform, in any tavern, barn or marketplace where they could set up their rickety stage, and then 'stalk upon boards and barrel heads, to an old cracked trumpet', as he sardonically phrases it.

Despite his association with this most famous of parts, Jonson's acting career was not illustrious. Aubrey records that 'he was never a good actor, but an excellent instructor' (HS I, 182), and Jonson's own estimate of his abilities is shown in the fact that he gave up acting as soon as he could. He was employed at the lowest level, as 'a poor journeyman player' (the name given to those actors who were not employed as members of a regular company, but hired like modern extras on an *ad hoc* basis) and, continued Dekker, 'hadst been so still, but that thou couldst not put a good face upon it' (IV.i) – this is one of many references to Jonson's ugly face, and by no means the un-kindest. Worse still, he acted in Paris Gardens. This place was one of the most disreputable haunts in London, where the theatre struggled unsuccessfully to retain some respectability among the rival attractions of bear-baiting and bordellos. The Duke of Newcastle, later one of Jonson's patrons and friends, wrote to Charles II that Paris Gardens 'will hold good for the meaner people'.[6] Never one to be comfortable when accused of keeping low company, Jonson afterwards came to regret that he had ever had anything to do with such a low dive, balefully castigating 'that accursed ground, the Paris Garden'.[7]

For better or for worse then Jonson's life was taking shape around him both professionally and personally. During the early part of 1596 his son Benjamin was born. That summer also saw the arrival in August of a princess to King James and Queen Anne, who continued the Tudor theme by naming her Elizabeth. The late 1590s while it accommodated the crescent fortune of the Stuarts saw too the disintegration of the old order that had been the triumph of the Tudors. One by one the links of the old Queen's golden chain of power and glory were giving way – in 1596 Sir Francis Drake, one of Elizabeth's most faithful knights, died on his last voyage to the West Indies. At last after so long there was change in the air, and all sorts of people were conscious of it.

Among those people was Ben Jonson. Despite the disadvantages and distractions that he laboured under, as the stepson of a brick-layer, an unsuccessful actor, a man without means and a newly-

28

created father, Jonson remained surprisingly in touch with the intellectual currents of his day. In 1595 came the publication of Sir Philip
Sidney's *Apology for Poetry*, which affected Jonson profoundly. This
radical critique made a systematic examination of the state of
English poetry, the first time that such an exercise had ever been
carried out. Jonson seized on it eagerly, absorbing not only Sidney's
ideas but even his phrases – these were to resurface in his first
successful play *Every Man In His Humour* three years later, parts of
which are a positive collage of Sidneyisms.

Most important for Jonson's development, however, was Sidney's
insistence on the teaching function of poetry. Sidney stressed the high
dignity of poetry both as a form and as an occupation. These lofty
critical standards and ideals were imprinted on Jonson sufficiently
powerfully to remain with him all his life. They passed through him
like wine through water, and altered the colour of his mind.

Jonson also kept a keen eye on the work of other poets. One who
particularly caught his attention was Edmund Spenser (?1552–1599).
Jonson never really liked Spenser's major work, the allegorical *Faerie
Queene*, finding it far-fetched and obscure. Others did too, and years
later Jonson had to explain some of Spenser's highly-wrought and
clouded meanings to Sir Walter Raleigh, who found it beyond him.
But Jonson took to an earlier work of Spenser, the series of linked
poems called *The Shepherd's Calendar* of 1597. It is fascinating that
Jonson, who was nothing if not urban to his fingertips, should have
been attracted to this delightful pastoral dealing with the country life
and the adventures of the shepherd swains and their shepherdesses.
But he liked it enough to learn some of it by heart and store it in his
phenomenal memory. He kept in mind an extract in praise of wine as
an aid to poetic inspiration:

> O if my temples were distained with wine,
> And girt in garlands of wild ivy twine,
> How could I rear the Muse on stately stage!

He also later possessed a 1617 edition of Spenser's complete works
which he copiously annotated. Notwithstanding his reservations
about Spenser's greatest poem, Jonson knew and enjoyed the pieces
with which Spenser charmed the literary public in the late 1580s and
1590s.

These intellectual exercises indicate that Jonson had from the first
wider mental horizons than the lowly occupation of player could hope
to satisfy. He probably only took up acting as an entrée into the
theatre, and his experiences as an actor obviously confirmed him in
his determination to exercise his talents as a maker rather than
re-creator of plays. This posed certain problems quite peculiar to his

day, which he was to wrestle with during all his life as a working dramatist.

For this was a composite audience, ranging widely over every social class, age, educational level and intellectual ability, from the upper classes sitting apart in the 'lord's room' to the 'penny stinkards' standing in the yard. The dramatist had to grab and hold the attention of all members of the audience, and ensure that no one section ever went too long unprovided for. The cultured minority would take delight in elaborate tricks of style, verbal inventiveness, and demonstrations of ingenuity. But those cracking nuts and swilling ale in the pit would look for something less rarefied.

Yet although the majority would be illiterate, they were not unintelligent. The people at large, in the era before the free dissemination of printed material, were highly-trained listeners. As part of their daily lives they were accustomed to proclamations, speeches and sermons, and consequently familiar with many intricate rhetorical forms and verbal devices.

There was too among high-born and low a tolerance of cruelty almost unbelievable to us today. It was part of the fabric of their everyday lives, of their notions of child-rearing, and their system of justice and punishment. The contemporary theatre was tied in to this, as the Hope, for example, alternated plays with bear-baiting (Jonson makes pointed reference to 'the bears within' and their powerful stink in the Induction to *Bartholomew Fair*). The appetite for physical violence was fed not only by scenes of death and mutilation but also by wild horseplay and knockabout farce. There were spectators who had to be sated with action, crowds, wrestling, singing, fighting, fooling and dancing. Ultimately, though, no generalisation can contain the diversity of the audiences of Jonson's day. They remained a conglomeration of highly differentiated individuals, as one contemporary dramatist at least was keenly aware:

> How is it possible to suffice,
>   So many ears, so many eyes?
> Some in wit, some in shows
>   Take delight, and some in clothes.
> Some for mirth they chiefly come,
>   Some for passion – for both, some;
> Some for lascivious meetings, that't their errant,
> Some to detract, and ignorance their warrant.
>   How is it possible to please
>   Opinion tossed in such wild seas?[8]

This last question is one that Jonson came to see as a crucial issue for the dramatist, as it determined the success or failure of his play. And although he protested that he recognised the audience's right to 'his or her own free-will of censure, to like or dislike at their own charge',[9] he never really solved this problem to his own satisfaction.

At the very outset of his writing career, however, Jonson ran into difficulties far more severe than those with the notoriously capricious Elizabethan audience. From being an unknown and unregarded player, he rocketed to national importance and the attention of the Queen's Privy Council through his involvement in a celebrated scandal. The cause of this was a play, staged just before 28 July 1597 and now lost, called *The Isle of Dogs*. Originally the brain-child of the irrepressible Thomas Nashe (1567–?1601), this satirical squib had been left unfinished. Nashe later claimed that he had 'begun but the Induction and the first act of it', and dismissed it as 'the imperfect embryo of my idle hours'. But the fragment he abandoned was taken up by the actors then playing at Langley's new playhouse, the Swan. As the Earl of Pembroke's Company this troupe had only been active since the spring of that year. They badly needed new material and a popular success. Nashe's opening was promising if it could be got up into a play. As Nashe later complained 'the other four acts, without my consent . . . by the players were supplied, which bred both their trouble and mine too'. Among the hands which contributed to the completion of *The Isle of Dogs* foremost was that of Ben Jonson.

Nashe himself was no stranger to trouble. As an undergraduate at Cambridge he was said to have 'flourished in all impudency' towards the dons and townspeople alike. He joyfully courted controversy throughout his London literary life. But even he must have been unprepared for what happened. It is impossible to deduce much from the title – the Isle of Dogs was a marshy peninsula across the Thames from Greenwich, and one of those frowstily dismal localities that lend themselves naturally to satire. But the play apparently attacked under thin disguise some person in high authority.

The exact nature of the offence cannot now be established. But information about it was laid before the Privy Council, and the Queen herself was very greatly angered. It is from the steps that the Privy Council took that Jonson's part in the business can be unravelled. The affair was handled at the very highest level in the land. At the Privy Council meeting to consider the matter in full on Monday 15 August those present included the Lord Treasurer, the Lord Chamberlain, the Chancellor of the Exchequer, the Comptroller of the Household, and the Secretary of the Council Sir Robert Cecil, later to be Earl of Salisbury. Having decided that this was a 'lewd play', 'containing very seditious and slanderous matter' (HS I, 217), the Privy Council closed in swiftly on those responsible. Orders were issued for the arrest and imprisonment of the authors of the play and also the chief actors who took part in the offensive performance. In the swoop that followed Nashe saved himself by headlong flight to the eastern counties and took refuge in Great Yarmouth. But his lodgings were searched and his private papers were handed over to the authorities. Robert Shaw and Gabriel Spencer, both actors and leaders of the troupe – sharers indeed in the newly-formed company which had only come together as the Lord Pembroke's Men in February of that year – were thrown into prison in the Marshalsea. Also singled out for incarceration by the same warrant was one who 'was not only an actor but a maker of part of the said play' (HS I, 217), Ben Jonson.

It is clear that the Privy Council was contemplating the arrest of the whole troupe, feeling that they should all be 'apprehended to receive such punishment as their lewd and mutinous behaviour doth deserve'. But in the event they had to content themselves with the ringleaders. The remnant of the shattered company took to the road, their speed to save their skins demonstrated by the fact that they were acting in Bristol before the end of this same month of July. But this was not the limit of the Privy Council's vengeance. On 28 July 1597 a letter was sent to the Justices of Middlesex and Sussex informing them that 'her Majesty hath given direction that not only no plays shall be used within London or about the city, or in any public place during this time of summer, but that also those playhouses that are erected and built for such purpose shall be plucked down'.[10] Playing was then inhibited within three miles of the city until All Hallows 1 November).

Meanwhile Jonson, Spencer, and Shaw remained in prison. Recollection of the fate of Thomas Kyd three years earlier cannot have made their imprisonment any easier to bear – especially as among those to whom their interrogation was trusted was Richard Topcliffe, Queen Elizabeth's notorious master-torturer. The prisoners were to be questioned as to where their fellows had got to; who had a part 'in the devising of that seditious matter'; who acted in it; what copies were given out, and to whom. The Privy Councillors were determined to root out all traces of the play – and they succeeded.

Despite all this panoply of intimidation, the spirit which had led Jonson to satirise the powers of authority with such stinging effect refused to allow him to knuckle under. It was a matter of pride with him later that 'at the time of his close imprisonment under Queen Elizabeth . . . his judges could get nothing of him to all their demands but "Aye" and "No" '. Frustrated, his inquisitors attempted to trap him into damaging admissions by the use of stool-pigeons; with a rumble of long-ago indignation, Jonson told Drummond that 'they placed two damned villains to catch advantage of him' in his cell (HS

I, 139). With that lifelong capacity always to make some friend at need, Jonson was lucky enough to get on the right side of the Keeper of the Marshalsea, who let him know what was going on.[11]

Another perennial characteristic revealed itself in Jonson's ability to coin his personal experience into poetry. He revenged himself upon the spies in an epigram whose central metaphor returned to him again and again:

> Spies, you are lights in state, but of base stuff
> Who, when you've burnt yourself down to the snuff
> Stink, and are thrown away. End fair enough.
>
> (Epigram 59)

Over two months went by before the authorities were satisfied that no serious offence had been committed. Finally on 3 October 1597 by order of the Privy Council a warrant was issued 'to the Keeper of the Marshalsea to release Gabriel Spencer and Robert Shaw, stage players, out of prison, who were of late committed to his custody'. A laconic rider adds, 'the like warrant for the releasing of Benjamin Johnson' (HS I, 218).

Jonson emerged from prison alive but facing an uncertain future. There was no hope of re-employment with the Earl of Pembroke's Men; this young company, only reorganised five months before the time of trouble, could not recover from such a blight upon its fortunes, and was utterly destroyed. Blasted too were Langley's hopes of profit from his smart playhouse, the Swan. The order for the razing of the playhouses issued in the first fury of retaliation had not been carried out and as the tempest of the Queen's rage blew over theatrical life began to raise its head again. But Elizabeth, with her Tudor capacity for animosity, would not forgive the Swan. Henceforth, by order of the Privy Council, licence to play would be granted to two companies only, the Admiral's Men at the Rose Theatre, and the Lord Chamberlain's (Shakespeare's company) at the Curtain. Effectively the Swan was wiped out.

Not everything was disastrous for Jonson at this time. From this early point of his career comes his first surviving full-length play, *The Case Is Altered*. Whether written before or after his imprisonment, it was well-known by the spring of 1598. It was commended by none other than Nashe, who was then writing his *Lenten Stuff*, in which he complimented 'the merry cobbler's cut in that witty play of *The Case Is Altered*'. The play was performed by the Children of the Chapel, a company of boy players descended from the troupe of choristers originally established to provide music for the sovereign. Their professionalism combined with the novelty value of their childhood contrived to 'berattle the common stages' and

33

threaten the adult companies, as Shakespeare lamented in *Hamlet*.

The connection with the Chapel Children marked the change in Jonson's career from player to playwright. The company was popular and fashionable and their very success bred a demand for new plays. Jonson got off to a good start with *The Case Is Altered,* an amiable comedy created from the blending of two Plautine originals into a rather old-fashioned romance. The Roman elements were familiar to the educated section of the audience, while the word-play and comical antics of the low-life characters Juniper and Onion had a different appeal, as Nashe's approval demonstrates. The play made a hit on its first appearance, and remained popular for some time in the Children's repertory, as the history of subsequent performance shows. For the next few years Jonson's services were to be devoted extensively to this company.

Extensively, but not exclusively; there was another regular call upon Jonson's nascent talent for playmaking. One man at least was shrewd enough to recognise the newcomer's ability – Philip Henslowe, owner of the Rose and manager of the Admiral's Men who played there. Henslowe had since 1595 been the owner of Paris Gardens, and it has been suggested that this was the origin of his connection with Jonson. In the aftermath of the *Isle of Dogs* affair Henslowe was not slow in snapping up those of the survivors who could be useful to him in his efforts to build up and profit from his theatrical ventures. Among the actors of the former company of Pembroke's Men whom he employed was Ben Jonson.

There was soon work for Jonson with Henslowe. Although play-acting was officially inhibited until 1 November, the pertinacious Henslowe managed to get permission to open his theatre again on 11 October. He had had contact with Jonson that summer just as the storm broke; he entered into his account book that on 28 July 1597 he had 'lent unto Benjamin Johnson, player, the sum of four pounds in ready money'.[12] Jonson would desperately have needed this cash not only to keep his wife and children afloat during his imprisonment, but also to pay for his necessities in the Marshalsea, under the iniquitous contemporary system whereby prisoners had to buy all their own food and comforts. But Henslowe was not a man of sentiment, and this substantial sum indicates the manager's business faith in Jonson as a paying proposition.

It was as Henslowe's debtor therefore that Jonson went to work for him after his release. But it was not as a 'player'. There is no further record of Jonson's ever acting again and all the subsequent references to him in Henslowe's account books are concerned with the preparation of play texts. Jonson's acting days were over. From now on, it would be not as a prentice but as a master-craftsman and playwright that he would make his mark upon the London scene.

CHAPTER 3

PLAYWRIGHT

JONSON the playwright lost no time in getting down to work. On 3 December 1597 Henslowe records giving him an advance of twenty shillings 'upon a book . . . which he showed the plot unto the company', as Henslowe noted. Having sold the idea to the actors, all that Jonson had to do was to write the play and he promised to finish it by Christmas. The play has not been identified and may be one of Jonson's many lost works – he told Drummond that 'the half of his comedies were not in print' (HS I, 143). But this shows that he had arrived at a point in his career where he was not only making plays but initiating dramatic projects with one of the two leading companies of his day.

For all the danger through which he had passed in this year, 1597 closed quietly for Jonson with only a trivial money matter on record. The Churchwardens' accounts of his old Westminster parish, St Martin's-in-the-Fields, show that he was assessed for a contribution to the upkeep of the pews in the last quarter of the year. This list at Michaelmas has Jonson's name together with that of Brett, his likely stepfather; Brett paid two shillings and Jonson eighteen pence. The implication is that the church officials still regarded him as a parishioner. But wherever he was living he was still working for Henslowe. The new year of 1598 opened with the record in Henslowe's diary of the payment to Jonson of five shillings on 5 January. Before the year was out he was amply to vindicate Henslowe's assessment of his dramatic ability.

The course of 1598 shows Jonson steadily increasing in experience and importance as a contemporary writer. By the summer of that year he had attracted attention from the commentator Francis Meres, who published an account of the contemporary drama, *Palladis Tamia*. When he came to the playwrights Meres named 'Benjamin Johnson' alongside Shakespeare as one of the foremost English dramatists, specifying that of all then writing he was 'among our best for tragedy'. Meres's book was entered for publication on the Stationers' Register on 7 September 1598. No play now survives to indicate how Jonson could have won esteem as a tragedian by that date; lost too is a comedy called *Hot Anger Soon Cold* dating from the summer of that year. Jonson was named as the author of this play with his fellow-dramatists Henry Chettle and Henry Porter in Henslowe's account book for 18 August 1598. In the absence of external evidence to illuminate or corroborate these allusions they remain tantalisingly obscure.

Henslowe recorded that the three men together received £6 for *Hot Anger Soon Cold*, so Jonson's share would have been £2. This gain has to be set against some indication of financial difficulty on Jonson's part. Earlier in the year on 2 April 1598 he had borrowed £10 from an actor named Robert Browne – a large sum, which he had no obvious means of repaying. As security for the money Jonson gave Browne a bill, by which he bound himself to repay the loan at Whitsuntide of that year, 27 May 1598. Meanwhile he carried on doing what he could for Henslowe – on 23 October of this year George Chapman was paid by Henslowe for writing 'four acts of a tragedy of Benjamin's plot'.

Within a relatively short space of time then Jonson had established himself as one of the group of Elizabethan dramatists whose members encompassed every shade of ability from hack to genius. At the lower end of the scale he had to work with journeyman scribblers like Chettle, whose professional competence did not include ideas like Jonson's about the status of poetry and the poet. George Chapman by contrast was a man after his own heart, a classicist and scholar whose main work was the translation of Homer later so admired by Keats. Jonson knew and worked with the actors, too; apart from Spencer and Shaw who had suffered with him over the *Isle of Dogs* affair, he was acquainted with William Bird (alias Borne) and Thomas Downton. These two were among those who had hired the Swan from Langley on 21 February 1597, and are named by Henslowe in his records as go-betweens in his transactions with Jonson in 1599.

Towards the end of this year Jonson produced a play which confirmed his early promise and his standing in the contemporary theatre. His comedy *Every Man In His Humour* was staged in the early autumn of 1598; a letter from a courtier to a friend in the country referring to it as 'a new play' fixes the date of its first performance as 20 September 1598. In view of Henslowe's previous nursing of the budding dramatist it is interesting that the play was given not by Henslowe's company but by the Lord Chamberlain's Men at the Curtain Theatre in Shoreditch. They had moved from their previous home The Theatre to the Curtain because of a wrangle with their landlord who would not renew their lease.

For Jonson this meant the opportunity to have his play put on by the premier acting company of his day. It is too his first recorded contact with the playwright who was his only real rival. A later tradition first noticed by Nicholas Rowe in 1709 declares that the play owed its stage life to the man known as 'sweet Master Shakespeare':

> His acquaintance with Ben Johnson began with a remarkable piece of humanity and good nature. Mr Johnson, who was at that time altogether unknown to the world, had offered one of his plays to the players, in order to have it acted; and the persons into whose hands it was put, after having turned it carelessly and superciliously over, were just upon returning it to him with an ill-natured answer, that it would be of no service to their company, when Shakespeare luckily cast his eye upon it, and found something so well in it as to engage him first to read it through, and afterwards to recommend Mr Johnson and his writings to the public. (*Some Account of the Life of Mr William Shakespear*, pp. 29-30)

This interesting anecdote may be no more than a romantic legend. But whether or not Shakespeare recommended the play, he certainly acted in it. The cast list appended to Jonson's 1616 Folio names Shakespeare, Burbage, Heminges and Condell as among 'the principal comedians'. Shakespeare is traditionally supposed to have played the old man's part, and Burbage the comic lead of the quick-witted servant. The contribution of such talented and experienced actors would have added immeasurably to the play's chances of success.

And a success it was. Aubrey later recorded that *Every Man In His Humour* was the first acknowledged triumph of Jonson's early writing career, the play in which he 'did hit it admirably well', 'his first good one' (HS I, 179). The title page of the 1601 quarto edition with its reference to the play's having been 'sundry times publicly acted' bears witness to its commercial viability. Approaches to *Every Man In His Humour* have been dogged by subsequent recognition of its importance – Jonson's, first and foremost. Despite the existence of previous plays Jonson later came to see this as the beginning of his career as a dramatist. Aware that he had produced a piece that was both significant and successful, he devoted much subsequent energy to polishing up both the text itself, and the ideas which lay behind it. Other people's interest, and his own natural pride in his achievement, led him into what was to prove a life-long habit, the *post-facto* theorising that has misled succeeding commentators.

Yet in the summer of 1598 it can hardly be doubted that Jonson's preoccupations were those of any aspiring dramatist – first to write the play and then to get it put on. The cheerful comedy of intrigue which Jonson produced owed a good deal, like its predecessor *The Case Is Altered*, to the grounding in Roman comedy that he had received at Westminster. What made the play distinctive, however, was the happy stroke of inspiration which stimulated him to combine Plautus with a boiled-down version of the medieval theory of the four bodily 'humours'. The handling of this subject in the play is casual and sporadic; the main impact of it is felt in the unusual and catchy title. But it caused a stir and created an interest which hardened into a fashion as Jonson chose to capitalise on it. One way and another he was to be living with the consequences of *Every Man In His Humour* for the next few years.

At the time however Jonson did not have long to savour his triumph. In one of those staggering reversals which marked his ever-eventful career the hero of the hour found himself in prison. Less than a year after he had escaped from the Marshalsea and the attentions of the dreaded Topcliffe, Jonson once again lay in grave peril. In the same month of September in which *Every Man In His Humour* was staged he was involved in a swordfight. He had come to a violent opposition with an actor in Henslowe's company, Gabriel Spencer. They had fought it out in the fields beyond Shoreditch, Spencer perished, and Jonson was arrested for his murder.

Like so many of this belligerent age, poets and artists not excepted, Spencer was no newcomer to brutal assault and sudden death. Had Spencer slain Jonson it would not have been his first victim. Two years earlier on 3 December 1596 a coroner's inquest found that Spencer had himself killed one James Feake with a rapier at the house of a barber in the parish of St Leonard's, Shoreditch.

Both Spencer and Jonson were men of an aggressive tendency and they had been much together over the last year or so. As one of the 'sharers' and leaders of Pembroke's Men, Spencer had played a large part in the *Isle of Dogs* scandal and had been imprisoned with Jonson then and shared his dangers. With Jonson again he was one of the few to escape the subsequent wreck of this company and both of them appear to have been taken on by the alert Henslowe at this time. Proximity fed antipathy. The quarrel broke out on 22 September 1598. The two antagonists took themselves off to Hoxton Fields beyond Shoreditch, home of the Curtain Theatre where *Every Man In His Humour* was being staged. There in the ensuing duel Jonson was accused by the subsequent indictment of having attacked Spencer with 'a certain sword of iron and steel called a rapiour, of the price of three shillings' (HS I, 219), giving him a wound six inches deep and one inch wide on the right side of the body. Spencer died instantly.

Whatever his faults Spencer was untimely cut off. He had been an actor of great promise and to judge from his management ventures not without business enterprise. He had earned the praise of the dramatist Thomas Heywood in his life and drew from Henslowe this lamentation on his leaving it: 'I have lost one of my company, which hurteth me greatly; that is Gabriel, for he is slain in Hoxton fields by the hands of Benjamin Johnson bricklayer'.

Such was Henslowe's complaint of this 'hard and heavy news' in a letter to his son-in-law the actor Edward Alleyn on 26 September 1598, four days after the event. Spencer had received burial in his home parish of St Leonard's Shoreditch on 24 September as the parish record shows, and Jonson was confined in Newgate Prison unable to vindicate himself. Inevitably Jonson's version of events differed from this. His account to Drummond was that he had been challenged to appear, 'appealed to the fields' by his adversary. There, Spencer enjoyed not only the advantage of youth over Jonson; he was, so Jonson claimed, armed with a sword which was ten inches longer than Jonson's. With this he contrived to wound Jonson in the arm before the fatal thrust penetrated his guard and dispatched him.

There are hints here of Jonson's favourite pastime of heroic self-mythologising, in the emphasis on his own blamelessness and convincing victory against the odds. While later critics have agreed that the dead man was probably the aggressor, the contemporary law seized on the outcome as murder. When Jonson was brought to answer to the charge at the Old Bailey in the hearings which followed the Gaol Delivery of 6 October 1598, a bill in the Middlesex Sessions Rolls records that he pleaded guilty. In this extremity, 'almost at the gallows' in his own words to Drummond, he only saved his neck by availing himself of the archaic practice of pleading 'benefit of clergy'. Of all that he had to thank Westminster School for the ability to read now purchased his survival, for this medieval remnant of the legislation designed to protect the clergy took no cognisance of the illiterate. Jonson was later commended for his reading aloud by the Duchess of Newcastle. But he never read to better effect than when he 'called for the book' (that is, the Bible), got through his 'neck verse', and satisfied the authorities that he had 'read like a clerk' (HS I, 219).

Jonson had saved himself from the gibbet, but life alone was all that he managed to bring off. His goods were confiscated according to the law and he was also branded on the base of the left thumb. This was not just a piece of gratuitous cruelty, but a device to identify killers who had pleaded benefit of clergy; no man could use this plea more than once. It was then as a destitute and a branded murderer that Jonson emerged from Newgate, alive but hardly unscathed. He was changed, too, in another significant particular. He had, in a way that was to develop into a characteristic pattern, reacted to his ordeal with an increase of assertion and conviction. His worldly loss and suffering he converted to spiritual gain. While in prison he took the measured but extraordinary step of converting from Protestantism to Roman Catholicism, 'turning papist'.

The direct cause of Jonson's conversion was one of that heroic band of Roman Catholic priests then working in England under circumstances of the direst terror, each one part-missionary, part-guerilla, trained in France for the likelihood of martyrdom and a hideous death. As Jonson recalled it to Drummond 'then took he his religion by trust of a priest who visited him in prison' (HS I, 139). In view of his current danger and also the not-too-distant serious difficulty with the authorities over *The Isle of Dogs*, this was a radically eccentric step for him to take. It was, too, a strange and ironic reworking of his father's story, the 'grave minister' having 'lost all' in his struggles against a stifling and state-enforced religious orthodoxy. In deliberately choosing to return to the old faith, that which his father had fought against, Jonson consciously committed an act which in political terms was identified as subversive, and whose consequences (non-attendance at Anglican worship) were proscribed as criminal.

Even as he left the Old Bailey then Jonson knew that this was not to be his last brush with the law. But the risks he ran were not to daunt his newly-established faith. Even though it had been born under such perils it was not simply an emotional reaction to the nearness of death but endured throughout Jonson's artistic and intellectual prime – he remained, as he told Drummond, 'twelve years a papist'.

1598 had been a highly-charged year for Jonson. His involvement in his own affairs would inevitably have diminished the interest he paid to other events: the slow winding-down of Queen Elizabeth's former glory and the breaking out of the Irish revolt which was to bleed on until 1603. One occurrence of national importance did however make its way into his crowded consciousness. William Cecil Lord Burghley died, Elizabeth's 'Fox' and her sagest counsellor, treasurer and friend. Born in 1521 he had steered a remarkable course through seventy-eight trying years and had lived to enjoy the stability of which he was in a large part the architect. Jonson later paid tribute to Cecil in lines whose strength of feeling warms up the conventional phrases evoking the public *persona*:

> Cecil the grave, the wise, the great, the good:
>   What is there more that can ennoble blood?
> The orphan's pillar, the true subject's shield,
>   The poor's full storehouse, and just servant's field.
> The only faithful watchman of the realm,

That in all tempests never quit the helm;
But stood unshaken in his deeds and name,
And laboured in the work, not with the fame . . .

(*Underwood* 30)

This epigram was later inscribed upon a gold plate, and presented to Burghley's son when he was Treasurer in his turn, as Jonson himself noted.

1598 closed with one final theatrical flourish which cannot but have appealed to the buccaneer in Jonson. The Lord Chamberlain's Men, fresh from staging *Every Man In His Humour*, came at last to the end of the road with their difficult landlord Giles Alleyn whose awkwardness over the leasehold of their Theatre had enforced their temporary residence at the Curtain. On 28 December Cuthbert Burbage, who with his brother Richard was a principal sharer in the company originally formed by their father James, 'got intelligence' that something was afoot; the unscrupulous Alleyn was planning to repossess the Theatre and convert the wood and timbers of it to his own use. The two Burbages decided to anticipate this action.

On 28 December, therefore, Cuthbert, aided by Richard, a 'chief carpenter', and twelve various 'labourers and such as wrought for wages', gathered at The Theatre in Finsbury Fields. The story is taken up by the outraged and outwitted Alleyn himself. The party, he said,

riotously assembled themselves together, and then and there armed themselves with diverse and many unlawful and offensive weapons, as namely swords, daggers, bills [hatchets], axes and suchlike, and so armed did repair to the said theatre . . . then and there pulling, throwing down and breaking down the said Theatre in very outrageous, violent and riotous sort.[1]

Armed with their timbers and building materials the perpetrators made good their escape across the river. There in the more hospitable though less respectable Bankside they used this valuable salvage to erect what was to become the most famous of all Elizabethan theatres, the great Globe.

1598 had been a mixed year for Jonson with success and setback in equal quantities. The start of 1599 found him involved in having to straighten out difficulties arising now from past neglect. Towards the end of January 1599 he was prosecuted in the Court of the Queen's Bench by his creditor Robert Browne. The aggrieved actor had not managed to extract from Jonson the £10 borrowed the previous April although he had had him repeatedly dunned. The money was now eight months overdue, and losing patience Browne had Jonson arrested and locked up in the Marshalsea in Southwark; the same prison in which Jonson had been held during the *Isle of Dogs* investigation. At the trial in Westminster Hall Jonson gave his attorney no instructions, and the case went against him by default; he may well not have appeared in person to expend vain energy defending a case where he was so clearly in the wrong.

Jonson must have come up with the £10 which he owed Browne in order to obtain his release from prison. He also had £1 damages awarded against him although Browne complained that prosecuting the case had cost him £5. Jonson was not temperamentally a cheat – even at the worst he tried to live by certain standards of honour – and this bilking of a fellow-theatrical suggests that his financial affairs, already shaky in the earlier part of 1598 when the money was borrowed, had utterly collapsed following his imprisonment and the loss of all his goods in October. The record of this prosecution has a further point of interest concerning Jonson's personal life; he is described there as 'citizen and bricklayer of London'. Since at the murder trial three months before Johnson was only a 'yeoman' on the indictment, he had during this interval been made a freeman of the Company of Tilers and Bricklayers. However much he had hated the 'craft' of his stepfather, he had maintained his connection with it. Henslowe's description of him as 'Benjamin Johnson bricklayer' and the later insults which he picked up were firmly grounded in reality now.

Whatever his feelings about the 'bricklayer' Henslowe continued to employ him. August of 1599 found Jonson collaborating with Dekker on a tragedy, now lost, called *Page of Plymouth*; on the tenth of this month Henslowe advanced forty shillings to the pair 'in earnest of their book which they be a-writing'. On 3 September 1599 Jonson was commissioned with Dekker, Chettle, 'and other gentlemen' to furbish up the tragedy of *Robert II, King of Scots*; again the payment was forty shillings between the lot of them. If the canny Henslowe was biffing up suitable dramatic material against the looked-for Scottish accession, the King of Scotland was also studying for his new role. Among the publications of this year was a book that Jonson certainly read, the reflections of King James on the nature and duties of kingship, *Basilicon Doron*. At the end of September Jonson received another twenty shillings as a further advance on the same play; any estrangement following Spencer's death was decisively over.

Jónson's overwhelming preoccupation during 1599 must have been to make some money in order to repair the ruin of his worldly fortunes. Hack work for Henslowe might keep the wolf from the door but it could never do much more than that. Jonson's personal situation was thrown into sharp relief by the passing of the greatest poet of the previous generation, Edmund Spenser. Spenser died on 16

January 1599 in Westminster, and Jonson both heard and believed the contemporary gossip 'that the Irish, having robbed Spenser's goods and burned his house (and a little child new born) he and his wife escaped; and after, he died for lack of bread in King Street, and refused twenty pieces sent to him by my lord of Essex, and said he was sorry he had no time to spend them' (HS I, 137).

During the first half of 1599 Jonson was becoming more and more deeply embroiled in the circle of professional writers which centred on Henslowe and his productions. Yet at the same time a determination was hardening that he must find another direction. This emerges clearly from his course of action. He decided to build upon the good fortune of *Every Man In His Humour* and attempt a sequel. The result, not so much a sequel as a companion piece and very different from its begetter, was *Every Man Out of His Humour*. The creation of this play was Jonson's main work in the second half of 1599. But it was more than just another drama. External events combined to lend dramatic productions of this period a more than theatrical significance.

The same fear that had led the secular authorities to restrain *The Isle of Dogs* was at work also within the church. Religious leaders had their own reasons to check the swelling spirit of criticism and dissent, and their disapproval fastened upon those whom they identified as the chief trouble-makers. On 1 June 1599 the Archbishop of Canterbury and the Bishop of London issued an order against the production of formal verse satire. This prohibited further printing of all work by Marston, Hall and Davies (Jonson's former acquaintance Nashe was also mentioned) and ordered that all copies of their work that could be found were to be brought to the Bishop to be burned. As a further precaution the Church Fathers decreed that 'no satires or epigrams be printed hereafter'. On 4 June a list was published of books which had been burned in accordance with the decree.

This action was directed at the producers of satirical attacks in verse, then reaching something of an epidemic. But a literary fashion is not to be arrested in midstream. The intervention of the Church authorities did not suppress satire, but redirected its flow. Jonson began work on *Every Man Out Of His Humour* soon after the restraining order of the Bishops. The drama had become the obvious vehicle for what poetry was no longer allowed to say. Jonson's new work then was more than just another play. It was a conscious attempt to give satire a dramatic form. It was by extension, as Jonson interpreted it, his contribution to the education of the time in manners, morals, stagecraft, and the writing of comedy. Its purpose was frankly didactic, its targets set far and wide, and its aim assured.

As this suggests, *Every Man Out of His Humour* contrasts strongly with its predecessor – the two plays are in fact linked only by their titles. In place of the good-humoured, rather old-fashioned characters and situations of its immediate predecessor, Jonson turned in a modernistic, experimental, plotless dramatic exercise whose central character, Macilente, is the embodiment of a malignant spirit of detraction, and envious 'humour'. Two futher experimental devices also helped to make the play remarkable. Jonson introduced a '*grex*' or Chorus, brought on between certain acts or scenes, to comment upon the action and to assess its correspondence with the rules of comedy as laid down by the ancients. More controversial than this was the play's original ending, which introduced Queen Elizabeth on to the stage at the climax of the action, as the object whose powerful effect cures Macilente from the poison of his envious humour. This created widespread adverse reaction, as implying disrespect to Elizabeth by impersonating her upon the public stage. Jonson, typically, was unrepentant, and firmly denied that his climactic piece of business was offensive:

> There was nothing, in his examined opinion, that could more near or truly exemplify the power and strength of her invaluable virtues, than the working of so perfect a miracle on so opposed a spirit, who not only persisted in his humour, but was now to come to the court with a purposed resolution (his soul as it were, new dressed in envy) to malign at anything that should front him; when suddenly (against expectation and all steel of his malice) the very wonder of her presence strikes him to the earth dumb and astonished. (HS III, 602–3)

This ending provided no problems when the company came to perform *Every Man Out Of His Humour* at court before the Queen during the Christmas season 1599–1600; it consorted well with the kind of compliment traditional in court performances, whose primary function was to praise and delight the monarch. But Jonson had to provide an alternative ending for the public theatre. How either of these two *finales* went is now unknown since all that he retained for the printed version of the play was the final speech in praise of Elizabeth.

Every Man Out of His Humour is a work of far greater significance in the development of Jonson's career than has generally been recognised. This was the first of his plays to cause him trouble with his fellow-theatricals and with theatre audiences. The previous brushes with the civic authorities were an occupational hazard for the dramatists of the period and various others besides Jonson endured scrutiny and suspicion. Only he of all the contemporary playwrights contrived to irritate and alienate professional colleagues and spectators too. The first hint of this is to be found in Jonson's account of the reception of the play; in his own words, 'many censures fluttered about it' (HS

III, 427). He had attempted something abrasively new and harshly unfamiliar and paid the price in terms of audience reaction. It proved no deterrent. From now on he never shrank from courting unpopularity if he was convinced on artistic grounds of what he was doing. *indly*

More important even than this is the critical point marked by *Every Man Out Of His Humour* at which Jonson's sense of a play in the theatre, and his awareness of it as a literary object, begin to divide. This was the first of his productions in any vein that he chose to publish. The likelihood is, given his combative personality and inability to tolerate being put in the wrong, that he decided to publish the play in order to quash the 'censures' it had attracted in performance. As he said himself the aim of publication was 'to give all leave and leisure to judge with distinction' (HS, III, 427). Underlying this apparently innocuous statement is an enormous confidence that the play would stand up to an extended and careful scrutiny.

It is difficult for modern readers to appreciate how brave and innovative this decision of Jonson's was. The drama in performance is the only literary form which permits of no checking up; the spectator cannot turn back to a previous episode, recall a scene or character to arrive at a considered opinion of its merits. Once launched it is in continuous flow, and only memory afterwards will imperfectly enshrine what happened. All Elizabethan dramatists take advantage of this fact, capitalising upon it to cover up lapses of concentration, carelessness, or downright shoddiness in construction. In offering his plays for close study, Jonson showed supreme confidence in his own dramaturgic and literary skills.

He further made another radical innovation by this action, the claim for a play text to be considered as a work of literature. *Every Man Out Of His Humour* originates Jonson's specifically literary career. The title pages of the three quarto editions all bear the words 'as it was first composed by the author, Ben Jonson, containing more than hath been publicly spoken or acted'. This demonstrates conclusively that Jonson was interested as no other dramatist had been so intensely before, in restoring and establishing the integrity of the text of his play which he conceived as something distinct from the stage performance that it had received. His addition to the play text of short character sketches of the *personae* also indicates his strong sense of the play's being read and studied by those who had not seen it on the stage as much as by those who had.

The publishing history of *Every Man Out Of His Humour* fully confirmed Jonson's faith in its prospects. The play text proved to be very much in demand, and it went through three editions between 8 April 1600, when it was entered on the Stationers' Register, and the end of the year.[2] Jonson's awareness of this success is evinced in his decision to publish both an earlier and a later play as soon as possible thereafter; the publication of *Every Man In His Humour* and of *Cynthia's Revels* was planned with title pages of the same format in the same year of 1600. From being a Henslowe hack, he had blossomed into a literary figure – more, into a 'humorist'.

For it is by this title that Jonson now gradually became known, following the popularity of the two 'humour' plays. He had decisively broken out of the mould of earlier dramatic forms and conventions; he had made himself into a leader, not a follower, of theatrical fashion. He had created the comedy of 'humours' and turned it into a vehicle for the kind of stinging satire forbidden in verse – the title page of the quarto edition carries the first recorded description by Jonson of one of his plays as a 'comical satire'. He had used it too as a personal instrument of definition, working through an analysis of the nature of poetry, the duties of the artist, and his relation to the audience. He had made it his task to 'strip the ragged follies of the time', as the main character declares, and was to find this role of humorist and satirist an all-engrossing one; it was to dominate the dramatic production of the next years of Jonson's career.

This then was the strange and demanding play which London theatre-goers were surprised by at the end of 1599. During the summer the Lord Chamberlain's Men had moved into their splendid new Globe theatre and *Every Man Out Of His Humour* was one of the first plays to be staged there.[3] With such a company, Burbage playing the lead as in *Every Man In His Humour*, and in such a place, the auspices for attention and comment if not for unalloyed success were good. And although the performance attracted some 'censures' the reception overall must have been good enough to encourage Jonson to think of publication.

As Jonson's professional career was gathering momentum so his personal life showed some significant developments. In early December of this year another son was born to him, a brother for three-year-old Benjamin. The new baby was baptised Joseph, a name redolent with biblical significance – in Genesis 42 and 46 Joseph is not only the brother of Benjamin but his only full brother of all Jacob's sons, as both were born to the beloved wife Rachel. The christening took place on 9 December 1599 at St Giles Cripplegate, the next parish to Shoreditch where Jonson had earlier been working with the Lord Chamberlain's Men at the Curtain theatre. It is also noteworthy that in August and September of 1599 Jonson had been collaborating with Thomas Dekker, and St Giles was Dekker's parish; he had his own daughters baptised there in 1594, 1598 and 1602.

It is also possible to recover something of Jonson's social life at this time, his personal circle outside the theatre world. Doubtless it was his stage work that had enabled Jonson to make these contacts – it is hardly likely to have been in bricklaying – but the Elizabethan theatre was not a self-contained unit and he moved through it to form an interesting range of acquaintance. Foremost among these were the law students of the Inns of Court, whose combination of ferocious intellectuality with gross licence found a ready echo in Jonson's own temperament. Most of the Inns of Court men outlived their undergraduate wildness to become pillars of the law and the state; as Jonson later wrote in the 1616 dedication of *Every Man Out Of His Humour*, 'when I wrote this poem [play] I had friendship with divers in your societies, who, as they were great names in learning, so they were no less examples of living'. Among Inns of Court members of the time were John Hoskyns, adopted by Jonson as his intellectual 'father', and the gifted and good-looking Richard Martin, the social leader of the group. This was also the time when Jonson probably met John Donne (who like Jonson himself was still struggling to make his mark on an indifferent world) and Donne's 'chamber-fellow' Christopher Brooke. Later Jonson was to boast of himself at this time as one who 'keeps gallants company';[4] and he described the Inns of Court as 'the noblest nurseries of humanity and liberty in the kingdom' (Dedication to the 1616 version of *Every Man Out Of His Humour*).

As this suggests, Jonson was moving into wider spheres than any he had previously known. In addition to the company of the fledgling lawyers he was making himself known in more elevated circles still. At the end of 1599 he noted the death of a woman who had had more than her share of griefs to bear and had found the burden beyond her strength. Within the space of a few months Margaret Radcliffe had suffered the loss of four of her brothers; Sir William and Sir Alexander were slain in Ireland in 1598 and 1599, and Edmund and Thomas died of fever in Flanders in 1599. Margaret pined away, refused food, and expired of her grief on 10 November 1599.

The Radcliffes were a titled family, and Margaret had been a favourite Maid of Honour of Queen Elizabeth. Yet Jonson knew them all, and wrote an epigram (93), to the surviving brother John. This movement into court circles and the acquaintance of the gentry was an uphill journey for one of his background and trade. But it was one that he was determined to make. He therefore used his poetic skills to smooth his way with such well-phrased and well-timed utterances as this acrostic to commemorate the passing of the unfortunate girl:

M arble, weep, for thou dost cover
A dead beauty underneath thee,
R ich as nature could bequeath thee;
G rant then no rude hands remove her.
A ll the gazers on the skies
R ead not in fair heaven's story
E xpresser truth or truer glory
T han they might in her bright eyes.

R are as wonder was her wit,
A nd like nectar ever flowing;
T ill time, strong by her bestowing,
C onquered hath both life and it.
L ife, whose grief was out of fashion
I n these times; few have so rued
F ate, in a brother. To conclude,
F or wit, feature, and true passion,
E arth, thou hast not such another.

(Epigram 40)

Jonson's determination to obtain recognition outside the limited world of the theatre was not only confined to attempts to win patronage by his verse. He began at this time to attract the attention of the *literati*, and to take the first steps towards becoming the presiding genius of English letters. This phase saw the first of his tributes to the work of others, a form that he was to become highly proficient in. He wrote a commendatory epistle to a botanical emblem book, Thomas Palmer's *The Spirit of Trees and Herbs*. Palmer had been the Principal of Gloucester Hall and Tutor in Rhetoric at Oxford University, until deprived of these posts because of his Roman Catholicism. Did Jonson get to know of Palmer and his work through his own membership of that harassed faith?

Jonson's first ventures outside his previously known worlds of private study or public theatre are recorded in his occasional verse, his epistles and epigrams. These are also the record of the growth of a series of truly outstanding friendships. From these beginnings he built up a quite unparalleled acquaintance, and the future range and richness of his friendships are already suggested here. Jonson had a genius for it, akin to his genius for poetry, as he began to discover; and from now until the time of his death, he was never without the support of someone who loved him.

CHAPTER 4

THE 'WAR OF THE THEATRES'

B UT as fast as Jonson was making friends he was also making
enemies. *Every Man Out Of His Humour*, intended to elevate
Jonson's claim to high seriousness as a writer and thinker, was
received in some quarters on a more personal level. One individual
was prepared to express his admiration for Jonson. John Weever, in
his *Epigrams in the Oldest Cut and the Newest Fashion* (1599), discovered in
Jonson 'so rich a style and wondrous gallant spirit' that he concluded,
'such wits must be admired'. Others did not hold this view, feeling
rather strongly that 'such wits' should be taken down from their
self-erected eminence.

Every Man Out Of His Humour seems to have inaugurated that
curious sequence of events which literary historians have come to call
the 'War of the Theatres' or the 'Stage Quarrel'. After the appearance
of this play Jonson became involved in a bitter and protracted
wrangle with some of his fellow-dramatists, notably John Marston
and Thomas Dekker. This personal dispute became by virtue of the
protagonists' occupation and position in London life a public matter.
All three eagerly embraced the opportunity to incorporate their
resentment into their plays, and over a period of some two years
London theatre-goers were treated to assorted sallies in this 'war'.

The source of the disagreement between the three men is a mystery.
Henslowe's records show that during 1599 Jonson had collaborated
with Dekker on two plays. Yet shortly afterwards Dekker was ranged
against him in a way that is difficult to explain. Dekker was not a
particularly obvious enemy for Jonson; indeed on a superficial level
there are many correspondences and shared experiences between
them. Both were born in or close to the year 1572; both are thought
to have 'trailed a pike' in the Low Countries; both first gained
employment from Henslowe and appear in his diary for the first time

in 1598. In that year too both men had known imprisonment; February of 1598 had found Dekker in the Counter, doubtless for debt, his besetting problem. Both were named by Francis Meres as tragedians in that same year although in both cases these early works were not sufficiently valued by their creators to ensure their preservation. Moreover Dekker was constantly referred to by contemporaries as a good-humoured and kindly man – even Jonson conceded in *Poetaster* that he was 'a simple honest fellow'. Yet somehow he contrived to enrage Jonson on personal, professional, moral and artistic grounds.

Marston's early part in the quarrel is likewise obscure. Before the hostilities Marston's affinity with Jonson is more apparent than any dissent between them. Like Jonson, Marston had made a stir in 1598 with his tortured but powerful satirical poems *The Metamorphosis of Pygmalion's Image* and *The Scourge of Villany*. He had engaged in a quarrel with the Cambridge satirist Joseph Hall whose exchanges had become so disturbingly vitriolic that they had precipitated the counteraction of the Bishops in restraining all verse satire. He shared with Jonson the experience of provoking the retaliation of the authorities upon his work and the free expression of his ideas. And as a satirist Marston shared many of Jonson's preconceptions. One of the 'University wits', an Oxford graduate, Marston was keenly alive to the satire of the ancient world. At times he very consciously modelled himself on Jonson, imitating both his methods and his style. But what the two men had most in common was the volatile combination of touchiness and truculence. Jonson later laid the blame for the origin of the quarrel at Marston's door, claiming to Drummond that the 'beginnings' of it occurred when 'Marston represented him in the stage' (HS I, 40). Which of Marston's plays caused the offence?

Ironically, it was one in which Marston may have intended to compliment Jonson, rather than to insult him. In the late summer of 1599 the boys of St Paul's presented *Histriomastix*, an old play that Marston had refurbished for them. Marston adapted one character, a Stoic professor of the arts, into a portrait resembling Jonson. This Chrysogonus is a 'translating scholar', a satirist and epigrammatist; he is a dramatist who demands £10 for a play and rails against inferior playwrights. Other objects of his scorn include the changeability of the despised multitude, a known Jonsonian *bête noire*.

Chrysogonus clearly evokes Jonson in some particulars. In representing a literary man Marston consciously or unconsciously drew on his knowledge of Jonson's behaviour and attitudes. But he reckoned without Jonson's hypersensitivity and irascible temperament; Drummond summed this up as 'jealous of every word and action of those about him', and concluded 'he interpreteth best sayings and deeds often to the worst' (HS I, 151). Perhaps Jonson simply did not like to feel that he was being 'staged', however well-meant the gesture. And despite his frequent protestations of impersonality in the classical mode he was not above descending to the personal in his satire. He struck back. For the character of Clove, a foolish fop in his next play *Every Man Out Of His Humour*, he drew upon Marston's speech and vocabulary.

Clove is not an attack on Marston himself. The ridicule of these few phrases is besides only one of Jonson's satiric targets. But even one sting of Jonson's lash must have been painful. Incited by this and possibly also by other passages of which nothing is now known, Marston declared war. As the century turned this skirmish evolved inescapably into open and wounding conflict. Marston, Jonson and Dekker were the principal but not the only figures. Some time in 1599 or 1600 Jonson revamped his earlier play *The Case Is Altered* to have a fling at the dramatist and 'pageant-poet' Anthony Munday.

Ironically this public and degraded debate occurred as Jonson was making headway in more rarefied circles altogether. Jonson had found a contact in a world far removed from the hurly-burly of the theatre. This was the Lady Elizabeth Rutland, daughter of the great romantic hero of the generation of Queen Elizabeth, Sir Philip Sidney. Sidney's *Apology For Poetry* had been among the formative texts of Jonson's literary apprenticeship, and nothing he found in the daughter diminished the respect he felt for the father.

The Lady Elizabeth had married early in 1599 and Jonson inaugurated the new century by sending her, on New Year's Day 1600, the characteristically Jonsonian present of a poem. The tradition of exchanging gifts on New Year's Day rather than at Christmas stretched back to the Middle Ages. A literary refinement of this custom was the sending of New Year poems. Jonson's offering to the Countess of Rutland bears all the marks of a carefully-wrought tribute, notwithstanding the fact that he describes its composition as 'hasty'. Beginning with an attack upon 'almight gold' as a prime motive force in life, the poet continues simply:

> I, that have none to send you, send you verse.
>   A present which, if elder writs rehearse
> The truth of times, was once of more esteem
>   Than this, our gilt, nor golden age can deem . . .
> With you, I know, my offering will find grace.
>   For what a sin against your father's spirit
> Were it to think that you should not inherit
>   His love unto the muses, when his skill
> Almost you have, or may have, when you will?
>   (*The Forest* 12, 19–24)

As a poet, then, Jonson offered his art in the expectation of an informed and sensitive response by a woman doubly gifted with the inheritance of her father's spirit and her own poetic gift. He is not merely flattering here; his regard was never slavish. His admiration of Sidney, although strong, was tempered by the opinion that Sidney was in breach of the rule of 'decorum' by 'making every one speak as well as himself' in his work. And many years later, long after the Countess had died and was far beyond the reach of earthly praise, Jonson told Drummond that she was 'nothing inferior to her father . . . in poesy' (HS I, 138). From the time and place of this compliment, as well as its position among Jonson's ample condemnation of other English poets, it is a reasonable inference that he meant it.

Jonson's poem employs a poetic figure which recurs frequently in his non-dramatic verse. The lady is assured that the gift is more than one of poetry pure and simple, but will also guarantee immortality for the recipient. The verse tribute will confer upon her that eternal fame that nothing else can afford. In developing this theme Jonson introduces another court lady to whom he was becoming known at this time, Lucy Countess of Bedford. He describes her as 'that other star' besides the Countess of Rutland in the court heavens. This lady, so Jonson states, 'hath won [his] grateful soul' through the 'timely favours' she had shown to his 'muse'. He had already employed 'some happy hours' in repaying her interest with occasional poems. These women, according to Jonson, deserved not the shallow treatment of 'tinkling rhymes of commonplaces', but those filled with 'high and noble matter'. He ended his New Year epistle to the Countess of Rutland by wishing her that the next twelvemonth would fulfil her mariage in the time-honoured way. He offers 'my best of wishes – may you bear a son'.

Parallel with these movements in Jonson's personal life were certain important developments in the theatre at large. 1600 opened promisingly when in the spring Henslowe and his son-in-law Alleyn began work on the Fortune theatre, intended to rival the great Globe. But there were further innovations yet to come. Enterprising Elizabethan moneymakers saw excellent prospects in reorganising the companies of boy players. The Children of the Chapel Royal had had a long and varied history when their fortunes took a new turn; on 2 September 1600 Henry Evans signed a lease of the Blackfriars theatre for twenty-one years with the intention of re-forming the Children of the Chapel Royal and getting their play-acting activities on a firmer footing. Concurrent with this revamping of the 'Blackfriars boys' as they were known was the revival of the Children of St Paul's.

The re-formation of these two companies of boy players led to important changes in the theatrical world. Plays were presented in the evening as against the daytime, daylight performances of the open-air public playhouses; and their presentation in smaller auditoria at rates of admission about three times higher than for the public theatres understandably created a more élite audience in which courtiers, students of the inns of court and other youthful or well-established sophisticates predominated. All these background circumstances contrived to fuel the 'War of the Theatres', and to give it both a direction and platform. The demand of the new companies was for a repertory of comedies with topical impact and satiric bite. The material lay close to hand. Within a few months of the production of *Every Man Out Of His Humour* in late 1599, Marston delivered his riposte in the first half of 1600. His play *Jack Drum's Entertainment*[1] was performed by the newly-activated Children of St Paul's, and one of the characters is a clear attack upon Jonson.

Brabant Senior is best described as a picture of Jonson as he appeared to his enemies. He is a 'censurer'. He jests at and makes fools of gulls (i, 353–428). He criticises all the literary men of his day but never himself (iv, 37–52). Certain passages very clearly score off Jonson:

> . . those bombast wits
> That are puffed up with arrogant conceit
> Of their own worth; as if omnipotence
> Had hoised them up to such unequalled height
> That they surveyed our spirits with an eye
> Only create to censure from above.
>
> (iv, 316-321)

At the end of the play the character is arraigned in terms which similarly evoke Jonson for us:

> Why shouldst thou take felicity to gull
> Good honest souls? And in thy arrogance
> And glorious ostentation of thy wit
> Think God infused all perfection
> Into thy soul alone, and made the rest
> For thee to laugh at? Now, you censurer,
> Be the ridiculous object of our mirth . . .
>
> (v, 16–21)

The character of Brabant Senior is not at one with Jonson's at all points. He is castigated as the 'prince of fools, unequalled idiot', something which could never be accurately laid to Jonson's charge. And in particular the plot features an intrigue in which Brabant tries to play a trick on another by introducing his own wife as a courtesan and gets roundly cuckolded for his pains. Since almost the only thing known of Jonson's wife is that she was 'honest' (chaste), there is unlikely to be any personal application in this part of the characterisation. Jonson is attacked through Brabant Senior more by some suggestive introduction of tones and techniques than by direct impersonation. But the slur is hardly likely to have been received with complaisance for all that.

Jack Drum's Entertainment launched the 'War of the Theatres' well on its way. This is a far more exceptionable representation of Jonson than that in *Histriomastix* and it was after this that Jonson felt free to respond in kind. His next play which followed Marston's in the autumn of 1600 was designed to incorporate two characters who were specifically formed to ridicule Marston and Dekker. It is possible that these were not Jonson's only targets in *Cynthia's Revels* – Jonson designated it, like *Every Man Out Of His Humour*, a 'comical satire', and critics have spotted other contemporary figures among the caricatures – but these were the two who rose most obviously to the bait. For these were the most clearly recognisable by theatre audiences when the play was staged by the rival company, the Children of the Chapel, at the Blackfriars.

Jonson had had the closing months of 1600 to work up his counterblast to Marston. When the new play *Cynthia's Revels* was staged by the Children of the Chapel at the Blackfriars around the turn of the year,[2] he had the satisfaction of having created two offensive but highly recognisable portraits of his antagonists. Marston was pilloried as Hedon (Pleasure), a shallow voluptuary, while Dekker appeared as his foul-mouthed down-at-heel side-kick Anaides. These are not of course the only characters or satirical targets in the play. But they are rendered with vigour and even today can still attract attention, while in their own day they certainly made the impact that Jonson desired.

Jonson had other aims in view too. This was the first occasion that he had worked for the re-formed boys' company and the move to the private theatre had certain definite advantages for him. In the public theatre the writer traditionally held a subordinate role both in the company and in the production of the play. Among the boys there was the opportunity for the dramatist to be actively engaged in the presentation and direction of his work. Jonson's life-long struggle for creative autonomy was more satisfied by this greater artistic freedom and control. His relish of the situation emerges clearly from the Induction to *Cynthia's Revels* where he makes two of the boy players quarrel over who shall speak the Prologue:

BOY 2:   . . . I think I have the most right to it, I am sure I studied it first.

BOY 3:   That's all one, if the author think I can speak it better.

(lines 5–8)

As this suggests, the boy players took their work seriously, and achieved a notably high standard of performance. Their quality is attested not only by the famous reference in *Hamlet* (II.ii.338–343), but also by the playwright Middleton's advice to a London gallant, to 'call in at the Blackfriars, where he should see a nest of boys able to ravish a man'.[3] Two of the young players in particular attracted Jonson's attention and won his regard. Salomon Pavy had the task of playing one of the main characters, Anaides, in *Cynthia's Revels*; although he was only eleven when Jonson met him, he had been on the stage for some time and his speciality lay in playing old men. Another 'leading man' of the boys' company was Nathan Field, later described by Jonson in *Bartholomew Fair* as the 'best actor.'

The more tender side of Jonson's personality comes out in his relations with these boys. Field in particular became a special *protégé*, and as such drew on Jonson's caring and his pedagogic impulses at the same time. Jonson told Drummond that 'Nid Field was his scholar, and he had read to him the satires of Horace and some epigrams of Martial' (HS I, 137). Despite his impressment in the despised career of player (he had been 'taken up' for the Children of the Chapel out of grammar school) Field was the son of an educated father and seems to have had a genuine desire to be educated. His early acquaintance with Jonson ripened despite the fifteen-year age gap into a life-long affection, as Jonson's had for Camden earlier in his life. Field later wrote commendatory verses for *Volpone* and *Catiline*, in the first describing Jonson as his 'worthiest master' but in the second as his 'worthy and beloved friend'.

To work with this talented and interesting company also answered another of Jonson's long-term aims, his desire to raise the status of the poet. The audiences of the Blackfriars, both more selected and selective, held out greater promise in this regard than the public of the Globe. Jonson could address himself there to the University wits, the Inns of Court men, the fashionable and sophisticated elements of London life. He could thereby hope to escape some of the odium which attached to writing for the theatres of the common people and appeal directly to a more elevated society which would respect his role as poet within it.

This desire seemed to be gaining some satisfaction when *Cynthia's Revels* received a performance before 'Cynthia' herself, Queen Elizabeth. On 6 January 1601 the Master of the Children of the Chapel took his boys to court to put on the play there. He had £5 for what is described as 'a show with music and special songs prepared for the

55

purpose' (HS IX, 188). There is some evidence, however, to suggest that the royal performance was not an unqualified success. By its title alone with the flattering reference to the Queen in her quasi-divine, heavily-mythologised role of the Virgin Goddess, the piece was an obvious bid for royal favour. Yet in no other way does it pay tribute to the Queen's known interests and preferences. On the contrary, it insists through the characters of Hedon and Anaides in parading Jonson's own undignified squabbles before Her Majesty and accompanies this personal satire with generalised but pointed satire upon courtiers and court affectations. Would it be surprising if this unflattering picture of courtly festivities ending in penance was not well received? Dekker shortly was able to indulge in some jibes at Jonson's expense, enjoying the moment 'when your players are misliked at court' (*Satiromastix* V.ii.324).

Jonson still retained enough faith in his play to want to publish it and it was entered on the Stationers' Register that spring on 23 May 1601. But not for the first time his wit had out-run his judgment. His rooted conviction that he was in the right blinded him to other more politic considerations. He had underestimated too his enemies' power of retort. Within a matter of a few months at most Marston struck back. His counter-attack *What You Will*, performed in March or April of 1601, figures a satiric poet who is recognisably Jonson as his detractors saw him. Jonson could hardly have relished the portrait which emerges.

For Lampatho in *What You Will* is a big-headed buffoon who reads his own verses aloud and begs for compliments on them. He has a foolish follower Simplicius Faber whose grovelling admiration is the mark of his dependency. Lampatho is poor and accepts money from others with unbecoming eagerness. His ready protestations of love for others are rapidly succeeded by curses and threats against them. He rails at the world, but loves his own jokes. Jonson is even arraigned for his appearance; he is always dressed in black, which heightens his 'tabor-faced look' – moon-faced, in modern English. At the end of the play the coarse satiric scholar is re-educated in civil and courteous ways. He is taught true humility and a proper estimation of himself (IV.i.370 ff). This disrespectful portrayal added fuel to Jonson's anger, but it was already burning strongly enough. The 'War of the Theatres' was moving to its climax. After completing *Cynthia's Revels* Jonson had wind of a projected riposte from Dekker this time and had set himself to forestall it. He was therefore at work shortly after *Cynthia's Revels* on what he clearly intended to be his final and crushing utterance. Writing at what was for him an unusually hot pace, Jonson completed *Poetaster* in only fifteen weeks. In the early summer of 1601, May or June, Jonson launched his counter-blow, *Poetaster*, upon the London public.

When *Poetaster* was performed by the boys' company at the Black-friars, Jonson described it in the Prologue as his 'forced defence' against 'base detractors and illiterate apes'. But by adopting this lofty attitude to his opponents and rivals he played straight into their hands. He put his revenge into the form of a classical fable, introducing characters like the poet Ovid and Caesar's daughter Julia. Other stars of the classical firmament also appear, like Virgil and Augustus Caesar. Jonson's decision to introduce himself into this exalted company was hubristic to say the least; and to cast himself in the role of his beloved Horace was vainglorious in the extreme.

This egregious piece of self-flattery was the more outrageous in comparison with the rough and contemptuous handling meted out to Marston and Dekker. Marston is projected as gushing, pretentious and inane, Dekker as thick and verminous to boot; each in his own way is intellectually and personally despicable. At the end of the play the Horace character is empowered by Augustus Caesar to administer an emetic to Crispinus (Marston); and in a violent episode of metaphoric action Crispinus vomits up on stage all the tortuous words and phrases that were a hall-mark of Marston's writing, the 'spurious snotteries' that insulted Jonson's conception of the plain style.

These powerful savage caricatures are instinct with Jonson's disgust and his conviction of his own rightness. But they were not the only elements in the play with the ability to bite. *Poetaster* was Jonson's third 'comical satire' and the one in which he most thoroughly exploited the implications of this generic title. Other targets of his satiric attention include the professions of soldiering, acting and the law. The satire here is to be distinguished from that on Crispinus and Demetrius Fannius (Dekker); it is more generalised and spasmodic, with the attack conducted rather through types than on individuals.

But in choosing to present his braggart soldier and his foolish actor as types, Jonson could not complain if his contemporaries found them typical. Wielding his satirist's scourge too freely, he succeeded in offending widely across the board of London public opinion. For those stung were not only his direct antagonists, Marston and Dekker. Jonson's generalised remarks and character-types enraged various important and influential sections of the population, especially members of the law. Others who felt sufficient grounds for resentment were representatives of the military and the acting professions.

Jonson had offended in so many disparate quarters that he could not hope to get away with his attack. Reaction was immediate. He came under so much pressure from the disgruntled parties that he was forced to compose an *Apologetical Dialogue*. This debate in blank verse between the author and others on the laws of satire and the merits of his position was added on to the original play and performed as an epilogue. It only succeeded in compounding the original offence since as an apology it reads like a defiant restatement of all the prior insults. According to Jonson, it was only once spoken on the public stage: 'all the answer I ever gave, to sundry impotent libels then cast out . . . against me, and this play'. But its reverberations were felt for all that.

Jonson could never sincerely apologise, perhaps because he could never whole-heartedly accept that he had been in the wrong. This unrepentant assertion of authorial defiance was an act either of courage and principle or of foolish bravado, given that Jonson had already twice in his short career felt the power of the state over the individual.

Official retribution now roused took its suppressive course. There were no further performances of the *Apologetical Dialogue* and when Jonson came to publish *Poetaster* the following year he was restrained 'by authority' from including the *Dialogue* with the play text. More seriously there was a threat of legal action. The authorities did not accept his protestations in the *Dialogue* that he had been the innocent party in the 'War of the Theatres', provoked by hostile poetasters until he had reluctantly been driven to his own defence. He was identified as the trouble-maker, and called before 'the greatest justice' in the land, the Lord Chief Justice Sir John Popham, who held office between 1592 and 1607 during which time he made his name a byword for severity.

But for a bricklayer Jonson had powerful friends. He was protected by the intervention of one of his Inns of Court contacts, the lawyer Richard Martin of the Middle Temple. Although now well on the way to what was to be a distinguished law career Martin had in former days known to his personal cost the tension of irreconcilable difference. The sudden collapse of the close friendship between Martin and Sir John Davies into Davies's violent unprovoked assault on him with a cudgel was one of the famous stories of the time, and Davies paid heavily, if not permanently, for injuring a man who was universally well regarded for his warmth of nature, personal beauty and graceful speech. He was expelled from the Middle Temple, imprisoned in the Tower, and subsequently banished from London for two years. Eventually however, Davies recovered from his peccadillo to become Lord Chief Justice.

Martin undertook to speak for the play and its author and to guarantee its innocence before the wrath of aroused authority, a service later acknowledged gratefully by Jonson by his dedication of the play in the 1616 Folio to this good angel. Martin's sweetness of speech and personality succeeded in smoothing things over, and there were no further proceedings against the troublesome Ben. The authorities however had some cause for concern. The dispute had by now outgrown its original limits and become a general point of interest. Outsiders were keen to get in on the act that was attracting so much attention. In August of 1601 an unknown poet published *The Whipping of the Satyr* in which the author, one 'W.I.', attacked Jonson and Marston as 'the Humorist' and 'the Satyrist' respectively.

The state authorities were not the only people concerned at this uncontrolled upsurge of satirical activity. Nicholas Breton indicated the feelings of some of London's literary circle with his attempt to placate all parties in the conciliatory *No Whipping No Tripping But A Kind of Friendly Snipping*. This intervention from one who had reason to wish Jonson well – Jonson had contributed an epistle commendatory on the publication of Breton's *Melancholic Humours* the year before – was entered on the Stationers' Register on 16 September 1601. But retaliation was inevitable within the satiric world. The anonymous retort to *The Whipping of the Satyr* was entered on the Stationers' Register just two months later, on 16 November 1601. Entitled *The Whipper of the Satyr His Penance in a White Sheet*, it may have been produced by Marston. But during 1601 currents of ill-will were running strongly and in a variety of directions; several hands could have penned it.

The players of course took their own revenge in their own way. As the spring had been enlivened by the appearance of *Poetaster* so the opening weeks of the autumn season provided a malicious treat for audiences in the shape of *Satiromastix*. This play, 'the whipping of the satirist' as its name means translated, was the response of the Lord Chamberlain's Men to their insults and injuries at Jonson's hands. It marks too the first clear appearance of Dekker in the 'War'. Jonson had of course identified him as an enemy along with Marston long before. But this is the first occasion on which Dekker took any action now known to deserve the appellation.

Dekker indeed protested, in the terms which Jonson had used (less convincingly) in the *Apologetical Dialogue*, that he had only been drawn into the quarrel in order to defend his own reputation. Jonson had undoubtedly slandered Dekker grossly. Dekker's fertility of invention and speed of composition had elicited from Jonson in *Poetaster* the caustic tribute that 'he hath one of the most overflowing rank wits in [London]' (III.iv.iii). 'Demetrius Fannius', as Jonson named Dekker, would libel any man for money. The portrait is a compound of coarseness, venality and stupidity. Dekker had reached the point at which he could no longer pocket up these slurs.

Jonson had informed his public in *Poetaster* that Dekker, a freelance writer like himself, had already been hired by the Lord Chamberlain's Men to write a play which should mount a satiric attack upon him. But the text of Dekker's *Satiromastix* makes it plain that Jonson's apprehension was not at that stage coming true. Dekker did not embark upon his retort until after the appearance of *Poetaster*. His play is full of reminiscences of and hits at Jonson's in a way that clearly demonstrates that Jonson's attack was Dekker's springboard, even though Jonson believed that it was the other way round. Nor does *Satiromastix* have the feel of a long-meditated and well-polished personal attack by Dekker. On the contrary the play is evidently one which has been hastily codged up to fit the needs of a pressing occasion. In its original form (and certainly under another name) Dekker had written a half-finished tragedy with a comic sub-plot. Its intrinsic feebleness offers a strong reason why Dekker had laid it aside. Onto this he had now grafted various new scenes, in which Jonson, under his own self-style of the great 'Horace', is made the subject of satire and ridicule. Numerous borrowings drawn from other plays in the 'War' act as aids to identification of the characters and issues. Jonson's own Captain Tucca, for instance, is transplanted whole from *Poetaster*, while Bubo links with Faber from *What You Will*. As finished then the play has three very distinct and totally inconsonant elements which indicate how Dekker worked up his revenge during the summer of 1601.

The staging of *Satiromastix* in the late summer of 1601 brought the 'War of the Theatres' to its climax. In writing the 'Horace' scenes Dekker permitted himself the luxury of amply fulfilling Jonson's baleful view of his capacity for hostility, and the picture of Jonson which emerges is a highly effective piece of hatchet work. Dekker's Horace is a pretentious oaf, who insists on reciting his verses aloud but will accept no criticism of them, only undiscriminating praise. He is taunted for his undistinguished history in the theatre and for his criminal past; he is arraigned as self-deluded and vainglorious in his protestations that he is in the right and his enemies always in the wrong. Jonson, who laid claim in his 'Horace' *persona* to be ranked alongside one of the greatest poets of the ancient world, is here twitted with writing 'strong garlic comedies' and being no more than a 'low-minded pigmy', a liar and a hypocrite.

Dekker had in fact proved adept at Jonson's own technique of dramatic caricature. While his play as a whole could not hold a candle to one of Jonson's in terms of structure and plot, nevertheless in the descent to personalities Jonson provided a much greater opportunity for satire than Dekker did. Jonson's aggressive individualism, his size, his appearance, and his larger-than-life temperament, made him a satiric target which could hardly be missed. Where Jonson had had some fun at the expense of Marston's red hair and Dekker's threadbare gown, he himself possessed a tanned pocky face, scraggy beard, skeletal frame and a variety of unattractive personal mannerisms.

Jonson's life history also presented a wealth of handles for a satiric grasp. As bricklayer, soldier if not braggart too, itinerant actor sacked from his company for lack of talent, homicide, jailbird and converted papist, Jonson is hounded through the scenes of the *Satiromastix* without mercy. But it is his defects of character that are most harshly censured. This Horace is vain, short-tempered and repetitious, a constipated rhymer, a compulsive slanderer, liar and coward. His toadying to noblemen and his cheating of naive gallants are admitted even by himself in the play. All these accusations must have had some resemblance to the truth, or basis in fact, to have any effective satiric purchase; and Dekker left no stone unturned in his comprehensive and venomous catalogue of Jonson's deformities. These were, in addition, given maximum exposure; Dekker's play was produced both by the boys of St Paul's and at the Globe by Shakespeare's company.

Satiromastix was the final salvo in the 'War of the Theatres'; a last raspberry, and at Jonson's expense. It is not hard to see why Jonson gave up the contest after this; the disapproval of the state authorities, the hostility of his non-theatrical friends among soldiers and lawyers, and a degree of personal injury, combined to convince Jonson that he should say no more on this score. The *Apologetical Dialogue* had been a valiant attempt to cover his retreat. Jonson undoubtedly went down fighting. But nothing further was heard from him on the subject.

We can only guess how it must have vexed his proud spirit to leave the field to his enemies. For the world perceived the outcome as a thoroughgoing defeat for Jonson. He had been made the laughing-stock of London, and when Dekker came to publish his *Satiromastix* he summed up the passage of events with the gaiety of complete triumph. In his preface 'To the World' he referred humorously to the 'War', 'lately commenced between Horace the second and a band of lean-witted poetasters':

> Horace haled his poetasters to the bar, the poetasters untrussed Horace . . . Horace questionless made himself believe that his Burgonian wit might desperately challenge all comers, and that none durst take up the foils against him; it's likely, had he not so believed, he had not been so deceived, for he was answered at his own weapon.

Dekker went on to protest at the 'lamentable merry murdering of innocent poetry' that had accompanied the war. He declared that he had only been criticised that in attacking Jonson, he did not go far enough – 'I did only whip his fortunes and condition of life, where the more noble reprehension had been of his mind's deformity'. In using

satire against Jonson, Dekker contended that it was not 'much im-
proper, to set the same dog upon Horace, whom Horace had set to
worry others'.

Such had been the stir caused by the 'War of the Theatres' that the
rumour of it had spread far beyond London's literary circles. Early in
1602 a play performed at St John's College Cambridge made explicit
reference to what had obviously ceased to be a private quarrel;

> Why, here's our fellow Shakespeare puts them all down, aye, and
> Ben Jonson too. O that Ben Jonson is a pestilent fellow – he hath
> brought up Horace giving him a purge that made him bewray his
> credit.
>
> (*The Return from Parnassus*, Part II, IV.iii.1766–73)

Discussion has failed to elucidate the full meaning of this quip. Does it
suggest that Shakespeare himself joined in the 'War of the Theatres'
and wrote a play to put Jonson down? Of various contenders, the front
runner here is *Troilus and Cressida*, but the hypothesis is open to
objection on several grounds.[4] Or does it simply mean that the Lord
Chamberlain's Men, Shakespeare's company, achieved this with
their performance of *Satiromastix*? At the least it implies that Jonson
was despised and that Shakespeare was in sympathy with the anti-
Jonson faction if not active on their behalf. Shakespeare is firmly
taken to have made a counter-attack of some sort.

Eventually both rumours and echoes died away. The 'War' was
over. But hostilities did not terminate without some scars. Marston
was silent for over two years while Jonson did not write another
comedy for nearly four. Ironically Jonson's withdrawal occurred just
as he was confirmed in his reputation as a comic dramatist by the
publication of the quartos of the Humour plays in 1600 and 1601. But
whatever the cost to the antagonists, the gain is posterity's. The
attacks upon Jonson in the 'War' have provided a picture of the poet
in his early manhood as he looked, moved, sat and wrote; they tell us
an enormous amount about his appearance, habits, friends and
opinions. On the surface level it is quite clear that to his enemies at
least he could appear quite exotically, extraordinarily ugly. Dekker
makes vivid reference in *Satiromastix* to his face, 'like a rotten russet
apple when it is bruised', with a 'terrible mouth'. Jonson himself
alludes to his distinctive facial colouring in the *Apologetical Dialogue*, where he talks of his 'dark pale face'. According to Aubrey
Jonson 'was (or rather had been) of a clear and fair skin' (HS I, 179).
But by the time of the 'War' his skin is specified as 'tanned' and he is
described as 'a copper-faced rascal', a 'poor saffron-cheeked sun-
burned gypsy'. As if this were not enough his face was further

disfigured with 'oylet-holes', the legacy of an early disease; he 'had one eye lower than t'other', as Aubrey heard, and Dekker jeers at his habit of pulling ridiculous faces. Perhaps because of his poor skin, he could not even cover up these deficiencies with a respectable manly facial growth, but is called 'a thin-bearded hermaphrodite'.

Nor did Jonson's physique compel admiration. He was enviably tall but absurdly thin, 'a starved rascal'. As Dekker informed him 'Horace was a goodly corpulent gentleman, and not so lean a hollow-cheeked scrag as thou art'. Jonson's scrawniness is monotonously insisted upon; he is called a raw-boned 'anatomy' (skeleton), always 'hungry-faced'. He was ungainly too and his lumbering motion is summed up in the comparison Dekker made between him and one of the most famous bears of London, Harry Hunks. Nor was he able to afford decent clothes to offset his physical short-comings. He is a joke among his aquaintances for having only one suit to his back, never owning a satin doublet but dressing always in 'rug', a coarse woollen fabric. Aubrey's version is somewhat kinder: 'his habit was very plain . . . he was wont to wear a coat like a coachman's coat, with slits under the armpits'. Finally Jonson was repeatedly damned for a lack of personal daintiness even by the standards of that unfastidious age; he is derided as a 'brown-bread mouth-stinker' and a 'lousy pediculous vermin'. The crack about lice recurs; Jonson is even supposed to have borrowed another actor's cloak and returned it lousy.

Dekker fills the reader in on Jonson's past history too. The many references to bricklaying – 'a poor lime-and-hair rascal', a 'mortar-treader' – would have no point unless Jonson had been at the trade both long and recently enough to give it some satiric purchase. A bricklayer, base and cringing, is Jonson's true métier, Dekker suggests; it is risible that he should aspire to the dignity of a satiric poet. 'Bricklayer' is thus a two-pronged sneer, managing to comprehend a reflection on Jonson's social and professional status at the same time. Jonson is further mocked for his involvement in the *Isle of Dogs* affair. But interestingly no mention is made of the Flemish adventure. Perhaps it seemed too brief and too remote to have much value as a joke.

What finally emerges is a complete public picture of Ben Jonson. He seems to have lived his life among groups of men – women are absent from the picture either as friends or lovers. He had, too, as a rule one admirer in attendance who seemed to some others to be an asinine toady. Yet for all this gregariousness there is as yet among this welter of malice and defamation no reference at all to Jonson's drinking which was to become so prominent later. The only introduction of this was made by Jonson himself, in the Induction to *Every Man*

Out Of His Humour, where he praises Canary as 'the very elixir and spirit of wine' in a picture of himself at this time:

> This is that our poet calls Castalian liquor, when he comes abroad now and then once in a fortnight, and makes a good meal among players, where he has *caninum appetitum* [a dog's appetite]; marry, at home he keeps a good philosophical diet, beans and buttermilk; an honest pure rogue, he will take you off three, four or five of these [glasses of wine] one after another, and look villanously when he has done, like a one-headed Cerberus . . . and then, when his belly is well-balanced, and his brain rigged a little, he sails away withal, as though he would work wonders when he comes home. (lines 334–345)

This fascinating insight into Jonson's habits throws into relief the contradiction between the sociable Jonson and the man who excelled at that most solitary of occupations, writing. The achievements of the last few years, the sheer amount of work that Jonson got through, had not been produced by sitting in taverns eating and drinking. His poverty at this time was such that he was straining to keep body and soul together, living on a peasant diet of brown bread, beans and buttermilk, and able to treat himself to a good meal and a drink once a fortnight, with luck. This kept him lean and hungry and confined him to his chamber where he struggled with his writing despite all difficulties. It obviously did not come easily to him. Apart from the many taunts about his slowness in the satires made on him, Jonson himself acknowledged his want of a Shakespearean flow. In the *Apologetical Dialogue* he described his compositions as

> Things that were born when nought but the still night
> And his dumb candle saw his pinching throes.

What Jonson had got out of the 'War of the Theatres' was a poor return on all this effort. Something which had begun as a high-spirited exchange had degenerated into a raucous brawl. But the protagonists were fortunate that things turned out no worse. Bellicose passages between Jonson and Marston were not confined to the stage. Jonson told Drummond that 'he had many quarrels with Marston' and that 'he beat Marston and took his pistol from him' (this boast was repeated to Drummond twice). An ineradicable aggression drew Jonson into this fight so soon after his fatal encounter with Spencer, who like Marston started out as friend and colleague. If Marston was lucky to escape Spencer's fate at Jonson's hands, Jonson was equally lucky to have escaped facing the consequences. No man could plead 'benefit of clergy' twice – no woman could plead it at all – and had he killed Marston, Jonson would have been for the rope's end.

The intense personal involvement of the War of the Theatres was never to be repeated in Jonson's professional career. While he had been so deeply engaged, important national events had been taking place, one of which was to cast a long shadow both for Jonson and for the nation as a whole. On 19 November 1600 the prince Charles Stuart was born to the King of Scotland James and his Queen Anne at Fife. Their second son and fourth child, the baby was a poor, sickly creature who was not expected to live. His future in any case could hardly command the interest lavished upon the heir-apparent, the handsome and promising Prince Henry. But he was to live, to give Jonson work, and to refuse him.

There were for Jonson two matters of a more immediate personal interest. In 1601 his former contact Thomas Nashe is referred to as dead. How, when and where Nashe died is unknown. It is clear from his last works that he had known poverty and that his tribulations had turned his mind to repentance. In the course of a long lifetime Jonson was to witness the passing of many friends and some dear enemies. But Nashe's was a particularly poignant loss. At thirty-three he was young to die even by the standards of his own time. In his youth he had been gifted with a unique sprightly personality and joyous irreverent wit. To trace his decline like that of his friend and mentor Robert Greene into his bitterness of rejection is painful.

Jonson was himself strenuously engaged in the struggle against poverty and neglect that had brought Nashe low. Despite the enormous effort of the 'War of the Theatres' he was still having difficulties in making enough to live on. The accounts of Henslowe for this period show that Jonson continued to work for him; on 5 September 1601 Jonson was paid £2 for additions to *The Spanish Tragedy*. This was the quintessence of hack work, to have to do re-writes on this old warhorse which was now only good for a laugh among the more sophisticated theatre-goers. The job took some time; on 22 June of the year following, 1602, Jonson received £10 from Henslowe, again for 'additions' to the same play. Although willing to spend money to keep this surefire old favourite on the boards Henslowe also needed new plays. In an entry of the same date he records that the £10 was further intended 'in earnest of a book called Richard Crookback'. This character is rather better known to later ages as Richard III and Shakespeare's outstanding success with a play on that character some years earlier is probably the reason that nothing was subsequently known of Henslowe's and Jonson's answer to it.

But although Jonson was having to work at hard and uncongenial tasks, he was not neglecting his friends. He had by this time established that nucleus of the friendships which were to carry him through his life (not that he ever lost the ability to make new friends when the occasion served). Apart from his friendships among the 'gallants', Jonson was becoming a valued member of a circle of older men, through his former schoolmaster, Camden. Camden was a prime mover in the Antiquarian Society which had been founded in 1572, the year of Jonson's birth. Among its members were such men as Cotton, Speed and Carew, with whom Jonson could share a studious and scholarly interest in matters far removed from the reverberating arena of the theatre. Despite his situation, beset by poverty and hostility, Jonson displayed his perennial capacity to attract and to cherish the attention of people of worth and distinction. This he sought to acknowledge as best he could. When his *Poetaster* was published he sent Camden a gift copy with the inscription, 'Alumnus olim, aeternum amicus' – 'a pupil once and now for ever a friend'. Another copy went to an equally important recipient in another way, his patron the Countess of Bedford. For this copy, Jonson had a special dedication printed and bound in with the text:

> Go little book, go little fable
>   unto the bright and amiable
> Lucy of Bedford; she, that bounty
>   appropriates still unto that County.
> Tell her, his Muse that did invent thee
>   to Cynthia's fairest nymph hath sent thee,
> And sworn that he will quite discard thee
>   if any way she do reward thee
> But with a kiss (if thou canst dare it)
>   of her white hand; or she can spare it.

> (HS VIII, 662)

Yet although making these efforts to develop his links with the worlds of learning and the court, Jonson did not lose touch with the boys' companies with which he had been so closely interwoven. Towards the end of July the Children of the Chapel suffered an unexpected blow; one of their little stars died, Jonson's former leading player Salomon Pavy. His burial at St Mary Somerset in London on 25 July 1602 elicited this delicately wrought epitaph from Jonson:

> Weep with me, all you that read
>   This little story,
> And know, for whom a tear you shed
>   Death's self is sorry.
> 'Twas a child that so did thrive
>   In grace and feature,
> As heaven and nature seemed to strive
>   Which owned the creature.

Years he numbered scarce thirteen
    When fates turned cruel,
Yet three filled zodiacs had he been
    The stage's jewel . . .

(Epigram 120)

Jonson was always ready to pay tribute to professionalism even in a thirteen-year-old child. But even as he was writing in this vein of the stage, he was seeking ways to leave it. His desire to quit this unprofitable trade had been expressed after the unwelcoming reception of *Poetaster* in 1601. The aggrieved poet, brooding on his wrongs in the *Apologetical Dialogue*, framed quite clearly the hope that he could somehow find the way to work on the higher products of poetry which he knew he was capable of, at a safe distance from the destructive malice or the crushing stupidity of the public at large:

I, that spend half my nights, and all my days
Here in a cell, to get a dark pale face,
To come forth worth the ivy, or the bays,
And in this age can hope no other grace –
Leave me. There's something comes into my thought
That must, and shall, be sung high and aloof,
Safe from the wolf's black jaw, and the dull ass's hoof.

(lines 223–239)

Soon Jonson was able to convert this emotional recoil from the public theatre into the creative retreat for which he pined. One of the friends whom he had made during this period came to his aid and provided him with a home and the means to live. For the first time he was free of Henslowe's treadmill; free, too, of his domestic responsibilities. In one of the periodic disruptions of his married life, Jonson left home. A law student John Manningham noted in his diary for February 1602 that 'Ben Jonson the poet now lives upon one Townsend, and scorns the world' (IIS I, 30).

This was a most welcome refuge for Jonson. Townsend was a well known friend to literary men; another protégé was Fletcher who saluted him as 'the perfect gentleman, Sir R.T.' in the Preface to *The Faithful Shepherdess*. Jonson could be hasty and careless, but he never forgot a favour. He later sent his patron one of the first fruits of his retirement, a copy of *Sejanus* inscribed 'the testimony of my affection, and observance to my noble friend Sir Robert Townsend, which I desire may remain with him and last above marble'.

The completion of *Poetaster* in 1601 marks the close of the first phase of Jonson's dramatic career. The years that followed before the production of another play and the opportunity to read, to study and

67

to develop had a profound effect upon his thought and practice. He
had lost the 'War of the Theatres'. But he had not lost faith in himself.
When he came to reckon up the progress and achievements of his
early years as a dramatist, Jonson found a firm basis for the confidence with which he now tackled the future.

CHAPTER 5

New Directions

T HE 'War of the Theatres' was over. London playgoers were no longer to enjoy the outbursts of vicious in-fighting that had gingered up the normal repertory of their playhouses. The patronage of Townsend with whom Jonson was living by the February of 1602 could hardly have come at a more fortunate time. It was followed by that of Esme Stuart, Seigneur D'Aubigny, a cousin of King James and a man 'no less noble in virtue than in blood', as Jonson described him in the dedication to *Sejanus*. This was the start of a long absence from home and a separation from his wife – as he told Drummond, 'five years he had not bedded with her, but remained with my lord D'Aubigny'.[1]

The patronage of such men offered Jonson more than just a living, welcome though that must have been. The implied compliment to his worth and standing supplied a much-needed salve for the injuries sustained in the 'War of the Theatres'. From this retreat Jonson could take stock of his position. And whatever knocks he had taken in the 'War', it is clear that he had suffered no permanent setback to his concept of his own purpose and vocation. On the contrary he seized the opportunity which his retirement provided to embark on a new artistic direction, that of tragedy. This resolve had been formed after the hostile reception of *Poetaster* in the summer of 1601:

> . . since the comic muse
> Hath proved so ominous to me, I will try
> If Tragedy have a more kind aspect.
> Her favours in my next I will pursue.
>
> (*Apologetical Dialogue*, 222–5)

Jonson was of course no novice to the form of tragedy. His *début* in the theatre had been as an actor in the most famous tragedy of the whole age, and he had also worked on *The Spanish Tragedy* as a writer when he had been commissioned to refurbish the old favourite for newer audiences. As early as 1598 Meres had effusively praised his powers as a tragedian, and among his named, if lost works are several which point to an interest in the history and tragedy of rulers of the past – *Robert II King of Scots* (1599) and *Richard Crookback* (1602) for example. Henslowe's accounts also mention a sketch by Jonson of the plot of a tragedy which was finished by Chapman.

But these were either prentice or hack works, so stigmatised by Jonson himself when he excluded them from the 1616 Folio. Just as *Every Man In His Humour* represented a breakthrough into the kind of comedy that Jonson wished to write, so *Sejanus* stands in relation to his concept of tragedy. The play is not only a very considerable tragic piece on its own merits; it embodies Jonson's mature convictions about the making of tragedy in particular and of the dignity of the poet's office in general. Jonson himself was conscious that he was embarking on a fresh and distinctive phase of his artistic development. He later referred to *Sejanus* as 'the first fruit of his retirement', the metaphor aptly summing up his hopes of further growth.

Jonson's assumption of a new direction in both his personal and professional life coincided strangely with a series of upheavals for the nation at large. In view of the excitements of 1602–3, it is doubtful that the fireworks of the 'War of the Theatres' can have been missed, as other events of a wider national significance soon obliterated coterie activity. The closing month of 1602 saw the onset of a highly virulent phase of that great leveller and ever-present menace, the plague. During the following twelve months over thirty-eight thousand people were to suffer death of the pestilence in London – almost a quarter of the estimated population. To sufferers and survivors alike, it seemed as if Armageddon had overtaken them.

Another blow, long awaited but nonetheless momentous, fell early in 1603. From the beginning of the new year it was clear that the Christmas festivities which Queen Elizabeth had just celebrated were to be her last. As she lay upon piles of cushions on the floor refusing to go to bed she abandoned her life-long reserve on the subject of the succession. To the demands of those about her that she should give her successor her 'dying voice', she enquired wearily, 'Who should it be but our cousin of Scotland?'

Elizabeth died in her great bedchamber at Richmond between 2 and 3 in the morning of 24 March 1603. Her passing seemed to her subjects to leave a gap in nature; after forty-five years, few then living could recall a time when she was not on the throne, the cynosure of all England. But while others hastened to express their feelings in appropriate verse, Jonson did not. His failure to comment upon this epochal event drew this explanation from a contemporary, Henry Chettle:

> His muse another path desires to tread;
> True satyrs scourge the living, leave the dead.
>
> *(England's Mourning*
> *Garment,* 1603)

It was precisely this reputation as satirical writer that Jonson was even then striving to undo. As he had declared at the end of the *Apologetical Dialogue,* 'There's something comes into my thought/That must, and shall, be sung high and aloof . . . '.

Jonson's new undertaking shared in a general time of hope. Elizabeth's death paved the way for a welcome change of government. Bacon's comments illustrate the widespread expectation which centred on the new King James, apparently possessed of so many natural advantages: 'in the strength of his years, supported with great alliances abroad, established with royal issue at home, at peace with all the world, practised in the regiment of such a kingdom. . . .' After forty-five years, as the worldly Bacon noted, there was inevitably a desire for change, and the King's own book on the art of government, *Basilicon Doron,* only intensified the hopes which were set on him. Unlike his immediate Tudor predecessors James came into a united and well-ordered kingdom, to a people exulting in the smooth transition of power; as Bacon summed up, 'the joy was infinite'. Jonson himself remarked on the peaceful transition by which the historic enemies England and Scotland were at last united:

> When was there contract better driven by fate,
> Or celebrated with more truth of state?
> The world the temple was, the priest a king,
> The spoused pair two realms, the sea the ring.
>
> (Epigram 5)

What were the implications of this succession for Jonson? He had every reason to hope for much from this scholar, poet and ruler. The man of whom it was written that 'he doth wondrously covet learned discourse' could not but strike a chord in Jonson's breast. The new king liked to parade his learning and engage in intellectual discussion so much that Sir John Harington rucfully compared an audience he had of him with his *viva voce* examination at Cambridge. Temperamentally, even physically too, Jonson and James were compatible. It was said of James that 'he naturally loved honest men, that were not over-active'. Drummond later recorded Jonson's declaration that 'of all styles, he loved most to be named *honest,* and hath of that one hundred letters so naming him' (HS I, 150). Did Jonson first develop

71

this estimation of himself from King James's often-professed delight in the virtue?

James's accession finally delivered England from her ancient nightmare of the menace from the North. Jonson was fortunate in being able to claim Scots descent when so many were rooting around for any shred of tartan that may have clung to a branch of their family tree. Jonson's entire professional future was to be bound up with James, Anne and their children. To him the King was able to present himself in some of his most-loved roles, not only as God's deputy, ruler and law-giver, but also as philosopher, scholar, fellow-author, royal master and friend. His little Queen proved to be Jonson's good angel in commissioning from him the masques in which she so delighted as expressions of that beauty and grace which her nature craved. As to the Princes Henry and Charles, and the Princess Elizabeth, hardly any significant event of their lives was to pass without some mark of the occasion from Jonson.

The King left Scotland for England almost immediately and the royal procession, swollen with hopefuls and hangers-on, made its way fairly leisurely into England. As he drew south so public excitement increased. 'Never came man more longed for, more desired', as Jonson was later to say; James 'won affections ere his steps won ground'.[2] Jonson himself however was set apart from the widespread public jubilation. He had been one of those lucky enough to escape from the plague in London by taking refuge in the country, and was staying with Camden's friend, Sir Robert Cotton, at his house just outside Peterborough in Huntingdonshire. Cotton was a former Westminster pupil one year senior to Jonson. He shared antiquarian interests with Camden who was also present on this occasion and the library of his town house was a literary centre of London. Jonson's own account of what happened there was given some fifteen years later to Drummond, but retains its vivid immediacy even today:

When the King came into England, at that time the pest was in London. He being in the country at Sir Robert Cotton's home with old Camden, he saw in a vision his eldest son (then a child and at London) appear unto him with the mark of a bloody cross on his forehead, as if it had been cutted with a sword; at which amazed, he prayed unto God, and in the morning he came to Mr Camden's chamber to tell him, who persuaded him it was but an apprehension of his fantasy, at which he should not be disjected. In the meantime comes there letters from his wife of the death of that boy in the plague. He appeared to him he said, of a manly shape, and of that growth that he thinks he shall be at the Resurrection.

(HS I, 139–40)

James left Edinburgh on 5 April and took a month over his progress to London. This event can therefore be dated in early May of 1603. Jonson's response took the form of a haunting valedictory remarkable for its blend of fortitude and grief:

Farewell, thou child of my right hand, and joy;
　My sin was too much hope of thee, loved boy.
Seven years thou wert lent to me, and I thee pay
　Exacted by thy fate, on the just day.
Oh, could I lose all father now! For why
　Will man lament the state he should envy?
To have so soon 'scaped world's and flesh's rage,
　And if no other misery, yet age?
Rest in soft peace, and asked, say here doth lie
　Ben Jonson his best piece of poetry.
For whose sake, henceforth, all his vows be such
As what he loves may never like too much.

(Epigram 45)

Jonson was not however allowed any protracted mourning for little Benjamin. He was soon caught up in the nationwide celebrations caused by the change of monarchy. In June 1603 he received what must have been a most agreeable commission, to write for the new royal family. Queen Anne and the heir apparent Prince Henry had set out after the King and were making a separate progress to London. They rested for several nights on their southward journey at the house of Sir Robert Spencer at Althorp, Northamptonshire,[3] where, among various 'laboured and triumphal shows', they watched an entertainment devised and written by Jonson, the piece later named *The Satyr*. The simple pastoral which Jonson produced on this occasion was a complete departure from his previous modes. It was based upon the woodland approach to the Spencer seat, newly weeded as the household accounts show by four women especially employed for the purpose.

As the Queen and Prince approached a playful satyr popped up out of a bush at the sound of the welcoming fanfares to demand to know what all the fuss was about and to express his intention of joining in the revelry. The subsequent appearance of Queen Mab and her attendant fairies contrived a delicate compliment to earthly royalty and their music and dance added grace to the humour of the satyr. The celebration continued with the donation of a jewel to Queen Anne and culminated with the presentation of the Spencers' eldest son to the royal party 'attired and appointed like a huntsman'. This led easily into the final part of the show, a stage-managed hunt when 'a brace of choice deer were put out, and as fortunately killed, as they were meant to be, even in the sight of her Majesty' (HS VII, i, 28).

Jonson's description of the event displays his satisfaction with the result, as well it might; this enchanting little piece, less than two hundred lines in length, possesses an assurance that belies his novitiate in the art of state entertainments. The occasion marked a very clear step forward for him. This was not only his first royal entertainment, the first of many such over the next thirty years, but also his first personal encounter with any members of the house of Stuart, with whose court and fortunes so much of his future working life was to be bound up.

For clearly the poet was in attendance at Althorp during the royal visit. As is plain from his notes and comments in the published text, Jonson not only watched his own show but was standing by during the weekend to supply whatever was necessary to the continuation of the festivities. For this entertainment of welcome was only part of the proceedings. It took place on the Saturday of the arrival of the Queen and Prince, 25 June,[4] after which (doubtless fatigued by the miseries of contemporary travelling) the Queen rested. She spent the Sunday quietly, and the first part of Monday, too; but 'after dinner' she was ready for a renewal of jollifications. The organisers had to cope with much beside the vagaries of the royal health and disposition. As happened everywhere at this stage of James's reign, Althorp was besieged by locals ranging from the landed gentry to the humblest members of the commonwealth, all of whom wished to warm themselves at the rising sun of the new monarchy and some of whom had prepared shows and entertainments of their own as a token of love and loyalty. Among these was what Jonson rather snootily calls 'a morris of the clowns thereabout, who most officiously presented themselves'.[5] When it was felt that this troupe (irresistibly reminiscent of Bottom and his fellows at the court of Theseus) needed some kind of introduction, 'there was a speech suddenly thought on', and Jonson wrote it.

Although produced to order at speed and under pressure, the speech is vigorously conceived and dramatically realised. 'The person of Nobody' was to appear, 'attired in a pair of breeches which were made to come up to his neck, with his arms out at his pockets, and a cap drowning his face'. The broad farce of this treatment consorted well with the subject-matter and provided an effective contrast with both the sprightly humour and airy fantasy of the main entertainment.

In the event however no one heard it, as the unfortunate speaker was drowned not only by the hat over his face but also by 'the throng of the country that came in'. The same fate also overtook Jonson's final contribution to the occasion, a carefully-written 'parting speech, which was to have been presented in the person of a youth, and accompanied with divers gentlemen's younger sons of the country'. This too was overwhelmed 'by reason of the multitudinous press' and perished unheard. But Jonson was sufficiently satisfied with it to have preserved it for posterity and to have felt that it was worthy of inclusion in his quarto of 1604.

Jonson became known to the Queen and to Prince Henry at Althorp. Shortly afterwards the opportunity presented itself to make an impression upon the King too. Jonson became involved in the preparations for the coronation which was to take place as soon as conveniently possible. Planning began early in April 1603 as soon as the new king was proclaimed, on the basis of the expectation that James would pass through the city in procession on his coronation day to show himself to the people and to receive their demonstrations of joy and regard. But as the summer wore on the intensification of the plague caused the suspension of all hopes of a public welcome.

When the coronation of King James and Queen Anne took place on 25 July, St James's day 1603, it did so quietly, overshadowed by the dread reminders of mortality. Almost fourteen hundred people died in London of the plague that week and this figure was to double in the weekly totals before the terror subsided. Londoners had to be forbidden to make the trip to Westminster to see the coronation and the celebrations there for fear of spreading the pestilence yet more widely. Panic and disorder inaugurated the new reign inauspiciously as the plague gripped ever tighter and the theatres were closed for nearly a year. This was a lean time for theatre people but most especially for writers. Actors after all were able to take to the roads, however unattractive a prospect that presented, and gain a living by hawking their old plays to country audiences.

The postponement of the coronation celebrations was Jonson's first experience of the delays and setbacks to which royal events were subject. The plans and preparations for the pageants and shows to greet the royal procession were kept alive for a month longer, then abandoned when it became clear that the King could not undertake a public engagement of this sort that summer while the plague raged unchecked. But Jonson was fortunate that he was spared the tribulations that befell some of his former colleagues. The patronage of D'Aubigny had preserved him from the exigencies of working for the public stage, and he was determined to produce something worthy of the favour.

Apart from the summer trip into the country to Sir Robert Cotton and the engagement at Althorp, Jonson was working steadily in 1603 on his new project. The 'first fruit of his retirement' as he described it himself was *Sejanus His Fall*, the first of the Roman tragedies in which

75

Jonson aspired to the full eminence of a tragic writer in the creation of a 'true poem'. The composition of this piece involved him not only in the planning and writing of the drama. His anxiety to present 'truth of argument' as a key requirement of authentic tragic writing, and his obsession to be correct in every detail of Roman life and customs, involved considerable amount of academic study. The prefatory address 'To The Reader' in the 1605 quarto cites numerous classical authorities and references in full (HS I, 252). Even allowing for Jonson's natural and constant tendency to aggrandise his effort by maximising his citations and sources, it is clear that he took the whole thing very seriously and devoted a good deal of effort to it.

The preface to *Sejanus* also hints at something of Jonson's private life. He dedicated this play to his patron in terms rather warmer than those of merely conventional gratitude. Clearly the relationship had outgrown the bonds of dependency and ripened into a true friendship. A further tribute, Epigram 127, breathes both gratitude and love:

> Is there a hope that man would thankful be
>   If I should fail in gratitude to thee,
> To whom I am so bound, loved Aubigny?
>   No; I do therefore call posterity
> Into the debt, and reckon on her head
>   How full of want, how swallowed up, how dead
> I and this muse had been if thou hadst not
>   Lent timely succours, and new life begot:
> So all reward or name that grows to me
>   By her attempt, shall still be owing thee.
> And than this same, I know no abler way
>   To thank thy benefits; which is, to pay.

D'Aubigny's 'benefits' had made possible for Jonson the 'new life' of literary scholarship which was not only devoted to the production of *Sejanus*. The 1605 quarto address 'to the Readers' spoke of Jonson's intention to publish 'shortly' his translation of Horace's *Ars Poetica* with his own preface to it. He never in fact published it. But its importance to him may be gauged from the fact that he recalled to Drummond fifteen years later that he had done the work 'in my lord D'Aubigny's house ten years since, *anno* 1604' (HS I, 134).[6]

This momentous year of 1603 closed with the staging of *Sejanus* by 'the King's Majesty's Servants', the former Lord Chamberlain's Men, Shakespeare's troupe.[7] One of King James's first acts as the ruler of England had been to place this pre-eminent company under his personal protection, so that Shakespeare and his colleagues walked in the King's livery in the coronation procession that summer. A note at the end of the 1616 Folio version of the play includes among 'the principal tragedians' Richard Burbage, who probably played the title role of the aspiring tyrant. Shakespeare, who may have played the lascivious Tiberius, and John Heminges and Henry Condell who were responsible for the Shakespeare First Folio in 1623 were also in the company.

Yet despite all these promising features the play was a dreadful flop. Jonson could not in so brief a space re-educate his old audience out of their preference for more popular subjects. *Sejanus* was hooted off the stage. William Fennor writing in 1616 still vividly recalled its fate at the hands of the 'stinkards':

> With more than human art it was bedewed
> Yet to the multitude it nothing showed.
> They screwed their scurvy jaws and looked awry
> Like hissing snakes, adjudging it to die;
> When wits of gentry did applaud the same
> With silver shouts of high loud-sounding fame.

In lines prefixed to the 1605 quarto another friend and admirer of Jonson addressed him with a heated description of the occasion:

> When in the Globe's fair ring, our world's best stage,
> I viewed the people's beastly rage,
> Bent to confound thy grave and learned toil,
> That cost thee so much sweat, and so much oil
> My indignation I could hardly assuage . . .

> (HS XI, 317)

Jonson himself grimly acknowledged his play's ill success in the dedicatory note to D'Aubigny: 'If any ruin were so great as to survive, I think this be one I send you . . . It is a poem that (if I well remember) in your lordship's sight, suffered no less violence from our people here, than the subject of it did from the people of Rome' (HS IV, 349).

To have his play booed, hissed and torn to pieces in the presence of his noble patron was a grim reward for Jonson's work and care. The play's failure must have been the more inexplicable to him because he had had in the composition of it the assistance of one of the choicer dramatic spirits of the age. As he informed the readers in the preface to the 1605 quarto 'a second pen' had 'a good share' in the original version. This ghost cannot be identified with certainty but scholars are agreed that the most likely collaborator for Jonson at this time was George Chapman.

Some twelve years older than Jonson, Chapman had a good deal in common with him. Originating like Jonson from a background that was neither wealthy nor distinguished, Chapman too had tried his fate as a soldier of fortune in the Netherlands before following the

77

career of a writer in London. Like Jonson again, Chapman was a passionate classicist and 1598, the year of Jonson's first success, had seen the publication of the initial instalment of Chapman's translation of Homer; this truly epic undertaking he described simply as 'the work I was born to do'. His skill ranged beyond epic verse. Comedies and tragedies of his hand survive, and Jonson further told Drummond that 'next himself only Chapman and Fletcher could make a masque' (HS I, 133).

Whatever the contribution of the second hand the play was substantially Jonson's. He seems to have borne alone the brunt of the popular distaste for the play. Nor was this the only unfortunate consequence of its production. Yet again as the result of his stage activities he came under official scrutiny. Given that direct comment on contemporary politics was forbidden and that Elizabethan and Jacobean minds were highly trained in analogy, a well-known expedient was to use classical or historical settings as a cover for topical discussion. A suspicious state saw the possibility of sedition everywhere and as Jonson told Drummond, he was 'called before the [Privy] Council for his *Sejanus*' (HS I, 141).

It is hard to discover in the printed text what was the source of the Privy Council's suspicion or what Jonson had to answer for. Drummond has a note that the charge was 'popery and treason', but in a play set in pre-Christian Rome the first charge is clearly irrelevant. 'Popery' must have been a separate black mark against Jonson brought forward at this time simply through its inextricable link in contemporary thinking with treason. Jonson later noted in his *Timber* (lines 1334–58) 'I have been accused to the Lords, to the King; and by great ones', in accusations based on extracts from his writings wrenched from context and maliciously misinterpreted to have a significance that they were never meant to carry. Past experience alone had taught their Lordships to be sensitive both to plays on the theme of bad government, and to plays by Ben Jonson. In this instance however Jonson coped with his difficulties and came off unscathed. Among Privy Council members was the Earl of Suffolk, the Lord Chamberlain, who was soon to renew his acquaintance with the troublesome poet.

Jonson himself believed that there was a personal animus behind the prosecution of the Privy Council against him. He saw in this move the hand of one whom he described to Drummond as 'his mortal enemy' (HS I, 141). This was Henry Howard Earl of Northampton, the second son of the poet Surrey. Jonson had been involved in a brawl one St George's day (23 April) with one of Northampton's attendants. The offended noblemen fastened upon *Sejanus* as the instrument of his revenge and lodged the charges upon which the Privy Council acted.

Popery seems an odd accusation against Jonson from a fellow-Catholic as Northampton was. Yet he was a crypto-Catholic who accompanied his secret machinations on behalf of his co-religionists with ostentatious anti-Catholic public activity. His faith did not prevent him from becoming actively engaged in the prosecution and martyrdom of the Jesuit Father Garnett in March 1606. He changed his religion several times and the attack upon Jonson came during one of his publicly Protestant phases. Yet he was suspected by his contemporaries of being 'a subtle papist inwardly' all along. He was in addition reputedly the most learned nobleman of the age and had been a lecturer at Cambridge. But his tortuous mentality betrayed itself in a style so convoluted that even King James who loved a rhetorical flourish found it 'Asiatic'. This deep and sinister man of power was hardly one to have as a 'mortal enemy'. But Jonson found his way out of the trap.

At all events, Jonson was never one to be intimidated by the name or presence of a lord. Early in 1604 came an example of his characteristically flamboyant and uninhibited behaviour. In the first week of the new year he had to be asked to leave a court performance of Daniel's Twelfth-night masque, *The Vision of the Twelve Goddesses*. In the company of his friend Roe, Jonson was ushered from the Great Hall at Hampton Court by no less a person than the Earl of Suffolk, the Lord Chamberlain himself. This must have been one of Jonson's first visits to the court – his previous commissions for the new royalty had all taken place elsewhere. The principal lady masquer was Lucy, Countess of Bedford, who had already favoured Jonson; his presentation to her of a gift-copy of *Cynthia's Revels* displays his gratitude. It is the more indicative of his ebullient and irrepressible nature that he could not avoid unseemly behaviour on this stately occasion.

Jonson's partner in outrage, Sir John Roe, was one of his dearest friends. How the acquaintance was first formed is unknown; this is the first reference to Roe in connection with Jonson in the contemporary accounts. But in after years Jonson touchingly recalled that 'Roe loved him' (HS I, 136). Like Jonson Roe was no stranger to wild escapades. Some nine years younger than the poet, Roe had had both the social and educational advantages denied to Jonson. He came of a good family, which boasted more than one Lord Mayor of London among its members as well as an ambassador, and he had studied at Queen's College Oxford.

But his temperament inclined him to an active life. Like Jonson he too had become a soldier and followed the wars, and he had in the way of that profession knocked about the taverns and bawdy houses (two further interests which he shared with Jonson). But he was also a man of honour and a noted duellist. More, he was a poet and an intimate of poets, being one of that circle of wits and writers which included both Jonson and Donne among its members. Through John, Jonson met others of the Roe family, like the gifted cousin Thomas, whose diplomatic career spanned both the court of King James and that of the Great Mogul of India. Thomas Roe has been associated with the admirer 'Th.R.', who contributed a congratulatory poem on the 1605 publication of *Sejanus*: 'To his learned and beloved friend, upon his equal work'. Jonson also knew William Roe, John's brother, and expressed respect and admiration for him, later even appearing for him in a lawsuit.[8] But his close friend and companion was John.

Roe seems in outline to be tailormade as a soul mate for Jonson. They were in the habit of exchanging verse epistles; a surviving example from 9 November 1603 plays lightly with ideas of great men whose standing raises them above the poor and vulnerable. Roe's poverty was a pressing problem. Jonson related to Drummond that Roe was 'an infinite spender, and used to say, when he had no more to spend, he could die' (HS I, 137). Had the two men been drinking heavily on Twelfth Night in 1604? Certainly Jonson's sense of decorum was overthrown and he felt badly about his behaviour afterwards. But Roe was unrepentant and comforted Jonson with a poetical reflection on the subject. He rallied Jonson with a couplet Jonson was able to quote to Drummond fifteen years later:

> Forget we were thrust out; it is but thus:
> Gods threaten kings, kings lords, as lords do us.
> . . . trust and believe your friend . . .

Roe went on to reassert his love for Jonson with the powerful observation that 'friends are our selves', and encouraged him to carry on in the face of misunderstanding and mockery: 'Let for a while the time's unthrifty rout/Condemn learning, and all your studies flout'[9]: eventually Jonson's worth would be recognised.

The author of this masque was Samuel Daniel whom Jonson later dismissed to Drummond as 'a good honest man, but no poet' (HS I, 132) adding that 'Daniel was at jealousies with him'. Jonson had, in fact, no great opinion of Daniel's work. He derided Daniel's *The Civil Wars between the Two Houses of Lancaster and York*, inaccurately informing Drummond that 'Daniel wrote civil wars, yet hath not one battle in all his book' (HS I, 138 and 163, note 211). As Jonson did not include Daniel in his list of those who beside himself had the talent and skill to 'make a mask', it is a fair assumption that Jonson reacted adversely to Daniel's *Vision of the Twelve Goddesses*.

The two men were in fact totally opposed in their attitudes to masque-making. Daniel insisted that masques should not be taken too seriously by their composers or they ran the risk of intellectual pretentiousness. In his dedication of *The Vision of the Twelve Goddesses* to the Countess of Bedford, Daniel declared:

> Whoever strives to show most wit about these [trifles] of dreams and shows are sure sick of a disease they cannot hide, and would fain have the world to think them very deeply learned in all mysteries whatsoever. And peradventure they think themselves so; which if they do, they are in a far worse case than they imagine.[10]

Nor was the disagreement between them confined to masque-making. To Drummond Jonson 'said he had written a discourse of poetry both against Campion and Daniel, especially this last, where he proves couplets to be the bravest sort of verses . . . ' (HS I, 132). Daniel by contrast considered that 'continual cadences of couplets . . . are very tiresome and unpleasing' (HS I, 152). The differences of opinion between Jonson and Daniel could be multiplied many times over. Some expression of Jonson's disdain obviously made itself felt.

Yet Jonson was not always so severe on writers less talented than himself if other interests, religious, for instance, came into play. In 1604 he wrote a dedicatory sonnet for Thomas Wright's *The Passions of the Mind in General*, a pedestrian treatise of expository prose. The only other tribute is by 'H.H'. – otherwise Hugh Holland, a prominent Catholic poet. Jonson also wrote a dedicatory poem for Holland's *Pancharis* in 1603, and Holland reciprocated with one for *Sejanus* on its publication in 1605. Wright came from a family of Catholic priests. His brother and his uncle were also in holy orders. Holland had like Jonson attended Westminster school and subsequently converted to Catholicism. Jonson's circle of fellow-Catholics was necessarily less public and noted than his friendships with gallants, wits and courtiers, given the dangers and disabilities that his co-religionists laboured under. But there are many hints like this that it was a significant part of Jonson's life nonetheless.

Early in 1604 Jonson was offered a chance to make a better impression upon the new King. The plans for the coronation celebrations of the year before, long deferred because of the plague, were revived. Jonson's was a major contribution to what has come to be called 'the Magnificent Entertainment' for King James as he passed in royal procession through 'his honourable city of London' – the other writer involved was Dekker. This elaborate civic pageant, which took place throughout the day on Thursday 15 March, consisted of a series of shows. At various places in the city 'triumphant arches' were built at which the royal party halted to receive speeches and greetings from various sections of the community; the Dutch merchants for example paid their respects at an arch erected near the Royal Exchange, their Italian counterparts at a show in Gracechurch Street.

Jonson, significantly, was responsible for the first and last parts of the 'Magnificent Entertainment'. In considering his invention, the central idea being the 'soul' of the pageant, he eagerly grasped the opportunity to create on the grand scale. The first arch, erected at Fenchurch Street, celebrated the theme of 'Monarchia Britannica'. A representation of the entire city of London was carved on top of the arch, and the structure was decorated with allegorical figures. Chief among these were the Genius of the City, and Father Thames, attended by six daughters of the Genius, whom Jonson describes as Gladness, Veneration, Promptitude, Vigilance, Loving Affection and Unanimity. All these were represented not by statues but by living individuals, seated in order on what must have been a very substantial edifice. The Genius and Thames were the only speaking parts out of twelve performers, each offering by turns long speeches of 'gratulation' to the King, the Queen, and Prince Henry.

Jonson's co-worker on the construction side was the master-joiner Stephen Harrison who afterwards published his own pictorial record of the event, *The Arches of Triumph* (1604). His was an important contribution. In the long history of English pageantry this was the first occasion in which the artificer was singled out for any attention. But Jonson was in modern terms the designer as well as the writer. He controlled not only the central concept but also such details as the costumes of the participants. Harrison's work and his record of it show his architectural and graphic skills – he was no mere carpenter.[11] Yet Jonson's was the shaping influence throughout. The final presentation in the Strand was also Jonson's; Electra spoke the parting blessing on the King from 'between two magnificent pyramids of seventy feet in height, on which were drawn His Majesty's several pedigrees' of England and Scotland. The performer playing Electra was suspended in the air 'in figure of a comet' – brave man! (HS VII, 106)

The 'Magnificent Entertainment' aroused tremendous public interest. Dekker enthusiastically contrasted the joyful crowded scenes with the desolation of the plague recently departed:

> The streets seemed to be paved with men; stalls, instead of rich ware were set out with children, open casements filled up with women . . . he that should have compared the empty and untrodden walks of London, which were to be seen in that late mortally-destroying deluge, with the thronged streets now, might have believed that upon this day began a new Creation.[12]

Londoners in fact enjoyed the day hugely with the abundance of shows, not to mention the free drink; 'the conduits of Cornhill, of Cheap and of Fleet Street, that day ran claret very plenteously, which

. . . ran the faster and more merrily down some bodies' bellies' (HS X, 389). But the King himself did not appreciate public displays of affection as Elizabeth had and Dekker records that 'a regard being had that His Majesty should not be wearied with tedious speeches, a greater part of those which are in this book set down, were left unspoken'. Jonson's published record similarly must reflect the performances as they should have been delivered not as they were (HS X, 387).

Jonson's pride in his achievement nevertheless is demonstrated by the lengthy and careful description of it which he later made for its publication. He was able too to work in a compliment to his old friend Camden as 'the glory and light of our kingdom' (HS VII, 84). Yet the great success of this public occasion could not harmonise all private discord. Echoes of the 'War of the Theatres' rumbled on. Dekker, who had written five of the seven episodes, published his own speeches and verses but omitted Jonson's contributions and did not even name Jonson as his co-worker. Additionally, he had a crack at Jonson's 'false flourish' of scholarship, deriding his learning as the 'borrowed weapons of all the old masters in the noble science of poesy', employed 'only to show how nimbly he can carve up the whole mess of the poets'. To compound the injury Dekker's volume went into a second edition which his publisher enthusiastically entitled 'The *Whole* Magnificent Entertainment'. Jonson's attempt to publish his work, carefully specified by his printer Edward Blount as 'a *part* of the King's Majesty's right royal and magnificent entertainment', was sabotaged by Dekker's printer – who by a mysterious piece of sharp practice managed to have Jonson's book suppressed and all remaining copies delivered into his hands.

Four days after the London welcome James made his first entrance to the Houses of Parliament on 19 March 1604. Again Jonson was involved. On this occasion he saluted the King with 'a brief panegyre', a 162-line speech of praise and welcome which blended congratulations with good counsel. Less than two months later Jonson again came to royal notice when he wrote a May Day entertainment for the King and Queen when they visited Sir William Cornwallis's house at Highgate. This was a private ceremonial in two parts. First came the welcome in the morning, pronounced by the household gods; then the entertainment resumed 'after dinner', when Jonson brought in Pan to introduce a more relaxed note into the proceedings. Pan, affecting not to recognise the royal visitors, praised the King as a good hunting man and advised the Queen cheekily to keep her eye on her husband – 'Look to him, Dame!'

This rural comedy was a strong but welcome contrast to the allegorical formality of the 'Magnificent Entertainment'. It went down well with the royal couple and the rest of the party. Jonson was making a good impression, and forming the contacts on which he could build a very different future from the despised craft of 'playwright'. The key to it all was King James – the centre of a new world and one which was drawing Jonson in, along with all the other stars that rise with the onset of a new reign.

CHAPTER 6

JONSON AT COURT

J AMES's reign, however well begun, had from the first its dangers and difficulties. Within months of his accession came a plot to overthrow him. Sir Walter Raleigh, whose security like his glory had died with the old Queen, was falsely implicated in this and thrown in the Tower. There were, too, coming signs of the division that were to split Elizabeth's united commonwealth. At the Hampton Court conference of 1604 James aggressively told the representatives of Puritanism that if they did not conform he would 'harry them out of the land'. But non-conformist opposition merely hardened under the harassment that followed. At the other end of the religious scale the Roman Catholics had not received the relief they had hoped with the change of monarchy. Their discontent, in the shape of the Gunpowder Plot, was to break out more swiftly than the Puritans'. But the slow-working anger of the last was to explode into a revolution that laid low the House of Stuart and changed the British nation forever.

Amid these ominous public developments Jonson's private fortunes were flourishing. Before the year was out he was given his own chance to try his hand at the form he was convinced that Daniel could not handle. He received the commission to write the Queen's masque for the Christmas festivities at court; the royal family had obviously been pleased with the previous work that they had seen. This choice of Jonson and the royal favour that it conveyed meant not only a great professional opportunity for him in the new and challenging form of the masque; in personal terms it gave him an entree into court circles, a new platform for his talents, and a new world to conquer far from 'the loathed stage'.

Jonson enthusiastically embraced the occasion of building on this closer contact with King James. Most unusually for a monarch James could legitimately approach a poet as a fellow-bard, having published

85

two books of poetry in his younger days. Jonson was keenly concerned with the new sovereign's poetical pretensions. In a superbly balanced epigram he linked James's worldly eminence with his eminence as a poet:

> How, best of kings, dost thou a sceptre bear!
>> How, best of poets, dost thou laurel wear!
> But two things rare the fates had in their store
>> And gave thee both, to show they could no more.
> For such a poet, while thy days were green
>> Thou wert, as chief of them are said to have been.
> And such a prince thou art, we daily see,
>> As chief of those still promise they will be.
> Whom should my muse then fly to, but the best
>> Of kings for grace, of poets for my test?
>
> (Epigram 4)

This epigram was a courtly gesture. Jonson was not so fond of the king's poetical taste as this suggests. Drummond noted that Jonson had 'said to the King, that his master, Mr G. Buchan, had corrupted his ear when young, and had learned him to sing verses when he should have read them' (HS I, 148). As Buchanan, tutor to the young King from 1570 to 1578, was a scholar of considerable repute, this was an amazingly candid observation (if Jonson made it) to a king who always demanded flattery rather than truth. But Jonson did the King the honour of taking his work seriously, even though this meant criticising it. He possessed copies of both of James's volumes of verse, the earlier annotated with his own corrections of the King's 'errors of orthography'. And Epigrams 35 and 36 show that he studied his royal master with care, balancing the required compliment against the need not to flatter too fulsomely one who craved uncritical adulation, yet flattered himself that he despised flatterers.

The entry into court circles also meant for Jonson the chance to deepen his acquaintance with those members of the nobility who had already had cause to mark out this emerging poet as an object of special interest. One of these was the Lady Elizabeth, Countess of Rutland, whom Jonson had honoured with a verse epistle as a New Year's gift in 1600. The intervening years had made him more familiar with the circumstances of the Countess's situation than he had been before and what he had discovered confirmed his early respect for her. Jonson's New Year's Day poem, written within a year of the Countess's marriage, had wished her the traditional blessing of the birth of a son. Rumour and gossip had subsequently brought forth in public a painful and private impediment; the Earl was impotent. With his strong heterosexuality Jonson was both keenly interested in the fact and sympathetically conscious of its effect on the Countess's life. In a lewd and gruesome moment he later told Drummond that 'the Count wanted the half of his' (HS I, 138). But in an epigram to the Countess, written during one of her husband's frequent absences abroad, he paid a delicate tribute to the Countess's distressing situation and to her conduct of it:

> The wisdom, madam, of your private life
> Wherewith this while you live a widowed wife,
> And the right ways you take unto the right,
> To conquer rumour and triumph on spite . . .
> Is of so brave example . . .
>
> (*Underwood* 50)

The poem goes on to develop a comparison of the Countess with Penelope awaiting the return of Ulysses, which enabled Jonson subtly to combine the idea of the Count's absence with his disability in order not to seem to be reflecting too plainly on the latter in his commiseration. But Jonson could and did openly commend the course which the Countess took in the face of all this, the development of her literary interests with extensive reading and study, enlivened by the company of poets and dramatists. This praise of the Countess's 'searching for knowledge', her efforts 'to keep /her mind . . . rich and refined' contrast strangely with his diatribes elsewhere against learned women as monstrosities and abominations of nature. Jonson also complimented her in the highest way that he knew by recalling the greatness of her family which she in no way diminished:

> That poets are far rarer birth than kings
> Your noblest father proved: like whom, before
> Or then or since, about our muses' springs
> Came not that soul exhausted so their store.
> Hence was it that their destinies decreed
> (Save that most masculine issue of his brain)
> No male unto him, who could so exceed
> Nature, they thought, in all that he would feign;
> At which she, happily displeased, made you:
> On whom, if he were living now to look,
> He should those rare and absolute numbers view
> As he would burn, or better far, his book.
>
> (Epigram 79)

Jonson was fortunate enough to be able to enjoy relations with the Sidney family in two of its generations. Although the great Sir Philip had died in 1586 while Jonson was still at school, he later came to know Sidney's brother Robert who had succeeded to the title. Sir Robert

Sidney, later Lord Lisle and eventually Earl of Leicester, despite his own insoluble financial difficulties offered Jonson both patronage and hospitality at his country house Penshurst in Kent, which Jonson came to love dearly. Sir Robert had three children, two daughters Mary and Philip (named after her famous uncle), and the heir, William; Jonson composed poetic tributes to all these, and to Mary's husband Sir Robert Wroth. Mary had been named after her aunt Mary Sidney, sister of Sir Philip and Sir Robert. This lady's marriage to the Earl of Pembroke had produced another Sidney cousin, William Herbert third Earl of Pembroke, another of Jonson's important patrons. Over the years Jonson had many varied contacts with these people, all of them closely related to the poet and critic who had been one of Jonson's earliest formative influences.

And Jonson soon won friendships among other members of the nobility too. Lucy Countess of Bedford who had already noticed him was a brilliant figure at court, and not only for her intelligence and beauty – she had an organisational talent that led to her taking charge of several great festive functions. Her educated visual sense made her a connoisseur of pictures and a great lover of gardens. But her real love was poetry, and she was a foremost patron of literary men, of Donne, Drayton and Daniel as well as of Jonson. Through her discerning patronage she 'made her country house at Twickenham a little court of literature' (HS I, 54). As Jonson was already friendly with Donne through mutual acquaintance among the law students of the Inns of Court, the shared connection with this generous and gifted woman brought the two men even closer together.

It was not however entirely plain sailing. Jonson, doubly handicapped by his lack of social training and by an inherent touchiness, had some difficulties in adjusting to a courtly circle. A letter from him to Donne alludes to one such episode, and at the same time gives a touching insight into the nature of the relationship between them. He begins with a tribute to Donne's concern and to his own desire to fall in with Donne's opinion:

> You cannot but believe how dear and reverend your friendship is to me . . . and therefore would I meet it with all obedience.

Some disagreement had arisen between Jonson and one of his noble female patrons and Donne was clearly trying to prevent Jonson from making matters worse. Jonson virtuously declared himself always ready to listen: 'my mind is not yet so deafened by injuries but it hath an ear for counsel'. But Donne had an uphill task. Jonson leaped to his own defence: 'I wonder how I am misunderstood; or that you should call that an imaginary right, which is the proper justice, that every clear man owes to his innocency'. As the outraged innocent, Jonson reserved the right to wax sarcastic:

> My lady may believe whisperings, receive tales, suspect and con-
> demn my honesty; and I may not answer, on pain of losing her; as if
> she, who had this prejudice of me, were not already lost.

Jonson could never see how a vigorous self-defence would only
compound the original fault: 'exasperations intend I none, for Truth
cannot be sharp but to ill natures, or . . . weak ones'.

Yet the second half of the letter undergoes a change in tone. Donne
had obviously written quite sternly to Jonson who expressed his
awareness that 'there is a greater penalty threatened, the loss of you
my true friend'. Jonson ruefully resolves,

> Well, my modesty shall sit down, and let the world call it guilt or
> what it will, I will yet thank you, that counsel me to silence in these
> oppressures, when confidence in my right and friends may aban-
> don me.

He concludes by counselling Donne to avoid any hazard of drawing
'jealousies of hatred' upon himself by being involved in this business,
and ends 'your ever true lover' (IIS I, 203–4).

Despite its pitfalls and setbacks the life of the court had much to
offer Jonson in the way of educated and cultivated friends. Among his
court contacts was Queen Elizabeth's godson, the roguish Sir John
Harington, poet, wit, and sanitary pioneer. Jonson had read Harington's translation of Ariosto's *Orlando Furioso*, and Harington sought
his opinion of his other verses. Jonson did not beat about the bush:

> When Sir John Harington desired him to tell the truth of his
> epigrams, he answered him that he loved not the truth, for they
> were narrations and not epigrams. (HS I, 133)

Jonson must have seen these epigrams in manuscript, for they were
not published until 1615, three years after Harington's death. And it
is further clear that Jonson must have both written and circulated a
number of his own epigrams at this stage, for his opinion as an
epigrammatist to have any weight.

One recipient of a Jonson epigram was Sir John Radcliffe, the
brother of that Margaret whose death Jonson had commemorated in
1599. Alone of his brothers, John had returned alive from Ireland,
and subsequently developed a long friendship with Jonson. Jonson
admired him deeply, declaring that he did not know 'a whiter soul'
Epigram 93). For his part, John Radcliffe demonstrated the valuation that he placed on the relationship in the way that Jonson
loved best; he presented to Jonson a vellum manuscript of Juvenal's
Satires and Horace's *Ars Poetica*, dating from the fifteenth century,

and later donated other texts to this great bookworm.

Nor were Jonson's contacts confined to the lower rungs of the court ladder, among the younger members or those still seeking to establish themselves. One of the rising stars in the court firmament was Sir Robert Cecil, who following in the footsteps of his father William Cecil had made himself indispensable to the monarchy. Robert Cecil had been the Secretary to the Privy Council which had investigated the *Isle of Dogs* affair and was soon to be made Earl of Salisbury on 4 May 1605. Undeterred by his earlier unfortunate brush with Cecil, Jonson decided that he was a man to cultivate and paid him this verse tribute:

> What need hast thou of me, or my muse,
>> Whose actions so themselves do celebrate?
> Which should thy country's love to speak refuse,
>> Her foes enough would fame thee, in their hate.
> 'Tofore [before], great men were glad of poets; now
>> I, not the worst, am covetous of thee;
> Yet dare not to my thought least hope allow
>> Of adding to thy fame; thine may to me,
> When in my book men read but Cecil's name;
>> And what I write thereof find far and free
> From servile flattery (common poets' shame)
>> As thous standst clear of the necessity.
>
> (Epigram 43)

Salisbury is commended again in Epigrams 63 and 64; and Jonson also expressed admiration of this conventional sort for Egerton, who was created Lord Chancellor in 1603 (Epigram 74). Considering that Jonson had escaped a life of manual labour to make his way into the world where he rubbed shoulders with the highest in the land, the wonder is that he did not find more difficulties and misunderstandings than he did.

All the evidence in fact combines to suggest that once entered on this circle Jonson felt thoroughly at home. The friendship of intelligent, sensitive and cultured people made a welcome addition to his previous set of theatre companions. But there was another side to the life of the court. The courtiers of James were not kept on such a tight rein as those of his predecessor, Queen Elizabeth, who was always likely to punish an infraction of manners or morals severely. King James possessed in paradoxical co-existence with his intellectual zeal and moral aspirations a coarse and vulgar streak like that in Jonson's makeup. There are many recorded instances of behaviour by the King that must have called up an echo of Jonson's own fiery temperament and his fondness for crudity in speech. Overcome by the people's desire to see him James once swore, 'God's wounds! I will pull down my breeches, and they shall also see my arse!' Contemporaries may have found this extraordinary Scot unkingly, but despite all the poet's poetic protestations about nobility and dignity, he was a king after Jonson's own heart.

Jonson certainly possessed in abundance the robustness of temper to endure court life, as Fulke Greville described it in his *Life of Sidney:*

> the state of favour, disfavour, prosperity, adversity, emulation, quarrel, undertaking, retiring, hospitality, travail, and all other moods of private fortunes or misfortunes.

He felt no false pride in accepting the help of those well able to afford it. And patronage was not simply a matter of money or gifts. It meant for the poet the existence of an intelligent and interested audience, the guarantee of being received by a cultivated taste. The assurance of this gave Jonson that sense of his own worth that enabled him to hold his own. However aware he was of the social standing of some of his new acquaintance, he was not intimidated by it. As he told Drummond, 'he never esteemed a man for the name of a lord' (HS I, 141). On the contrary, he raised his expectation of a man in direct proportion to the possession of wealth, title and privilege. In keeping with his neo-classical philosophy, of the best only the best was to be expected. On these grounds then the worst of all beings was 'a worthless lord', while 'clothes and titles' were 'the bird-lime of fools'.

Nor were the court ladies protected by their sex from Jonson's censure. As he grew familiar with the court and its prominent personalities, Jonson fell foul of a famous court beauty, Cecilia Bulstrode, a kinswoman of the Duchess of Bedford. When the lady expressed her displeasure with Jonson by criticising him publicly, Jonson responded violently with a long epigram of a mercilessly personal nature (Underwood 49). Beginning roundly by calling Mistress Bulstrode 'the Court Pucelle' [whore], Jonson proceeded to attack her both directly and by innuendo. He derided her social habits, her conversation, her religious observance, her dress. He insinuated that her chamber was a home to 'the prime cocks of the game', and with an ingenious perversion of his classicism claimed that in writing poetry Bulstrode, as a woman, was guilty of a lesbian rape (the muse of poetry being a female, and therefore properly accessible only to masculine advances). No insult however obvious or brutal was disdained – Jonson not only raked up her past history but informed the reader that 'her face there's none can like by candlelight'. The combination of vicious invective with obscene denigration at such a pitch of hysterical intensity can only make us wonder what was the nature of Bulstrode's offence to Jonson. Whatever it was, he did not enjoy the satisfaction of this literary revenge but fetched down trouble on his own head – the poem was 'stolen out of his pocket by a gentleman who drank him drowsy, and given Mistress Bulstrode, which brought him great displeasure' (HS I, 150).

Jonson's first Christmas at court in the winter of 1604–5 was fortuitously a special one. The Yuletide revels on this occasion were unusually joyful and prolonged with the King's Men well to the fore in the ceremonial. Of eleven plays presented before the King by his newly-elevated company seven were by Shakespeare and two were Jonson's. But the highlight of the season both for the playwright and the courtiers was the performance of Jonson's first royal masque.

Jonson's commission from the Queen to create her masque proved to be the inauguration of a remarkable series in this specialised dramatic form. For the production on 6 January 1605, the last official event of the court's Christmas season, Jonson had devised an arresting and powerful piece which could not fail to stir interest. On her side, Queen Anne spared neither trouble nor expense in the preparation of her show, and court circles were full of it:

> We have here great preparation for the Queen's masque; wherein besides Her Majesty will be eleven ladies (Bedford, Suffolk, Susan Vere, Lady Dorothy Rich, a daughter of my lord Chamberlain's, Lady Walsingham, Lady Bevill, and some other which I have forgotten for haste). But the Lady of Northumberland is excused for a sickness, Lady Hertford by the measles, Lady of Nottingham hath a polypus in her nostrils which some fear must be cut off. The lady Hatton would fain have had a part, but some unknown reason kept her out; whereupon she is gone to her [country] house. (*JAB* 39)[1]

Also among the masquers though unrecorded here was the daughter of Sir Robert Sidney, Lady Mary Wroth, another of Jonson's patrons and then newly married.

Apart from the difficulties with the cast which anyone experienced in amateur performance will instantly recognise, contemporary accounts stress the enormous cost of the production. It was canvassed in advance as 'a gallant masque, which will cost the Exchequer £3000' while the Venetian ambassador writing on 29 December 1604 also found the expense the most noteworthy point of the whole venture: 'Her Majesty is preparing a masque which will cost twenty-five thousand crowns' (*JAB* 39). Such extravagance in the teeth of the grave financial difficulties of the kingdom was central among the factors which cost the Stuarts their crown. But for the present, Jonson had no cause to feel that 'the first of his studies in this sort' had had other than a lavish and open-handed staging.

The masque, when seen at the old Banqueting House of Queen Elizabeth in Whitehall, proved to be controversial both in itself and in its wider state implications. The spectators were startled, some even disgusted, that the central device of the piece consisted of the Queen and her ladies appearing as 'Moors' – 'blacking up', in theatrical parlance. Politically, too, there were repercussions. As King James declined to make any decision on the much-disputed matter of whether the French or the Spanish ambassador should have precedence on state occasions, the Lord Chamberlain had to see to it that all the ambassadors were invited privately. Nevertheless on hearing that the French ambassador was not to attend, the Spanish ambassador agitated vigorously for a public invitation. His efforts met with success, at which state of affairs the French ambassador was exceedingly put out. One inveterate letter-writer who frequently included Jonson in his gossip sent the following account of the proceedings to an acquaintance:

> On Twelfth-Day . . . at night, we had the Queen's masque in the Banqueting House, or rather her pageant. There was a great engine at the lower end of the room, which had motion, and in it were the images of sea horses, with other terrible fishes, which were ridden by Moors; the indecorum was, that there was all fish and no water. At the further end was a great shell in the form of a scallop, wherein were four seats; on the lowest sat the Queen with my lady Bedford; on the rest were placed the ladies . . . their apparel was rich, but too courtesan-like for such great ones. Instead of vizards, their faces, and arms up to elbows, were painted black, which was disguise sufficient, for they were hard to be known; *but it became them nothing so well as their own red and white, and you cannot imagine a more ugly sight than a troop of lean-cheeked Moors.* The Spanish and Venetian Ambassadors were both present, and sat by the King in state; at which Monsieur Beaumont [the French Ambassador] quarrels so extremely that he saith the whole court is Spanish . . . the night's work was concluded with a banquet in the great chamber, which was so seriously assaulted that down went tables and trestles before one bit was touched. (*JAB* 41)

Yet despite – or indeed because of – this spice of malice and scandal, the masque went very well. Jonson was launched upon an artistic form which was to occupy his attention intermittently for the next thirty years – between 1605 and 1631 he wrote twenty-five masques. This was indeed a full and gratifying season for him. In addition to the masque, the accounts book of the Master of the Revels records that the King's Men gave *Every Man Out Of His Humour* two days later on 8 January, following it with a revival of

Every Man In His Humour at Candlemas (2 February).

Yet in keeping with the extraordinary see-saw pattern of these early years, having found royal favour Jonson came near to throwing it all away. King James had triumphantly concluded peace with Spain after a nineteen years' war but he was in no particularly pacific mood at home. He was besides notoriously intolerant of personal criticism – Shakespeare in *Measure for Measure* (1604) had found it prudent to observe that 'slandering a prince' deserved 'pressing to death, whipping *and* hanging' (v.i.520–522). In an ill-judged venture Jonson sailed too near the wind and rapidly discovered the fragility of the King's self-esteem.

Ironically Jonson's new difficulties proceeded from the resolution of a former set. 1604 had seen the final closure of the wounds inflicted and received among the playwrights during the earlier 'War of the Theatres'. In publishing his play *The Malcontent* during that year Marston had equipped it with a dedication to Jonson making reference, in stylish and rotund Latin, to his friend's supereminence among poets. In the epilogue he intensified the compliment by describing Jonson as the possessor of 'art above nature, judgement above art'. One of the fruits of the new-found amity was a resumed collaboration. Dekker and Webster had been working together on plays entitled *Westward Ho!* and *Northward Ho!* Towards the end of 1604 Jonson and Marston sat down with Chapman to produce their own version. The result was the tendentious and ill-fated piece *Eastward Ho!*

In itself this play is an amusing and apparently harmless comedy of Jacobean city life with a basic plot of virtuous young love contrasted on all sides with ignorance and greed. But it contained some satire upon the Scots, and some comment upon James's inventive remedy for his sorely depleted Exchequer of raising money by selling honours. Two excerpts were found particularly objectionable. In the first, a knight is ridiculed who has stolen his knighthood, and the speaker also mocks James's Scots accent in the line 'I ken the man weel, he's one of my thirty-pound knights'. In the second, Virginia is described as peopled only by 'a few industrious Scots, perhaps, who indeed are dispersed over the face of the whole earth', people who are notable friends to England 'when they are out of it'. This was too much for the sensitive Scot. The King found his nation derided, his practices openly censured, and by extension the divinity of his monarchy and the exercise of his prerogative seditiously undermined. When the play was staged in 1605 by the Children of the Queen's Revels at Blackfriars word of it was carried to the King and the heavy machinery of royal power swung into action.

Jonson later identified to Drummond the man who had informed on him as Sir James Murray. Murray had only just received his own knighthood, on 5 August 1603, and may have resented the specific thrust in the play at James's 'thirty-pound knights'. He was ambitious of court favour, embarking as he was on a career which was to make him a gentleman of the Privy Chamber to Prince Henry by 1610. There is no indication of any personal animus against Jonson or any of the playwrights. But the result of Murray's action was none the less disastrous for all that.

For as with the *Isle of Dogs* trouble seven years previously the authorities attempted to lay hands upon all involved. Marston, as Nashe had done earlier, made good a timely escape. But Chapman was arrested, and Jonson as he later told Drummond, apparently disdaining Marston's recourse, 'voluntarily imprisoned himself' along with his colleague. To make matters worse, the play had been put on without the licence from the Lord Chamberlain that was technically required, although such a course was not unprecedented among the acting companies.

The wrath of the authorities had been roused not only by the staging of the play but also by its publication; it was entered on the Stationers' register on 4 September 1605. However slight the offence, in any matter of this sort where the personal authority of the King appeared to be flouted the penalties could have been severe, even for the previously blameless Chapman – 'the report was that they should then have their ears cut, and noses' (HS I, 140). Jonson, as a man with a history of encounters with the law and one who still bore the Tyburn brand on his thumb, could hardly have relished another experience of the Jacobean judicial processes of torture and mutilation. But no breath of fear is to be detected in the letters he wrote from this position of jeopardy. Seven of these survive from Jonson's imprisonment. He turned to any member of the nobility who might advance his cause; all the letters are to lords, except one to an unnamed lady, most probably the Countess of Bedford. The letters help to put together a picture of the business. The seriousness of the danger is clear from the numbers of letters Jonson wrote, and the high station of those whom he addressed. His apprehension doubtless proceeded from the fact that the King had interested himself personally in it because he felt himself to be personally outraged. Jonson referred to 'His Majesty's high displeasure', and in another letter observed 'the anger of the King is death (saith the wise man) and in truth it is little less with me and my friend, for it hath buried us quick [alive]'.[2]

The King's rage had found swift expression and one which Jonson was quick to point out was against the principle of natural justice. He protested that he had been committed to a vile prison, 'unexamined or unheard', 'a right not commonly denied to the greatest offenders'. His guilt had been prejudged. He grieved at the offence to the King ('for which I am most inwardly sorry') but refused to accept the responsibility: 'how I should deserve it, I have yet I thank God so much integrity as to doubt'. As he wrote to the one lady whose help he invoked, in a mood of bitter sarcasm:

> And our offence a play, so mistaken, so construed, so misapplied, as I do wonder whether their ignorance or impudence be most who are our adversaries.

Jonson also wrote to the Earl of Salisbury, the King's right-hand man, to whom he gave the fullest outline of his present situation, making reference to his previous brush with the authorities over *The Isle of Dogs* in 1597:

> My noble lord, they deal not charitably who are too witty in another man's works, and utter sometimes their own malicious meanings under our words. I protest to your honour, and call God to testimony, since my first error (which yet is punished in me more with my shame than it was with my bondage) I have so tempered my style that I have given no cause to any good man of grief . . . . I beseech your lordship, suffer not other men's errors, or faults past, to be made my crimes; but let me be examined both by all my works past, and this present . . . whether I have ever (in any thing I have written, private or public) given offence to a nation, to any public order or state, or any person of honour or authority, but have equally laboured to keep their dignity, as my own person, safe; if others have transgressed, let me not be entitled to their follies.

This glancing reference is the only direct mention of the writer whom both Jonson and Chapman held responsible for the offensive phrases, Marston. Despite Drummond's later record of Jonson as saying that Marston and Chapman were imprisoned with him, it is clear from the letters that Chapman, described by Jonson as 'a gentleman', his 'worthy friend', and 'a learned and honest man' was the only sharer of his fate – 'I am here . . . and with me a gentleman . . . one Mr George Chapman.'

Jonson tried hard to mobilise all his influential acquaintances, and just as he had established his innocence before Salisbury in 1597, when as Sir Robert Cecil the statesman had been one of the Privy Council who conducted the investigation of the play, so he expected to be able to do again. But there is a marked difference in tone when Jonson was writing to those lords who were also his friends and patrons. Letters 5 and 7 (HS I, 198 and 199) tentatively identified as to D'Aubigny and Pembroke, have a much warmer and more confident feeling. Jonson felt able to express the 'lasting gratitude' he had 'conceived in soul' towards 'one who hath so far and freely adventured to the relief of our virtue'; to the other he wrote, 'you have ever been free and noble to me, and I doubt not the same proportion of your bounties'. There is a strong consciousness of social distance and of the present situation – Jonson regrets having to 'profane the lady's free hand with prison-polluted paper', and apologised to Salisbury for having been involved with a play: 'the word irks me, that our fortune hath necessitated us to so despised a course'. But there is absolutely no grovelling. He wrote to the Earl of Montgomery, 'I know it is now no time to boast affections, lest while I sue for favours, I be thought to buy them'. And as always there is the stubborn insistence on his own worth in spite of all: 'I appeal to posterity that will hereafter read and judge my writings.'

Chapman adopted a much more submissive tone than this in his petition to the King on behalf of both offenders:

> Vouchsafe, most excellent sovereign, to take merciful notice of the submissive and amendful sorrows of your two most humble and prostrated subjects for your highness's displeasure, George Chapman and Ben Jonson, whose chief offences are but two clauses, and both of them not our own.

Chapman went on to express the hope that the two dramatists' past 'manners and lives' would stand them in good stead in their current hour of need (on the face of it a rather unsafe refuge for Jonson in view of his history). Chapman's was however a particularly abject conclusion; 'in all disjection of never-enough iterated sorrow for your highness' displeasure,' he promised, 'we cast our best parts at Your Highness's feet, and our worst to hell'.

Chapman then wrote to the Lord Chamberlain in similarly complimentary and self-abasing terms, expressing his regret that the regulations had been breached when 'our unhappy book was presented without your lordship's allowance'. Jonson also wrote to the Lord Chamberlain, that very official who had thrown him out of the 1604 masque with Roe, noting grimly that 'it hath ever been my destiny to be misreported and condemned on the first tale'. On this occasion though, Suffolk stood his friend and it was to his intervention that the two writers eventually owed their release, although Jonson's host, patron and friend D'Aubigny had also been active in the case.

Jonson and Chapman were finally set free through a combination of their own protestations of innocence, the intercession of powerful friends, and their own relatively good standing. Despite the mildness of their crime, they had stood in danger of a hideous punishment and humiliating disfigurement. Jonson's relief and joy expressed itself socially. He told Drummond that 'after their delivery he banqueted all his friends; there were Camden, Selden and others' (HS I, 140). Jonson had continued to enjoy the regard of his schoolmaster – in his *Remains Concerning Britain* the great antiquary had listed Jonson among 'the most pregnant wits of these our times, whom succeeding ages may justly admire' (*JAB* 33). Selden was a newer friend, though one of Camden's circle. This great jurist and linguist was summarised by Jonson as 'the law book of all the judges in England, the bravest man in all languages.' It was a strong mutual respect; Selden was 'taught by Ben Jonson, as he used to brag, to relish Horace' in his 'sallies into poetry and oratory' (HS I, 149 and XI, 57).

Along with Camden another of the guests dated from Jonson's very earliest days. This celebration gives the only glimpse on record of Jonson's mother. At the high point of the feast, so Jonson told Drummond, his old mother raised her glass and drank to her son. She then proceeded to show him a small paper packet which she had with her, full of 'lusty strong poison'. Her intention had been to administer this to her son, 'in the prison among his drink', to cheat the authorities of their shameful revenge upon him if the dreaded sentence of disfigurement were to be carried out. To show the quality of her strength and purpose, 'that she was no churl', she planned 'first to drink of it herself' (HS I, 140). The spirited, even histrionic nature of this anecdote (not to mention the fact that Jonson thought well enough of his mother to have her at such a gathering of his friends, when there is no mention of his wife) makes her absence from elsewhere in Jonson's memoirs the more to be regretted.

Jonson and Chapman, then, were both exonerated. Jonson soon repaid Suffolk by beginning work on a nuptial masque to celebrate the wedding of Suffolk's daughter. Marston, whom both men had impeached as the sole author of the offending passages in *Eastward Ho!* was beyond reach and retribution. Punishment fell, therefore, on the men in control of the Children of the Queen's Revels who had put on the play. It proved to be a mortal blow for the 'Blackfriars Boys', Jonson's little protégés. This company which had reorganised following the death of Queen Elizabeth had enjoyed earlier success with the King and had been summoned to play at court. Marston had been allowed to become a sharer in this organisation and was retained as one of their regular playwrights. With poets like him, Chapman and Jonson, the future looked promising.

But in attempting to present topical and sophisticated entertainment the company over-reached itself. The year before in the spring of 1604 a Samuel Daniel play acted by the boys, *Philotas*, had attracted the attention of the authorities who had scented in it covert references to the Essex rebellion. But Daniel seems to have established his clearance with the Privy Council and the little actors escaped retribution on this occasion. Now, however, for presenting the play and for neglecting to secure the Lord Chamberlain's allowance, the manager Kirkham and others in charge of the boys were prohibited from having any further connection with the playhouse in the Blackfriars. The playhouse itself was closed down for a while and the company was denied the patronage of Queen Anne. No longer 'the Children of the Queen's Revels', they dwindled into 'the Children of the Revels', or simply 'the Children of Blackfriars'.

Once more then Jonson emerged from prison with his fortunes in disarray and no immediate prospect of an obvious remedy. Queen Anne had given birth to her second daughter Princess Mary on 8 April and as a consequence there was no masquing at court. But Jonson was continuing with the struggle to establish himself as a 'true poet'. That autumn brought the publication of *Sejanus*, now re-written to be free of the collaborative hand. It had been entered in the Stationers' Register in November of 1604, but Jonson's various difficulties had delayed its appearance for almost a year (the same fate seems to have overtaken *Eastward Ho!*, entered on the Stationers' Register in September of 1605).

The publication of *Sejanus*, equipped with dedication, preface, argument, and commendatory verses, gives some insight into Jonson's standing at this time. Chapman for instance wrote a long poem of one hundred and ninety lines, taking the opportunity of publicly supporting the 'good friend' with whom he had endured so much. In it he compared Jonson with a fine jeweller: 'thy work, in itself, is dear and rare'. He echoed Jonson's own sense of being set apart from the common herd; Jonson's 'chaste muse', he stated, could only show her spirit when 'nobly cherished'. Chapman accurately observed, too, how Jonson's assumption of superiority drove him on in a belief that he could and should reform others. Could he have put his finger upon the play's lack of success with the general public in the following comment?

> Thy poem [play] therefore hath this due respect
> That it lets pass nothing without observing
> Worthy instruction; or [what] might correct
> Rude manners . . .
>
> (HS XI, 309–13)

Many others of Jonson's well-born or scholarly friends also rallied round to contribute some line of verse to launch the publication on its way: Hugh Holland, Marston, William Strachey, 'Th. R.', 'Philos' and 'Cygnus', among others. All commend the play's wit and workmanship and reassure Jonson for the play's popular failure with the conviction that both his play and his fame will outlast marble.

Jonson took pride in his volume and in the demonstration that despite its stage failure a group of discerning friends and practising dramatists had found it good. One quarto was presented to his patron Sir Robert Townsend, inscribed in his own hand; another went 'to my perfect friend Mr Francis Crane, [to whom] I erect this altar of friendship, and leave it as the eternal witness of my love'. Crane was a coming man in the Stuart government. He became in 1606 the clerk to Parliament and was later secretary to Prince Charles, with the reward of a knighthood. Once again the enormous range of Jonson's friends and contacts can be seen. As 1605 drew to its close fate unexpectedly provided Jonson with a chance to convince the state authorities of his true allegiance to them and to the King. Like many others (though few so distinguished in other fields as he) Jonson became involved in the aftermath of that extraordinary event which has retained its hold on the public imagination ever since, the Gunpowder Plot. He jumped at the chance to display his patriotism in this emergency with the vigour which he brought to all his activities.

How Jonson was originally involved is not clear. Following the discovery of the 'Great Treason' on 5 November, the capital and its executives were thrown into the confusion of deep panic. It is remarkable how little for the first two or three days the government appears to have known. Guy Fawkes baffled all interrogation with heroic fortitude, and other channels of intelligence proved unproductive or deceptive. The authorities were desperate to unravel the true nature and extent of the conspiracy and to root out the conspirators. Their transaction with Jonson took place during this period of darkness and dread.

Jonson was, despite his literary claims, a natural suspect. He was a Catholic – from the Protestant point of view one of the worst kind, as a convert – and a known friend of Catholics. These were not only literary men and bookish priests, like Hugh Holland and Thomas Wright. On about 9 October 1605, less than a month before the day of the 'Gunpowder Treason', 'in the beginning of the [Michaelmas] term', Jonson was guest at a supper party at a house in the Strand given by the arch-conspirator Catesby himself (HS XI, 578). Of the seven guests, Thomas Winter was also a principal in the plot, John Ashford was his brother-in-law, Henry Lord Mordaunt was later imprisoned for a year in the Tower on a charge of complicity in the plot, and Francis Tresham was the man supposed to have sent the warning letter to his cousin Lord Monteagle which betrayed the whole enterprise. Jonson, himself not long released from prison, must have seemed from the outside to be in the bosom counsels of dangerous and desperate men.

Fawkes himself may have been unwittingly responsible for involving Jonson. When he was taken from under the Houses of Parliament

Fawkes, like the experienced undercover agent that he was, gave a false name. He called himself John Johnson, and it was by that name that he was for the first few days known and investigated. This was in the contemporary spelling the same name as the playwright's. To strengthen the link both men were professed Catholics; both had fought in the Low Countries; both had given vent to adverse comments upon the King's Scottish followers (Fawkes deposed that one object of the Plot was to blow them all back to Scotland). The authorities would have been negligent indeed not to follow up a lead like this, however flimsy the connection in reality.

Jonson appeared before the Privy Council on 7 November. He was known to all the members from his recent difficulty over the *Eastward Ho!* affair. Whatever the nature of the interview Jonson left it having undertaken to play an active part in the investigations that were going on. His mission was to make contact with a certain Roman Catholic priest and to act as a go-between and safe-conduct in bringing this man before the Privy Council. The priest had apparently offered his services, or some information in the country's hour of need, and Jonson's specific responsibility was to assure him that if he came forward he would not be trapped or imprisoned. Jonson was furnished with documentary proof of his authority in the matter and of their Lordships' integrity:

> 7 November 1605
> A warrant unto Benjamin Johnson to let a certain priest know (that offered to do good service to the state) that he should securely come and go to and from the Lords, which they promised, in the said warrant, upon their honours. (HS I, 203)

Jonson meant well. But his mission was from the first doomed to failure. It was even under normal circumstances a capital offence to be a Roman Catholic priest in England, and at least one such met his death during every year of James's rule.[3] And in this extremity of anti-Catholic hysteria any man however remotely connected with the old faith had gone to ground. No priest obliging enough to comply with the Privy Council's request was to be found.

Jonson's letter to the Privy Council, written in his own hand on the following day, makes it clear that he had tried hard enough. He had straightaway made contact with one of the few Catholics licensed to remain openly in England, a chaplain to a foreign ambassador, in this case the Venetian. The Chaplain had readily agreed with Jonson that both conscience and patriotism should incline any priest to co-operate with the lawful authorities in this emergency; and he had further volunteered to find the man for Jonson's purpose. Soon, however, he returned the answer that 'the party will not be found'.

This proved to be the story wherever Jonson tried. He could not make contact with any Catholic priests in person, 'they being all either removed or concealed upon this present mischief'. By resorting to what he calls a 'second means' (doubtless relying upon those contacts which he must have built up as a practising Catholic for the last seven years) Jonson managed to make the request generally known. But all he received by way of answer was a series of evasions. Chief among these was the excuse that any priest would have to ask permission of the 'arch-priest', one George Blackwell, the supreme Roman Catholic authority in England, before he would be able to assist. On 8 November Jonson reported to Salisbury his difficulties and eventual failure.

A certain anxiety about this is very evident from Jonson's opening words: 'May it please your Lordship to understand that there hath been no want in me either of labour or sincerity in the discharge of this business'. To have been able to complete the mission 'to the satisfaction of your Lordship and the state', would have been the perfect answer to the suspicions of unsoundness which *Eastward Ho!* had aroused. Jonson's disappointment and disgust shines through his narrative of events. He gloomily surmises that all the Catholic priests are somehow 'enweaved' in the Plot and predicts that they will lose five hundred of their followers in a week through their base conduct. Jonson's personal involvement in the whole thing bursts out in an emotional conclusion:

> For myself, if I had been a priest, I would have put on wings to such an occasion, and have thought it no adventure [hazard] where I might have done (besides his Majesty and my country) all Christianity so good service – and so much have I sent to some of them. (HS I, 202)

Jonson did not simply content himself with letting some of these slippery clerics have a piece of his mind. He renewed his offer of service to Salisbury in whatever form it would be most useful. But the crisis was passing. The framework of the plot had been exposed and the architects of it hunted down and rounded up. Jonson had no more to do in this matter. One final point of interest lies in the fact that among the many items of gossip and anecdote which Jonson shared with Drummond, he apparently made no mention of this episode.

Jonson's behaviour had left no doubt as to where his allegiance lay. Nor did he underestimate the importance of these critical events in the life of the nation. When the dust had settled Jonson made his own poetic record of them. Upon reflection Jonson identified the key figure in the whole crisis as the man who first uncovered it, Lord Monteagle. Monteagle's reception of an anonymous warning letter sparked off the timely discovery of the gunpowder, and resulted in his being regarded as the saviour of Parliament. Jonson in his personal tribute went further, chiding the state authorities for their failure to mark Monteagle's act with some public commemoration:

> Lo, what my country should have done – have raised
>   An obelisk or column to thy name,
> Or, if she would but modestly have praised
>   Thy fact, in brass or marble writ the same –
> I, that am glad of thy great chance, here do!
> And, proud my work shall outlast common deeds,
> Durst think it great, and worthy wonder, too:
>   But thine, for which I do it, so much exceeds!
> My country's parents I have many known,
>   But saver of my country thee alone.

(Epigram 60)

For all its excitements this varied year still had a small sting in its tail for Jonson. In November 1605 *The Queen's Arcadia* by Samuel Daniel was entered on the Stationers' Register. The piece had been performed before Queen Anne at Oxford and for its publication Daniel had prepared a dedication to her Majesty. In this preface Daniel made some curious observations upon

> the impropriety of men who, being 'below the sphere of action and exercise of power' presume to comment on their conduct of state affairs. They will inevitably be wrong in their conclusions, and may sow sedition in the minds of the people.

These vague and self-righteous pronouncements strongly hint that Daniel had Jonson in mind. The publication of *Sejanus* recalled Jonson's being called before the Privy Council to answer for it when it first appeared, and however reassuring it may have been to Jonson at this point the publication had hardly been timely with the recent disturbance over *Eastward Ho!* still reverberating. Daniel implies that this claimant to court favour had forgotten his lowly station and had bombastically ventured his opinion on high and grave matters, where his intervention was at best foolish, and at worst dangerous.

These remarks may seem out of place in the mouth of one who had himself suffered a Privy Council inquisition on suspicion of making seditious comments under cover of historical drama in *Philotas*. But Daniel was proclaiming both his innocence of that charge and his humble duty and loyalty to the state in general. On a personal level he was also using the opportunity presented to him to strike another blow in the running war between himself and the rival who had derogated his poetry, laughed at his masques, and proclaimed his own superiority in all things.[4]

Jonson however could afford to rise above Daniel's slings and arrows. He had other literary interests to cultivate, such as the contribution of a set of commendatory verses to the translation by Joshua Sylvester of Guillaume du Bartas's *Divine Weeks and Works* (1605). This poetic tribute was an act of good will only – Jonson knew no French at all at this stage. Sylvester was a groom of Prince Henry's chamber, so this argues against Jonson's efforts to win the favour of those at court. Jonson later dismissed du Bartas as a poet, stigmatising him as 'a verser, because he wrote not fiction' (HS I, 135); du Bartas, that is to say, did not satisfy the requirement of Horace for a true poet. He also told Drummond that he thought 'that Sylvester's translation . . . was not well done'.

All in all, despite its upheavals Jonson had cause to feel satisfaction with these opening years of the new reign. He had gained the interest of the King which had proved strong enough to withstand his periodic lapses from grace. The phase of his writing career that had begun unpromisingly with the defeat in the 'War of the Theatres' had proved unexpectedly rewarding. As Jonson slammed the door on the public theatre, others had opened on prospects that he could not have anticipated. The future looked bright for Jonson at court.

CHAPTER 7

ROYAL MASQUE-MAKER

THE year 1606 opened triumphantly for Jonson with a performance on Twelfth Night of his *Hymenaei*. This elaborate masque was written to celebrate the marriage of the Lady Frances Howard with Robert Earl of Essex. Jonson was repaying his debt of gratitude to Lady Frances's father the Earl of Suffolk who had intervened to help him and Chapman over *Eastward Ho!* The masque was magnificently given with unparalleled sumptuousness. But even so it was only part of the whole entertainment. On the night of Sunday 5 January a pageant was staged at the Banqueting House, Whitehall, followed by Jonson's masque. This was an allegory of Marriage in which Reason or Knowledge had to quell the Riot of Affection or Humour.

Then on the second night the 'solemnities' of the masque gave way to the exertions of a contest at the barriers. 'Barriers' can best be described as a combination of sport and play. It had descended from medieval jousting, assuming over time a more stylised and less dangerous kind of movement than those of its rough-and-tumble origins. But the emphasis was still very much on the physical prowess of the performers. Two teams of men, fifteen a side, contended on behalf of the bride and groom for the honour of Virginity and Marriage, respectively. The inclusion of the barriers was prompted by Prince Henry's enthusiasm for the sport. Although only eleven he tilted in this competition, showing here as elsewhere the precocious skill that was never to come to fruition. Another unfelt shadow on the house of Stuart was present on this occasion – among the combatants was Sir Oliver Cromwell, uncle of the future revolutionary and regicide. Among those taking part of more interest to Jonson were his new friends at court Sir Henry Cary and Sir Henry Goodyere, whom he had come to know and like through John Donne.

This order of procedure exactly followed that of the wedding

masque which King James had composed for the Marquis of Hunt-
ley's marriage in 1588. James's masque had consciously looked to the
past for its sources and inspiration – the court of Scotland became the
court of King Arthur, and the formal masquing then had been
followed by a sporting interlude, in this case the antique sport of
tilting at the ring. Jonson's very similar structure and composition
look like the kind of literary compliment to the Royal Poet that James
would particularly have relished – Jonson had not omitted to study
the poetical productions of his new royal master and James was
hardly likely to forget his one-and-only venture into masque-making.
The masque was subsequently published with a battery of detailed
notes; there are some ninety-five references to the variety of classical
sources Jonson had used in writing it.

Hard on the heels of this triumph however came another threat to
Jonson's peace. In January 1606, in the ecclesiastical jargon of the
time, Jonson was 'presented' for 'correction' by the Church authorities in the Consistory Court of London. The charge, which also
included Jonson's wife, was brought on the grounds that the couple
had absented themselves from communion, the taking of which
through all the troubled religious history of the period was a political
as well as a religious imperative. Despite repeated admonishments, so
the indictment ran, Jonson had continued in this course 'since the
King came in' (that is, since James had acceded to the throne in
1603). Even more dangerous to Jonson, however, in view of the
savage laws and penalties against Catholics which had been rushed
onto the statute book in the wake of the Gunpowder Plot was the
laconic observation on the charge sheet that 'he is a poet, and by fame
a seducer of youth to the Popish religion' (HS I, 220–2).

The full hearing of the case took place on 26 April 1606. In his own
defence Jonson declared that both he and his wife did 'ordinarily' go
to church, naming 'his own parish church' as St Anne's Blackfriars.
There, he deposited, he had worshipped regularly for the last six
months, thus indicating that it had been the 'Gunpowder Treason', in
November of 1605, that had precipitated his regular attendance at
Anglican worship. Admitting that he had refused to receive communion, he attributed this to religious scruple, and made efforts to
dissociate his wife from this serious charge. It is not clear from the
evidence quite how close Jonson's knowledge of his wife was at this
time or even whether or not they were living together. His first
statement that 'he and his wife' went to church, 'and to his own
church', suggests that they went together. But later in the deposition
Jonson testified that his wife 'for anything he knows' had gone to
church, continuing that 'she always used to receive the communion',
both phrases indicating that he was out of touch with his wife and her

habits of worship. Yet in his final reference to her, Jonson told the authorities that she 'is appointed to receive the communion tomorrow', so clearly some contact had taken place between them.

Anne Jonson by the mere act of taking the holy sacrament would place herself out of danger. Jonson's case was more serious. From the time of Elizabeth the effect of the laws governing religion had been to identify Roman Catholicism with treason. To attempt to withdraw an Englishman from what was seen as his natural allegiance to Protestantism, was legally defined as high treason, and carried the barbarous penalty devised for that offence. Admittedly these laws were only spasmodically enforced; there was nothing like the systematic and sustained campaign of persecution which England had suffered under Mary Tudor. The majority of Roman Catholics to die for their faith under the Stuarts were priests active in holy orders rather than laymen like Jonson. But there were martyrs among the ranks of the laity, and Jonson was vulnerable.

He met the danger head on, categorically denying that he 'ever went about to seduce any [body] to popery'. He further denied the truth of any such 'fame' or rumour about him to that effect, 'he never giving the cause thereof'. Challenging his accusers for proof, Jonson expressed himself 'desirous the Churchwardens or anybody should justify how they should charge him' in the matter. On this reasonable, not to say legal request, the judge adjourned the case to enable the evidence to be brought against Jonson. In the meantime, on Jonson's expressing his readiness to submit his religious scruples against taking the communion to further consideration, the judge issued a list of several eminent divines, including the Dean of St Paul's and the Archbishop of Canterbury, for Jonson's consideration. He was ordered to choose one of these men and to attend twice a week for religious instruction and debate to resolve his doubts. Jonson agreed to this. Yet characteristically even in this tight corner he reserved the right of freedom of conscience in the last resort; he promised 'to conform himself *according as they shall advise and persuade him*' – the last clause reserving the ultimate vital decision to himself.

The case dragged on all through the first half of 1606, with six appearances in all in the court records. The churchwardens and 'swornmen', who originally 'presented' Jonson, failed to produce any evidence against him on the charge of being a seducer of youth. However Jonson fared with his religious re-education, it did not make him change his faith. But the authorities evidently decided that this dauntless spirit was not essentially malignant. The matter against Jonson was allowed to drop, although it is significant that it was not completely closed – the case is marked 'stayed at seal', the phrase used to mean that no final decision had been taken.

Jonson appears to have come off well from this difficult situation in such a troubled time. The country at large was still unsettled in the aftermath of the Gunpowder Plot, and in the absence of swift and reliable communication rumour often fed the desire for information. Jonson himself commemorated one such occasion when the story that the King had been stabbed while out hunting got abroad and caused widespread alarm. Although not himself free of his entanglement with the Church authorities at this time (22 March 1606), he hailed his sovereign with a confident and courtly poem, 'To King James on the Happy False Rumour of his Death':

> That we thy loss might know, and thou our love,
>   Great heaven did well to give ill fame free wing;
> Which, though it did but panic terror prove,
>   And far beneath least pause of such a king,
> Yet give thy jealous subjects leave to doubt,
>   Who this thy 'scape from rumour gratulate
> No less than if from peril; and, devout,
>   Do beg thy care unto thy after-state.
> For we, that have our eyes still in our ears,
> Look not upon thy danger, but our fears.

(Epigram 51)

Another important preoccupation of Jonson around this time was the writing of *Valpone*. Despite the attractions of court life he had been drawn back to writing for the stage. The play has been assigned to the early weeks of 1606, and he tells us in the prologue that five weeks of intense labour produced it in time for public performance in February.[1] A later apocryphal tradition suggests that Jonson's inspiration and composition were artificially stimulated; he is supposed to have declared, 'I laid the plot of my *Volpone*, and wrote most of it, after a present of ten dozen of palm sack from my very good Lord Treasurer. That play I am positive will last to posterity and be acted (when I and envy are friends) with applause' (HS I, 188). What is certain is that the performance of *Volpone* by the King's Men at the Globe Theatre with Burbage in the title role reversed the trend of Jonson's ill fortune on the public stage. The play was acted to great acclaim as a later admirer of Jonson related, recalling the time

> When that thy *Fox* had ten times acted been
> Each day was first, but that 'twas cheaper seen.[2]

In other words, each performance was as successful as the first and only distinguishable from it by virtue of being less expensive to see (a reference to the contemporary custom of reducing admission charges after the initial showing of a new play). *Volpone* was later given at

Oxford and Cambridge; the quarto edition's dedicatory epistle to the Universities, with its reference to the 'love and acceptance' that the play won there, also points to an unqualified success.

The summer of 1606 brought more court occupation for Jonson. King James was entertaining his brother-in-law King Christian IV of Denmark, and if one royal presence was a cue for ceremony, two kings regnant called for something exceptional. Jonson was involved with the ceremonies when James and Christian stayed with the Earl of Salisbury at the great house of Theobalds at Cheshunt in Hertfordshire as the guest of the Earl of Salisbury from 24 to 28 July 1606. Jonson wrote the welcoming addresses in the King's honour which he subsequently printed in the 1616 Folio. Accounts among the Cecil papers record that a payment of £13 6s 8d was made to 'Ben: Iohnson the Poett' as part of the 'chardges of ye Showe at Theoballs'. Inigo Jones was also involved, his fee and expenses amounting to £23. As Jonson's remuneration seems too large for the short welcoming speeches which he had written even with the addition of the Latin epigrams he had composed which were hung on the walls by way of compliment, it seems likely that Jonson must have had some further part in the 'very learned, delicate and significant shows and devises' which went to make up the four-day entertainment of the foreign visitor.

It is not known if Jonson was employed in the writing of the masque with which the King of Denmark was honoured, *Solomon and the Queen of Sheba*. If he were he would have had every reason to suppress his connection with it thereafter. This notorious show ascended through drunken debauchery to a climax of disaster. Sir John Harington has left a justly famed account of the grisly proceedings:

> The lady who did play the Queen's part, did carry most precious gifts to both their Majesties; but, forgetting the steps arising to the canopy, overset her caskets into his Danish Majesty's lap, and fell at his feet, though I rather think it was in his face . . . His Majesty then got up and would dance with the Queen of Sheba; but he fell down and humbled himself before her, and was carried to an inner chamber and laid on a bed of state; which was not a little defiled with the presents of the Queen which had been bestowed on his garments; such as wine, cream, jelly, beverage, cakes, spices and other good matters. The entertainment and show went forward, and most of the presenters went backward, or fell down; wine did so occupy their inner chambers. Now did appear, in rich dress, Hope, Faith, and Charity: Hope did assay to speak, but wine rendered her efforts so feeble that she withdrew. . . . Faith was then all alone, for I am certain she was not joined with good works, and left the court in a staggering condition: Charity came to the King's feet, and

seemed to cover the multitude of sins her sisters had committed; in some sort she made obeisance, and brought gifts. . . . She then returned to Hope and Faith, who were both sick and spewing in the lower hall. . . . Victory . . . after much lamentable utterance . . . was led away like a silly captive, and laid to sleep in the outer steps of the antechamber. Now did Peace make entry . . . and much contrary to her semblance, most rudely made war with her olive branch, and laid on the pates of those who did oppose her coming.[3]

As this suggests, masques for the court, like plays for the stage, were not always attended by that high seriousness that Jonson so craved. He was occupied during 1607 in further attempts to consolidate his literary and dramatic standing. Early in the year he prepared his *Volpone* for the press. This emerged in an interesting quarto which tells us something of his life and thought at the time. In dedicating it to 'the most noble and equal sisters, the two famous universities' of Oxford and Cambridge, Jonson took the opportunity to express his appreciation of their support of his work and, by a Jonsonian extension, of poetry in general. To do this he decided to re-use some of the material from a former piece, the *Apologetical Dialogue* from the 'War of the Theatres'. This speech, only once spoken on stage and intended for inclusion in the 1602 edition of *Poetaster*, had been suppressed by authority because of its tendentious nature. With his usual tenacity Jonson had hung onto the offending document until such time as he had a chance to reintroduce it.

The 'two sisters' of Oxford and Cambridge were therefore treated to a vigorous reworking of some of the main preoccupations of the earlier quarrel. Jonson was at pains to establish his disinterested concern for the dignity of poetry which he proceeded to defend from 'ribaldry, profanation, blasphemy, all licence of offence to God and man'. In unfolding a series of rhetorical questions Jonson further demanded of his readers an acquittal on the charge of personal satire, proclaiming his own innocence with 'what broad reproofs have I used? Where have I been particular? Where personal?'

Jonson signed this piece of self-justification 'from my house in the Blackfriars this 11 of February 1607'. He was living, that is, once more under his own roof and in the heart of the private theatre district. The Consistory Court proceedings of the year before suggest that he had resumed at least some contact with his wife. His patron Lord D'Aubigny was to be married in 1607; had the awareness of the forthcoming match necessitated a removal for Jonson from the house of the man with whom he had lived as he told Drummond for five years? And had Jonson in his own house taken his wife to him once more? The *Volpone* quarto is silent on this point. More illuminating is the picture it provides of Jonson's friendships. The dramatist Francis Beaumont contributed prefatory verses, commending Jonson's 'bold and knowing muse', as did his partner John Fletcher, and Chapman, Donne and Field, the former boy player. Jonson's satisfaction with the book may be seen from his making a gift of it to another special friend. To the dedicated Italian teacher and scholar Jonson presented a copy inscribed 'to his worthy father and loving friend Mr John Florio, the aid of his muses, Ben Jonson seals this testimony of friendship and love' (HS VIII, 655). The relationship both filial and pedagogic implied in the use of the term 'father' is one which Jonson himself was later to enjoy with younger poets, while this description of Florio as 'the aid to [Jonson's] muse' indicates the contribution made by this gifted educationalist and translator to Jonson's dramatic and intelletual endeavours.[4]

Despite the dangerous rumours of the previous year about his 'popish' tendencies Jonson remained in royal favour. Early in 1607 he was again commissioned to write an entertainment for the King at Theobalds; it was presented on 22 May 1607 to celebrate the transfer of this magnificent house and estate from the Cecil family to the King. The entertainment, which Jonson later published in full in the 1616 Folio, consists of a short dialogue between the Genius of the House, Mercury, and the Three Fates – five speaking parts in all. Surviving accounts suggest that the show, however brief, was mounted with great attention to visual effect, with the Genius swathed in 'five yards of yellow tinsel' and Mercury in 'one ell and three quarters of blue taffeta'.[5] Overseeing this aspect of the work was Inigo Jones once again.

The 1607 entertainment differs from Jonson's earlier attempts in this form in a way that clearly shows the influence of Jones on Jonson's stagecraft. Jonson's previous versions of this traditional Elizabethan form of compliment and welcome were not so much stage pieces as outdoor pleasantries. They consisted of encounters between the visiting royalty and various classical or allegorical figures in a pastoral landscape. The 1607 show however makes the transition from an outdoor reception to a fully staged performance. Jones's varied skills in architecture, scene and costume design, stage lighting and 'machines', created the preconditions for a more developed dramatic conception on Jonson's part. The simple fact of the removal indoors (the show was put on after dinner in the long gallery) made possible an opening *coup de théâtre*; a traverse curtain drawn back revealed 'a gloomy obscure place' inhabited by the Genius of the House seen drooping sadly in the gloaming light of a solitary candle. Suddenly the scene changed to 'a glorious place' where a monumental classical setting, brilliantly lit, gave onto a distant perspective with clouds riding in the sky.

Jonson was now becoming clearly associated in the public mind with the preparation of these short but highly important ceremonials. In the same summer of 1607 he was consulted by Sir John Swinnerton acting on behalf of the Merchant Taylors' Company. The Company had received word that the King, the Queen, Prince Henry and various nobles intended to dine with them in their hall on the occasion of the annual election of their Masters and Warders. Concern with 'the reputation and credit' of the Merchant Taylors' Company had led its council to take professional advice. Accordingly Swinnerton was 'entreated to confer with Mr Ben Jonson the poet about a speech to be made to welcome his Majesty, and for music and other inventions which may give liking and delight to his Majesty, by reason that the company doubt that their schoolmaster and scholars be not acquainted with such kinds of entertainments.'

This resolve was taken on 27 June. Jonson was not allowed much time for his preparations. But the event, on 16 July, succeeded happily and justified the company's proceedings. The royal party was 'splendidly entertained with great variety of music, vocal and instrumental, and speeches, in a chamber called the King's chamber'. For the welcoming speech Jonson turned again to one of the boy performers for whom he always had a soft spot:

> At the upper end of the Hall there was set a chair of state, where his Majesty sat and viewed the hall; and a very proper child, well spoken, being clothed like an angel of gladness, with a taper of frankincense burning in his hand, delivered a short speech containing eighteen verses, devised by Ben Jonson, which pleased his Majesty marvellously well.[6]

Jonson received £20 for 'inventing the speech to his Majesty, and for making the songs, and his directions to others in that business' – not the only hint of Jonson's desire and ability to take the more active part of a producer than the conventional image of the writer allows.

1607 drew to its close with another much more important royal occasion for Jonson. He received the commission to write the Queen's masque for the Christmas revels at court. This was the second masque that Jonson had been asked to make for the Queen and he was expected to link it with its predecessor, *The Masque of Blackness*, and to repeat the earlier success. As the time of the performance approached interest ran high on all sides and seemed to some observers to be quite out of proportion to the occasion. The Venetian ambassador who often found King James neglectful of state affairs in favour of hunting noted disapprovingly that 'the King . . . and the court are entirely absorbed in the festivities, and in the Queen's masque. She is giving it great attention in order that it may come up to expectation' (*JAB* 61).

The Masque of Beauty required in fact an enormous amount of trouble and expense. In the first week of January 1608 one courtier wrote to another out of town that the masque had had to be put off for a few days as it had proved impossible to have everything ready on time. The richness of the show was to surpass all previous experience:

> Whatsoever the device may be, and what success they have in their dancing, yet you should be sure to have seen great riches in jewels, when one lady (and that under a baroness) is said to be furnished for better than a hundred thousand pounds; and the Lady Arabella goes beyond her; and the Queen must not come behind (*JAB* 62).

As before, the masque was a source of political trouble. This was another reason for its being put off for a few days, the Venetian ambassador reporting with glee that it had caused the greatest chagrin to the French ambassador that the Spanish ambassador had also been invited. Yet when it was eventually performed on Sunday 10 January 1608 it managed to live up to all the excitement that had been generated. It had a splendid setting; the King intended it to 'consecrate' the new Banqueting House which had just been completed, and which was in every way larger and more gracious than the building it replaced, the old timber structure of 1581. Even to the previously critical Venetian ambassador it was an unqualified triumph:

> I must just touch on the splendour of the spectacle, which was worthy of her Majesty's greatness. The apparatus and cunning of the stage machinery was a miracle, the abundance and beauty of the lights immense, the music and dance most sumptuous. But what beggared all else, and possibly exceeded the public expectation was the wealth of pearls and jewels that adorned the Queen and her ladies, so abundant and splendid that in everyone's opinion no other court could have displayed such pomp and riches. So well composed and ordered was it all that it is evident that the mind of her Majesty, the authoress of the whole, is gifted no less highly than her person. She reaped universal applause, and the King constantly showed his approval (HS X, 457).

This account furnishes a premonitory glimpse of Jonson's later difficulties with the masque form, and specifically with his collaborator Inigo Jones. For as this stresses, the spectators were hopeful of and impressed by extravagant show. There is no word here of the poet as maker – indeed, Queen Anne is celebrated as 'the authoress of the whole'. Amid the chorus of praise which greeted the masque only one voice, that of Rowland Whyte writing to the Earl of Shrewsbury on 26 January 1608, recognised the poet's contribution to the overall success of the performance. Yet as his comment shows, Jonson was given no time either to rest on his laurels or to reflect upon the project he had just completed. He was plunged immediately into another commission:

> The Masque [of Beauty] was as well performed as ever any was; and for the device of it, with the speeches and the verses, I had sent it to your lordship ere this, if I could have gotten those of Ben Jonson. But no sooner hath he made an end of these, but that he undertook a new charge for the Masque that is to be at the Viscount Hadington's marriage (*JAB* 64).

John Ramsey Viscount Haddington was a Scot and one whom the King delighted to honour – he had, according to James, saved the King's life during the bloody and mysterious fracas which became known as the Gowrie conspiracy of 1600. Jonson alludes to him as having had 'the honour to be the saver of his king'. Part of his reward was that he 'got to his bedfellow one of the prime beauties of the kingdom, daughter to Robert Earl of Sussex'.[7] Although not a royal wedding the marriage was celebrated on Shrove Tuesday, 9 February 1608, with an almost royal extravagance, and the crowning event of the magnificent proceedings was the nuptial masque in the evening, which was attended by the King and the foreign ambassadors.

The Hue and Cry After Cupid, as the Haddington masque was later called, is generally reckoned to have been one of the most brilliant and costly of Jonson's masques. Although following hard upon the *Masque of Beauty* it was not therefore neglected; indeed in the dead days after Christmas Whyte noted that 'the great masque intended for my lord Hadington's marriage' became 'the only thing thought upon at court'. No expense was to be spared either by those staging or those performing the masque; as to the latter, five English and seven Scots lords, their participation, so Whyte informed his correspondent, 'would cost them £300 a man'.

Expense and effort conjoined to produce a stunning show and one which incorporated two scenic devices previously unrecorded. The setting itself was spectacular with two pilasters on either side of the scene 'and overhead two personages, Triumph and Victory, in flying postures, and twice so big as the life, in place of the arch'. Above, at the sudden signal of loud and solemn music (which both added to the atmosphere and distracted the audience by covering any grinding and clanking that took place as the scene was shifted) a miraculous transformation took place. A bright sky appeared to break forth from the clouds and 'there was discovered first two doves, then two swans with silver gears [harness] drawing forth a triumphal chariot'. Another thrilling effect was achieved later, when on Vulcan's cry 'cleave, solid rock, and bring the wonder forth', a cliff, the central scenic feature of the stage, 'parted in the midst, and discovered an illustrious concave, filled with ample and glistening light, in which was an artificial sphere, made of silver, eighteen feet in the diameter, that turned perpetually' (HS VII, 257–8).

Again the court was ravished by the show, the actors and performance also coming in for praise. To one observer 'especially the motions were well performed; as Venus, with her chariot drawn by swans, coming in a cloud to seek her son; who with his companions Lusus, Risus and Jocus, and four or five wags, were dancing a *matachina* [sword dance], and acted it very antiquely, before the Twelve Signs, who were the master-maskers, descended from the Zodiac, and played their parts more gravely, being very gracefully attired' (*JAB* 64–5). It is not hard to recognise here the union of Jonson's sense of occasion with his careful classicism; Venus and her son Cupid are associated with the spirits of jollification and merry-making Lusus (Sport), Risus (Laughter) and Jocus (Jest), as befits the season and the time. When all these 'wags' were cavorting about in the buffoonish '*matachina*', later superseded by the grave and graceful 'master-maskers' (among whom were Jonson's patrons D'Aubigny and Pembroke), the effect was striking and memorable.

In strong contrast to this glorious public occasion was an event which occurred immediately before it. Unheralded and unsung another son of Jonson slipped quietly into the world. The baby boy was named Benjamin after his father and baptised on 20 February 1608 at St Anne's in the Blackfriars, the parish of Jonson's residence. As Jonson's first son Benjamin had died Jonson was following a common contemporary practice in calling another infant by the same name (Shakespeare's parents did the same with their daughters Joan). Like so many others of the period the child's entrance is also his exit; there is no further record of him. Jonson would have been an extremely unusual Jacobean father if he had been much concerned with a newborn baby; and he was at this time particularly heavily involved in these ephemeral but highly demanding royal entertainments.

Yet even after this work was completed Jonson had not finished with ceremonial occasions for 1608. In the early summer of that year he was involved along with Inigo Jones in the creation of an entertainment for King James at Salisbury House in the Strand. This house was the Westminster residence of the Cecil family, whose household bills for 1608 contain the only reference to this event. Jonson published no text of the entertainment and no other accounts of it are in existence. From the evidence of the surviving invoices both Jonson and Jones received £20 for their part in the show, which was held in the library of Salisbury House especially refurbished for the occasion.

Other payments to painters, drapers, tailors, joiners and musicians suggest that the show was carefully and lavishly prepared. The exact date cannot be determined, but the invoices prove that it must have occurred between 5 and 11 May 1608. In addition, the location of the show, together with the fact that one of the invoices is written in Salisbury's own hand, suggest that it may have been connected with Salisbury's appointment to the position of Lord Treasurer on 4 May 1608.

One distinguishing feature of this entertainment was the appearance in it of the great actor Edward Alleyn. Jonson hailed Alleyn's achievement in an epigram comparing him with the famous dead of the antique world:

> If Rome so great, and in her wisest age,
>   Feared not to boast the glories of her stage,
> As skilful Roscius and grave Aesop, men
>   Yet crowned with honours, as with riches then,
> Who had no less a trumpet of their name
>   Than Cicero, whose every breath was fame:
> How can so great example die in me,
>   That, Alleyn, I should pause to publish thee?
> Who both their graces in thyself hast more
>   Outstripped, than they did all that went before;
> And present worth in all dost so contract
>   As others speak, but only thou dost act.
> Wear this renown.'Tis just that who did give
> So many poets life, by one should live.
>
> (Epigram 89)

Officially retired from the stage for some years, Alleyn had nevertheless taken part in the coronation procession of James I in 1604 and his participation in this entertainment was highly prized. He was paid £20, the same as Jonson and Jones, and like them was accorded the honour of dining with Lord Salisbury. The value placed on his appearance is also suggested by the gorgeous costume prepared for him. His robe was especially made of five ells of rich crimson taffeta costing £3 10s, with open sleeves of fine white silk tissue, and a girdle of white taffeta. Yet Alleyn in all his glory was only one element of what was clearly an impressive show. Records of payments for skin coats and cloven feet indicate the presence of satyrs, whose boisterous dancing and tomfoolery would well offset the gravity and power of Alleyn. Other unusual effects were provided by a juggler, whose remuneration of £10 suggests that his part was important, a conjurer and a 'flying boy'.

Again the prominence if not predominance of the visual and scenic aspects of the show foreshadow the future conflict between Jonson and Jones over the 'soul' and 'body' of these performances. For the moment, however, although Jones was allowed extra expenditure for his materials and workmen, both he and Jonson received exactly the same payment from the Earl of Salisbury for their services. This sum was in comparative terms bounteous, each £20 representing more than one tenth of the overall cost of the entertainment, £170. In comparison with a much more elaborate court masque, whose overall cost amounted to more than £2000, yet which never paid Jonson or Jones more than £50, this was an excellent reward. To the playwright who grumbled to Drummond that he had never made as much as £200 from all his plays together, £20 for one small entertainment must have seemed a small miracle.

Characteristically Jonson paid tribute to Salisbury with what he regarded as far more valuable than money, his own work. Offering the fruits of his love and the treasure of his art Jonson took a bold, unservile tone in Epigram 64, 'To Robert Earl of Salisbury: upon the accession of the Treasurership to him':

> Not glad, like those that have new hopes or suits
>   With thy new place, bring I these early fruits
> Of love, and what a golden age did hold
>   A treasure, art: contemned in age of gold;
> Nor glad as those that old dependents be
>   To see thy father's rites new laid on thee;[8]
> Nor glad for fashion; nor to show a fit
>   Of flattery to thy titles; nor of wit.
> But I am glad to see that time arrive
>   Where merit is not sepulchred alive;
> Where good men's virtues to them honours bring
>   And not to dangers; when so wise a king
> Contends to have worth enjoy, from his regard
>   As her own conscience, still the same reward.
> These, noblest Cecil, laboured in my thought
>   Wherein that wonder, see, thy name hath wrought;
> The whiles I meant but thine to gratulate
>   I've sung the greater fortunes of our state.

As 1608 drew on, other events in the world of the public theatre held importance for Jonson. During the summer of that year the King's Men, Shakespeare's company of players, took over the lease of the Blackfriars Theatre, a private indoor playing area very different from their famous Globe. This group overshadowed all others in the quality and consistency of their work. But like the others it had suffered from previous difficulties – the restraint upon playing

117

brought about by the *Isle of Dogs* affair had forced them into travelling throughout the summer of 1597 and on into early autumn. The King's Men were now enduring in 1608 a time of desperate plague that struck at the very heart of the public playhouses.

Among the decisions that the company members were taking in the face of their grave difficulties was the resolve to build up the new theatre. Essential to this purpose was the acquisition of new plays, and a new type of play, that would be acceptable to the more sophisticated playgoers of the private theatre. Among those procured for service was Jonson. Before 1608 Jonson had written only four plays for the King's Men; three, nine, and ten years previously. After this he wrote all his remaining plays for this company except one.

Jonson was of course a natural choice for the new managers. He had had earlier connections with the theatre itself; he had written plays for performance there when it was used by the boy players who staged his *The Case Is Altered, Cynthia's Revels, Poetaster* and *Eastward Ho!* Jonson had also shared some of the responsibility for directing the boys' performances in this playhouse, as the induction to *Cynthia's Revels* and his personal statements about individual boys indicate. He was familiar with the Blackfriars audience too – sophisticated and worldly, certainly, but not necessarily as aristocratic as has sometimes been deduced from the high cost of entry (the cheapest seat at the private theatres cost, at 6d, six times more than the 'penny stinkards' paid to gain entry to the Globe, for example). Jonson categorised them sardonically in lines written to accompany Fletcher's *The Faithful Sheperdess* which was published in the same years as this transaction (1608):

> Gamester, Captain, Knight, Knight's man,
> Lady or Pusil [whore], that wears mask or fan,
> Velvet or taffeta cap, ranked in the dark
> With shop's foreman, or some such brave spark
> That may judge for his sixpence . . .

Nevertheless the courtly element was prominent among the Blackfriars audience. Again Jonson would be a considerable acquisition for these playgoers, as a name well known in court circles following his masques and entertainments for the King and the nobility. Finally he had by this time built up through his writing and perhaps even more important through the publishing of his work a following among the *literati* and critics, writers and students, the educated and intelligent section of contemporary society which it was hoped to attract to such a playhouse.[9]

As the Blackfriars secured the service of one playwright, so it lost another. On 8 June 1608 John Marston was committed to Newgate

Prison in a renewed purge by King James of offending dramatists and dramatic companies. He disappeared from the Blackfriars and from London literary life, leaving his current play, *The Insatiate Countess*, unfinished and selling his share in the Blackfriars management. He ended his career as a poet and playwright and unexpectedly turned country parson. He already had a close relative in holy orders, if Jonson's later pronouncement to Drummond was any more than a joke, that 'Marston wrote all his father-in-law's preachings, and his father-in-law his comedies' (HS I, 138). Marston's work consistently displayed a sustained capacity for moral thought together with a deep vein of disgust for modern life which would appear to fit him for his new calling. He was in any case granted many years in which to pursue it. He was ordained by December of 1609 and lived until 1634, almost as long as Jonson. But he never wrote for the stage again and there is no further record of any contact between the two men.

For the Blackfriars management it was at this stage in the summer of 1608 a question of policy-making only. The ferocity of the plague prevented the King's Men from making their new acquisition operational until the end of the following year, 1609. As a writer rather than as a member of the company Jonson had no part in these deliberations. One of the greatest disadvantages of his career as a dramatist was that he never became as Shakespeare did a sharer in a prosperous and well-established company, a 'house-keeper' as the holders of theatre shares were known. Such a position preserved Shakespeare from the insecurity and penury that blighted Jonson's closing years.

Johnson constantly had, however, other concerns both professional and personal. 1608 provides the record of a grievous blow, the death of his friend Sir John Roe, with whom he had been thrown out of the Daniel masque in 1604.[10] Roe had led a dangerous life. As a duellist he had risked himself successfully in two encounters and while soldiering in Ireland had been described as 'sore hurt in the head' in October of 1605 (HS XI, 6). Yet he survived all these to fall to a common bacillus and died of the plague in London. Jonson's deep grief and sense of loss appears from his having written no less than three epitaphs for Roe. He borrowed from Seneca for the simplest and finest of these:

> I'll not offend thee with a vain tear more,
>   Glad-mentioned Roe; thou art but gone before
> Whither the world must follow. And I now
>   Breathe to expect my when, and make my how.
> Which if most gracious heaven make like thine
>   Who wets my grave can be no friend of mine.
>   (Epigram 33)

119

The concluding couplet touchingly tells us that Roe made a good death. However he died Jonson was uniquely placed to know about it, since Roe died in his arms. Jonson followed this last dear act of friendship with the last rites of respect. In the absence of anyone else, he furnished the dead man's funeral expenses, giving his friend a substantial £20 ceremony, a sum later reimbursed to him by Roe's family.

But once again the demands of work soon claimed Jonson's attention. In November of 1608 John Donne wrote to his friend Sir Henry Goodyere that the King had gone from London but 'hath left the Queen a commandment to meditate upon a masque for Christmas, so that they grow serious about that already' (*JAB* 68). This is the first mention of what was to become Jonson's *Masque of Queens*. Letters and warrants flew to and fro in connection with the preparations – Sir Thomas Lake wrote to Salisbury, the Lord Treasurer, on 27 November 1608, that he should 'enlarge' the King's warrant for £1000 'to some reasonable increase as [he] should think meet'. Salisbury can hardly have found this request 'meet', in view of the government's accelerating difficulties with money which he was already trying vainly to curtail, and which were already casting long shadows of the darkness to come across the house of Stuart. But the King was not to be crossed; the Queen was not to be disappointed; the Banqueting House at Whitehall was made ready at the cost of £78 0s 8d; and the poet was commissioned and set to work.

Jonson's third masque for Queen Anne shows Jonson incorporating matters of interest to other members of the Royal Family. The anti-masque of witches was a courtly gesture directed at the King, who had an almost obsessional belief in the subject. He had published a study of it, his *Demonology* in 1597, and he was firmly convinced that he had personally been the object of the evil practices of the so-called Witches of Berwick, who had been accused of raising the great storm at sea when James was trying to bring home Anne of Denmark as his bride in 1589. The introduction of Hecate and her hags into the *Masque of Queens* was therefore an allusion to a romantic and dramatic episode in the life of his royal patron, as well as a compliment to the King's learned studies.

Equally interested in Jonson's work was the King's son Henry, now fifteen years old. Unlike the majority of spectators Prince Henry was not simply taken by the show but expressed his appreciation of the poet's contribution by asking Jonson for an annotated copy of the text. The request from the discerning and well-educated young prince was a signal mark of esteem of the kind that Jonson most valued, and even the most unworldly of poets could not fail to recognise the importance of attracting the attention of the heir-apparent. Jonson's dedication of the masque to the Prince expresses his sense of all this.

The fulfilment of the task, however, involved Jonson in an enormous amount of work, which must have carried over into the early weeks of the new year, 1609.

For Jonson had to annotate some 450 lines of text, giving his classical sources, his references and cross-references. The amplitude with which he carried out the assignment shows that this was to him no exaction but a labour of love. *The Masque of Queens* is so massively annotated that the text bears the appearance of a full Renaissance commentary upon a classical text. Line after line of fine script, a parade of Greek and Latin quotations, all demonstrate Jonson's revelling in the panoply of scholarship. The battery of learning is sometimes more apparent than real; Jonson often relies on secondary sources, or conceals the origins of his borrowings. But the erudition displayed is never merely a mechanical collection of facts nor a surface acquaintance with the names and works of ancient writers. What it may lack in depth and accuracy it makes up in the varied and vigorous uses to which Jonson puts it. Among the names of the authors cited, the young prince would have seen that of his father King James, whose work *Demonology* Jonson could hardly have ignored. And Prince Henry received too a book that is almost a work of art in itself, a little masterpiece of fine calligraphy, in Jonson's lovely regular handwriting. This unique text of a masque exactly as Jonson wrote it has its touching features – the odd misquotation or mistake in Latin, some spelling variations in difficult classical names. But this is a fair and good-looking text, remarkably free of errors, truly a gift fit for a prince. It is still preserved in the British Museum.

This recognition in the Prince's action to Jonson of the masque's permanent status as literature contrasts strongly with its reception in other quarters. Among the politicos of the court it was seized upon as an opportunity to ventilate temporal and topical grievances. While the Queen was, in the Venetian ambassador's account, 'deeply engaged' in the preparations and 'sparing no expense to make it as fine as possible', the Spanish and Flemish ambassadors were involved in manoeuvres designed to wangle themselves formal invitations to attend, thus marking their predominant status among the diplomatic personnel. Meanwhile the French ambassador who had felt himself to be slighted the previous year declared that he would withdraw from the court entirely if he were not invited.

The complications of this situation, with the possible ramifications of any action he were to take, resulted in the King's decision to delay the masque until the Spanish ambassador took his leave as he was expected to do early in the new year. Undeflected by this move, the Spaniard lingered on and on in London and did all he could to secure the invitation which he felt was his due. He succeeded thereby in having what was designed as the Twelfth Night masque (6 January) postponed until it could celebrate the Feast of the Purification on 2 February. The anxious Queen had to while away the tedious weeks of delay with daily rehearsals and trials of the machinery. The eventual performance in the Banqueting House at Whitehall cannot, whatever else, have suffered from being under-rehearsed.

Jonson's own account in the introduction to Prince Henry's edition gives a vivid sense of the occasion:

> First then, his Majesty being set and the whole company in expectation, that which presented itself was an ugly hell, which flaming beneath smoked unto the top of the roof. . . witches, with a kind of hollow and infernal music came forth from thence. First one, then two, and three, and more, till their numbers increased to eleven, all differently attired: some with rats on their heads, others with ointment-pots at their girdles: all with spindles, timbrels, rattles or other venefical [mischief-making] instruments, making a confused noise with strange gestures.

This splendidly theatrical opening in which the grotesquerie of the anti-masque set off the grace, order and beauty of the masque proper must have done much to ensure the success of the enterprise. Jonson's witches are lovingly conceived and written up with the greatest attention to detail. He was clearly satisified with the contribution of his collaborator in the realising of his 'invention': 'the device of their attire was Mr Jones's,' he informed Prince Henry and the reader, 'only I prescribed them their properties, of vipers, snakes, bones, herbs, roots, and other ensigns of their magic'. Equally important was the choreography of their 'magical dance, full of preposterous change and gesticulation'. Jonson wanted them to 'do all things contrary to the custom of men, dancing back to back, hip to hip, their hands joined and making circles backward, to the left hand, with strange fantastic motions of their heads and bodies'. To his satisfaction 'all [these] were excellently imitated by the maker of the dance, Mr Jerome Herne, whose right it is here to be named' (HS VIII, 301).

This spirited action was cut off at its height. In the midst of their wild dance the witches were surprised and dispersed by the character of Heroic Virtue who with his daughter Fame ushered in the masque of queens on what Jonson calls their 'night of nights'. Each of the eleven court ladies[11] took the part of a famous queen of antiquity; the Queen herself personated 'Bel-Anna' (the prefix a Jonsonian allusion to her beauty), the Queen of the Ocean and supreme head of all the others as 'the worthiest queen' who 'possessed all virtues'. The ladies were initially revealed in an allegorical pageant showing their place in the House of Fame. From this structure they descended in chariots accompanied by music and torches to drive ceremoniously around the stage and subsequently to dance. A novel device came at the end of the third dance when the masquers finally arranged themselves in a formation which spelled out the name of Charles, the King's second son (then the eight-year-old Duke of York, but later Charles I). More dancing and revelry concluded this, one of the most elaborate and expensive of the court masques, costing over £3000.

1609 opened promisingly for Jonson and the promise was not delusive. He was soon in demand again for another royal entertainment, once more at the command of the Earl of Salisbury. The occasion which the Lord Treasurer sought to honour was the visit of the Royal Family on 11 April to the opening of a new building in which he had an interest, Britain's Burse, later known as the New Exchange. This was a splendid new commercial centre in Westminster. Once again the Venetian ambassador fills in the background:

> Hard by the court the Earl of Salisbury has built two great galleries decorated, especially outside, with much carving and sculpture. Inside each of these galleries, on either hand, are rows of shops for the sale of all kinds of goods. This will bring in an immense revenue. Last week he took the King, the Queen and the Princes to see them. He has fitted up one of the shops very beautifully, and over it ran the motto, 'All other places give for money, here all is given for love'. To the King he gave a cabinet, to the Queen a silver plaque of the Annunciation worth, they say, four thousand crowns. To the Prince he gave a horse's trappings of great value, nor was there any one of the suite who did not receive at the very least a gold ring. The King named the place 'Britain's Burse'.[12]

The entertainment which Jonson devised for the proceedings took its cue from the essentially mercantile nature of the whole event. The text of the performance unfortunately is not extant; the only evidence for it survives among the accounts of the Cecil family. These reveal that the three principal characters were a shop-keeper, his apprentice, and a key-keeper. This, taken with the fact that the accounts show no expenses for staging or lighting effects, indicates that the show took place in the new building itself without benefit of special staging and by daylight, its function being to provide a formal framework for the elaborate present-giving on which the Earl of Salisbury had lavished so much attention and money.

Yet this is not to be regarded as a trivial or casual piece. The payment of the substantial sum of £13 6s 8d to 'Iohnson the Poett', and the same to 'Inigo Iohnes', shows that a considerable amount of work had gone into it. Another interesting feature lay in the hiring of professional actors to perform the entertainment itself; the principals were William Ostler as the shop-keeper, Giles Gary as the apprentice, and Nathan Field as the key-keeper. All these actors were well-known to Jonson. Ostler had as a boy been a member of the Children of the Queen's Revels and had acted in Jonson's *Poetaster* in 1601. Gary and Field were both members of the current company of the Children and therefore were to work with Jonson again before the year was out, appearing in his *Epicoene* at the Whitefriars theatre. Ostler too crops up in a Jonson play at a later date – by 1610 he was a member of the King's Company, who performed Jonson's *Alchemist* in that year.

Of the three Jonson had had a special relationship with Field, his former 'scholar'. Yet being Jonson's protégé seems to have had a double-edged effect for Field who was carrying burdens above and beyond an actor's call of duty. One of the bills for the 1609 expenses relates to the fact that Field 'sat up all night [writing] the speeches, songs and inscriptions'. But apart from his admiration for Jonson, Field had his own reasons for going along with this. He was desirous of leaving the performing side of the profession for the creative, and was only twenty-two when he decided to become a writer. He contributed prefatory verses to Fletcher's *Faithful Shepherdess* which disclose his ambition to write and contain a veiled compliment to his mentor Jonson:

> O Opinion, that great fool, makes fools of all,
> And once I feared her, till I met a mind
> Whose grave instruction philosophical
> Tossed it like dust upon a strong March wind.
> He shall for ever my example be
> And his embraced doctrine grow in me.

Jonson himself of course always paid his literary debts. In 1609 his commendatory lines to Clement Edmondes's translation of Caesar's *De Bello Gallico* were published, although they had probably been written earlier when the book was first completed in 1604. Edmondes was then in the primary stages of what was to be a distinguished career of legal and public service, and he repaid Jonson with a signed copy of the 1609 edition of his work inscribed 'Clement Edmondes commendeth himself to Ben Jonson, and dedicateth this book to his virtues and his love to Clement Edmondes'. In the same year of 1609 Jonson performed the same literary service for the man whom he described as 'my loved Alphonso', the Spaniard Ferrabosco, music master to Prince Henry. Jonson and Ferrabosco had worked together on several different ventures, and in 1609 Ferrabosco published a collection of his *Airs* which included the music for the songs in *Volpone* and several of Jonson's masques. Jonson also wrote a poem to accompany Ferrabosco's second publication in 1609, his *Lessons*; both were later reprinted as Epigrams 130 and 131.

Whatever the pleasure and distraction afforded by private moments such as these, 1609 continued its course as a very heavy year for Londoners. With the theatres closed as plague deaths mounted the players dispersed, some taking to the road, others seeking different and securer employment. Some embraced this as their time to 'leave the loathed stage'. Shakespeare, for instance, at forty-six already outliving many of his contemporaries, had received in 1608 two particular reminders of his mortality. In that same year he had experienced the death of his mother and the birth of his first granddaughter; in 1609 he had undergone the vexation of the appearance of an unauthorised quarto of the 'sugared sonnets' which he had written for circulation among his 'private friends', as Meres had related in 1598. It is hardly surprising, then, that Shakespeare's involvement with the stage that he had served so outstandingly for almost thirty years now entered its final phase.

Among the many casualties of this terrible year one woman died whose passing called forth from Jonson a remarkable expression of regret. She was Cecilia Bulstrode, the court beauty, friend and kinswoman of Jonson's patron the Countess of Bedford, at whose house she died on 4 August 1609. In life the lady had been a special object of Jonson's satire; he had attacked her venomously as 'the Court Pucelle' (*Underwood* 49). But her death at the age of only twenty-five was one of great suffering both of body and mind. Jonson heard of it from Donne's friend George Garrard; Donne had visited her on her death-bed and reported her condition.

Jonson was deeply struck to hear the news of Cecilia Bulstrode's dying. He wrote to Garrard that it had made him 'a heavy man'. He wished that he had seen her before she died, so 'that some that live might have corrected some prejudices they have had injuriously of me'. This sense of remorse moved Jonson to grieve for her loss and to recall her virtues in a vein of almost hyperbolical exaggeration. Even for Jonson a complete revolution from 'whore' to 'virgin saint' is quite extraordinary. He produced this epitaph under the impression of the immediate receipt of the news and sent it to Garrard with a covering note explaining that it had been written in haste and sorrow while Garrard's man waited at the door:

> Stay, view this stone; and if thou beest not such
> Read here a little, that thou mayst know much.
> It covers first, a virgin; and then one
> That durst be that in court: a virtue alone
> To fill an epitaph. But she had more:

She might have claimed to have made the muses four,
Taught Pallas language, Cynthia modesty,
As fit to have increased the harmony
Of spheres, as light of stars; she was earth's eye;
The sole religious house and votary,
With rites not bound, but conscience. Wouldst thou all?
She was Cil Bulstrode. In which name, I call
Up so much truth as, could I it pursue,
Might make the fable of good women true.

(Ungathered Verse, 9)

   The tone and phrasing of this indicate Jonson's familiarity with the court circles in which he was no longer a newcomer but an established member. His increased status as the chief royal masque-maker made him even something of a luminary. Critics of Jonson have tended either to ignore Jonson's masques or to dismiss them as trivial, irrelevant to his main achievement as a writer. There is no evidence at all that Jonson felt this way. On the contrary his writing of masques brought him the financial, social, professional and personal rewards that his plays never did. From this point of view the pity is that he could not continue in this fortunate situation for the rest of his working life.

CHAPTER 8

RETURN TO THE STAGE

J ONSON enjoyed to the full his twin roles as courtier and royal masque-maker. Yet the drama still exerted its old fascination over him. As 1609 progressed he was once more drawn away from court circles to return to the stage. The company of boy players with whom he had had close working relations earlier in his career, especially during the 'War of the Theatres', had had to surrender their Blackfriars playhouse to the owner after a dispute over the lease in 1608. Undeterred, the management of the Children of the Queen's Revels had reorganised at the Whitefriars theatre. Among their first actions was to procure their former dramatist to write a play for them, thus ending Jonson's three-year break from the stage following *Volpone*.

Jonson must have started work soon after finishing his annotated edition of the *Masque of Queens* for Prince Henry, a tremendous task which would have occupied the early part of 1609 at least. The play which became *Epicœne, or The Silent Woman* was composed and written without the usual pressure on the playwright. It luckily escaped having to slot into the process of continual production that constituted the working conditions of the Elizabethan theatre. For the continuing violence of the plague had put a stop to almost all theatrical activity and the boys could not open at their new playhouse until plague deaths had dropped below forty a week. So all that could be done, through the second half of 1609, was to have the playwrights prepare new plays – and wait.

The delay must have favoured Jonson, who was legendarily slow in composition. The writing of *Epicœne* in fact ushered in a three-year burst of creativity during which he brought a play to fruition every year, two of which are regarded as among his finest works. *Epicœne* shows him capitalising on the skills of the boy actors with a sensational device at the heart of the drama – the final revelation that the

127

'silent woman' is in fact a real boy. In other respects he made no concessions to the boys' youth and inexperience, writing here at the top of his form a play with a ferocious topical and satiric bite. The company's satisfaction with the piece appears from the fact that it was among the first to be staged early in 1610 when the theatre was at last allowed to open its doors to the public after the first week in December 1609.

As a play *Epicœne* is a triumph of Jonson's art. But as a piece of contemporary theatre once again it sailed rather too near the wind for the authorities' comfort. In keeping with a drama that satirised fashionable London life Jonson had made reference to a notable figure of the time, an enterprising con-man self-styled 'The Prince of Moldavia' who was claiming to be engaged to be married to the King's cousin, Lady Arabella Stuart. Jonson's allusion is brief and apparently uncompromising; indeed it is ambiguous, since it is not at all clear whom he meant by 'the Prince of Moldavia's mistress'. But Lady Arabella was already in disgrace with the King for embroiling herself in an unauthorised liaison – the careful monarch ensuring that the suitor of today would not become the usurper of tomorrow – and Jonson discovered that she objected strongly to any reference to this episode. Although she could not have seen the play herself, since she was living under restraint imposed by the King both as a punishment to her and as a safe-guard to himself, the lady heard of the play. According to the Venetian ambassador she made formal complaint that 'in a certain play the playwright introduced an allusion to her person and the part played by the Prince of Moldavia'. As a result, he continued, 'the play was suppressed. Her Excellency is very ill-pleased, and shows a determination this coming parliament to secure the punishment of certain persons . . .'.[1]

The new parliament opened on 9 February 1610. But Jonson, stung, had reacted to the accusation by turning off a defiant prologue insisting that his work obeyed the rules of true satire, and that he would not submit to the wrenching of a personal application from his work:

> The ends of all who for the scene do write
> Are, or should be, to profit and delight.
> And still't hath been the praise of the best times
> So persons are not touched, to tax the crimes.
> Then in this play which we present tonight
> And make the object of your ear and sight,
> On forfeit of yourselves, think nothing true
> Lest you so make the maker to judge you.
> For he knows poets never credit gained

> By writing truths, but things like truths, well feigned.
> If any yet will, with particular sleight
> Of application, wrest what he doth write
> And that he meant or him or her will say
> They made a libel, which he made a play.

Jonson felt, on this occasion as on so many others, that he had been unjustly handled. When he came to dedicate the play in the 1616 Folio, he spoke darkly of the 'certain hatred of some' against him, and the 'contumely' done to him. Perhaps because of this breath of official disapproval the play did not achieve the public success of its predecessor *Volpone*. The response seems to have been cool where not positively hostile. As the very last of his numerous observations of Jonson's statements and his own opinions, Drummond set down that 'when his play The Silent Woman was first acted, there were found verses after, on the stage against him, concluding that the play was well named the Silent Woman. There was never one man to say Plaudite to it' (HS I, 151). 'Plaudite' is a Horatian term to denote the applause in the theatre at the end of the play to signify the audience's enjoyment and approval. Once more Jonson had received the cold shoulder from the capricious contemporary audiences.

In returning to the drama Jonson did not, however, lose his connection with royal entertainments. Coinciding with the presentation of the new comedy were the preparations for a lavish ceremonial in which Prince Henry rather than his father the King was the centre of interest. The event was the creation of the heir apparent as Prince of Wales. It took place in the first week of January 1610, and was attended with many masques and triumphs. Jonson's contribution was the entertainment called *The Speeches at Prince Henry's Barriers*, an assignment which must have taxed his creative skills to the utmost.

For the form of the 'Barriers', this strange hybrid of sport and dance, was thrust upon him by the prior choice of the young prince. Henry delighted in physical activities; his warlike disposition and skill in martial arts contrasted strongly with the King's timorousness, a quality bred in him through the combination of weak legs and a calculating intelligence. Jonson, who could not be accused of either of these shortcomings, was still by no means an uncritical admirer of military matters or attitudes. But Prince Henry had issued a challenge to all the knights of the realm under the mythological name of Meliadus, a lover of the Lady of the Lake. Jonson therefore had recourse to the legends of King Arthur in order to build round the Prince's original concept a show of some meaning and significance. In so doing he contrived to stand the form on its head, translating the combative form to its opposite, a classical love of peace and

129

moderation. He represented the ancient Golden Age as the equivalent of the age of chivalry in England and, mindful not to overlook the reigning monarch in his homage to the rising sun, included King James with the compliment of making him the new Golden Age's restorer.

The ceremony of the Barriers was a great success at a particularly fruitful time for Jonson. Early in the new year of 1610 he was working upon what was to become his best-loved play, *The Alchemist*. As his *Epicœne* had been given by the Children of the Queen's Revels at Whitefriars, this was Jonson's first return to the public stage since his *Volpone* of four years earlier in 1606. The commercial scene and the setting recall those of the entertainment at the opening of Britain's Burse in the spring of the year before, here satirically exaggerated by Jonson into a world where everyone is on the make, from the highest to the lowest.

Meanwhile there were fresh developments in Jonson's largely unrevealed personal life. There are two births registered in 1610 which point to him as the father but which clearly relate to two different women. On 25 March 1610, a little girl was baptised at St Mary Matfellon, Whitechapel, as 'Elisib. daughter of Ben Jonson'. This first appearance of the familiar abbreviation of Jonson's forename would seem to make the baby his, although of course Jonson need not have been living in Whitechapel, where the parish of St Mary Matfellon was located, nor the child have been by his wife.

Less than two weeks later, in early April, another child was born whose connection with Jonson is even plainer. 'Beniamen Jonson fil. [son of] Ben' bears the distinctive first name in conjunction with the shortened form of it which Jonson made famous. The little boy was also baptised on 6 April 1610 in the church of St Martin's-in-the-Fields where Jonson according to tradition had first attended school, and where he was certainly a parishioner in 1597 when he was assessed for his contribution to the upkeep of the pews.

If Jonson fathered these children they must have had different mothers (they may well have had different fathers, and neither of them Jonson). But his paternity is at least possible on his own admissions of his irregular life and sexual habits. As he told Drummond he was living apart from his wife for a prolonged period at a time of his life when he was 'given to venery' [sexual indulgence]. His anecdotes to Drummond reveal a variety of sexual encounters, and the experienced man's preference for married women, along with an apparently untroubled morality. Given the desperate nature of contemporary contraceptive practice, the wonder is that Jonson did not add even more to the stock of Elizabethan and Jacobean bastards in his philanderings.

The summer of 1610 brought the staging of *The Alchemist* by the

King's Men at the Globe. Once again Burbage played the leading part of Face, a wonderful role for an actor, and a contemporary account states that Lowin (Shakespeare's Falstaff) played Sir Epicure Mammon (HS IX, 225). The performance must have taken place before 12 July 1610 when the theatres were again closed down by the ever-present plague. Even with actors of this quality in the cast Jonson was by no means sure of a good reception – some years later the poet Herrick attacked the ignorance of those 'who once hissed / At thy unequalled play, *The Alchemist*'.[2] Yet despite the opposition of one or two hostile spirits, the play had obviously gone well. When the King's Men left the capital on their enforced summer tour, *The Alchemist* was one of the plays they took with them. They gave it in Oxford in September of 1610, 'to the greatest applause, in a full theatre' – while narrow souls were outraged at the profanity put into the mouths of the religiously satirised characters Ananias and Tribulation Wholesome, scholars and divines flocked to see the performance. During the next month the play was entered in the Stationers' Register on 3 October 1610, showing a desire to bring the play before a wider audience.[3]

During the writing of *The Alchemist* in the early summer of 1610, Jonson's delineation of sharp practices took on an unexpectedly personal application. Although his friend Sir John Roe was dead, Jonson had remained in touch with the family. He was now called upon to help in a difficult situation. Roe's younger brother William had been only a minor when he inherited the estate. It seems likely that the inheritance was in bad shape; Roe had travelled extensively and roistered his life away, leaving the management in other hands. He was too, in Jonson's words to Drummond, 'an infinite spender', quite careless of the consequences of his prodigality.

Whether for these or other reasons young William had been prevailed upon to sell one of the properties of the estate for considerably less than its market value. The buyer had worked his way into the confidence of the boy heir, visiting him at school and later at college with presents and tips, finally obtaining a lawful deed of sale two or three days after William came of age. The family had eventually decided to go to law to recover the house and lands which the young man had parted with so ill-advisedly.

Jonson was among the witnesses called for the Roe family when the case opened in the High Court of Chancery on 5 May 1610. After other depositions had been taken, Jonson gave his evidence on 8 May. In response to a set of interrogatories, Jonson testified in support of the family's claim that the defendant Walter Garland had used undue pressure to influence William Roe to the sale. Jonson fully recalled what had passed and gave a vivid account of Garland's blandishments to William. Having obtained the youth's promise to sell Garland then followed this up with what can only be described as moral blackmail; Jonson related Garland's repeated insistence that 'noblemen and gentlemen' always honoured to the full any promise they had made in their minority.

But Garland was clearly a pragmatist as well as a rhetorician; Jonson told the court that among Garland's battery of 'allurements' came an offer to him as William's friend, to induce Jonson to persuade the youth 'to be good unto' the verbal agreement to sell. When this failed Garland offered Jonson 'a Nag of £10 price' to press his case. Garland was of course spared the trouble of finding a horse capable of carrying Jonson's increasing weight. Jonson deposed that for his part, 'faith, he was ever against it, utterly refusing to be any witness thereunto'. It was a 'matter which he never desired should come to pass' and he had further attempted to safeguard William's interests by urging him 'to do nothing without good advice' (good advice in itself, which William ignored). Garland, in Jonson's view, summarised in the light of that intelligence which was currently engaged in the creation of the master-rogues Face, Subtle and Doll, was 'a crafty fellow, and indirect in his practices'. Had Jonson's view prevailed earlier with the susceptible heir much distress, expense and litigation would have been spared.

The loyal Jonson, having done his best for his young friend in court (a situation where he would have been at home, in view of his numerous court appearances on his own behalf), did not lose touch with or faith in William Roe. Epigram 70 is a moral admonition addressed to him, urging him not to waste his life. Despite the theme it is not a reproof from on high and Jonson generously gathers himself into the concluding couplet along with Roe:

> Then since we (more than many) these truths know,
> Though life be short, let us not make it so

Later when William, like his elder brother John Roe before him, was about to leave England for foreign travel Jonson gave him his envoy in a sonnet-like epigram which breathes affection and encouragement:

> Roe (and my joy to name) thou 'rt now to go
>   Countries and climes, manners and men to know,
> To extract and choose the best of all these known,
>   And those to turn to blood and make thine own.
> May winds as soft as breath of kissing friends
>   Attend thee hence; and there may all thy ends,
> As the beginnings here, prove purely sweet,
>   And perfect in a circle always meet.

So when we, blest with thy return shall see
  Thyself, with thy first thoughts, brought home by thee,
We each to other may this voice inspire:
  This is that good Aeneas, passed through fire,
Through seas, storms, tempests; and embarked for hell
  Came back untouched. This man hath travailed well.

(Epigram 128)

The Roe trial is a welcome addition to the picture of Jonson at this time. Apart from the strong loyalty to friendship which is such a consistent feature of his behaviour, we learn that he was still living in the Blackfriars district and had become sufficiently well-established to be referred to in the legal record as 'a gentleman'. His age is recorded as 'thirty-seven years or thereabouts'; this taken with the remarkable creativity of these years suggests a man in the prime of life at an age when the majority of his contemporaries were already old men.

Another pointer to Jonson's state of fulfilment at this time was the vigour of his social life. Time had deepened and ripened the friendships he had built among the nobility, and he was on easy terms in several great houses, like Penshurst in Kent, the home of the Sidney family since 1552, and Sir Robert Wroth's Durrants, his estate in Enfield.[4] One of Drummond's anecdotes gives a glimpse of the sort of relationships Jonson enjoyed there:

> Pembroke and his lady discoursing, the earl said that women were men's shadows, and she maintained them [upheld the women's cause]. Both appealing to Jonson, he affirmed it true, for which my lady gave a penance to prove it in verse: hense his epigram (HS I, 142).

This was the piece which Jonson entitled 'Song: That Women are Men's Shadows' (*Forest* 7). A substantial number of his verse productions were written for his court circle. He had continued in the good graces of 'Lucy the Bright', the Countess of Bedford, and of the members of the Sidney clan – Drummond was treated to the outline of a pastoral called *The May Lord* which Jonson wrote for this group, with each individual being given an appropriate character (HS I, 143). Other court ladies who noticed Jonson and were honoured by him in return were the daughter of Sir Edmund Carey (Epigram 126); Susan Herbert, Countess of Montgomery and married to the brother of Jonson's patron (Epigram 104); and the Countess of Rutland and Lady Wroth as before. Jonson was equally gifted at forming friendships with men. He recorded a warm tribute to the 'all-virtuous' Sir Edward Herbert, brother of the poet George Herbert, in Epigram

133

106, and Herbert's own poetic contribution to the friendship is printed as his 'Satyra Secunda: Of Travellers; from Paris', written in September 1608. Others, not so lustrous, were Sir William Jephson and Sir Ralph Sheldon, two knights of James's court who received their honours in 1603 and 1607 respectively. Sheldon, as a Roman Catholic, was nearer to Jonson's own persuasion, but both are respectfully handled in Epigrams 116 and 119. Through Pembroke Jonson met Benjamin Rudyerd (Epigram 121); he was a close friend of the earl, and later wrote poems with him which were published in 1660. Jonson was also still in touch with Sir John Ratcliffe, as continuing presents of books show.

For Jonson was no social climber, interested in men only for 'the name of a lord'. Despite the glamour of these courtiers, Jonson was careful to keep his old friendships and more discerning contacts in good repair. 1610 saw the publication of Selden's work *Jam Anglorum Facies Altera*. When the author presented a copy of the book to his old friend, it was copiously annotated by Jonson with a warm tribute to the friendship that had produced it. Jonson was, too, at this stage of his life, winning golden opinions from his fellows in the literary world. One contemporary commentator in his summary of the London writers listed Jonson among 'the chief' of English stylists for his 'proper graces' and use of 'the most warrantable English'.

Among fellow writers Jonson had continued and enriched his intimacy with John Donne. The two poets shared a patron, as Lucy Countess of Bedford displayed her generosity and intelligent interest to both; on one occasion, commemorated in Epigram 94, Jonson sent her a copy of his friend's satires, with a complimentary poem praising the book and its recipient. The Countess of Montgomery also favoured both poets. But the principal bond between the two men was a mutual delight in each other's work. Donne, who never condescended to praise any other contemporary poet, contributed some very flattering Latin verses to the quarto edition of *Volpone*. On his side Jonson declared Donne to be in himself an absolute standard for poetry in the opening couplet to Epigram 96:

> Who shall doubt, Donne, whe'er I a poet be,
> When I dare send my epigrams to thee?

Donne's pre-eminence is again insisted upon in Epigram 23 where he is described as 'the delight of Phoebus and each muse'. Although there is an element of courtly extravagance in Jonson's encomiastic verse, he correctly identified the key factors of Donne's genius in his wit and singularity. The criticism later made to Drummond should not obscure a picture of regard which led Jonson to read and consider Donne's poems very thoroughly, and to commit certain pieces and extracts to memory; as he told Drummond, 'he esteemeth John Donne the first poet in the world in some things' (HS I, 135).

Through Donne, Jonson made the acquaintance of Sir Henry Goodyere of Polesworth in the Forest of Arden. Goodyere had been knighted in 1599, and was made a Gentleman of the Bedchamber to King James after his accession. He was a dear friend of Donne and his passion in life was hawking. Although not a sporting man himself Jonson was always interested in other people's activities. On his own account he observed Goodyere in the field with a keen curiosity and drew a very Jonsonian allegory from the scene:

> Goodyere, I'm glad and grateful to report
>   Myself a witness of thy few days' sport,
> Where I both learned why wise men hawking follow,
>   And why that bird was sacred to Apollo:
> She doth instruct men by her gallant flight
>   That they to knowledge so should tower upright
> And never stoop but to strike ignorance;
>   Which, if they miss, they yet should re-advance
> To former height, and there in circle tarry
>   Till they be sure to make the fool their quarry.
> Now, in whose pleasure I have this discerned,
>   What would his serious actions me have learned?
>
> (Epigram 85)

In addition to his court acquaintance and literary friendships, Jonson was becoming from this time onwards a leading figure in London tavern gatherings. Here he encountered all sorts and types of men, feeding his appetite for human variety and establishing himself as what he would be for the rest of his life, a most clubbable man. It is from this phase of Jonson's life that the first mention of his drinking comes in, and it comes in thereafter so regularly that Jonson's social habits have become legendary; whatever else, he established a lasting reputation for conviviality. Winstanley's account is typical of many such anecdotes that have attached themselves to Jonson:

He having been drinking in an upper room, at the Feathers Tavern in Cheapside, as he was coming downstairs, his foot slipping, he caught a fall, and tumbling against a door, beat it open into a room where some gentlemen were drinking canary. Recovering his feet, he said, Gentlemen, since I am so luckily fallen into your company, I will drink with you before I go.

He used very much to frequent the Half Moon Tavern in Aldersgate Street through which there was a common thoroughfare. He coming late that way, one night, was denied passage; whereupon going through the Sun tavern a little after, he said:

Since that the Moon was so unkind to make me go about,
The Sun henceforth shall take my coin, the Moon shall go without.[5]

Aubrey too repeats the information about Jonson's drinking habits, remarking that 'he would many times exceed in drink (Canary was his beloved liquor)'; this sweet white wine crops up very frequently as Jonson's favourite tipple. Yet clearly Jonson enjoyed these gatherings as much for the company as for the alcohol, and the pleasure was not his alone. Francis Beaumont, writing to Jonson from the country where he and Fletcher had retreated one summer to escape the plague and to finish two comedies which they had in hand, nostalgically recalled their joyful encounters and lamented the work 'which deferred their merry meetings at the Mermaid':

> In this warm shine
> I lie, and dream of your full Mermaid wine . . .
> What things have we seen
> Done at the Mermaid! Heard words that have been
> So nimble, and so full of subtle flame,
> As if that every one from whence they came
> Had meant to put his whole wit in a jest
> And had resolved to live a fool the rest
> Of his dull life . . .

Beaumont sees an educative purpose in the relentless wit – it has an instructive value for 'our young men', who 'like trees . . . have growing souls'. Beaumont is obviously pining for such company in his country solitude. He calls himself 'banished' from his friends, and concludes with this wish:

> Fate once again
> Bring me to thee, who canst make smooth and plain
> The way of knowledge for me, and then I
> Who have no good but in thy company,
> Protest it will my greatest comfort be
> To acknowledge all I have to flow from thee.
> Ben, when these scenes are perfect, we'll taste wine;
> I'll drink thy Muse's health, thou shalt quaff mine.

> (*JAB* 65–7)

Jonson always responded very readily to professions of admiration in a literary vein, and turned off a courtly response to the younger poet and dramatist:

136

How do I love thee, Beaumont, and thy muse
  That unto me dost such religion use!
How do I fear myself, that am not worth
  The least indulgent thought thy pen drops forth!
At once thou mak'st me happy, and unmak'st;
  And giving largely to me, more thou tak'st.
What fate is mine that so itself bereaves?
  What art is thine that so thy friend deceives?
What even there where most thou praisest me
  For writing better, I must envy thee.

                                 (Epigram 55)

Jonson's poem is complimentary rather than literal, and his self-deprecation in particular is not to be taken too seriously. Nevertheless the gatherings at this famous tavern in Cheapside were of such quality and regularity that they and the Mermaid itself have passed into legend. Some details of the meetings can be gleaned. The traveller Thomas Coryate, well known to Jonson, wrote from India to 'the High Seneschall of the Right Worshipful Fraternity of the Sirenaical Gentlemen, that meet the first Friday of every month, at the sign of the Mermaid in Bread Street in London'.[6] The membership of the 'Fraternity' is not given, but Coryate sends greetings to Jonson, Donne, Sir Robert Cotton, Inigo Jones and Hugh Holland. As other frequenters of the Mermaid included lawyers like Hoskyns and Martin, and Sir Francis Stuart, a relative of the King and of the Lord High Admiral, it is clear that this was not a literary club but rather a gathering of men about town who came together to drink, to joke, and to enjoy one another's company.[7]

Jonson did not confine his social life to public taverns. He often dined out, where he must have been a valuable addition to any table if a somewhat rumbustious guest. At one such private party, as he afterwards told Drummond, 'at a supper where a gentlewoman gave him unsavoury wild fowl, and thereafter (to wash) sweet water, he commended her that she gave him sweet water, because her flesh stinked' (HS I, 145). Jonson also liked to play host, and his conception of this role is outlined in one of the most sweet-tempered and graceful of the epigrams:

Tonight, grave sir, both my poor house and I
  Do equally desire your company;
Not that we think us worthy such a guest,
  But that your worth will dignify our feast
With those that come; whose grace may make that seem
  Something, which else could hope for no esteem.

It is the fair acceptance, sir, creates
   The entertainment perfect, not the cates.
Yet you shall have, to rectify your palate
   An olive, capers, or some better salad
Ushering the mutton . . .
      . . . Howsoe'er, my man
Shall read a piece of Virgil, Tacitus,
   Livy, or some better book to us,
Of which we'll speak our minds, amidst our meat;
   And I'll profess no verses to repeat . . .
Digestive cheese and fruit there sure will be;
   But that which most doth take my muse and me
Is a pure cup of rich Canary wine,
   Which is the Mermaid's now, but shall be mine . . . .
      . . . No simple word
That shall be uttered at our mirthful board
Shall make us sad next morning, or affright
   The liberty that we'll enjoy tonight.

(Epigram 101)

What Jonson was expressing through this range of activities was his gift for friendship, an attribute which he possessed in both depth and breadth. The entry into the wider world of court and city brought him many more chances to exercise it, and during this time Jonson seems to have enjoyed a great number of warm and sustaining relationships. Even one who was not in Jonson's close circle, Sir John Davies, could write in his *Scourge of Folly* (1611) 'To my well-accomplished friend, Mr. B.J.':

I love thy parts; so I must love thy whole:
Then still be whole in thy beloved parts.
Thou'art sound in body; but some say thy soul
Envy doth ulcer; yet corrupted hearts
Such censurers may have. But if thou be
An envious soul, wouldst thou could envy me . . . .

A newer contact and one which Jonson prized was the friendship of Sir Thomas Overbury, celebrated in Epigram 113. This knight who was rising with the rising star of King James's favourite, Robert Carr, held as Carr's secretary an influential place where he shared his master's good fortune if not his accommodating morality.

Perhaps as a result of Jonson's drawing nearer to the great ones of church and state there came another characteristically Jonsonian revolution. In a development which he never explained he abandoned the Catholic faith and returned to the Protestantism of his father, his

children and his wife. This spiritual development he characteristically celebrated in a physical and public manner: 'after he was first
reconciled with the Church, and left off to be a recusant, at his first
Communion, in token of true reconciliation, he drank out all the full
cup of wine' (HS I, 141). The flamboyant gesture still kindles the
imagination after all the intervening centuries.

Again, and in Jonson's own account, comes a reference to his
drinking habits. Posterity has relished this picture of the gregarious,
bibulous dramatist swilling liquor in the Mermaid surrounded by
friends and fellow-poets. There is no account from this period of his
habits of work, only Aubrey's later anecdotal testimony that after his
drinking bouts, 'then he would tumble home to bed, and when he had
thoroughly perspired, then to study. I have seen his studying chair,
which was of straw [wicker-work] such as old women used' (HS I,
179). But Jonson was working, and steadily too. As 1610 drew to its
end his services as a masque-maker were very much in demand and
he was commissioned to write for both the Queen and Prince Henry.

King James was as usual favourably inclined to these ventures. But
as court gossip indicates, neither of these projects could be staged as
lavishly as in the previous year: 'The King is pleased that at the
approaching Christmas [the Queen] should give another masque of
the Ladies; it will precede the Prince's masque, and neither will be as
costly as last year's, which to say sooth were excessively costly' (*JAB*
73). Some courtiers suspected that the King would be hard-pressed to
find the money required, even if things went forward on a more
modest level: 'I think my Lord will be in some pain even to furnish the
expense of the approaching feast; yet doth the Prince make but one
masque, and the Queen but two, which doth cost her Majesty but
£600' (*JAB* 74). Jonson was working now within a framework which
allowed for two masques only a fifth of what had previously been
spent on one; and this for a series of masques designed particularly to
honour the presence in court of the Marshal de Laverdin who had
come over for the swearing of a highly important treaty with France.

Of these ventures Jonson clearly had the greatest success with his
Masque of Oberon for Prince Henry. This was performed on the first day
of the New Year of 1611 at the Banqueting House in Whitehall to the
general admiration of the court:

> Upon New Year's Night, the Prince of Wales being accompanied
> with twelve others, viz., two earls, three barons, five knights and
> two esquires, they performed a very stately masque, in which was
> an excellent scene, rare songs, and a great variety of most delicate
> music, in the beautiful room at Whitehall, which room is generally
> called the Banqueting House. (*JAB* 74)

Another contemporary account described the performance in full:

> When their Majesties entered accompanied by the princess and the ambassadors of Spain and Venice, flageolets played and the curtain was drawn discovering a great rock with the moon showing above through an aperture, so that its progress through the night could be observed. Old Silenus mounted on this with some dozen satyrs and fauns who had much to say about the coming of a great prince to be followed by a thousand benefits, in the hope of which the fauns danced about joyfully, exciting great laughter. Then they danced a ballet, with appropriate music with a thousand strange gestures, affording great pleasure. This done the rock opened discovering a great throne with countless lights and colours all shifting, a lovely thing to see. In the midst stood the prince, with thirteen other gentlemen chosen as famous dancers of the court. Before passing into the hall ten musicians appeared each with a lute and two boys who sang very well some sonnets in praise of the prince and his father. Then ten little pages dressed in green and silver with flat bonnets *à l'antique* danced another ballet with much grace. During this the cock crew ten times, standing on the rock, and then, according to the prophesy of Silenus, there came the gentlemen in short scarlet hose and white brodequins [buskins] full of silver spangles coming half way to the calf, some wearing jackets with wide folds, as the Roman emperors are represented and the sleeves the same, all in gold and silver cloth, white and scarlet feathers on their heads and very high white plumes, and black masks. Each one wore a very rich blue band across the body, except that of the prince, whose band was scarlet to distinguish him from the rest. They entered dancing two ballets intermingled with varied figures and many leaps, extremely well done by most of them. The prince then took the Queen to dance, the Earl of Southampton the princess, and each of the rest his lady. They danced an English dance resembling a pavane. When the Queen returned to her place the prince took her for a coranta which was continued by others, and then the gallarda began, which was something to see and admire. The Prince took the Queen a third time for *los branles de Poitou*, followed by eleven others of the masque. As it was about midnight and the King somewhat tired, he sent word that they should make an end. So the masqueraders danced the ballet of the sortie, in which the satyrs and the fauns joined. (HS X, 522–3)

Jonson was able to incorporate a good deal of himself into this masque. Within the conventional framework the dance of the satyrs and their boyish antics express the frolicsome and exuberant side of his artistic personality. This is however balanced and controlled by the use of Silenus, much rehabilitated from his gross classical *persona* into a very Jonsonian pedagogue. Jonson had in fact employed the idea of the masque of satyrs two years previously, in the 1608 entertainment for the King at Salisbury House. On this occasion, given a fuller treatment and a court setting, they made such an impact that Shakespeare himself borrowed the motif wholesale, and incorporated it into *The Winter's Tale*, which was given some months later in 1611 at the Globe. In this play the satyrs' dance is introduced with the sly little in-joke, 'One three of them, by their own report, sir, hath danced before the King' (IV.iv.337–8).

The appearance of Oberon was the central concept of the masque and Jonson was fortunate in his leading actor. Prince Henry's real love was sporting activity. The Venetian ambassador observed sourly that the Prince 'would have liked to present this masque on horseback, could he have obtained the King's consent'. But he was also a confident and accomplished dancer, so that to one contemporary 'the masque was very beautiful throughout, very decorative, but most remarkable for the grace of the prince's every movement' (HS X, 518–19). The load was not too heavy for the sixteen-year-old prince to bear as an amateur performer in accordance with the convention he was not called upon to speak at all, and even when the customary flattery has been set aside, it is clear that he acquitted himself well.

If the Prince's masque occupied the centre point of the Christmas revels, the Queen's was scheduled for its triumphant finale, the Twelfth and last night. But Jonson's *Love Freed From Ignorance and Folly* suffered an unexpected delay. Court gossip variously blamed this on the unreadiness of the stage machinery and effects or on the King's desire to avoid another diplomatic clash between the foreign ambassadors. The show was eventually given on the Feast of the Purification, Sunday 3 February. Despite enforced financial cutbacks the masque was evidently not a skimped affair. Accounts of the royal exchequer reveal that Jonson received £40 for his 'invention', as did Inigo Jones. Some idea of relative values may be drawn from the fact that the dancing master, 'for teaching all the dances', had £50, while money was spent lavishly on 'copper lace', silk stockings, 'flesh-coloured satin' and 'crimson taffeta', the last item alone costing more than the poet or the architect were paid at £46 15s.

Yet mere expense cannot supply the place of flagging inventive vigour. Side-by-side with the emergence of the new heir and rising star must come the waning of the old. Jonson's central device of the masque is limp in comparison with others. The inspiration derived from the King and Queen in the earlier years of the reign was fading. This was, too, the last masque ever danced by Queen Anne. From this time forth, the little Danish woman who had found so much delight and fulfilment in masquing left these glittering 'toys' to others.

As in the two previous years, Jonson followed a Christmas of court activity with the preparation of a play for the public stage. With the past successes of *Epicœne* and *The Alchemist* assured, the artist, classicist and pedagogue in him all combined to dictate a change of direction. For his next play Jonson abandoned the London of his own day and his special form of satirical comedy. With a conscious determination to elevate both his own art and the audience's understanding, he returned to Roman tragedy to write *Catiline*. His tragedy of the Roman conspirator was performed before the end of August by the King's Men. Burbage, now in his forties, probably played the senior lead part of Cicero rather than the title role, and the gifted boy actor 'Dicky' Robinson appeared, most probably in the part of Sempronia.

The result was an unmitigated disaster. Although the first two acts went well, the spectators gradually took against the character of Cicero, and particularly resented his lengthy oration in the fourth act. Jonson later admitted with great animosity that the play had attracted 'all bitterness of censure' when it was performed. It proved to be a serious misjudgment on his part, being rejected by the groundlings and the sophisticated alike among theatre-goers. There was a personal as well as an artistic significance to this. In 1605 Jonson had been a committed Catholic. By 1611 he had abjured that faith and regained a Protestant perspective. *Catiline*'s ambitious design has been interpreted as a 'classical parallelograph', in which the ancient Roman conspiracy of the disaffected nobleman would shadow forth the Gunpowder plot.[8] But this design, if it existed at all, proved too subtle and slender for the multitude and the play failed in its aim.

Some voices were lifted to censure the degraded taste of the age:

> A general folly reigneth, and harsh fate
> Hath made the world itself insatiate.
> It hugs these monsters and deformed things
> Better than what Jonson or Drayton sings
>
> (*JAB* 80)

But later gossip was not inclined to credit Jonson with the lofty motives which he claimed. He is supposed to have given this version of the composition of his tragedy:

The first speech in my *Catiline*, spoken by Scylla's ghost, was writ after I had parted from my boys at the Devil Tavern; I had drunk well that night, and had brave notions. There's one scene in that play which I think is flat; I resolve to mix no more water with my wine. (HS I, 188)

Clearly Jonson had learned nothing from the lesson of *Sejanus* eight years previously. If anything, the new play confirmed the former refusal to woo the groundlings, the earlier determination to address himself to none but those who preferred oratory to action and whose taste was formed by the highest classical standards. The public rejection of *Catiline* carried also therefore the sting of a rebuke – he had massively misjudged his audience, his theme, even his own skills.

The sense of injury which Jonson experienced as a result of this contemptuous response to his work is evinced by his subsequent action. He brought out a fully corrected quarto version of the play within the year, in order to afford the discerning contemporary intelligence that chance to appreciate the piece which the rage of the theatre-going populace had denied. He dedicated it to his patron the Earl of Pembroke, with a volley of insults directed at the ignorance of the age and an outburst about the impossibility of discrimination in 'these jig-given times'. He defended *Catiline* as 'a legitimate poem' and 'the best' of his productions in the tragic vein.

Not content with this vindication of his play, Jonson also equipped the quarto with two further dedications of a quite extraordinary character. The first, 'To the Reader in Ordinary', gets off a series of hostile directives to the reader in which jibes at the average person's incapacity sit uneasily with pompous self-glorification: 'if I were not above such molestation now, I had great cause to think unworthily of my studies . . . . ' Only to 'the Reader Extraordinary' (the subject of the final dedication) will Jonson submit himself and his work. These prefaces, statements quite without parallel in the long history of relations between author and public, show how grievously he resented the reception of *Catiline*; hysterical rage is throughout contained but not concealed by transparent bombast.

The only consolation for Jonson lay in the fact that his friends rallied round to give the printed edition of the play the send-off which might in some degree make up for its reception on the stage. Beaumont, Fletcher, Field, and others all contributed commendatory verses which combined to exalt the play and to damn its public. Beaumont reassured Jonson that his *Catiline* was truly drawn according to the classical models and that his outstanding ability placed him beyond the reach of the average understanding:

> Thou hast squared thy rules by what is good
> And art three ages yet from understood.

For Beaumont, the need was that Jonson's audience's should 'grow up to' his wit. Fletcher was similarly consoling. Calling Jonson his 'dear friend' he assured him that 'thy labours shall outlive thee', being 'like gold/Stamped for continuance' and always current. Field, too, addressing his 'worthy and beloved friend' reflected that

> . . in this age, where jigs and dances move
> How few there are that thy pure work approve . . .
> Each subject thou, still thee each subject raises . . .

The classical trope in the last line is as much a compliment to Jonson in his capacity as a teacher as it is to his dramatic powers, which Jonson could not have failed to appreciate.

Once again, then, Jonson had cause bitterly to regret his connection with 'the loathed stage'. Nor was this a temporary estrangement between the poet and his public as had happened before. *Catiline* proved to be a watershed in Jonson's dramatic career. Never again was he to enjoy a success equivalent to that of *Volpone* or *The Alchemist*. Indeed he had no further popular success of any kind, since virtually all his later plays were given their one introductory performance only. What the Globe audience had brought about was not merely the dismissal of one play but the demolition of Jonson's career as a popular dramatist.

Even then the year 1611 had not finished with Jonson. In November of that year his second son Benjamin died only three months short of his fourth birthday. The little boy was buried at St Anne's Blackfriars, the parish of his father and the church of his own baptism. The parish records note simply the interment of 'Benjamin Johnson son to Benjamin'. What became of the third little 'Beniamen', who had been baptised on 6 April 1610 at St Martin's-in-the-Fields, is not known. But as Jonson was certainly alone in his old age it is likely that he, too, died before reaching his maturity.

There were other losses for Jonson too. 1611 was effectively Shakespeare's last year as a working dramatist; the world of the Jacobean theatre saw the retirement of two titans at the same time. Jonson was not to attempt the stage again for another three years and from then on till his death he had only one more well-regarded play, *Bartholomew Fair*. In wider circles came an even more serious falling off. The court of King James was losing its lustre as disorders and scandals began to accumulate and to add their weight to the gathering difficulties. King, court and nation had also seen the best of their hopes in Prince Henry, on whom Jonson was focusing so much expectation. His fates were even then busy spinning out his thread and the young prince had little longer to live.

Jonson at the end of 1611 could not have foreseen all this. Yet any realistic appraisal of the situation (and Jonson was never a man to dodge harsh personal truths) could not fail to point to the great flowering of his last few years, the output, the variety, the high level of achievement, and to wonder if Jonson could ever match this accomplishment again.

CHAPTER 9

'THE POET'

THE year 1611 had been unkind to Jonson. It had brought him public failure and private grief. Nor did the New Year begin on any more encouraging footing for him. As had now become customary he had contributed a new masque for the Christmas festivities at court; in 1612 it was the Twelfth Night masque for Prince Henry, ostensibly the high spot of the season's merry-making. But there were adverse circumstances quite beyond Jonson's control. King James was in particularly acute financial difficulties at this point after negotiations with Parliament had become so exacerbated that he had severed all relations for the time. Even the King who revelled in both the graceful dancing of the courtiers and the high compliment to himself and his court which lavish masquing implied, was forced therefore to economise.

The total expenditure on Jonson's 1612 masque, *Love Restored*, was allowed to come to no more than £280 8s 9d (HS X, 533) – less than a tenth of what had been spent in less straitened times. Jonson himself glanced humorously at this state of affairs with a reference in the masque to one 'pretty fine speech' by 'the Poet' – 'which if he never be paid for now, 'tis no matter' (lines 11–12). One immediately obvious result of the shortage of money was the poverty of the setting. The only scenery was a chariot in which Cupid entered, a drastic reduction after the magic globes and moving mountains of earlier years. Another reflection of the current situation was Jonson's inclusion in the text of some debate about Puritan attitudes to masques. Despite his inveterate opposition to Puritanism in all its aspects, Jonson's treatment implies that the voice of the enemy was beginning to make itself heard.

The inability of the paymasters to provide the usual ample funding need not in itself have undermined the masque beyond hope of recovery. Jonson was always determined to make his masques more than simply sparkling entertainments, brilliant to the eye but nothing to the mind. He could as before call upon his poetic skills, his management of key symbols, his vigorous classicism, to offer the court another of his lucid and thoughtful comments upon itself. But the spirit of enthusiasm was absent this year and it was a lacklustre proceeding. In the event the Prince himself lent his patronage rather than his active participation. The masque was subsequently described as being 'given by Gentlemen, the King's servants'.

This dismal little show was a definite decline for Jonson from the previous standard of his masque-making and the esteem that had accompanied it. His was never a temperament to adjust to inferiority and this was to be his last court function for almost two years. Equally Jonson had exerted himself tremendously in the theatre's service, producing three plays in as many years (a feat never matched before or after this in his dramatic career) only to see his last play founder ignominiously as if his previous successes had never been. In the same way as he had reacted after the 'War of the Theatres' he retreated in disgust from the public arena, and once again he found shelter under the patronage of a noble friend.

This was Sir Walter Raleigh. The 'great Machiavel' was himself no stranger to far worse difficulties than ever Jonson laboured under. Falling foul of the new king after the death of Elizabeth, he had narrowly escaped execution when suspected in 1603 of plotting against the throne. He had been held a prisoner in the Tower ever since then, fending off stagnation in this lengthy detention by writing and by pursuing his interest in natural sciences through a variety of experiments. It was a poor substitute for the life of action which his multifarious talents fitted him for. As Prince Henry observed, 'Who but my father would keep such a bird in a cage?' From the Tower, Raleigh continued to oversee his affairs and those of his family. He decided to send his son Walter on a visit to Europe, in the care of Ben Jonson as his tutor.[1]

Raleigh had had previous occasion to prove Jonson's ability for himself. Jonson had prepared for him to assist his reading an explanation of the various allegorical figures in Spenser's oblique and highly-wrought poem, *The Faerie Queene*. Jonson had also had a hand in Raleigh's great work, *The History of the World*, a massive undertaking with which Raleigh was attempting to occupy the long slow years of incarceration. Jonson claimed to Drummond that he had written for Raleigh a piece on the history of the Punic Wars which Raleigh had altered and included in the text as his own.[2] He also gave it as his opinion that 'the best wits of England were employed for making of [Raleigh's] history' (HS I, 138). Despite the faint note of resentment in this, the two men had extensive literary and historical interests in common. Young Wat, however, lacked something of his father's cultivated style. As an undergraduate at Oxford he had been noted for his addiction to violent exercise and strange company; he was described as 'a handsome lusty stout fellow, very bold and apt to affront'. With his mother's support he had played off his tutors one against another and was both unruly and given to practical jokes. Jonson was to be the governor of this ungoverned and ungovernable young man.

The new position for Jonson offered a number of definite advantages. First came the opportunity to get away, to leave the small and tightly-knit world of literary London at a time when his current ventures were not enjoying the success which he desired. Again, for an adventurous spirit like Jonson who had not been out of England since his brief foray as a soldier over twenty years before, the chance to travel abroad must have been enticing. A main attraction though would have been the job of 'governor' itself. Throughout his life Jonson manifested both a fondness and an aptitude for the role of pedagogue and it is clear that he had at different times had various younger men and boys as his 'scholars'. Aubrey tells of 'the gentleman that cut the grass under Jonson's feet, of whom he said, "ungrateful man! I showed him Juvenal!" ' (HS I, 181). Another eminent divine, a 'man of the long robe', is said to have refused Jonson a request, at which Jonson commented, 'why, the ungrateful wretch knows very well that before he came to preferment, I was the man that made him relish Horace' (HS I, 184). This however would be the first time that Jonson was to be officially appointed and paid for the job.

To undertake the commitment meant for Jonson deferring plans of his own. On 15 May 1612 a collection of his *Epigrams* had been entered for publication on the Stationers' Register. At this stage Jonson was intending to publish a selection of the poems with which he had occupied his time, practised his art, and honoured his friends and patrons over many years. With his departure abroad however the project had to be shelved; he was not the writer to see a cherished work published uncorrected in his absence. The *Epigrams* in fact were not to come before the public until they appeared with Jonson's other works in the Folio collection of 1616. But their surfacing at this point in Jonson's life suggests a desire on his part to consolidate his position, to upgrade his poetic and literary achievements by putting them in the more permanent and accessible form of a book. He wished in fact to raise himself above the level of the dramatists with whom he was customarily associated, even though he was usually given the gratifying status of *primus inter pares*. Webster expresses this attitude in his description of his contemporaries:

I have ever truly cherished my good opinion of other men's worthy labours; especially of that full and heightened style of Master Chapman, the laboured and understanding works of Master Johnson, the no less worthy composures of both worthily excellent Master Beaumont and Master Fletcher, and lastly (without wrong last to be named) the right happy and copious industry of M. Shakespeare, M. Dekker and M. Heywood.[3]

Other contemporary writers too strove to add to the praises which Jonson was now beginning to receive. John Taylor the Water Poet addressed his 'dear respected friend Mr Benjamin Jonson', in *The Sculler Rowing From Thames to Tiber* (1612):

> Thou canst not die, for though the stroke of death
> Deprives the world of thy worst earthly part,
> Yet when thy corpse hath banished thy breath
> Thy living muse shall still declare thy art.
> The fatal sisters and the blessed graces
> Were all thy friends at thy nativity
> And in thy mind the muses took their places
> Adorning thee with rare capacity.
> And all the worthies of this worthy land
> Admires thy wondrous all-admired worth;
> Then how should I that cannot understand
> Thy worth, thy worthy worthiness set forth . . .

Jonson held a very low opinion of Taylor's verse, and must have cringed at the dreadful badness of these lines. But nothing can impugn the sincerity of the compliment intended.

One task that Jonson fulfilled before leaving was the payment of a literary debt. His patron D'Aubigny had married in 1609 and his wife was now expecting their first child. Jonson greeted her in a long verse epistle (*Forest* 13), praising her virtues and demeanour and the modesty of her 'soft blush'. He wrote to wish her a safe delivery of 'the burden' she was going with, since the birth would take place while he was away. On this occasion Jonson's good wishes came true. Before he left France Lady D'Aubigny was safely brought to bed of the first of the four sons she bore to her husband. The baby was named James, after his king and kinsman.

Around the time of his fortieth birthday in the midsummer of 1612 Jonson and his charge left England and travelled to France. Jonson knew no French and had never visited the country before; he describes himself in Epigram 132 as 'the child of ignorance / And utter stranger to all air of France'. By the early September they had got as far as Paris where it is clear that Jonson had not abandoned his own intellectual interests while engaged in the struggle to cultivate a younger mind. Some members of the community of English expatriates in the French capital had arranged a debate between representatives of the Protestant and Catholic religions. The subject was to be the vexed issue which was one of the fundamental divisions between the two religions, that of transubstantiation, or the Real Presence in the host at communion – in plain English, was God really present in the bread and wine at the moment of communion (as Catholics believed), or were the bread and wine symbols of God's body and blood rather than the actuality (as Protestants thought)? The venue for the debate was to be the private chamber of one of the English residents and there on 4 September the company met.

Among them was Ben Jonson. He was probably the only one of the men present who had been a member of both the Protestant and the Catholic religions; this would however maximise his enjoyment of the proceedings rather than the reverse. A report of the debate was subsequently written up by one of the Englishmen present, one John Pory, who is said to have been a 'burgeois' in 'the first Parliament in King James's time'. In writing his account Pory later demonstrated the trust reposed in Jonson as a Protestant witness of the proceedings. He called on Jonson to check and verify his version of events and his use of the notes of one of the disputants as his source. Jonson was quite ready to do this: 'I profess,' he wrote, 'that all things in narration delivered and quoted . . . are all true out of my examination. And of the rest, I remember the most, or all: neither can I suspect any part – BJ' (HS I, 65–6).

Young Walter Raleigh was not present at this conference on religion. Jonson's pupil, as 'knavishly inclined' it appeared as in the Oxford days, was readier to turn his attention to tricks than to texts. In one prank Raleigh took advantage of Jonson's fondness for alcohol to contrive an elaborate practical joke at his expense. The resulting escapade also incorporated a thoroughly Protestant sideswipe at the religious practices of the host country:

> He [Raleigh] caused him [Jonson] to be drunken, and dead drunk, so that he knew not where he was; thereafter laid him on a car, which he made to be drawn by pioneers [labourers] through the streets, at every corner showing them his governor laid out, and telling them, that was a more lively image of the crucifix than any they had. (HS I, 141)

When the news of this scene reached England, young Raleigh's mother was delighted with the sport, 'saying his father, young, was so inclined'. But Sir Walter, who had himself suffered from his son's coarse and disrespectful humour,[4] abhorred it. Jonson's own boisterous sense of the ridiculous enabled him to take the episode in his stride and he later shared the joke with Drummond (HS I, 140). This was it seems only one of various 'pastimes' which the young man undertook.[5] Jonson himself did not maintain an uncritically reverent attitude to the Roman Catholic practices of the French. He later told Drummond that 'the greatest sport he saw in France was the picture of our Saviour with the Apostles eating the Pascal lamb – it was all larded [greasy]' (HS I, 145).

By March of 1613 this rumbustious pair had been in France for almost a year. Another encounter of Jonson of which only a brief record remains was with a Frenchman celebrated in a number of different fields. Cardinal Duperron was a prominent Roman Catholic and an ecclesiastical politician at a high level, famous for triumphing in just that sort of debate which Jonson had witnessed. But this worldly, witty and stylish man also had literary ambitions and pretensions. As a young man he had been chosen to pronounce the funeral oration for Ronsard, and he had written satires, ballads, and translations of Virgil and Horace.

Somehow Jonson was introduced to this distinguished man, as he told Drummond, during his stay in France in 1613. The cardinal showed him his translations of Virgil which had won the applause of King James, among others. The proud author must have been considerably surprised when Jonson bluntly told him that 'they were naught'; that is, worthless. The Cardinal's version had been advertised as 'une traduction libre', and a free translation was the last thing to appeal to the literal-minded orthodox translator, Jonson. But this frankness is little short of breathtaking in these circumstances; once again Jonson demonstrated his resolute refusal to flatter.

From Paris Jonson resolved to direct their travels to Brussels and to ensure a welcome in the Belgian capital he providentially equipped himself with letters of recommendation to English residents there. Part of his motive as one letter makes clear was to prevent or counteract 'the rumour of some cross business wherein he hath been interested here [in Paris]'. Jonson did not want to be preceded by an undesirable reputation. He had, however, with his great gift for friendship, made a sufficiently good impression to draw forth the warmest commendations to his proposed new acquaintance in the low countries. Not surprisingly he was admired for 'his extraordinary and rare parts of knowledge and understanding which make his conversations to be honoured and beloved in all companies, especially for the commendation he hath not to abuse the power of his gifts, as commonly other overflowing wits use to do . . . '.

Jonson was promised, in this letter, 'the best cup of claret that Brussells shall afford, to remember the healths of his friends here'.

151

When he travelled to Brussels to receive it both he and Raleigh went by sedan chair. There they remained for about a month. By the beginning of April 1613 they were in Antwerp and in financial difficulties. They succeeded however in prevailing upon Raleigh's agent there to bail them out of their situation; the unfortunate man was so 'earnestly importuned' (if not browbeaten) that when he cashed their bills of exchange he advanced them £10 over and above the value.[6]

In the early summer of 1613 Jonson brought his wayward charge back to England and restored him to his mother. Walton comments that he had heard that 'they parted (I think not in cold blood), with a love suitable to what they had in their travels (not to be commended)' (HS I, 181). Jonson returned to London to discover a profound change in the capital and in the life of the nation. His country had sustained some serious losses during his absence abroad. Most sorrowful and unlooked-for was the death of the heir to the throne, Prince Henry. This vital and gifted young man, only eighteen years old, had fallen ill and sank rapidly, defying the hopes of the nation and his physicians' frantic attempts to recover him. This event on 6 November 1612 had serious and ever-widening implications. The boy destined to restore England's Tudor greatness, as his name implied, had developed easily and naturally the traits most becoming in a royal prince and future leader of men. He had grown with time into the very heart of his country's aspirations for the future, a future ever darkened by James's increasing difficulties, while his awkward and undeveloped younger brother Charles had never learned the management of those skills of which he was now to have such need.

In literary and cultural terms too the loss made itself felt. Jonson was among the poets who had experienced Prince Henry's enlightened patronage; as early as 1609 Jonson had written to the young prince, 'your favour to letters, and these gentler studies that go under the title of humanity, is not the least honour to your wreath'.[7] Jonson's *Love Restored* had proved to be the last masque with which the young prince was connected. But he did not lend his voice to the wailful choir of lamentation in which the Prince's death was universally if somewhat tritely mourned. This does not imply any indifference on his part to the fate of the Prince whom he had known and praised so lavishly in his lifetime. His long absence in Europe would rob any contribution that he cared to make of any immediacy or impact. But it is equally likely that he would avoid the performance of such an obvious and commonplace gesture, as he did in 1603 when his failure to herald the passing of Queen Elizabeth caused contemporary comment.

For Jonson the loss of Prince Henry's patronage was not an

immediate financial threat. He had other noble friends and other sources of income. For his friend and fellow-classicist Chapman however the national disaster was also a personal catastrophe. Chapman had been dependent on the Prince for material assistance with his major work of translating Homer. The sudden end of his allowance brought upon Chapman poverty and insecurity from which he was never again able to free himself. The damage to Jonson's career made itself felt more slowly and subtly. Prince Henry had been the only one of the Stuarts who combined the very real intellectual gifts of the family with any grace or style. James and Anne were ageing, and James's once-bright regal image was becoming tarnished as his coarser streak prevailed over his taste and judgment. A certain disillusion was setting in; hopes and ideals began to pall. Jonson's earlier images of god-like majesty, harmony and unity were becoming less and less serviceable, more and more impossible to sustain in and through James alone. The death of Henry robbed Jonson of the rising sun by which he had already begun to set his course in *The Masque of Oberon* and thereafter. It dashed too his aspirations to use the masque form in the Sidneyan manner, to raise the mind to virtue through delight. The older Stuarts were beyond such developments; the young Charles not yet capable. Jonson lost at this time the impulse to produce masques that combined fantasy and imagination with learning. After 1612 his masques increasingly settle into conventional forms, while his fertility of invention expends itself on the anti-masque.

Prince Henry's death had one further consequence for Jonson's future career. His former colleague in masque-making, Inigo Jones, had held a Surveyorship to the Prince. Deprived of this post Jones took advantage of this natural break in his career to return to Italy for further study of art and architecture. It was to be as a more widely-travelled and deeply-studied man that Jones would eventually return to the English court. The two men had been able to work together on masques in the past. But in becoming a more considerable artist Jones developed too into a more formidable and eventually irresistible opponent and adversary.

As the nation lost a son in 1612, it lost also a father. The Earl of Salisbury, another of Jonson's patrons, died. His death deprived James and the country of an elder statesman whose shrewdness had succeeded in restraining the worst of his monarch's egregious financial indiscretions. Gone too was another link with the reign of Elizabeth — the Cecils father and son had served the crown for over sixty years, through some of the most troubled years of its history. Jonson's relations with Salisbury had been problematic. His initial enthusiasm for the Secretary of State as evinced in the encomiastic Epigram 43 had survived Cecil's aggrandisement to an earldom and his accession to the Treasurership in 1608. But disillusion had set in. It was never enough for Jonson simply to be taken up by those whom fortune had placed in a higher station than his own; it was an article of faith with him that 'he never esteemed of a man for the name of a lord' (HS I, 141). What he sought was a personal rather than a merely social contact.

This is clearly borne out in one anecdote of the relationship. Jonson had been invited to dine with Salisbury; this may have been the occasion in 1608 when the Cecil accounts record that Jonson, Inigo Jones and Edward Alleyn were summoned to dine with the Earl during the preparation of the entertainment at Salisbury House to celebrate Salisbury's appointment to the position of Lord Treasurer. At the meal Jonson found himself seated at the end of the table with Inigo Jones. His resentment at being placed so far away from his host and from the positions of honour nearby communicated itself to the top of the table. Salisbury himself called down to demand of Jonson why he was not merry. Jonson's reply was restrained, but to the point: 'My lord, you promised that I should dine *with* you, but I do not' (HS I, 141). For Jonson, being seated so low, and as was the custom served with different meat from that which his Lordship received, was, in effect, not to be dining with him at all.

Jonson became convinced eventually that Salisbury was no more than an exploiter of others' abilities, that he 'never cared for any man longer [than] he could make use of him' (HS I, 162). But the poet, as Jonson constantly reminds both himself and his reader, has the last word. In preparing his epigrams for the press Jonson followed two in praise of Salisbury (63 and 64) with a passionate piece upbraiding himself for writing poetry in praise of 'a worthless lord'. This juxtapositioning leads to the irresistible conclusion that Salisbury is intended here, as the 'great image' in the service of whom Jonson feels with evident self-disgust that he has prostituted his poetic gift. The poem ends with Jonson's pledge to himself henceforth only 'to write /Things manly, and not smelling parasite'. In view of his supremely derogatory picture of the parasite Mosca in *Volpone*, this must have been a deep anger to make him abuse himself so.

Yet personalities apart, Jonson knew Salisbury not merely as a man, but as one of the main props of state. His passing could not but leave the whole edifice the shakier. A less public but more personal loss was the death from smallpox on 3 December 1612 of Sir William Sidney, the eldest son of Jonson's patron Lord Lisle of Penshurst.

This young man was a junior member of that lustrous family whose chief ornament had been Sir Philip Sidney in the old Queen's time, and whom Jonson had delighted to honour with many literary tributes. William had, most poignantly, died just at that point of his illness at which hope for his recovery was stirring: 'the small pockets were well out, and yet he went away on the sodain'.[8] Only a year before in November 1611 Jonson had greeted the young man with an ode especially composed for the occasion of his twenty-first birthday. In this poem (*Forest* 14), Jonson mingles his congratulations with the reminder that much will be expected of the bearer of such a famous and well-loved name. He wishes that William may grow in honour, reputation and love, burning brightly as an inspiration to others. As with his benign hopes of a child for the Countess of Rutland, Jonson was once more to see a malignant fate turn his words to bitter irony. And as with the death of Prince Henry he did not join those poets who hallowed William Sidney's death with their elegies.

A less natural and explicable casualty during Jonson's absence was Sir Thomas Overbury. Born in 1581, Overbury died in 1613 in circumstances that were not fully understood at the time. Jonson had come to know and admire Overbury who was making his way at court to become the secretary and close adviser of James's first favourite in England, Robert Carr. The two men had a common interest in literature; Overbury was a writer too, and his *Characters*, thumbnail sketches drawn with wit and clarity of familiar contemporary types, continued in popularity long after his death. Jonson's Epigram 113 dates from this earlier warm stage of their acquaintance, with its free praise of Overbury's contribution to the court's 'wit' and 'manners' through his knowledge of 'letters and humanity'.

But Overbury had proved to be another instance in Jonson's life of regard decaying into estrangement and antagonism. Jonson recorded that Overbury 'was first his friend, then turned his mortal enemy' (HS I, 137). The reason behind this violent reversal of feeling is suggested by a further comment to Drummond. Overbury had fallen in love with the Countess of Rutland, in whose house Jonson was a welcome visitor. Overbury so far enlisted the help of Jonson in his courtship as to succeed in getting the poet to read poetry on his behalf to the lady (Jonson's excellence in reading aloud, doubtless formed in his early days as an actor, never failed to win him 'golden opinions'). The poem chosen was one of Overbury's own, and Jonson was sufficiently pleased with his own performance to inform Drummond that he had read 'with an excellent grace'; he had further commended the author magnanimously to the Countess. The following morning however Overbury had requested Jonson to act for him in pressing the relationship further, a paradoxical development in view of the fact that Overbury's poem, *A Wife*, was a long moral piece which preached chastity both before and within marriage. Jonson could never approve of other people's adultery. He refused to be involved as go-between in 'a suit that was unlawful' and quarrelled with

Overbury who never thereafter forgave either the refusal or the implied rebuke which it contained (HS I, 138).

The object of Overbury's illicit passion had herself died in 1612, not thirty years of age, and only two months after her husband. Jonson's relations with the Countess had done much to mitigate his anti-feminism, providing for him an audience and an occasional refuge as well as a poetic subject. Like that of Prince Henry this was a complex loss. For this lady Jonson had maintained the respect and admiration with which he had first saluted her in his New Year verse epistle of 1600. He had considered her 'nothing inferior to her father', the legendary Sir Philip Sidney, in poetry; he had commended her mind, her manners and her morals as expressions of her rising above her less than satisfactory private life, her marriage rendered void by her husband's impotence.

On one occasion when Jonson was dining with the Countess her husband came in and accused her of 'keeping table to poets', that is, offering hospitality to her inferiors. The Countess wrote to Jonson after this scene, presumably some words of apology or excuse. But Jonson's anger was not to be assuaged and he returned a strong reply. The jealous husband intercepted this and the memory of its contents caused Jonson to fear a challenge from Rutland by way of reprisal. In this circumstance it never came but it is interesting to observe that despite his experience of other hostile passages, Jonson never lost his taste for confrontation and his carelessness of consequences.

The years 1612 and 1613 had seen some major readjustments in the everchanging kaleidoscope of Jonson's personal circle. One significant gain however to some extent balanced these losses. Into Jonson's life after the return from Europe came Richard Brome. Originally Jonson took Brome on as his 'man', this employment suggesting that Jonson was no longer enjoying his wife's domestic services. It is possible that the long continental trip finally brought down Jonson's rickety marriage structure, or he may have been widowed. Ageing then and without a regular establishment Jonson would have needed some domestic assistance.

Brome, in his early twenties, came from humble origins and had had no chance of academic training. But he was quick, keen and adaptable. This combination of qualities seems to have called upon the pedagogue in Jonson again, and as a pupil Brome was far more promising than young Walter Raleigh despite his formal handicaps. Jonson found in his manservant one whose abilities were to enable their possessor to fulfil a far wider variety of tasks than the purely menial and whose importance in his master's life increased proportionately.

Jonson was back in London by the early summer of 1613. He had been absent from a revival of *The Alchemist* which took place at Court earlier in the year. But he had not, as it turned out, missed all the excitement. On 29 June 1613 (St Peter's day, as every former Westminster schoolboy would know) the great Globe theatre caught fire and burned to the ground. This fine edifice had been much admired by Jonson, who described it in *Every Man Out Of His Humour* as 'this fair-fitted Globe'. It had been the last word in theatre architecture for its time.

Jonson was present on this occasion which set the whole town astir. It was a warm, sunshiny afternoon and the theatre was filled with people gathered to see the performance of a new history play, *All Is True* (better known today as Shakespeare's *King Henry VIII*, a label which eclipses Fletcher's major contribution to its composition). The play was being staged with spectacular opulence and attention to historical verisimilitude. This in fact was the cause of the disaster. On the King's entrance in the fourth scene of the first act two cannon discharged a royal salute. One of the charges lodged in the thatch of the roof where it gained hold unnoticed.

The resulting conflagration was swift and savage. Within an hour nothing was left of the stately Globe. Jonson later recorded his experience of the event with a note of disbelief:

> . . . the Globe, the glory of the Bank
> Which, though it were the fort of the whole parish,
> Flanked with a ditch and forced out of a marish [marsh],
> I saw with two poor chambers [cannon shot] taken in
> And razed, ere thought could urge, This might have been!
> See the world's ruins, nothing but the piles
> Left! and wit since to cover it with tiles.[9]

Jonson further observed ironically how ready the Puritans were to seize upon the fire as an evidence of divine judgment against the players. But miraculously the only casualties were 'a few forsaken cloaks' and one pair of breeches, soon doused by their wearer with a providential bottle of ale. The spectators were left to contemplate the ruins, nothing but the smouldering piles of London's greatest theatre, famed throughout the civilised world.

This was not the only misfortune endured in 1613 by theatre people. Jonson's old adversary from the 'War of the Theatres', Dekker, had succumbed to his financial distresses and was imprisoned for debt in the King's Bench prison. Lacking the influential friends who had been mustered to deliver Jonson from durance, Dekker could not contrive his own release and was imprisoned for the next six years. But as Dekker sank to the lowest point on the wheel of fortune, so Jonson was riding high in esteem at this time. His *Volpone* (1606) had grown in the affection of theatre-goers and readers alike while *Sejanus* (1603), after a poor start, had made surprising headway in public esteem. Numerous warm references testify to the contemporary popularity and esteem of these two plays, which held their place in the forefront of critical attention even in the decade which also produced *Othello, King Lear, Macbeth* and *Coriolanus*.[10] As a practical demonstration of his plays' popularity, the Lord Treasurer's accounts record performances for the Royal household – both *Eastward Ho!* and *The Alchemist* were given at court in 1613. In view of the offence that *Eastward Ho!* originally gave to the King, its performance at court is a remarkable tribute to Jonson's advancing status.

But Jonson was never quite to be without the abrasive reminder of the carpers and cavillers around him. Henry Parrott, in his 1613 work *Laquei Ridiculosi, or Springes for Woodcocks*, revives among other sneers the old jibe of bricklayer:

> Put off thy buskins, Sophocles the great,
> And mortar tread with thy disdained shanks.
> Thou thinkst thy skill hath done a wondrous feat,
> For which this world should give thee many thanks.
> Alas! It seems thy feathers are but loose,
> Plucked from a swan, and set upon a goose.
>
> (*JAB* 84–5)

It is interesting to observe that Jonson's legs were still remarkable enough to merit a crack of their own, as in the 'War of the Theatres'. There cannot have been a good deal wrong with their function as they had just completed a tour of Europe and five years later were to bear the 'mountain belly' all the way to Scotland and back. It is obvious, though, that Jonson's legs must have wanted something aesthetically, if they were so unsightly and ill-proportioned as to be capable of being made a laughing-stock in this way.

But Jonson could afford to rise above these slings and arrows. On Monday 9 August 1613 the Lady Elizabeth's Men staged *Eastward Ho!*, the play having passed to them from the Children of the Queen's Revels. And as 1613 drew to its end he was once again employed in the preparation of a new masque for the forthcoming Christmas at court. This was to be an unusually full season. The highlight was the marriage just after Christmas of the King's favourite Carr, now Earl of Somerset, to the Countess of Essex. Jonson contributed two entertainments to the festive season of 1613–14. His first piece was *The Irish Masque at Court*, performed first on Wednesday 29 December and liked well enough to be revived on the following Monday, 3 January. This performance had not been bedevilled by the lack of money; one contemporary commentator had heard little or nothing about the masque, 'only that it was rich and costly'. Some of the more discerning spirits at court considered that the central device, 'a mimical imitation of the Irish', was both tasteless and inappropriate: '[this is] no time (as the case stands) to exasperate that nation by making it ridiculous' (*JAB* 86). But Jonson's introduction of masquers disguised as Irishmen, after the masque convention of the wandering strangers seeking the court, was generally well received, and the masque's success carried it forward to a second performance.

On New Year's Day 1614 came the performance of Jonson's *A Challenge at Tilt* to celebrate the Somerset-Essex wedding. Ten courtiers in mulberry and white for the bride contended with ten for the groom in yellow and green; among them was Jonson's friend, Sir Henry Cary. Once again in James's increasingly degenerate court all behaved as if the proceedings gave no offence in the world. But the path to the altar for this glamorous couple had been far from straight and narrow. Jonson knew this as well as any man since it was he who had written the masque of *Hymenaei* for the bride's first marriage six years before. The Countess had been a married woman when she first attracted the attention of Somerset. Since then the couple had driven forward ruthlessly towards this union, treading down all obstacles and opposition with the shameless connivance of the King. In order to escape from her existing marriage in an era before divorce, the Countess had to establish that her marriage was null through her husband's physical incapacity to consummate it. The suit which she consequently brought was vigorously resisted by the Earl, who not unnaturally did not wish to be branded as impotent. The commission which was set up to adjudicate upon the issue was evenly divided. At this juncture the King appointed new members, carefully chosen to obtain the annulment which his favourite Carr so desired. This packing of the commission gave great scandal to lawyers, divines and laymen alike. Jonson's constant claim to an unswerving morality receives a check from the verses which he wrote to commemorate this occasion, 'To the most noble, and above his titles, Robert, Earl of Somerset' (*Ungathered Verse* 18). In this piece Jonson pulls out all the stops to praise and honour 'virtuous Somerset', and to 'pray [his] joys as lasting be as great'. He even incorporates without apparent sense of inappropriateness lines which he had previously used in *Hymenaei*;[11] the Countess must have had a short memory.

Poets of course are hired for their couplets not for their consciences and Jonson certainly gave value for money on this occasion. After these ceremonies, on 25 January 1614 the Lady Elizabeth's Men gave his *Eastward Ho!* at court. These were for Jonson welcome successes, and from them he enjoyed a return of confidence and creative vigour. By Hallowe'en of 1616 Jonson was ready once again to try his fate upon the 'loathed stage'. In March of the previous year his old employer Henslowe had gone into partnership with the manager of the Whitefriars theatre Philip Rosseter. Their agreement was to join Rosseter's troupe, the Children of the Revels, with the Lady Elizabeth's Men, then under Henslowe's management, in order to form a company strong enough to compete with the King's Men.

A new company called for a new theatre. Accordingly, the old Bear Garden was torn down and the Hope theatre built in its place. The stage was made removable to permit animal baiting in the same arena. This took place only one day in every fourteen but the inmates of the stables, kennels and bear dens inevitably made their presence felt all the rest of the time too. Jonson made jokes about this, observing 'the place being as dirty as Smithfield, and as stinking every whit'. For he was one of the playwrights approached to be involved in this young enterprise.

Jonson's *Bartholomew Fair* was staged at the Hope theatre on the Bankside on 31 October 1614. On the following day, All Saints, it was presented at court with a new prologue for the occasion; the Lord Treasurer's account records that £10 was paid to Nathan Field and his fellows for this special performance. Jonson had not forgotten nor forgiven the London audience's reception of his *Catiline* three years before. In a lengthy and careful induction to his new play he was at pains to instruct his listeners in the correct attitudes by establishing himself as strong presence within the play; a threatening presence, in fact, and a heavily implied control on the audience's responses. The induction has as its central character the Stage Keeper (rather like the stage manager in today's theatre). Jonson makes him talk extensively of the playwright, stressing his shortness of temper and tendency to violent retaliation when crossed. The audience is constantly reminded of the playwright's insistence on his own artistic standards and his own judgment, while scorn is cast upon the popular taste and the conventions of popular comedy. The tone of all this is humorous and good-natured, but the message to the spectators is clear: shape up, or else.

Not satisfied with this, though, Jonson prolongs the Induction by including a contract between the poet and the audience. This curious conceit, unique in the drama of the period, is his way of trying to forestall another mutual disappointment between himself and his audience. This lengthy 'contract' (over one hundred lines) is authoritarian in manner and sardonic in tone. It seems at times more of a rebuff than a welcome to the play. This brusquerie, though, scarcely conceals Jonson's determination that this time his play must and will please. A sense of past hurts is never very far below the surface of the writing, and it is covered with a humour that is only skin deep.

In the event *Bartholomew Fair* was a success for Jonson. With this piece, perhaps the most amiable of all his productions, he succeeded in the aim professed in the prologue delivered before King James, of giving an experience of 'true delight'. There is a tradition that the immemorial phrase with which he is most associated, 'O rare Ben Jonson!', was first heard as a cry raised by the gratified audience at the end of the performance. The warmth of this reception must have done much to compensate him for the coldness which had greeted his *Catiline* three years earlier. *Bartholomew Fair* is also of interest in that it affords us a brief glimpse of Jonson's servant Richard Brome. Brome is humorously referred to in the Induction as lurking behind the arras in the playhouse, acting as his master's ears. He had obviously been in Jonson's service by now for long enough to be universally known to theatre audiences as Jonson's 'man'. His duties had clearly progressed beyond the purely domestic, if he was being included in Jonson's working life in the theatre. Brome's later divergence into drama on his own account shows that these early experiences were not wasted on him.

Although occupied with his play, Jonson did not neglect his literary duties. From the Tower Sir Walter Raleigh had at last brought out his *History of the World* (1614). Jonson had had an active interest in this project all along and for the book's publication he contributed an introductory poem. This piece is a description and commentary upon what is represented in the frontispiece, an allegorical design showing the importance of 'grave history' in the life of man. A faith in the power of history to bring all truths to light must have been one of the few consolations available to Elizabeth's old courtier in his protracted imprisonment.

Another publication of 1614 throws an interesting sidelight upon Jonson's life at this time. His friend Selden brought out his *Titles of Honour*, in the preface of which he describes one of the circumstances of its composition. He happened to want to look up a passage in Euripides's *Orestes* but did not have a copy of the book. So as he writes 'I went for this purpose to see it in the well-furnished library of my beloved friend that singular poet Mr Ben Jonson, whose special worth in literature, accurate judgement, and performance, known only to that few which are truly able to know him, hath had from me, ever since I began to learn, an increasing admiration' (IIS I, 250). The two men examined the passage together and Selden was confirmed in his first opinion.

A verse epistle written for the *Titles of Honour* by Jonson speaks feelingly of the love, friendship and ease of understanding between the two men:

> I know to whom I write . . .
> Your book, my Selden, I have read, and much
> Was trusted, that you thought my judgement such
> To ask it . . .

Jonson sets the trust that he enjoys with Selden against his experience of other men:

> . . . I confess (as every muse hath erred
> And mine not least) I have too oft preferred
> Men past their terms, and praised some men too much;
> But 'twas with purpose to have made them such.
> Since, being deceived, I turn a sharper eye
> Upon myself, and ask to whom, and why,
> And what I write? And vex it many days
> Before men get a verse, much less a praise.

> (*Underwood* 14)

One man for whom Jonson never had cause to regret his admiration was the Earl of Suffolk. This man, who had rescued Jonson and Chapman from imprisonment in 1605 and whom Jonson honoured in Epigram 67, was made Lord Treasurer in 1614.

1614 closed for Jonson as so many years had now with the writing of the royal masque for the Christmas season at court. The now endemic shortage of money was once again a factor in the equation but it was not to be allowed to spoil the festivities. One courtier commented sardonically on the reason behind this:

> Yet for all this penurious world we speak of a masque this Christmas toward which the King gives £1500, the principal motive whereof is thought to be the gracing of young Villiers and to bring him on the stage. (*JAB* 86)

George Villiers, the son of an insignificant Leicestershire squire, had made his way out of nowhere into the King's good graces. The court was as charmed as the King by his good looks and winning ways, intrigued, too, to discover how the old favourite, Carr, would fare in the face of this unforeseen challenge. Given that Villiers was a gifted and graceful dancer, that he had been sedulously practising his skill since he came to court, and that the whole event was spiced with malice and mischief, the literary aspect of *The Golden Age Restored* went unnoticed. The masque went well. It was performed on 6 January, Twelfth Night, and two nights later on 8 January.

But Jonson was not to rest on his laurels. 1615 brought back into court circles his only rival in masque-making, Inigo Jones. Jones now returned from his second visit to Italy and succeeded to the Sur-

veyorship of the King's Works, in effect to the position of royal
architect and designer. Like Jonson himself Jones was now older,
more experienced, and hardly less opinionated than he had been in
former years. The ease of the earlier collaboration was no longer
possible for either man. Yet difficulties at this stage lay ahead. Jones
rejoined on his return the group of friends whom he had known
before. He had previously been a member of the Mermaid Club, as
Coryate recorded; Jonson remained its presiding genius. The two
men were thrown together socially as well as professionally.

Yet Jonson was not spending his time entirely in quaffing and
conversing at the Mermaid. He was working, and very seriously too –
not on a new play but on his major legacy to future ages. Jonson had
decided to collect and publish his works and was engaged in seeing
them through the press. The rumours which now began to make their
way around the town about Jonson's non-dramatic writings were not
always received by others in a cordial spirit. To some Jonson's
poetical pretensions were a joke. One commentator, hiding behind
the initials 'R.C.', observed sourly, 'Jonson, they say's turned Epigrammatist'. 'R.C.' takes leave to doubt this, on the grounds that
Jonson does not possess so much as 'a dram / Of wit befitting a true
epigram'; he pieces out his 'broken stuff' with scraps of playbooks so
that his work resembles a patched coat. 'R.C.' concludes with the
dismissive direction:

> Then write no more, or write with better grace.
> Turn thee to plays, and therein write thy fill;
> Leave epigrams to artists of more skill.
>
> *(JAB 90–91)*

But Jonson also had at this time the encouragement of his friends as a
counterbalance to such ignorant condescension. On 28 February
1615 Selden wrote affectionately to Jonson praising his mind and his
abilities: 'you best know, being most conversant in the recondite parts
of human learning . . . your own most choice and able store cannot
but furnish you with whatever is fit that way to be thought. Whatever
I have here collected, I consecrate to your love, and end with the hope
of your instructing judgement'. With the support of friends like this
Jonson was able to move ahead in his work.

Among other projects at this time Jonson picked up something
begun ten years previously, his translation of Horace's *Ars Poetica*.
After *Bartholomew Fair* he expanded the critical commentary which
formed the preface to the translation by including 'an apology for a
play of his, *St Bartholomew's Fair*', as he later told Drummond (HS I,
134). The conjunction of the greatest poet of the classical era with the
pemier poet of the present day struck certain of Jonson's acquaintance

as peculiarly apposite. Lord Herbert of Cherbury later made an
epigram upon the subject. 'Upon his friend Mr Ben Jonson, and his
Translation':

> 'Twas not enough, Ben Johnson, to be thought
> Of English poets best, but to have brought
> In greater state to their acquaintance one
> So equal to himself and thee, that none
> Might be thy second, while thy glory is,
> To be the Horace of our times and his.

(HS XI, 352)

But despite these friendly auspices Jonson was not satisfied with his
translation. It lay among his papers unpublished, and eventually
perished years later in the fire of 1623 in Jonson's lodgings.[12]

Although at this time leading a largely literary life, Jonson remained
in demand for formal public occasions. In March of 1615 King James
was to visit the University of Cambridge. Robert Lane, the President
of St John's College, making special arrangements for the royal
descent upon St John's, went to London. From there he reported back
to the other Fellows that 'we have been with Mr Johnson our
musician, and entreated Ben Jonson to pen a ditty, which we expect
on Saturday'. As this letter was written on a Thursday it gives a good
idea of the speed with which Jonson could work at times.

Jonson's settled and stable life at this period contrasts strongly with
that of the court. There, where according to Jonson's masque for-
mulation harmony and virtue ought to prevail, discord and wickedness were breaking out. The marriage two years earlier in 1613 of the
Countess of Essex to the King's favourite the Earl of Somerset had
caused a great scandal as an adulterous liaison was violently wrenched into the semblance of a Christian union. But now it came to light
that the couple had been guilty of breaking more than social laws.
Jonson's former friend Overbury, then the Earl's secretary, had
vigorously opposed the match; he had accurately foreseen that his
master would be putty in the hands of this terrifyingly self-willed
woman. This course of action, as it now transpired, had made the
Countess his vicious and inveterate enemy and had finally cost him
his life. Not content with bullying the King into having Overbury
imprisoned she took steps to silence him altogether. When Overbury
met his mysterious death in the Tower in 1613 it was because the
malice of the Countess had pursued him there and struck him down.

The revelation of these dreadful facts and the ensuing trial of the
guilty engrossed all London. The outrage was increased rather than
diminished when the King pardoned the two titled malefactors while
their low-born agents went to the gallows. Once again Jonson had a

private and personal involvement in a public and national affair. His
art had twice been placed at the service of the murderous Countess on
the occasion of her two marriages; his acquaintance and fellow-poet
Overbury had paid with his life for flying too near this flame. Despite
his own less-than-scrupulous private life Jonson never abandoned a
stern, almost Old Testament morality. What he felt about the fact that
his pen had been employed in the celebration of such ill-starred
wedding rites may be gathered from his subsequent course of action.
He took the only step open to him, a literary revenge. When he
prepared his collected works for the Folio publication Jonson ex-
punged the names of both the bride and groom from the wedding
masques *Hymenaei* and *A Challenge At Tilt*.

The choice of subject for a court still recovering from these shocks
and scandals required some care. Jonson's device for the Christmas
masque of the 1615–16 season was cast in the form of a triumph, in
which the hero achieves vindication through victory. The figure of
Mercury, badgered and beset in the anti-masque, wins through at the
end. *Mercury Vindicated From The Alchemists At Court* was given on
Monday 1 January 1616 and repeated on 6 January because of a
precedence quarrel of almost unparalleled ferocity between the
foreign ambassadors. As the French ambassador had taken deep
offence at being invited along with those of Venice and Savoy the
friction could only be eased by giving him his own invitation to a
special Twelfth Night performance staged especially for his benefit.

How Jonson must have chafed at these petty and irrelevant inter-
ruptions, so far removed from the dignity of 'the Poet'! Yet he was
never the man to be deflected from his sense of purpose by worldly
considerations. Even as he hung about the court to accommodate the
tantrums of the ambassadors, events were in train which would
ensure that all his endeavours were coming to an enduring fruition.
Now at last could he clearly see the prospect of the name of 'Ben Jonson,
poet' living for all eternity.

CHAPTER 10

LAUREATE

1616 brought a decisive change in Jonson's status. At the start of the new year he received the reward for his long and brilliant court service in a way that meant far more to him than mere money. At last he was granted official public recognition of his contribution to the life of the court and of his standing as a man of letters. By an Act of 1 February 1616 King James granted to his 'well-beloved servant' a life pension of one hundred marks a year 'in consideration of the good and acceptable service done by him'. This annuity, to be paid every quarter, 'at the feast of the Annunciation of the Blessed Virgin Mary, the nativity of St John the Baptist, St Michael the Archangel, and the birth of our Lord', both rewarded Jonson's past endeavours and confirmed his future status as the King's poet.

By this act Jonson was created the first Poet Laureate in the history of the English monarchy. The award also promised to relieve him of the unremitting pressure of financial need – since a mark was worth two-thirds of a pound (13s 4d), the grant was therefore equal to what he would have made had he sold six plays at Henslowe's rate of £10 each. His triumph would undoubtedly have impressed his old employer. But Henslowe had at last been forced to relinquish his own inveterate money-making by his death just before this in January of 1616.

The early part of this year brought a fatal change for another of Jonson's acquaintance. As a court correspondent noted, 'Sir Walter Raleigh was freed out of the Tower last week, and goes up and down seeing sights and places built or bettered since his imprisonment'. Raleigh had been shut up for thirteen years, a time still not long enough to defeat the King's implacable hostility to him. He owed his release now only to James's increasingly desperate need for money. The idea was that Raleigh should be set at liberty in order to renew his search for a gold mine in Guiana, which he had been on the track of twenty years before during a previous expedition. Nothing short of a miracle of this order would have restored Raleigh to James's favour. As he had warned Carr before his fall, 'I had rather a conformable man, with but ordinary parts, than the rarest man in the world that will not be obedient'. It was too late for Raleigh to become 'conformable' or 'obedient'. His future turned on this last throw. But he was defeated before he began. For James, turning against him, furnished the enemy Spain with full details concerning the size and destination of Raleigh's expedition and so ensured its failure.

As Raleigh was preparing his fleet for the eventual sailing in June another friend of Jonson's met a much swifter and more unexpected doom. Francis Beaumont died in March 1616, still a young man and at the height of his career as a dramatist. Jonson later commented to Drummond on Beaumont's youth: 'Franc: Beaumont died ere he was thirty years of age'. Jonson was in fact inaccurate – Beaumont was in his thirty-second year when he died – but still too young, even for those days. Like Jonson, Beaumont had enjoyed his best years in the decade between 1606 and 1616. This was the time of his famous friendship with Fletcher, when gossip credited the two men with being so close that they shared everything, be it an idea, a cloak, or a woman.

Jonson had in the past admired their work. He told Drummond that 'Fletcher and Beaumont ten years since hath written *The Faithful Shepherdess*, a tragicomedy well done'. His feelings for Beaumont were not over-warm, and he criticised him to Drummond on the grounds that 'he loved too much himself and his own verses'. But evidence abounds that Beaumont on his side had a strong feeling of regard for Jonson and the friendship had clearly flourished, despite some discrepancy in affection. Later gossip continued to link the two men in their professional context too. Dryden stated that Beaumont 'was so accurate a judge of plays that Ben Jonson, while he lived, submitted all his writings to his censures and 'tis thought used his judgement in correcting, if not contriving, all his plots' (*JAB* 343). As critic, colleague, or friend, therefore, Jonson lost a member of his personal circle when Beaumont was laid to rest in Westminster Abbey. He was besides too shrewd not to recognise a wider impoverishment of the stage in the loss of one of its younger luminaries.

In the next month of the spring of 1616 news reached Jonson from the country of another loss. On 23 April Shakespeare died. He had been retired from the theatre to his great house in Stratford-on-Avon for five years or so, and since his own going into France Jonson could have seen little of his old friend, colleague and arch rival. Yet posterity has continued to yoke these two men together, in their lifetimes and after.

For what is known as a skeletal account of their working relationship has consistently been bodied out by rumour and anecdote.
The tradition was already in existence by the time of Shakespeare's
death that he had been invited to be the godfather of Jonson's child.
After the baptism he is reported to have said to the father, 'Now you
expect a great matter [that is, the traditional christening gift]. But I
shall give you a latten spoon, and you shall translate it.' The quip here
plays upon the contemporary meaning of 'latten' as a type of metal
alloy, and Latin, the language. The story is somewhat vitiated by the
existence of a parallel version in which it is Jonson who is the
godfather to a child of Shakespeare and thus Jonson who makes the
joke. But the first is certainly the likelier version of the two, since
Jonson had more children than Shakespeare; his wife and children
were already in London, where Shakespeare might more readily
attend a Blackfriars baptism; and Jonson was the more famous for his
classical knowledge and fondness for translating Latin.

Another tradition records that Jonson and Shakespeare made
merry at a tavern together, on which occasion the following epitaph
was supposedly made upon himself by Jonson:

> Here lies Ben Jonson
> That was once one ('un).

Alternatively, the epitaph reads:

> Here lies Ben Jonson
> That was one's son.

To this Shakespeare is supposed to have added:

> Here lies Benjamin
> With short hairs upon his chin,
> Who while he lived was a slow thing
> And now he's dead is no thing.

> (*JAB* 92)

The incomparable feebleness of these lines does not automatically
debar the possibility of their having issued from the imaginations of
the two premier wit-and-wordsmiths of the day – even the most
powerful muse does not swim well in alcohol. What these traditions
enshrine is a relationship between the two men which went beyond
the professional contact. Perhaps the most famous of all is Fuller's in
his *Worthies of Warwickshire*:

> Many were the wit-combats betwixt him and Ben Johnson, which
> two I behold like a Spanish great galleon, and an English man-of-
> war. Master Johnson (like the former) was built far higher in

learning; solid, but slow in his performances. Shakespeare, with the English man-of-war, lesser in bulk but lighter in sailing, could turn with all tides, tack about and take advantage of all winds, by the quickness of his wit and invention. (HS XI, 510)

Yet the two men were not thought of as operating wholly upon the cerebral plane. An eighteenth-century anecdote tells of 'Shakespeare [who] seeing Jonson in a necessary-house, with a book in his hand, reading it very attentively, said he was sorry his memory was so bad that he could not shite without a book'.[1]

Jonson's own comment is all the valediction needed. He recorded in *Discoveries* that he 'loved the man'. He had known him for eighteen years at least, and Shakespeare had acted in his first real success, *Every Man In His Humour*. Gossip pursued them to the end. Shakespeare was subsequently said to have contracted his fatal 'ague' (chill and fever) as a result of a 'merry meeting' with Jonson and the poet Michael Drayton in Stratford. From this time on Jonson's friends gradually become younger men – one such was the poet William Browne, to the second volume of whose *Britannia's Pastorals* in 1616 Jonson contributed commendatory verses, 'to my truly-beloved friend Mr Browne'. Browne's poem, a fluent narrative interspersed with lyrics, was written in Jonson's favourite form of couplets.

For Jonson, then, in 1616 personal losses had to be balanced against professional gains. The mark of approval signified by the granting of his pension confirmed his status as the court poet. 1616 also saw the last real demonstration of his supereminent powers as a dramatist of the public stage. During this year was produced the last of the plays in the miraculous decade following on the production of *Volpone* in 1606. The new play *The Devil Is An Ass* was performed by the King's Men at the Blackfriars theatre in the autumn of 1616. Topical and harshly satiric, the play indicated that Jonson had lost none of his concern with the immediate and growing social abuses of the time.

For the first quarter of the seventeenth century through which England was now passing was the period of the greatest economic confusion in our history. Throughout Europe this was a time of currency disorder; trade crises were common, and monetary confusion prevailed everywhere. But in England the general difficulties were given an added edge by the King's response to them. His policy was inept and his tampering with the coinage mischievous. The British economy proved to be too delicate a mechanism to be left to the royal amateur economist and his self-interested associates. In *The Devil Is An Ass* Jonson put his finger on a contemporary practice which highlights social as well as economic malpractice. This was the custom not unknown under Elizabeth but given a far wider currency

under James whereby a courtier lent his 'countenance' to a business-
man. The result was a union of place and influence with capital and
enterprise, for the production of profit. 'Countenance', however, was
neither given nor lent for nothing, nor did courtiers usually initiate
these projects, for which their help was eagerly sought. Yet so
important was the contribution of the courtier's 'countenance' that
businessmen would flatter, cheat, or bribe to secure it.

In this practice Jonson found the new equivalent of Volpone's
feigned malady, or Subtle's alchemical fraud, the device by which the
greedy shark draws the blind fish into its ever-open jaw. The combination of rampant greed with a runaway economy made for some
gross abuses of which even the blinkered King could not be unaware.
In an attack on such business practices as early as 1604 James had
condemned these money-spinning 'projections' in terms which included the condemnation of the projector as a 'viper' and a 'pest'.
Jonson was therefore in his derogation of these entrepreneurs echoing
the previously-expressed views of his royal master. But the situation
had deteriorated since then, and the ground covered by Jonson in this
play had become contentious. Two of Jonson's own patrons, the
Countess of Bedford and the Earl of Pembroke for example, were
involved in one such enterprise, the Somers Island Company.

Jonson was then running the risk of alienating powerful people by
handling this issue in *The Devil Is An Ass*. And in accordance with what
he always claimed was his (and classical) satiric practice, he generalised his attack to incorporate the vice itself, not just the author of it.
Many could therefore feel themselves attacked under the cover of
speeches like this:

> Promise gold mountains, and the covetous
> Are still most prodigal . . .
>
> (I.iii.)

There were all too many at James's court whom this cap fitted. They
were not however the sort who would bear such a reflection upon
themselves in silence. Jonson's play caused a disturbance at court,
and once again he was, as he told Drummond, 'accused', informally, of
venturing to censure the establishment. Who raised this storm is not
known, but it went as far as the highest in the land. King James
himself sent for Jonson and 'desired him to conceal it' – what, is not
clear. But the royal intercession in itself was a sure sign that the
dramatist had hit a nerve.

And his play was not merely topical but prophetic. On the immediate level the central device of the play (the reclamation of land under
water) served as a metaphor for any other 'projection'; such economic
practices were live and relevant to Jonson's Blackfriars audience. But

in 1637, the year of Jonson's death, one John Smythe, a steward of the Berkley estates, was involved in a lawsuit concerning land reclaimed from the River Severn, while in the same reign of Charles I Sir Edmund Verney was also involved in a project for the reclamation of 'drowned' Fen land.[2]

It is therefore a marked tribute to Jonson's courage and to his independence of mind that in the very year that he was most bound to the King by the granting of the royal pension he did not hold back from attacking a contemporary source of corruption in which the King was implicated and which he personally pressurised his poet to leave alone. This was however to be Jonson's last blast against the iniquity of the times. Almost twenty years had passed since he had first undertaken the correction of his compatriots through the agency of comical satire. After this final and swingeing assault 'the poet' withdrew once again from the public stage. It was to be another decade before London theatre-goers would see again a play from Jonson's pen; and never again would his dramas crackle with this angry fire.

Undoubtedly though, the major event of 1616 for Jonson was the appearance of his collected *Works*. Mindful of posterity in a way that Shakespeare never was, Jonson had worked long and hard upon this project. He had begun upon the preparation not long after the failure of *Catiline* in 1611 and had completed it by 1613.[3] The great book had been three years going through the press as the printer, William Stansby, had another massive volume in hand, Raleigh's *History of the World*, which had been licensed in 1611 and was not published until 1614.

Jonson now had the satisfaction of bringing to fruition a scheme as daring in concept as it had been difficult in execution. His was an age in which plays were published casually if at all, and regarded as different in kind from works of literature. The idea then of producing a collection of contemporary ephemera was radical and innovatory. By his insistence that plays were worthy of the kind of formal treatment and attention that had previously been reserved for other literary productions, Jonson made an incalculable contribution to the raising of the drama's status in England. He was the first of the Elizabethan dramatists to make this claim, and his action in collecting and issuing all the pieces that he wished to preserve of his life's work to date undeniably set the precedent which resulted seven years later in the publication of Shakespeare's works in the now world-famous First Folio of 1623.

The first thing that Jonson was careful to ensure was the standard of the texts. With attentive proof-reading and correction he provided for succeeding ages excellent and reliable texts of all his major works. This then facilitated another development – once good and reputable texts are established and available as a basis of study and scrutiny, what we think of as literary criticism also becomes possible. But Jonson's literary legacy was also prepared for the public with equal care given to non-literary factors. As a bibliophile he knew that the appearance of a book is as important as its contents. His Folio therefore came upon the world as a good-looking leather-bound volume, large and handsome, with an elaborate allegorical title-page. The publication of the Folio enabled Jonson to discharge some of his intellectual and personal debts. Each of the plays, for instance, was specifically dedicated to some person or institution to whom he felt an especial gratitude or respect. In chronological order they are:

Every Man In His Humour	– William Camden
Every Man Out Of His Humour	– The Inns of Court
Cynthia's Revels	– The Court
Poetaster	– Richard Martin
Sejanus	– Lord D'Aubigny
Volpone	– The Universities
Epicene	– Sir Francis Stuart
The Alchemist	– Mary, Lady Wroth
Catiline	– The Earl of Pembroke.

Pembroke is also the dedicatee of the *Epigrams*.

As Jonson was making these professions of his duty and regard, so his friends took this as an opportunity to demonstrate their affection. The Folio was ushered into the world with the support of laudatory verses from many of Jonson's friends – Selden, Chapman, even Beaumont before his death had all contributed good wishes and congratulations. Selden made his encomium in Latin, while Edward Hayward wrote in English – but Latin was also the language chosen by Abraham Holland for the verses he wrote to accompany the engraved portrait of 'the poet' which was prefixed to the 1616 Folio, and later used again for the 1640 Folio (reproduced as the frontispiece to the present work). This portrait was also printed and sold separately, which gives some indication of Jonson's popularity and the public interest in him at this time.

Jonson also used his great book as a present to those of his circle whom he particularly wished to reward. One such copy, dedicated in Jonson's own hand, went to 'my worthy and deserving brother' Alexander Glover, 'as a token of my love. And to the perpetuating of our friendship I send this small but hearty testimony', Jonson continued, 'and with charge that it may remain with him

> Till I, at much expense of Time and Taper,
> With chequer ink, upon his gift, my paper,
> Shall pour forth many a line, drop many a letter,
> To make these good, and what comes after, better.

Glover was a clerk in the Royal Exchequer. Jonson's whole-hearted response to his interest and to his small gift are indicative yet again of his extraordinary capacity to make friends on every social level.

But the Folio is chiefly interesting for the picture it gives of Jonson's idea of his work as a whole. Of what we know was a much larger dramatic output, he chose only these nine of his plays for inclusion. The others were rejected as unworthy of preservation. He followed these in order of sequence in the Folio with his collected *Epigrams*. These had originally been licensed for publication in 1612 but circumstances having delayed their appearance then, the sheets were conveniently incorporated into the Folio. Jonson quite clearly conceived of this collection of epigrams as only a beginning; he entitled it 'Book I', and planned a sequel which never materialised.

These poems, 133 in number, provide a fascinating cross-section of Jonson's life. Each one is like a snapshot with an individual, an event, or a response caught and set down for posterity. Jonson believed as part of the classical foundation of his thought that the epigram should deliver truth. He plainly thought that he had succeeded in this aim, as he described the *Epigrams* as 'the ripest of my studies'. This, from the man who 'would not flatter, though he saw death', ensures that the epigrams conduct the reader in a series of striking vignettes through his life and acquaintance, with his opinions of both.

Jonson's London swarms with life. His poems depict the entire city scene, from honest traders like his bookseller to every kind of scoundrel and cheat. Fine Lady Would-Be jostles with the whores of the 'new hot-house' sardonically observed by Jonson; his doctors and lawyers are but slenderly divided from the depraved and the diseased to whom they minister. Lucre and lechery are the obsessions of all, from Bank the Usurer to Sir Voluptuous Beast, and he does not hesitate to attack those who debauch themselves in either cause. In contrast with the streets of London brought to the reader in all their tawdry vitality are the scenes from court life. Here in his treatment of such persons as the King himself, the Lord Chancellor and the Earl of Suffolk, Jonson seeks to establish the standard of the great and the good by which lesser mortals are to be judged and found wanting. But his is not an attitude of uncritical adulation. The lines to Sir Henry Neville (Epigram 109), written when he was out of favour, show that Jonson was not only interested in flattering the rich, powerful and fashionable members of the court, nor was he afraid to attack those whom he disliked. Although policy compelled his veiling the identity of individuals under typical names, the portraits of 'Censorious Courtling', 'Court-Parrot' and this on 'Court Worm' can hardly be accused of being uncomplimentary:

All men are worms: but this no man. In silk
  'Twas brought to court first wrapped, and white as milk;
Where afterwards it grew a butterfly
  Which was a caterpillar. So 'twill die.

(Epigram 15)

Less formal in tone and manner than the court pieces are those in which Jonson addresses members of his immediate personal circle – Camden, his two lost children, his friends Roe and Donne. Towards the children he was able to express a tenderness which is not generally thought of as part of his personality. His sense of childhood's vulnerability comes out again in his epitaph on Salomon Pavy. At the other end of the scale from this child of promise was the achievement of one like Sir Henry Savile (Epigram 95). Savile was a distinguished academic whose intellectual interests closely followed Jonson's; he had translated and edited the classics, while taking on a wide range of other subjects. After an Oxford career he had become the Provost of Eton, and was reputed to be the most learned Englishman of the time. In his friendship Jonson found many echoes of his own themes of thought and study.

The *Epigrams* are, however, much more than simply a procession of Jonson's acquaintance. There is a teasing element of abstract thought which runs through, originating in the necessity to generalise some of the satirical attacks, and fed by Jonson's experience of masque-making and allegorisation. In this vein he reflects upon life and death, on the union between England and Scotland, and handles such topics as 'one that desired me not to name him' (Epigram 77). Writing in this mode he is capable of some strange and powerful effects, resulting in a kind of poetry which the reader can only regret that he produced so rarely, like this, 'On Something that Walks Somewhere'.

At court I met it, in clothes brave enough
  To be a courtier, and looks grave enough
To seem a statesman. As I near it came,
  It made me a great face; I asked the name;
A lord, it cried, buried in flesh and blood,
  And such from whom let no man hope least good,
For I will do none; and as little ill,
  For I will dare none. Good Lord, walk dead still.

(Epigram 11)

Such moments are not the least provocative in this collection. As stimulating is the tension between Jonson's defensive protestations about what he calls 'my chaste book', and the strongly sexual nature

174

and tone of the material which he incorporates. Partly this proceeds from the time-honoured classical stance of satirical disgust; the 'voluptuous beasts' of the contemporary scene are anatomised as a moral lesson. In the presentation of such as 'Sir Cod the Perfumed' (Epigrams 19 and 20) with the stress upon bodily odours and the stench of decay Jonson discovers a rare sensuousness. But equally his imagination is stimulated by the contemplation of degraded sexual pleasure, unnatural vices, and the corruption of the innocent. There is an excitement, a quickening of the pace of the writing when he creates the revenge of a bawdyhouse-keeper on a client who bilks her:

> But see! the old bawd hath served him in his trim –
> Lent him a pocky whore. She hath paid him.
>
> (Epigram 12)

These strains of irregular sexuality and its concomitant diseases unite to fuel a strong and steady anti-feminism in this collection. To Jonson all women are whores, either 'pocky' or pretending not to be. Gypsy, the whore turned bawd, is arraigned for her 'quaint' practice in Epigram 41; the coarse pun (quaint/cant) expresses what elsewhere is implied, that it is in the nature of women to be sexually rampant, unfaithful; woman is the one through 'false play' 'gets all', in the fullest sense. Against this background of violent revulsion from the female sex, the complimentary epigrams to court ladies like the Countesses of Bedford, Rutland and Montgomery sit very uneasily and carry little of the conviction of the overtly hostile pieces.

The tensions and contradictions within Jonson make themselves felt in a number of ways in this collection. Jonson works hard to establish an image of himself as a serious poet of the highest and most ancient sort, a Christian philosopher dedicated to preserving the eternal values, human and divine. But apart from the inclusion of a good deal of lurid sexual material, the decision not only to write but to include the joyously scatological 'Famous Voyage' (Epigram 133) indicates Jonson's own desire to question and to undermine this pious stereotype; this 'merd-urinous' celebration of all the excrement of London with its enthusiastic attention to privies, buttocks, farts and stinks is rather the product of a Rabelaisian than a religious disposition.

This process is carried further in the second collection of poems which were incorporated in the Folio, *The Forest*. These fifteen pieces, situated immediately after the *Epigrams* to heighten the contrast, are very different from them in tone and temper. The collection as a whole is more varied than the *Epigrams*; free from the constraint of the formula to deliver truth with a witty incision, Jonson was able to strike a greater range of notes from the humorous to the elegiac. He is able too to take

his self-examination further than in the *Epigrams*. The same elements
are constant, but presented with a rueful irony that makes 'the poet'
seem very much more human. The man who emerges from these lines
is no longer the aggressive youngster of the 'War of the Theatres'. He
is much nearer to the Ben Jonson of tradition, the hearty man's man,
the boastful boozer and Great Cham of the Jacobean period. In
reality the self-portrait is subtler, with its dark and sombre side. The
poetic conceit of *Forest* I, 'Why I write not of love', begins playfully
enough but ends with the monosyllabic desolation of

<blockquote>When Love is fled, and I grow old.</blockquote>

Similarly Jonson adduces it in praise of Lord Lisle's hospitality in 'To
Penshurst' that 'here no man tells my cups . . .' (*Forest* 2). Evidently
from this he had had the humiliating experience of having his liquid
intake noted and rationed by begrudging spirits.

Jonson's insistent irony is such however that too much emphasis
should not be placed upon a literal or personal interpretation of the
poems. In *The Forest* he works through his singing robes, adopting
different *personae* at need. In 'To the World' (*Forest* 4) he speaks with
the voice of a broken-hearted 'gentlewoman, virtuous and noble',
achieving a wistful, understated, yet impressive monologue from the
arresting opening 'False world, good night'. And in the final poem of
this collection, 'To Heaven' (*Forest* 15), there are metaphysical flashes
when he seems to address God in the pure accents of Donne:

<blockquote>
As thou art all, so be thou all to me,
  First, midst and last; converted one in three;
My faith, my hope, my love; and in this state,
  My judge, my witness, and my advocate.
Where have I been this while exiled from thee?
  And whither rapt, now thou but stoopst to me?
Dwell, dwell here still; Oh, being everywhere
  How can I doubt to find thee ever here?
</blockquote>

Jonson's location of this poem in the terminal place of honour
demonstrates the value which he placed upon it. *The Forest* and the
Epigrams taken together provide an invaluable record not only of his
thoughts and feelings but also of the range and grace of his poetic skill.

Last in Jonson's great Folio stood the masques and entertainments
that he had written for numerous occasions over the years. These had
obviously been hurriedly assembled; he had not been able to attend to
the proofs with the care he had given to the earlier sections of the
book. Unlike the rest of the Folio the masque texts were carelessly
printed and the Latin and Greek footnotes are so full of errors that
Jonson cannot have been given the chance to work over the galleys.

Printing was rushed towards the end of this mammoth project. Publication was in sight, and nothing was allowed to slow it down.

Publication of the Folio created a stir that was slow to die away. Inevitably Jonson's critics made sport with the book, its title, and the idea that lay behind it. The contemptuous notion of plays as slight and trivial was very hard to uproot, and Jonson was attacked as arrogant and pretentious for trying to promote his plays to a higher literary league. During the next year a satirist Henry Fitzgeoffry sneered at 'books made of ballads; works, of plays'. The same point was made more plainly by another writer, John Boys, who complained that 'the very plays of a modern poet are called in print his *Works*'. Nor was the amusement quickly forgotten. As late as 1633 Thomas Heywood in his *English Traveller* remarked loftily:

> My plays are not exposed unto the world in volumes, to bear the title of *Works* (as others), in numerous sheets and a large volume; but singly, as thou seest, with great modesty and small noise.

Jonson was also subjected to the humour of the would-be epigrammatists:

'To Mr Ben Jonson demanding the reason why he called his plays works'

> Pray tell me, Ben, where doth the mystery lurk,
> What others call a play, you call a work?

Thus answered by a friend in Mr Jonson's defence:

> The author's friend thus for the author says,
> Ben's plays are works, when others' works are plays.
>
> (HS IX, 13)

Fortunately Jonson had as always the encouragement of his true friends. As Edmund Bolton observed:

> But if I should declare mine own rudeness rudely, I should then confess that I never tasted of English more to my liking nor more smart, and put to the height of use in poetry, than in that vital, judicious, and most practical language of Benjamin Jonson's poems. (*JAB* 109)

In the midst of the excitement of this achievement Jonson remained in demand for royal entertainments. On 14 June 1616 King James was feasted by Alderman Cockayne and the New Company of Merchant Adventurers who presented the royal visitor with £1000 in a basin and ewer of gold. To entertain the King certain dyers, 'cloth dressers with their shuttles' and 'Hamburgians' were presented to him, and in welcome and greeting 'spoke such language as Ben Jonson put into their mouths' (*JAB* 94).

It is hard not to see 1616 as the pinnacle of Jonson's career. He had attained in this year a height of achievement to which he had been steadily building and on which he must have hoped to rest his declining years. In an age when the average life expectancy was not more than forty years at best, he was already an old man. In receiving the King's grant he had had public recognition of his status in life; in publishing his works he had given to the world his literary legacy to last after death. With these two events coming together in the same year his future and his standing seemed assured.

The year closed for Jonson as it had begun, with a masque to write; in this season, two. First came *Christmas His Masque*, which resembles nothing so much as an old-fashioned mumming. The show was presented at court at the Christmas of 1616 and the warmth and good humour of the piece make it considerably less grandiose and more accessible than Jonson's higher flights of fancy. Early in the new year of 1617 came another Jonson masque, this time of a more ambitious kind. For the traditional Twelfth Night climax to the revelry he had prepared *The Vision of Delight*. This had first been noticed before Christmas in a letter from one courtier to another containing the dry observation that the new masque would 'increase the King's debt £2000'. At the performance on 6 January the star of the show was the new-made Earl of Buckingham, George Villiers, who had replaced the former favourite Carr (later Somerset) in the King's affections. The Earl danced with the Queen, displaying to great advantage his good looks and grace of movement. Jonson's masque was also honoured by the presence of an unusual visitor, as a contemporary account relates:

> The Virginian woman Pocahontas with her father counsellor have been with the King and graciously used, and both she and her assistant well placed at the masque. She is upon her return (though sore against her will) if the wind would but come about to send her away. (*JAB* 99)

Small wonder that Pocahontas was reluctant to depart, being so favoured by the King as to be granted a special place at the masque, and enjoying a performance of Jonson's work. This legendary woman from the earliest days of the British colonisation of America aroused Jonson's interest, as well she might; she was the only Indian princess he was ever to meet and he observed her doings in London closely enough to remember them for a long time. When he was writing *The Staple of News* ten years later in 1626 he referred to one of her London adventures:

> .. I have known a princess, and a great one,
> Come forth of a tavern ... The blessed
> Pocahontas (as the historian calls her)
> And great King's daughter of Virginia
> Hath been in womb of a tavern.

(II.v.119-24)

Pocahontas was not the only one who enjoyed the masque. It was sufficiently well received to be revived for another performance on 19 January. The following month saw the preparation of yet another Jonson masque. On Saturday 22 February 1617 *Lovers Made Men* was presented in Essex House, home of Lord Hay. The performers were 'divers of noble quality, his friends' and the occasion was arranged 'for the entertainment of M. the Baron de la Tour' according to the title page. The presiding genius was a patron of Jonson who doubtless helped him to the commission; as one comment had it 'the Countess of Bedford is Lady and Mistress of the feast'. The guest of honour, Baron de la Tour, was the French ambassador and a man of great eminence – this was the only masque of Jonson not written to be performed in the presence of royalty. The French ambassador was the man who had preferred Lord Hay to the King's service, and the masque now presented was in repayment of this debt of gratitude. With the extravagant Lord Hay supplying the funds, and the experienced Countess at the helm, the masque was organised as a suitably glittering occasion to which all the court was invited.

Yet despite his intense involvement with the masque at this time – never before nor afterwards did he see three of his masques staged within eight weeks of one another – Jonson was not too busy to try a small act of kindness, on this occasion at the opposite end of the social scale from the nobility and the gentry. He took it upon himself to intercede on behalf of a 'poor man' with the Lord Chancellor, as he recorded in *Underwood* 31 and 32. He wrote to the eminent justice's secretary whom he addressed as 'my honoured and virtuous friend' in these terms: 'Sir, I am bold, out of my trust in your friendship, to request your help in the furthering this gentleman's suit ... who (of my knowledge) is a most honest man, and worthy of a much better fortune than he sues for ... Let him find, I pray you, that I have credit with you by your undertaking what you can for him cheerfully: and I will take care you shall not repent it ...' (HS I, 20).

This was a busy time for Jonson. In addition to these calls upon his time and interest he had not entirely abandoned his theatrical connections. In the summer of 1617 he performed an office of friendship when he became engaged with Fletcher in the writing of a tragedy called *Rollo, or, the Bloody Brother*. It must have been very hard for Fletcher to have to learn how to continue his writing career alone after the marvellous years of his partnership with Beaumont – and to whom would he more naturally turn than to the old friend and colleague of them both? Jonson's contribution to the finished play was small; most scholars are agreed that he had a hand in no more than two or three scenes. The first two scenes of the important fourth act have been felt to be the most Jonsonian, dealing as they do with the theme of deception and the actions of rogues and sharks, scenes which afforded Jonson scope for the kind of character work that he had made his own. But he had had the experience of working in collaboration before, when he had been one of Henslowe's hacks at the dawn of his career in the theatre, and however small, his contribution assisted the completion of the this play during the summer of 1617.

Jonson was, however, becoming ready for a substantial change in his life once more and it would not lie in the direction of a collaborative partnership with Fletcher. The suggestion came from an action of the King himself with whom Jonson was now on terms of some kind of affection, even familiarity. One small piece from this period shows that Jonson did not always write for his king in term of high-flown courtly compliment and gives some indication of the pleasure which James could obtain from 'his poet':

'A Grace by Ben Jonson
extempore before King James'

Our King and Queen the Lord God bless,
The Palsgrave and the Lady Bess,
And God bless every living thing
That lives and breathes and loves the King.
God bless the council of estate
And Buckingham the fortunate;
God bless them all and keep them safe:
And God bless me, and God bless Ralph.

(*Ungathered Verse* 47)

Aubrey comments on this: 'The King was mighty inquisitive to know who this Ralph was: Ben told him it was the drawer at the Swan tavern, by Charing Cross, who drew him good canary. For this drollery His Majesty gave him a hundred pounds.' In the spring of 1617 James had returned to Scotland for a long visit. This was his first return to his native land since his accession to the throne of England in 1603, despite his assurances made at the time that he would often come back among his people. James entered Scotland on 13 May 1617 and stayed until August. The trip caused a vast sensation throughout the British Isles.

Among those who were thereby put in mind of Scotland was Ben

Jonson. Much had been heard and spoken (some of it by Jonson himself) about Scotland and the Scots since the King had descended from there to assume the sovereignty of Scotland's southernmost extremity. But the King's tour and the interest is provoked brought all this into a sharp contemporary focus. Jonson decided to go and see it all for himself. If he could in addition devise literary projects more attuned to his royal patron's race and nation then so much the better. The first mention of Jonson's trip to Scotland comes in a letter of 14 June 1617: 'Jonson is going on foot to Edinburgh and back, for his profit' (*JAB* 100).

Before the idea of the trip to Scotland developed any further, another Christmas season intervened and with it the obligatory round of court festivities. At the end of 1617 Jonson received a special commission. He was engaged to write the climactic Twelfth Night masque for Prince Charles. The importance of this occasion to the newly created Prince of Wales was that this was to be Charles's first appearance in a masque of his own as chief masquer. It was there-fore a milestone in the attempts of the sober, formal little prince, then just seventeen years old, to efface memories of his dead brother Henry who had been so talented in all such matters. Nor was this simply to be a court affair. The Spanish ambassador was to be the principal guest, as a marriage between Prince Charles and the Infanta of Spain was on the horizon.

Evidently neither trouble nor expense was spared to ensure the success of the venture, Charles personally sending his Groom of the Chamber from Whitehall to Blackfriars to bid 'the Poet to come to the Prince'. King James had recently received £50,000 from the East India merchants to relieve his increasingly dire financial situation. It says much for the royal order of priorities that while £12,000 was earmarked for Ireland, £8,000 for artillery and so on, somehow £4,000 found its way to those responsible for funding 'the Prince's masque'. Jonson's invention then had to take account of the King's still-central position while incorporating themes relevant to the rising prince. The final product, *Pleasure Reconciled to Virtue*, offered a lofty example of the altruism expected of a ruler. James was represented as Hesperus and linked with his 'brother' Atlas, his importance suggested through myth and allegory.

Scenically at least the masque was impressive. Its dominating feature was Atlas, a mountain formed in the likeness of an old man with a white beard, who thanks to the efforts of Inigo Jones could roll his huge eyes very cleverly. But despite the work and worry of all concerned, the masque did not please. The account of the Venetian ambassador's chaplain, the fullest description that exists of a court masque, may suggest why:

On the 6th of January, his Excellency was invited to see a masque which had been prepared with extraordinary pains, the chief performer being the King's own son and heir, the Prince of Wales, now seventeen years old, an agile youth, handsome, and very graceful . . . Whilst waiting for the King we amused ourselves by admiring . . . such concourse as there was . . . every box was filled notably with the most noble and richly arrayed ladies, in number some 600 . . . the dresses being of such variety in cut and colour as to be indescribable; the most delicate plumes over their heads, springing from their foreheads or in their hands serving as fans; strings of jewels on their necks and bosoms and in their girdles and apparel in such quantity that they looked like so many queens, so many stars. During the *two hours of waiting* we had leisure to examine them again and again . . .

Finally the King appeared, seemingly as jaded as the audience. What followed next, the written part or 'soul' of the masque, struck the Venetian as mere 'mummeries'. Even the climactic dancing of the courtiers fell flat:

Twelve cavaliers, masked, made their appearance . . . They performed every sort of ballet and dance of every country whatsoever such as passamezzi, corants, canaries, like Spaniards, and an hundred other very fine gestures, devised to tickle the fancy. Last of all they danced the Spanish dance, one at a time, each with his lady, and being well-nigh tired they began to lag, whereupon the King, who is naturally choleric, got impatient and shouted aloud, 'Why don't they dance? What did they make me come here for? Devil take you all, dance!'

Upon this the Marquis of Buckingham [the former George Villiers] his Majesty's favourite, immediately sprang forward, cutting a score of lofty and very minute capers, with so much grace and agility that he not only appeased the ire of his angry lord, but rendered himself the admiration and delight of everybody. . . The King embraced and kissed him tenderly, and then honoured the Marquis with extraordinary affection, patting his face. . . .

But the King's anger had put everyone in a bad mood. The party afterwards turned into a rout:

The repast was served on glass plates or dishes, and at the first assault they upset the table; and the crash of glass platters reminded me precisely of a severe hailstorm at midsummer smashing the window glass. The story ended at half-past two in the morning, and half-disgusted and weary we returned home. (*JAB* 103-6)

Taking its cue from the disgruntled King, court gossip rapidly disseminated the news of the masque's ill success. One courtier wrote from town to inform his country correspondent that he found 'the conceit good' but 'the poetry not so'. On 10 January he amplified this:

> There was nothing in it extraordinary, but rather the invention proved dull. Mr Comptroller's daughter bore away the bell for delicate dancing, though remarkable for nothing else but for a multitude of jewels, wherewith she was hanged, as it were all over. (*JAB* 107)

Many other comments along the same lines were heard, including the resuscitation of the old personal insult to Jonson: 'the masque on Twelfth Night is not commended of any. The poet is grown so dull that his device is not worth the relating, much less the copying out. Divers think fit he should return to his old trade of brick-laying again' (HS X, 576).

Jonson did not bear all this censure alone. Sir Edward Sherburn, while agreeing that the masque 'came far short of expectation', singled out the designer as responsible rather than the dramatist: 'Mr Inigo Jones hath lost in his reputation, in regard [that] some extraordinary device was looked for'. Considering that this was the Prince's first masque, 'a poorer was never seen' (*JAB* 108). Charles himself survived the temporary wreck of the reputations of his poet and architect; though he can hardly have been pleased with this reception, he had enough faith in the project to wish to keep it alive. As the Queen had been ill, and had not been able to see the performance on Twelfth Night, it was arranged that the masque should be given again for her at Shrovetide.

The intervening weeks provided at least one sensation for the blasé courtiers when the banqueting house at Whitehall burned down on 12 January. They also gave Jonson the chance to try to correct the masque's deficiencies with some rewriting to try to make up for its initial lack of success. The 'improvements' were laconically described by one observer in unenthusiastic terms: 'The Prince's masque was shown again in court . . . with some few additions of goats and Welsh speeches'. What Jonson had written was a new anti-masque *For the Honor of Wales* into which he had introduced some Welsh countrymen as a vehicle for the kind of rustic humour and uncomplicated banter that the King enjoyed. But it would have taken more than 'goats and Welsh speeches' to tickle the jaded palate of the court audience. The verdict came down: 'On Shrove Tuesday the Prince's masque for Twelfth Night was represented again, with some few alterations and aditions; but little bettered' (*JAB* 108). As with Jonson's Irish masque, there was a suspicion of a racial slur – it was said to be 'sufficient to make an Englishman laugh, and a Welshman choleric' (HS X, 577).

This event cannot but have strengthened Jonson's resolve to take his leave for a time from this hothouse atmosphere of the court, and from London itself. He had a heroic adventure planned, and his last commission fulfilled. It was time to be gone.

CHAPTER 11

THE JOURNEY TO SCOTLAND

SHORTLY after the summer masque Jonson set out on his historic journey to Scotland. His going was attended with great interest and comment, most of it of a good-natured sort. Typical of the contemporary reaction was this:

'To Mr Ben Jonson on his Journey'

When wit and learning are so hardly set
That from their needful means they must be barred,
Unless by going hard, they maintenance get,
Well may Ben Jonson say the world goes hard

'This was Mr Ben Jonson's answer of the sudden'

Ill may Ben Jonson slander so his feet,
For when the profit with the pain doth meet,
Although the gait were hard, the gain is sweet.
(*Ungathered Verse* 46)

Jonson himself enjoyed the spirit of good fun enough to pass on one of the jokes to Drummond when he arrived. He recounted that 'at his coming hither Sir Francis Bacon said to him that he loved not to see poesy go on other feet than poetical dactyls and spondees' (HS I, 141).

What had induced England's poet laureate with forty-five years on his back and twenty-odd stones' weight (mostly in front) to undertake this four-hundred-mile adventure? Jonson himself left no clear reason for his action. James's Scottish visit had given a fresh stimulus to English interest in the terrain to the north of its boundaries and Jonson was clearly hoping for some inspiration from his trip of a suitably Caledonian nature. The suggestion has also been made (by David Masson in his *Drummond of Hawthornden*, 1873) that as Jonson believed himself to have descended from the celebrated Borders clan renowned in song and ballad he was obeying a 'salmon-like instinct' to ascend to the place of his ancient origins.

Jonson left London in the summer of 1618 at the end of June or early in July. He took the eastern route to Scotland, travelling the Great North Road which meant passing through the villages of Islington, Highgate, Finchley and Barnet. From there he traversed Hertfordshire, Bedfordshire, Northamptonshire, Leicestershire and Nottinghamshire, until he reached Yorkshire. At Darlington ('Darnton', in the contemporary pronunciation) his shoes gave out and he had to buy a new pair. These, as he complained to Drummond, took some breaking in and for the first two days afterwards his feet were painfully blistered and skinned.

From Darlington Jonson made for Edinburgh,[1] and by mid-August had arrived in the Scottish capital. There he made contact with some of the Scottish lairds and gentlemen whom he had known in London at the court and who were now back at their Scottish homes for the summer. While Edinburgh and Leith were clearly his headquarters there was both time and opportunity for him to have made other forays. He was absent from London for almost nine months, six of which were spent in Scotland. A Scots historian offers this imaginative recreation of Jonson's stay:

> One fancies his great figure seen day after day, for a month or two in that winter, in the fields between Leith and Edinburgh, or climbing the old Canongate and High Street from Holyrood to the Castle, or seen in Andro Hart's shop, or descending some of the closes for a call, or sauntering out as far as the College, or again, in various directions, to Musselburgh and Pinkie, Craigmillar and suchlike spots of local fame in the neighbourhood.[2]

Although fanciful, this picture of Jonson's activities is not implausible. The summer months were vacation time for court and government in the Scottish capital, and he would have had to make his own amusement. It is, though, a fair assumption that this did not take the form beloved of so many Scottish gentlemen from James downward of roaming the glens and mountains to enjoy the hunting. There is no firm evidence that Jonson ever budged from Edinburgh, Leith, and the vicinity.

Jonson's welcome was not confined to private individuals. While in the capital he was honoured with its highest award. On 20 September 1618 the Edinburgh Town Council authorised his admission as an honorary 'burgess and guild brother', in effect granted him the freedom of the city. In October they entertained him to a banquet formally to mark the occasion. This event was royally celebrated. The amplitude of the feast is witnessed by the account of the cost in the Treasurer's records: two hundred and twenty-one pounds Scots, six shillings and fourpence. Finally the company presented Jonson with a 'burgess ticket, gilded and choice written'.

At the end of September Jonson was to be found staying in Leith some miles down the estuary from Edinburgh towards the North Sea. His host was one John Stuart, a well-regarded citizen who held the office of Water-Baillie of Leith. Here he received a visitor who although a fellow-countryman was not entirely welcome. The visitor was another Londoner and self-styled fellow-poet, John Taylor. Taylor was a Thames waterman who had discovered and capitalised on a talent for producing rough and ready verse. His combination of high-flown literary pretension with lowly occupation caught the fancy of fashionable London, and he was nicknamed 'the Sculler' and 'the King's Majesty's Water Poet'. For such was the vogue for Taylor's work that it was read by the King himself, who in a fit of poetical appreciation declared that 'Sir Philip Sidney was no poet, neither did he see ever any verses in England [which could be compared] to the Sculler's' (HS I, 142). In emulation of Jonson's feat Taylor too had made the journey northward, arriving in Edinburgh a week or two after Jonson on 13 August.

Since then the two men had been moving separately around Edinburgh, and having decided on a much shorter stay than Jonson's, Taylor had now tracked Jonson down to bid him goodbye. Taylor has left his own account of the meeting in *The Penniless Pilgrimage* (1618):

> Now the day before I came from Edinburgh, I went to Leith, where I found my long approved and assured good friend Master Benjamin Jonson, at one Master John Stuart's house; I thank him for his great kindness toward me: for at my taking leave of him he gave me a piece of gold of two and twenty shillings to drink his health in England. And withal, willed me to remember his kind commendations to all his friends: so with a right friendly farewell, I left him as well as I hope never to see him in a worse estate; for he is among noblemen and gentlemen that know his true worth, and their own honours, where, with much respective love, he is worthily entertained.

But Jonson's friendly, even generous response to Taylor was only part of the story. In reality Jonson deeply suspected Taylor's motives. The man who had despised and censured genuine poets like Daniel, Drayton, even occasionally his friend Donne, had no time for Taylor's doggerel, and he wondered, too, why Taylor had copied him in undertaking a Scottish trip. Taylor himself in his later account of his

187

travels protested vigorously against the suggestion that there was a covert motive to his actions, attacking his 'shallow-brained critics' who 'lay an aspersion on me, that I was set on by others, or that I did undergo this project, either in malice or mockage of Master Benjamin Jonson. I vow by the faith of a Christian that their imaginations are all wide, for he is a gentleman to whom I am so much obliged for many undeserved courtesies that I have received from him, and from others by his favour, that I durst never be so impudent or ungrateful, as either to suffer any man's persuasions, or mine own instigation, to incite me to make so bad a requital, for so much goodness formerly received' (*JAB* 110–11). Jonson himself had entertained these suspicions, which had hardened into conviction. To Drummond Jonson confided his fears of a cruel joke against him by his London enemies; Taylor, he concluded, 'was sent along here to scorn him'.

Yet there remained for Jonson episodes of interest and delight. During his visit on the night of 18 November 1618 Edinburgh witnessed the greatest comet in memory, of prodigious brilliance and size, which endured for a month. And at the end of this time Jonson was experiencing the high point of his Scottish stay, his visit to Drummond of Hawthornden. He may have met this distinguished Scot before accepting his hospitality, at the house of another of his hosts. He had certainly taken up residence with the Scots laird by the end of December 1618.

The two men were already known to one another by reputation. Jonson was a now-legendary genius; no name was better known than his among those who took any interest in books, plays and poetry, and there was no writer whose critical judgments were more often quoted. Drummond too in his quieter way had established wide reputation as a man of letters. There was at the time a regular traffic between Edinburgh and London of Scots who had gone south in attendance upon King James yet frequently returned to their own kingdom. Among these were Drummond's bosom friend Sir William Alexander, now Gentleman Usher to Prince Charles, and his other friends Sir Robert Kerr, Sir Robert Aytoun and Sir David Murray. Kerr, Alexander and Aytoun were all among Jonson's acquaintance. He somewhat tactlessly complained to Drummond that Alexander 'was not half kind to him, and neglected him'; the truth was that Alexander patronised Drayton, whom Jonson despised. Jonson got on better with Aytoun, who, he told Drummond, 'loved him dearly'. With such mutual friends in common, Jonson and Drummond were partly known to one another already.

Jonson was invited to stay with Drummond at his historic castle and family home and accepted. Accordingly he travelled the nine miles from south Edinburgh to the densely-wooded estate where

Hawthornden castle lies high above the river North Esk in Midlothian. This ancient and impressive edifice was to be his home for the next two or three weeks of his Scottish trip, a visit which has passed into history thanks to Drummond's scholarly and methodical habits. Legend has clung around this encounter of the leading English and Scottish poets. One such account goes as follows:

> Better than most myths of the kind is the myth which would tell us exactly how the visit began. Drummond, it says, was sitting under the great sycamore tree in front of his house, expecting his visitor, when at length descending the well-hedged avenue from the public road to the house, the bulky hero hove in sight. Rising and stepping forth to meet him, Drummond saluted him with:
>
> 'Welcome, welcome, royal Ben!'
>
> To which Jonson replied:
>
> 'Thank ye, thank ye, Hawthornden!'
>
> And they laughed, fraternised, and went in together.[3]

Drummond must have been endowed with more than his share of the legendary hardiness of his race if he could sit outside waiting for a visitor in Scotland in December.

Of all Jonson's new Scots acquaintances Drummond had the most to offer in terms of literary interests. Although leading at thirty-three the retired life of a Scots laird of modest income, Drummond was both by education and inclination a man apparently very much along Jonson's line. He had had the advantage, which Jonson always respected, of a university education, having graduated from 'the Tounis [Town's] College' (Edinburgh University) in 1605. He subsequently travelled to London and thence to France where he visited Paris and studied jurisprudence at Bourges university. On returning to Scotland in 1608 Drummond settled down to live the life of a Renaissance gentleman and in particular to study and to write. He had at this time several volumes of verse to his credit with which it is safe to assume that Jonson was familiar.

Drummond was, then, a much more cultivated man than most of those in his society whom Jonson would have met. He had also worked hard at his poetry; he was one of the first of his countrymen to write in English and he had been careful to eliminate from his verse any trace of Scotticisms as a mark of the provincialism into which a Scottish laird might easily fall. Like Jonson again Drummond was a confirmed monarchist whose loyalty was expressed through poetical connections with the royal house. His panegyric 'Forth Feasting' had been written to welcome King James's return to Scotland in the previous year (1617). Later, in the next reign, Drummond was to be involved in writing the entertainment with which Edinburgh greeted Charles I on his Scottish visit in 1633.

Naturally his poetic gift was not of the same magnitude as Jonson's. His output had been small. He had published his tribute on the death of Prince Henry, *Tears on the Death of Meliades* (1613), and his collected *Poems* (1616). In addition, his was not an original voice. Even in an age when critical theory encouraged imitation, Drummond was a great follower and borrower of others' forms, ideas, phrases. His best known piece of prose, *A Cypress Grove* (1619), has been characterised as 'a mosaic of echoes', and in his poetry he emerges as 'a faithful follower of Petrarch, an imitator of Ronsard, a paraphraser of Sidney and a translator or thief of a host of other poets, Italian, French, Spanish, English and Scottish'.[4] This slender and derivative talent has been somewhat roughly handled in a work whose very title relegated Drummond's achievement; Sir Walter Scott in his *Provincial Antiquities of Scotland* (1819–26) said of Drummond that 'his own powers did not exceed a decent mediocrity'.

Drummond has had the misfortune to become a footnote in English literary history as the recorder of another man's opinions. His name survives, but the lamp of his own fame has burned low. This is not entirely a merited fate. Although he borrowed more heavily than many poets and certainly much more than Jonson did, he was not devoid of ability. His verse is smooth, melodious and accomplished in its chosen manner, he could handle literary conventions and the appropriate attitudes that went with them, and within his narrow emotional range he is particularly adept at evoking a poignant or melancholy mood. To Jonson in 1618 he was one of Scotland's leading literary lights and a man whose studies in poetry if not his attainment in it would forge an obvious bond with England's poet.

If Drummond could find common ground with Jonson the poet he could also meet Jonson the bookworm, and on a high level. Drummond was pre-eminent as a book collector and his library was one of the small miracles of the age. Described as 'a slice of intellectual history' of its time and place, it was a unique assembly of around fourteen hundred books in English, French, Spanish, Italian, Latin, Greek, and Hebrew. It is both a personal and a representative sample of early seventeenth-century tastes. Drummond was eclectic enough to pick up what pleased him and modern enough to pick up what was fashionable in contemporary literature. But he did not neglect to supply as a counterweight examples of the respected academic authorities of the day.

Nor was Drummond simply a collector. Like the genuine bibliophile that he was he devoured his books' contents, putting his library to such good use that he undoubtedly became one of the best-read men of his time. He bought good texts in small, cheap, second-hand editions of the great humanist scholarly printers like Aldus and Plantin, and he worked through them methodically. A number of his self-prescribed 'reading lists' for successive years survive, and provide convincing evidence of the pleasure he took in reading widely in English and European literatures. He had kept his classical scholarship in good repair too, and read very extensively in Latin using both Latin and neo-classical texts.

Drummond's guiding principle in the formation of his library was the Miltonic belief that 'a good book is the precious life blood of a master spirit'. As he expressed it himself, 'wits, however pregnant and great, without books, are but as valiant soldiers without arms, and artisans destitute of tools' ('Of Libraries', *Works*, 1711). For Jonson this impressive collection would afford the intellectual and spiritual nourishment rarely available in a private house; Drummond's library was truly an oasis in the desert. Jonson would not have made much of the works in French, Italian and Spanish – the literature of contemporary Europe never exerted a very strong pull on his imagination.

But he would have felt thoroughly at home with Drummond's extensive section on Aristotle; Drummond possessed texts, commentaries, and various examples of the opposed schools of critical thought. Undoubtedly Jonson would have missed his beloved Horace; and Martial, Catullus and Propertius were not among Drummond's books. But here, probably for the first time since leaving England, Jonson could meet again Ovid, Virgil, Plautus, Terence, Seneca, and the racy pornography of Petronius Arbiter's *Satyricon*. Well represented too were the classical historians, backed up by a sizeable number of grammars and dictionaries. All these masters of the ancient world were to be found alongside the modern works of Jonson's friends and acquaintances like Donne, Dekker, Marston and Middleton. Contemporary plays were in fact well represented, with Day's *Law Tricks* and Shakespeare's *Midsummer Night's Dream* as examples of Drummond's lighter reading. Finally Jonson could not but be pleased to see a 1607 quarto of *Volpone* and his 1616 Folio on Drummond's shelves. When Jonson left Scotland he left with at least one memento of this great collection – Drummond presented him with a 1586 edition of George Buchanan's *Rerum Scoticarum Historia* signed by both poets at the moment of exchange.

A library of this quality would absorb a good deal of Jonson's time and interest. It is likely too that Drummond would invite other gentlemen and friends from Edinburgh and the neighbourhood out to Hawthornden to meet his famous guest. There is no evidence at this or any other point in Jonson's life of an interest in outdoor activities which would have enabled him to share Drummond's passion for hunting; the 'mountain belly' must have been built up rather by sitting at a table than astride a horse. Largely therefore the entertainment provided for Jonson was domestic, and unpretentious hospitality at that. Drummond's was a bachelor establishment, for he was unmarried at this time following the sudden death of his betrothed shortly before the wedding was due to take place.

The two men spent much of their time together in conversation. Drummond's subsequent record of their talk, eliminating as it did his own contribution, has made it sound as if the whole visit consisted of a barrage of opinionated prose from Jonson.[5] Further, Drummond's contractions and omissions for the sake of brevity in note-taking make Jonson come across as more trenchant and brutal in his utterances than may well have been the case – 'Shakespeare wanted art'; 'Spenser's stanzas pleased him not'. Yet even passed through the filter of another man's consciousness these observations retain a distinct impression of Jonson. The topics covered range over his known acquaintance and areas of interest. They reveal his literary preoccupations and techniques. They present an enormous amount of material of great value, loose, gossipy and scattered as it is.

Predictably enough what these two writers spoke of most was the work of other writers. Jonson's beloved classics were well to the fore in discussion, with Jonson recommending to Drummond authors ranging from Suetonius to Hippocrates, 'for health'. Jonson boasted to Drummond that 'he was better versed, and knew more in Greek and Latin, than all the poets in England', which was probably true. But his classicism was as always no mere parade of names; he read aloud to Drummond an ode of Horace and an epigram of Petronius in his own translation. This raises an interesting speculation – had Jonson worked on these translations during his stay, or had he arrived equipped to perform, his translations ready in his pocket? European writers too came into the talk, and Jonson delivered his views on Petrarch, Guarini and Ronsard. These were among Drummond's best-known poets and sources and he was not impressed with Jonson's mastery of his pet subject, commenting dourly, 'all this was to no purpose, since he doth neither understand French, nor Italian'.

But it was the world of Jonson's poetic colleagues and contemporaries which engrossed the attention of the two men. Jonson was free with his censures of those whose efforts 'pleased him not'. Of all translations, Sir John Harington's *Ariosto* was 'the worst', and his epigrams mere 'narrations'. He 'scorned' Sir John Davies, and found some of Shakespeare's devices quite ridiculous:

Shakespeare in a play brought in a number of men saying they had suffered shipwreck in Bohemia, when there is no sea near by some 100 mile.

At times Jonson's condemnation descended from poetry to personalities, and became crushingly dismissive:

Sharpham, Day and Minshew were all rogues. Abraham France was a fool . . . Markham was a base fellow, so were Day and Middleton.

Most strenuously attacked was Jonson's colleague in masque-making:

He said to Prince Charles of Inigo Jones, that when he wanted words to express the greatest villain in the world, he would call him an *Inigo*.

But Jonson's criticisms were not all destructive. He was careful to try to distinguish the capacities of his contemporaries – Daniel was 'a good honest man . . . but no poet'. Drayton's *Polyolbion* was 'excellent' in conception, but fell short of its promise in the execution; Drayton's gift was not for extended or epic verse. Jonson could also give credit where it was due. He warmly praised Hooker's *Ecclesiastical History* and the work of his friend Selden whom he described to Drummond as 'the law-book of the judges of England' and 'the bravest man in all languages'. And reflecting on the martyred Jesuit and poet he remarked with a touch of wistfulness 'that Southwell was hanged, yet so he hath written that piece of his 'The Burning Babe', he would have been content to destroy many of his'. As this suggests Jonson did not spare himself from adverse criticism. The conversation took him back over his literary past He recalled that he had contributed commendatory verses to Sylvester's translation of Du Bartas in 1605 and now confessed to Drummond that he thought that the translation was 'not well done'. He had written his poem before he understood enough French to compare Sylvester's work with the original.

Of all his contemporaries the man who emerges most frequently in this record is John Donne. The long-standing friendship between them was to Jonson no reason for sparing the lash. He told Drummond that 'Donne's *Anniversary* was profane, and full of blasphemies', and that Donne himself, 'for not keeping of accent, deserved hanging'. This was no mere back-biting; like a true friend, Jonson would tell Donne what he thought of him to his face and related to Drummond the occasion when he took Donne to task over his presentation of the female, 'to which Donne answered that he described the *idea* of a woman, and not as she *was*'. Jonson's discussion with Drummond of a fragmentary poem of Donne shows that Donne shared work in progress with Jonson. All these comments are to be set against a background of Jonson's strong admiration for his friend's work: 'he esteemeth John Donne the finest poet in the world in some things', Drummond observed. Drummond also noted the pieces of John Donne that Jonson had troubled to learn by heart, another important sign of his appreciation.

Jonson and Donne had been friends for over fifteen years and had grown from young men about town into pillars of the establishment together. Jonson's sense of the passage of this time is responsible for the occasional introduction of an elegiac note into his remarks. Drummond noted without comment that Jonson 'affirmeth Donne to have written all his best pieces ere he was twenty-five years old'. Now, twenty years later, 'since he was made Doctor', as Jonson told Drummond, Donne 'repenteth highly, and seeketh to destroy all his poems'. Donne's work, Jonson feared, 'for not being understood, would perish'.

Naturally Jonson did not give all his attention to the works of others. He spoke to Drummond too about his own pet literary theories and ideas. Poetry should be forward-moving and direct; the verses should stand or fall by their 'sense', unadorned by stylistic or metrical tricks. To this Drummond added, 'which yet at times he denied', a plaintive reminder of the difficulty in following Jonson in full flood of developing and refining his thoughts. The comment certainly holds up as a general Jonsonian principle; he was blistering about fancy rhymes and rhythms, like the alexandrine and the hexameter, sticking out for the honest couplet as the only true and necessary verse form.

Jonson's stylistic principles were to be employed, so he informed Drummond, on a variety of new projects which he fully outlined to his host. Of the most immediate interest was one based upon Scotland itself: 'he hath an intention to perfect an epic poem entitled *Heroologia* of the worthies of this country,[6] roused by fame, and was to dedicate it to his country. It is all in couplets, for he detesteth all other rhymes'. Drummond thought this important enough to set it at the head of his record. Drummond heard, too, a good deal about Jonson's ongoing translation of Horace's *Ars Poetica*; Jonson read to him the preface which he had prepared and which he called his 'Observations', by now amplified with an 'Apologia' for *Bartholomew Fair* and a discussion of poetry couched as a dialogue between him and Donne. He recalled a piece from the past, *The May Lord*, a pastoral written for his circle of noble patrons and friends; Jonson himself, the Countesses of Bedford and Rutland, Lady Wroth, Pembroke, and Overbury all had parts in it. This was going back at least six years, since the Countess of Rutland had died in August 1612, and Overbury a year later. But Jonson remained interested in the form and told Drummond that 'he hath intention to write a fisher or pastoral play, and set the stage of it in the Lomond Lake'. Immediately however 'he is to write his foot pilgrimage hither, and to call it "A Discovery" '. It is interesting that Jonson also spoke of his abandoned and unsuccessful works; he was not continually boasting. He spoke of his 'intention to have made a play like Plautus' *Amphitrio*', a story of two pairs of identical twins, 'but left it off, for that he could never find two [actors] so like others that he could persuade the spectators they were one'. (This scruple had not of course inhibited Shakespeare from using the same device in *The Comedy of Errors*.)

This summary reduces what in the original was clearly the extended talk of many hours. But Jonson did not only produce conversation. His fondness for reading aloud and more particularly for reciting must have turned many of these occasions into a performance. He was unashamedly given to repeating his own work. Drummond names seven of Jonson's poems as the subjects of such attention, including some of the favourites of posterity like 'Drink to me only with thine eyes' (*Forest* 9). Strangely, the unusual 'Musical Strife', a pastoral dialogue, was 'the most commonplace of his repetition'. But this was not just a parade of self-indulgence. The ability of Jonson at his age effortlessly to recall poems by Spenser, Donne, Chapman and others is a throwback and credit to his Westminster training. Among his store were pieces of great nobility and power like this poem of Sir Henry Wotton:

> How happy is he born and taught
> That serveth not another's will,
> Whose armour is his honest thought
> And silly truth his highest skill . . .
>
> This man is free of servile bands,
> Of hope to rise, of fear to fall;
> Lord of himself, though not of lands,
> And having nothing, yet hath all.

Not all the moments that the two men shared were on such an elevated plane as this. Jonson passed on to Drummond any amount of gossip and anecdote together with a number of jokes, some of which are very colourful. Jonson enjoyed talking bawdy, and was highly intrigued by any unusual or irregular sexual activity. The 'Conversations' resemble the *Epigrams* in their evocation of Jonson's London world, at once stately and sordid. These elements come together in Jonson's assurance to Drummond that Queen Elizabeth had only stayed a virgin because she 'had a *membrana* . . . which made her uncapable of a man, though for her delight she tried many'. Some of Jonson's tales are much more lewd and gruesome than this, such as the one he told the King about a man who being 'consumed' with a disease, 'occupied his wife with a dildo, and she never knew of it', until one day, being sleepy, he forgot to remove it afterwards. Jonson also had a simple streak – he repeated innocent riddles, bits of doggerel and silly verses. But the talk frequently reverted to the sexual, inevitably perhaps in the absence of women.

There was clearly little reserve between Jonson and Drummond on this subject, strangers though they had been till now. The frankness with which Jonson imparted to his new-found acquaintance some very compromising details of his personal life is remarkable. His disgrace with Roe, his public exposure at young Raleigh's hands, were escapades Jonson revealed to Drummond. Jonson also liked to play practical jokes on his own account. Once, he said, 'he with the consent of a friend cosened a lady, with whom he had made an appointment to meet an astrologer in the suburbs, which she kept; and it was himself, disguised in a long gown and white beard by the light of dim-burning candles, up in a little cabinet reached unto by a ladder'. We are left to imagine what kind of a fortune Jonson told her.

Jonson was equally open with Drummond about matters of a much more painful nature. He related to the Scottish laird (who in his social position could never have shared these experiences) his humiliation at the hands of various 'worthless' lords; his recurrent money difficulties which had caused him from time to time to part with his books in order to raise some ready cash; and his irregular marriage, with its separations. He confided, further, details of his pre- and extra-marital amours:

> In his youth given to venery [sexual indulgence]. He thought the use of a maid nothing in comparison with the wantonness of a wife, and would never have another mistress. He said two accidents strange befell him: one, that a man made his own wife to court him, whom he enjoyed two years ere he knew of it, and one day, finding them by chance, was passingly delighted with it; one other, [he] lay divers times with a woman who shew him all that he wished, except the last act, which she would never agree unto.

To contrast this with Jonson's professed desire to be a churchman is to have some insight into the extent of Jonson's conflicts. And the other side of this picture of cheerful harmless fornication is to be found in Jonson's story of the 'good man' who catching Jonson in the act with his wife said 'I would not believe you would abuse my house so'.

The impact of all this upon Drummond was formidable. His had not been a life of stainless purity, nor was he the mealy-mouthed Scottish puritan that he has sometimes been represented. He had in fact fathered a family of bastards before his betrothal. But his engagement had been a conscious attempt to settle down with a woman of his own rank and intellectual interests, and when the marriage was thwarted Drummond had resigned himself to a life confined to aesthetic pleasure and high seriousness.[7] Nothing in his life had prepared him for the encounter with a character of such forcefulness as Jonson's, living such a self-determined, unfettered and physically indulgent life. Jonson obviously found Drummond unassuming and unsophisticated by his standards: as Drummond notes, 'he said to me that I was too good and simple, and oft a man's modesty made a fool of his wit'.

Yet Drummond's divergence from Jonson came rather over literary than personal matters. Superficially the two men had much in common. Both were fond of literary trifles like anagrams and impresas; Drummond was as attached to the epigram as Jonson was, and had written a number of them himself. Like Jonson again Drummond loved puns, witticisms and funny stories and had made a collection of them in his own manuscripts, although his recording of his guests' 'jests and apothegms' is so solemn as to rob them of their zest. More importantly they shared the whole world of literature, of which they had both scaled the known peaks. But this was a case of a fundamental difference of approach. Drummond's was a well-formed and well-furnished mind. But his cast of thought was conventional and his wisdom ultimately derivative. In addition the conventions upon which he had so studiously modelled his life and work were in most cases already outmoded. His sonnets for instance, published in 1616, were following a fashion that was in England about twenty years out of date. An innate conservatism restricted his vision so that although he read so widely among the latest authors his views remained unmodified and old-fashioned. His training, his reading, and his habits of mind inclined him to the classical, the artificial, the decorous, and the safe.

Jonson, by contrast, was nothing if not a fearless risk-taker. His interest in conventions lay in stretching them to test their continuing validity and usefulness. Never content simply to reproduce, he sought a literary method by which he could fill his chosen form to bursting point, to remould and extend his material and sources. For him the adoption of some element of a classical writer was part of the work of forging a modern meaning, and not a vacant act of ancestor-worship.

Drummond's summary of his visitor appears at the end of his notes of Jonson's remarks:

He is a great lover and praiser of himself, a condemner and scorner of others, given rather to lose a friend than a jest,[8] jealous of every word and action of those about him (especially after drink, which is one of the elements in which he liveth) a dissembler of ill parts which reign in him, a bragger of some good that he wanteth, thinketh nothing well but what either he himself or some of his countrymen hath said or done. He is passionately kind and angry, careless either to gain or keep, vindictive, but, if he be well answered, at himself.

He is for any religion, being versed in both. Interpreteth best sayings and deeds often to the worst. Oppressed with fantasy, which hath overmastered his reason, a general disease in many poets. His inventions are smooth and easy, but above all he excelleth in translation.

Drummond's chilly résumé gives us Jonson, warts and all. It is not an attractive picture of the poet 'vapouring' on about himself, running others down, venting nationalistic prejudice to a host of another country, and all this in such a welter of alcohol that Drummond is inclined to think it his natural element like water to a fish. The effect on Jonson of years of heavy drinking was obviously beginning to tell. In another suggestive confidence he told Drummond that 'he hath spent a whole night in lying looking at his great toe, about which he hath seen Tartars and Turks, Romans and Carthaginians, fight in his imagination'. There are, too, strong hints of cruelty in Jonson's wit, and more than a trace of paranoia in his mental makeup.

Yet Jonson had very clearly tried to be an amiable guest. He had told Drummond that his verses 'were all good', even though he must have spoiled the effect of his compliment when he could not resist adding, 'save that they smelled too much of the Schools, and were not after the fancy of the time'. He admired Drummond's 'Forth Feasting', a panegyric written to celebrate King James's return to Scotland in 1617, and told Drummond that 'he wished, to please the King, that "Forth Feasting" had been his own'. But by the end of the visit Drummond had built up a strong antipathy to this turbulent personality.

Eventually, however, the visit came to an end. Jonson had left Hawthornden by the middle of January 1619. Drummond's civility overcame his resentment, and he wrote to Jonson on 17 January in courteous terms:

To his worthy friend, Mr Benjamin Jonson:
Sir,
Here is that epigram which you desired, with another of the like argument. If there can be any other thing in this country unto

which my power can reach, command it; there is nothing I wish more than to be in the calendar of them who love you. I have heard from the court that the late masque was not so approved of the King as in former times . . . . Thus, to the next occasion, taking my leave, I remain,

Your loving friend
Hawthornden
(HS I, 204–5)

Jonson was not far away – he had not yet left Scotland – and he was able to reply almost by return on 19 January 1619. With his letter he sent two of his poems (later *Underwood* 8 and 9) as a parting gift to Drummond. The two lyrics were introduced with a studied compliment to Drummond, and a formal declaration of the bond between the two poets:

To the honouring respect
Born
To the friendship contracted with
The right virtuous and learned
Mr William Drummond
And the perpetuating the same by all offices of love
Hereafter
I, Benjamin Jonson
Whom he hath honoured with the leave to be called his
Have with my own hand, to satisfy his request
Written this imperfect song
On a Lover's Dust, made Sand for an Hourglass

The second of these two lyrics in particular, 'My Picture left in Scotland', presents a very different Jonson from the coarse and egotistical braggart of Drummond's notes:

I now think Love is rather deaf than blind
For else it could not be
That she
Whom I adore so much should so slight me,
And cast my love behind.
I'm sure my language to her was as sweet
And every close did meet
In sentence of as subtle feet,
As hath the youngest he
That sits in shadow of Apollo's tree.

Oh but my conscious fears
    That fly my thoughts between,
    Tell me that she hath seen
    My hundred of grey hairs
    Told six-and forty years
Read so much waste, as she cannot embrace
    My mountain belly and my rocky face;
And all these through her eyes have stopped her ears.

This poem Jonson described to Drummond as 'a picture of himself'. Doubtless it represents with a merciless accuracy his ravaged appearance. Of greater interest is the introduction of these facts to create an engaging literary *persona*, half-hopeful, half-rueful. The feeling in Jonson which could result in poetry of this quality had not communicated itself to Drummond. He entered the two pieces in his Jonson notes without comment.

Jonson's stay in Scotland was even then drawing to its close. On 25 January 1619 he set out from Leith, in the same pair of shoes that he had bought in Darlington five months before and with the resolution that they should carry him at least as far as Darlington again. On his side he seems to have been unaware of any feeling of aversion Drummond may have had towards him and viewed his contact with him as more than an ordinary friendship. He had in effect designated Drummond as his literary executor while he was in transit, leaving instructions that if he were to die *en route* for England the papers that he had written about Scotland during his visit were to be sent to Drummond exactly as they were. He had also arranged with Drummond that the Scot was to forward to him in London descriptions of Edinburgh and of the countryside around Loch Lomond, to further Jonson's plans of writing up his Scottish adventures in fictions of some kind. Jonson clearly envisaged here the start and continuance of a significant literary connection.

Jonson returned south as he had gone, breaking his journey in stages. He had waited out the worst of the winter in Scotland, and by the time that he was back in London spring was under way. So ended one of Jonson's most interesting and inexplicable ventures. He was never again to return to Scotland. Yet it is to the impulse of this strange journey, and the fortunate collision of his course with Drummond's, that we owe much of our knowledge and understanding of Jonson's life and work.

CHAPTER 12

FATHER BEN

Jonson returned to London to find that many changes had taken place in his absence. As on his visit to France the Royal Family had again suffered a personal loss. On 2 March 1619 while Jonson was on his return home from Scotland, Queen Anne died. At forty-four she had had a good life by contemporary standards, and the time had passed when she could provide the focus for a masque as she had done a decade or so previously. But she had been one of his most important patrons, by virtue both of her position and her great love of masquing. Her death was therefore a professional, if not a personal, loss for him. The little queen had not long survived another portentous event, the destruction by fire of Queen Elizabeth's banqueting hall at Whitehall. Originally built in 1581 it had been the site of most of the court masques of those days. Sadly Anne did not live to see the great new banqueting hall raised up in its place by Inigo Jones between 1619 and 1622.

The death of the Queen had serious repercussions for the theatre. All play-acting was immediately suspended for a period of public mourning; the players were forbidden to act while the Queen's body lay above ground. As her funeral did not occur till 13 May 1619, the playhouses had to be closed for eleven weeks. This period of the theatre's mourning also served coincidentally to mark the passing of a principal member of the stage's aristocracy. On 13 March Richard Burbage died. Jonson had known him in both his theatrical roles, as one of the owners of the Globe and Blackfriars playhouses and as the leading actor of the day whose participation in Jonson's plays had been commemorated by the playwright himself in the 1616 Folio. Despite the encroachment of years Burbage had remained actively interested in the theatre until his death and his loss too would be felt.

More grievous was the fate that overtook Jonson's former employer,

Sir Walter Raleigh. His son and Jonson's former pupil, the young Walter Raleigh, had been killed early in 1618 while in Guiana with his father on Raleigh's final expedition, although the news did not reach England until the bereaved father's return in the midsummer of the same year. Nor was this the worst of Raleigh's distresses. His expedition failing, the old hawk was whistled back to his unloving master and the delayed sentence of death upon him was put into effect. In the final process against Raleigh on 28 October 1618 the Attorney-General pronounced his doom: 'He hath been as a star at which the world gazed. But stars may fall, nay they must fall, when they trouble the sphere wherein they abide'. On 29 October 1618 Raleigh was executed in the Tower of London.[1]

Naturally these momentous happenings did not eclipse the memory of the Scots visit nor of the friends Jonson had made there. To one of these, a Mr Fenton, Jonson had despatched a note from one of his resting places on the journey south. Fenton was a distinguished man in Scottish life, having been head of the office of the Scottish Comptrollery since 1582. He was about sixty years of age at this time but still held a high reputation for activity and business ability. He was, too, an acquaintance of Drummond, since Drummond had heard of Fenton's receipt of Jonson's letter soon after its arrival. Drummond refers to this welcome event when he wrote to Jonson himself on 30 April 1619:

> *To my good friend* BEN JONSON:
> Sr. – after even a longing to hear of your happy journey, Mr Fenton shewed me a letter from you, remembering all your friends here, and particularly (such is your kindness) me. If ever prayers could have made a voyage easy, yours must have been, for your acquaintance here in their thoughts did travel along with you. The uncertainty where to direct letters hath made me this time past not to write; when I understand of your being at London, I shall never (among my worthiest friends) be forgetful of you. I have sent you the oath of our knights as it was given me by Herald Drysdale. If I can serve you in any other matter, you shall find me most willing. [What a loss it were to us if aught should have befallen you but good]. Thus wishing that the success of your fortunes may be equal to your deserts, I commit you to the tuition of God.[2]

In consulting the Scottish Herald about the form of the oath of allegiance to the crown made by the Scottish lords of antiquity, Drummond was carrying out Jonson's historical research for him at the very highest level. Drummond's letter also establishes that Jonson had given up his previous residence in the Blackfriars when he undertook his journey and at that time had no fixed address in

London to which correspondence could be directed. Nevertheless Drummond's letter found him out where he had taken up his abode and he replied promptly on 10 May 1619 reporting his safe arrival and the King's pleasure at seeing his poet again:

> To my worthy, honoured and beloved friend, Mr William Drummond, Edinburgh:
> Most loving and beloved Sir:
> Against which titles I should most knowingly offend, if I made you not at length some account of myself, to come even with your friendship. I am arrived safely, with a most Catholic welcome, and my reports not unacceptable to his Majesty. He professed (I thank God) some joy to see me, and is pleased to hear the purpose of my book; to which I most earnestly solicit you for your promise of the inscriptions at Pinky, some things concerning the Loch of Lomond, touching the government of Edinburgh, to urge Mr James Scot; and what else you can procure for me with all speed; especially I make it my request, that you will enquire for me, whether the students' method at St. Andrews be the same with that at Edinburgh, and so assure me, or wherein they differ. Though these requests be full of trouble, I hope they shall neither burden nor weary such a friendship, whose commands to me I will ever interpret a pleasure. News we have none here, but what is making against the Queen's funeral, whereof I have somewhat in hand, which shall look upon you with the next. Salute the beloved Fentons, the Nisbets, the Scots, the Levingstons, and all the honest and honoured names with you; especially Mr James Writh, his wife, your sister, etc. And if you forget yourself you believe not in
>
> your most true friend
> and lover
> Ben Jonson.
> (IIS I, 207)

Jonson was clearly pleased with the general good wishes that had greeted his return and minded to put his new literary projects into shape with all speed. What these were the letter to Drummond affords some clues. The reference to Pinkie, the great battle of 1547 against the English and a landmark of Scottish history, supports the idea that Jonson was interested in writing 'a history of the worthies of this country', Scotland, 'all in couplets'. He was also writing a verse account of his Scottish trip with all his adventures, as the 'Execration upon Vulcan' (*Underwood* 43) makes clear. The reference to Loch Lomond demonstrates that the Scottish pastoral play set in the Lomond region, which Jonson had mentioned to Drummond during his stay, was still alive in his mind. What use he intended to make of the information on the government of Edinburgh and the course of study of the St Andrews' students remains obscure, but such facts would fit into any projected historical commentary upon Scotland and her great political and educational institutions.

At the point of writing however Jonson had had to set these projects aside in favour of making some literary contribution to the Queen's funeral. It is doubtful that Jonson finished this funerary tribute, although he promised to send Drummond a copy in his next letter. No trace of it survives among his works. He concludes his letter with sending good wishes to numerous Scots – an indication of the warmth of the hospitality that he had received. Early in July 1619 Drummond replied with some of the fruits of his labour on the poet's behalf. In a long and involved letter he makes reference to the various points which Jonson had asked for, and includes too a lengthy description of the designs upon a bed of state 'wrought and embroidered all with gold and silk by the late Queen Mary, mother to our sacred sovereign' (HS I, 208–10). This, Drummond impressed on Jonson, 'will embellish greatly some pages of your book' – presumably the projected history of Scotland. The enormous detail in which Drummond wrote shows how seriously he was taking his duties as Jonson's authority on Scotland and her antiquities.

Yet here strangely enough the correspondence seems to have died. No further letters between the two men have survived. As it turned out Jonson did not apply himself immediately to these literary designs since he had a busier summer than he might have anticipated. In the same month of July 1619 he paid a visit to Oxford where he stayed with a former pupil of his old school, Westminster. This friendship was characterised, like so many of Jonson's, by a substantial age gap. The Oxford contact, Richard Corbett, was ten years younger than Jonson. He was, though, well known to him. Corbett was at this point Senior Student of Christ Church. Later he became Bishop of Oxford and subsequently of Norwich.

Despite the suggestion of ecclesiastical gravity in all this, Corbett was a man of great humour and conviviality. As early as 1605 when he took his MA he had been esteemed one of the most celebrated wits in the University. He had spent his time at Oxford writing satires, verse epistles, epigrams and other trifles, relieving the strain of composition with practical jokes, ballad-singing and tavern escapades. He shared with Jonson both a partiality for the bottle and a hostility to Puritans, whom he consistently attacked in his verse. Anecdote subsequently linked the names of Jonson and Corbett in a way suggestive of the witty playful nature of the relationship between them:

Ben Jonson was in a tavern and in comes Bishop Corbett (but not so then) into the next room. Ben Jonson calls for a quart of raw wine, gives it to the tapster: 'Sirrah', says he, 'carry this to the gentleman in the next chamber and tell him I *sac*rifice my service to him'. The fellow did so, and in those words. 'Friend,' says Dr. Corbett, 'I thank him for his love, but prithee tell him from me he's mistaken, for *sac*rifices are always burnt.' (*JAB* 140)

Doubtless this was only one of many jokes and many cups of sack, whether served plain or mulled and flaming, that passed between the two men.

Corbett was, too, a poet in his own right, and as he had recently lost his father on 29 April 1619 he had marked the occasion with an elegy. Jonson read Corbett's valedictory on this visit, some six weeks after the event, and stimulated both by Corbett's poem and by his own warm memories of the old man Jonson composed his own epitaph – borrowing, incidentally, the four-beat verse line that Corbett had employed in his poem. Corbett senior had been a remarkable man. Although by birth a gentleman of some property he had devoted himself to the simple life of a nurseryman of Twickenham, cultivating and experimenting on trees, fruits and plants. He had successfully cultivated too the virtues often missing in those of far greater place and education, and which Jonson always respected. Yet Jonson's epitaph on this splendid octogenarian, although reverent, is not cold or impersonal, and the genuine feeling finds its expression through the short verse line to convey a real sense of informality and affection:

> . . for I both lost a friend and father
> Of him whose bones this grave doth gather:
> Dear Vincent Corbett, who so long
> Hath wrestled with diseases strong
> That though they did possess each limb,
> Yet he broke them, ere they could him . . .
> . . . Pray, who shall my sorrows read
> That they for me their tears will shed;
> For truly, since he left to be
> I feel I'm rather dead than he!
>
> (*Underwood* 12)

Jonson had found in old Corbett a kindred spirit despite the discrepancy between their background and pursuits. He had admired Corbett's brave fight against his final defeat as much as his 'life that knew nor noise nor strife'. The old gardener had been gifted with a sweetness of temper denied to Ben and in his circumscribed existence had achieved what was to the poet a classical standard of order and decorum: 'His mind as pure and neatly kept/As were his nurseries', so that his 'very manners' 'chid the vice, yet not the men'. In his summary on this gentle soul Jonson's truly egalitarian spirit shines through:

> Much from him I profess I won,
> And more, and more, I should have done . . .

Jonson's presence in Oxford promoted a public as well as a private welcome. On 17 July 1619 Jonson's patron, the Earl of Pembroke and then Chancellor of the University, proposed in a letter to Convocation that the degree of Master of Arts should be conferred upon Jonson. Accordingly two days later on 19 July he was formally received into the bosom of the university at a ceremony in full Convocation. This tribute honoured him both as a poet and as a scholar who had laboured so long and so hard to elevate the profession of letters. Although only a formality in itself – it did not offer Jonson a course of study, nor give him any rights of residence in the university – it undoubtedly set the final seal on his unique status in British life. He stood without peer at the very forefront of English literature.

Jonson was enjoying at this time the sort of life which was consonant with this status and which he had always striven for. The evidence abounds of his bookishness and scholarly pursuits; lending and borrowing texts from friends, working on through the classics, and discussing the finer points of translation with fellow-linguists. But his interests were not purely classical. From the books that he owned it is possible to build up a picture of his reading and study in a way that brings out the enormous range of his intellectual curiosity. He mastered topics as diverse as farriery, witchcraft and hunting in the course of the background work for different artistic productions in these years.

Equally varied as always was Jonson's personal circle. This underwent many changes over the years, but he was never alone. The loss of his patron and friend Raleigh was compensated for by the acquaintance of the Duke of Newcastle. Newcastle was a brilliant and dedicated horseman, who worked hard at the theory and practice of equitation, published on this theme, and later established a famous riding school. He was also a man of marked literary sensibility and following his patronage of Jonson also took an interest in Brome, Davenant, Dryden, Shirley and Hobbes. Jonson's first recorded contact with this unusual man occurred when he wrote an epitaph on Newcastle's father, who died on 4 April 1619; it was engraved upon his monument in the ancestral chantry of the Cavendishes at Bolsover. Subsequently he got to know the whole family and paid various members verse tributes of one sort and another.

As with patrons, so with friends. Jonson never lost the capacity to attract people to him. In his laureateship he became the mark by which other writers desired to set their course, and by force of his achievements and personality he drew the new generation of university wits and Inns of Court men into his company. From these friends of the later period, which at different times included men-about-town and poets such as Lucius Cary, Thomas Randolph, Shackerley Marmion, William Cartwright, Richard Lovelace and Robert Herrick, emerged the inner circle who were privileged to style themselves those 'sealed of the tribe of Ben' as his 'sons'.

The centre of this circle during these years was the Devil Tavern. This ancient edifice, strictly 'the Devil and St Dunstan', had stood between Temple Bar and Middle Temple Lane since 1464, distinguished by its sign of the Devil pulling St Dunstan's nose with a pair of tongs. Its landlord was Simon Wadloe, dubbed 'Simon the King' and 'Duke Wadloe' by Jonson in *The Staple of News*; when Jonson was in the house Wadloe personally served wine to the company. Within this tavern on the first floor was the Apollo room where he met his friends and presided over an informal drinking club of poets. These gatherings were conducted with some ceremony. Jonson as presiding genius had a seat raised above the body of the room, which was in every way furnished as befitted the dignity of the company. It was appropriately equipped with a bust of the god of poetry, Apollo himself, and the walls were hung with rich hangings. A minstrels' gallery allowed for the provision of music but the bands of peripatetic fiddlers who traipsed about from tavern to tavern were always refused entrance. As Jonson noted to Drummond 'the best banquets were those where they [needed] no musicians to chase time'. His was the controlling hand throughout. The newcomer first encountered over the doorway, painted in gold and black, verses of welcome composed by Jonson himself:

> Welcome all who lead or follow
> To the oracle of Apollo . . .
> All his answers are divine,
> Truth itself doth flow in wine . . .
> 'Tis the true Phoenician liquor,
> Clears the brain, makes wit the quicker,
> Pays all debts, cures all diseases,
> And at once three senses pleases.
> Welcome all who lead or follow,
> To the oracle of Apollo.
>
> (HS VIII, 657)

Jonson was the self-styled and undisputed '*arbiter bibendi*', a phrase from Horace denoting 'master of the drinking'. As the leader he drew up a set of what he called '*leges conviviales*', 'laws of the feasting'. These twenty-four rules for convivial procedure were engraved in Latin over the mantelpiece in the Apollo Room itself. A contemporary verse translation of the *leges* runs as follows:

> Let none but guests or clubbers hither come;
> Let dunces, fools, sad sordid men keep home . . .
> The cook and purveyor must our palates know;
> And none contend who shall sit high or low.
> Our waiters must quick-sighted be, and dumb,
> And let the drawers quickly hear, and come . . .
> And let our only emulation be
> Not drinking much, but talking wittily . . .
> Let none of us be mute, or talk too much;
> On serious things or sacred let's not touch
> With sated heads and bellies; neither may
> Fiddlers, unasked, obtrude themselves to play . . .
> Insipid poems let no man rehearse,
> Nor any be compelled to write a verse.
> All noise of vain disputes must be forborne,
> And let no lover in a corner mourn . . .
> Let none by drinking do or suffer harm,
> And while we stay, let us be always warm.[3]

Whatever the arrangements the festivities there were such as to pass into legend. Years later in *Fragmenta Aurea* (1646) Sir John Suckling playfully set down what he had heard of the celebrated wit-encounters, and of the behaviour of the chief wit in particular:

'A Session of the Poets'

> A session was held the other day,
> And Apollo himself was at it, they say,
> The laurel that had been so long reserved
> Was now to be given to him best deserved.
>
>   And
> Therefore the wits of the town came thither,
> 'Twas strange to see how they flocked together,
> Each strongly confident of his own way,
> Thought to gain that laurel away that day. . . .
>
> The first that broke silence was good old Ben,
> Prepared before with canary wine,
> And he told them plainly he deserved the bays
> For his were called works, where others were but plays.

And
Bid them remember how he had purged the stage
Of errors that had lasted many an age,
And he hoped they did think *The Silent Woman*,
The Fox and The Alchemist outdone by no man.

Apollo stopped him there, and bade him not go on,
'Twas merit, he said, and not presumption
Must carry't, at which Ben turned about,
And in great choler offered to go out.

But
Those that were there thought it not fit
To discontent so ancient a wit;
And therefore Apollo called him back again,
And made him mine host of his own New Inn.

Even after the great schism of the Civil War and the subsequent upheaval of the Restoration in 1660, memories of these feasts of wine and wit lingered on. Dryden in his 1668 'Defence of the Epilogue' gibes at 'some few old fellows' with memories of the Blackfriars Theatre who 'can tell a story of Ben Johnson, and, perhaps, have had fancy enough to give a story in the Apollo, that they may be called his sons; and because they were drawn in to be laughed at in those times, they think themselves sufficiently entitled to laugh at ours'. Shadwell even later in his *Bury Fair* (1689) makes a character declare 'myself, simple as I stand here, was a wit in the last age; I was created Ben Johnson's son, in the Apollo'.

Certainly the wit was very closely connected with the wine, and although the Devil was Jonson's headquarters it was not his only haunt. His devotee the poet Herrick makes this plain in an Ode he wrote on this Bacchanalian theme:

Ah Ben!
Say how, or when
Shall we thy guests
Meet at those lyric feasts
Made at the Sun,
The Dog, the Triple Tun?
Where we such clusters had,
As made us nobly wild, not mad;
And yet each verse of thine
Outdid the meat, outdid the frolic wine.

Inevitably, with the regular indulgence in quantities of wine and food, Jonson had become very fat. This comes to be reflected with

209

increasing prominence in his verse. In *Underwood* 52 he comments almost with surprise 'I seem of a prodigious waist', adding

> 'Tis true, as my womb swells, so my back stoops,
> And the whole lump grows round, deformed, and droops.

On one occasion Jonson was asked to dine with friends in order to settle for a merry wager the question of his weight. Who the friends were is not known but 'a merchant's wife is regent of the scale', as he described the proceedings in *Underwood* 54. In the event his weight proved to be two pounds short of twenty stone. He was made painfully aware of the consequences of this vast bulk, chiding himself for being

> a tardy, cold
> Unprofitable chattle, fat and old,
> Laden with belly [who] doth hardly approach
> His friends, but to break chairs, or crack a coach . . .
>
> (*Underwood* 56)

As time went by Jonson's reputation for hard drinking spilled over into one for hard living too. A later anecdote links this with a supposed patriotism to give a version of the traditional Jonson which we all recognise:

> Father Ben (when one . . . swore he had got a clap, which he called the French pox) was worthily wroth at the expression, and in a fume, said, 'Why not, Sir, the *English* pox? We have as good and as large as they have any'. (*JAB* 304)

These tales of hard drinking and loose living are as always at variance with other aspects of Jonson's crowded and often contradictory life. On New Year's Day 1620 he met the Dutch scholar Joachim Moers (Latinised by Jonson as 'Morsius'). This distinguished historian and antiquarian was Professor of History and Greek at Leyden University. He visited Jonson, who inscribed his autograph book in Latin very warmly and signed it with a flourish, 'Poeta Regius', the Royal Poet'.

As 1620 opened Jonson was beginning to pick up the traces of this occupation again. He was commissioned to write the Prince's masque for the end of the Christmas festivities and the young Charles took it all very seriously indeed. Among the royal accounts there survives a bill from a Groom of the Chamber to Prince Charles for carrying 'two messages two several times from the court at Whitehall into London by Cripplegate, to warn Mr Ben Johnson the Poet, and the Players at the Blackfriars, to attend his Highness that night following, at court, which several services being done, he returned each time with answer' (HS I, 235). This is the only hint of Jonson's residence since his return from Scotland. It is possible that he had resumed living in Blackfriars near the players. Aubrey however has a different version: 'I have heard my uncle Danvers say (who knew him) that he lived without Temple Bar at a comb-maker's shop about the Elephant and Castle'.

Wherever he travelled from, the 'royal poet' had to be on hand to fulfil his court duties. The masque for the close of the Christmas festivities in 1620 was *News from the New World Discovered in the Moon*. It was given on 17 January in the presence of 'the great Monsieur of France', the ambassador Marshal de Cadenet, who had received his first audience of the King on New Year's Eve. The masque was conducted with even more formality than was customary. Any courtiers below the rank of baron were forbidden to attend. Prince Charles was the chief masquer, and the entertainment lasted for more than three hours. In keeping with this great state as well as with his own improved status Jonson received £100 for writing this masque. It was given again on Shrove Tuesday (11 February) at which the Spanish ambassador appeared, the eternally vexed question of precedence having prevented his attendance at the first performance.

In writing this masque the poet as he often liked to do had worked in a sly reference to himself, making one of the characters, a printer, say 'one of our greatest poets went to Edinburgh o' foot, and came back; marry, he has been restive, they say, ever since, for we have had nothing from him; he has set out nothing, I am sure'. Yet Jonson was in demand again. His prospects and employment at this time contrast strongly with those of some of his fellows in the worlds either of the public theatre or of court masquing. During 1619 his old foe Dekker had been released from the King's Bench prison after six years of imprisonment for debt, while on 4 October 1619 his former rival Samuel Daniel died.

In early spring Jonson had another court commission. This was an entertainment to celebrate the baptism of the Earl of Devonshire's second son, born 20 May 1620. This was a great occasion which took place at the Blackfriars in the presence of Prince Charles; the baby was named after his royal godfather. But as he had done before he went away, Jonson was trying to combine his professional work with serious private scholarship. And whenever a group of men interested in letters came together, Jonson's name was invariably on their tongues. For one such group, interest crystallised into a positive proposal about this time. From about 1617 the idea had been mooted to found an English Academy. The general concept seems to have been not an academy in the educational sense so much as a knightly order of learned men akin to that of St George. Its purpose was nothing less than the bringing together of all those who were working in the fields of literature, history, philosophy and science, under the aegis of the King, in an 'Academy Royal' at Windsor Castle.

The author of the proposition was Jonson's friend Edmund Bolton, and the men nominated by him to form this elect order included Jonson, Chapman, Sir Robert Cotton, Sir Kenelm Digby, John Selden and Sir Henry Wotton. All these were known to Jonson as friends and patrons, if by no closer link; Cotton's was the house at which Jonson was staying in 1603 when his son died, and Digby was to be his literary executor. Other names about whom Jonson felt less warmly were those of Michael Drayton and Inigo Jones. The former, so Jonson told Drummond, was afraid of him, and Jonson's opinion of Drayton's work was low. But among the eight-odd others, who included the most hallowed names in the kingdom, there were many that Jonson could respect.

While the idea was taking shape during 1620, Jonson had a welcome summer commission. The masque *Pan's Anniversary*, most probably written for the celebration of the King's birthday on 19 June, deified James as Pan and exalted him as central to the life of the nation. But this was fast becoming a literary fiction as the real exercise of power passed into the hands of Charles, who was himself in the hands of Buckingham. An old man now, James became increasingly helpless for the last years of his reign. As a result the 'College and Senate of Honour', the 'English Olympus', which would have fed both the scholarly and the sociable sides of Jonson's nature, came to nothing.

In September 1620 one of Jonson's chief patrons suffered a great loss. Mistress Philip Sidney, the daughter of Robert Earl of Leicester and master of Penshurst, died. She was only twenty-six and untimely cut off like her famous uncle whose name she bore. Jonson had known her for years and had saluted her beauty and her descent in Epigram 114. But he left no epitaph for her as might have been expected. Jonson usually preferred to honour the living rather than to mourn the dead. On 26 January 1621 Lord Bacon celebrated his sixtieth birthday. Jonson had deeply admired him both as an essayist and as a statesman, the public and the private occupations equally affording exercise for his acute brain and pellucid prose. Jonson, who possessed a 1620 copy of Bacon's work, greeted the occasion of his anniversary with an enthusiastic poem (*Underwood* 51) in which Bacon's greatness is derived from his distinguished father and published as the 'fame and foundation of the English weal'. Now Lord Chancellor, Bacon stood at this time at the height of his power and honour; his had been a life, as Jonson justly observed, 'whose even thread the fates spin round and full'.

Subsequent events were to load Jonson's phrases with unintended irony. Within the same year of 1621 Bacon had, in the violent way of contemporary politics, fallen from grace and office. He was impeached in the House of Commons on a charge of taking bribes from suitors as an inducement to pervert the course of the law. Bacon made no attempt to deny that he had accepted presents but strenuously affirmed that he had never had 'the troubled fountain of a corrupt heart in a depraved habit of taking rewards to pervert justice'. One man who believed him was Ben Jonson. Jonson's regard for this great man was not shaken by the loss of temporal power and glory. He felt Bacon's fall as a personal grief and as he later recorded 'in his adversity I ever prayed, that God would give him strength; for greatness he could not want'. His consolation was the firm belief that in the last resort 'no accident could do harm to [Bacon's] virtue; but rather help to make it manifest'.

Bacon was of course only one of the many caught in the cross-fire between the King and Parliament as the former sought to retain and redefine the ancient powers of the monarchy while the latter doggedly and by degrees asserted its prerogative. Even had Jonson been other than he was, the course of his working life had aligned his interests ineluctably with those of the monarchy. His work therefore in this second half of his career often points outside its immediate context to the events of political significance underlying it. One such piece was a masque made by Jonson in the summer of 1621, *The Gypsies Metamorphosed*.

The occasion of *The Masque of Gypsies* was the visit of King James to Burley in Rutlandshire. There the King was to be entertained by his favourite Buckingham, who had organised 'a great provision of plays, masques, and all manner of entertainment' for his doting and capricious master. George Villiers, a country squireen before becoming successively Earl, Marquis and now Duke of Buckingham, had originally won his way into James's affections through his grace and skill in dancing. What more natural then on this important visitation that he should seek the opportunity to display his prime accomplishment? Jonson's masque *The Gypsies Metamorphosed* proved to be the perfect vehicle for Buckingham and the perfect show for the occasion. This was in fact something of a family affair. Away from the formality of the court, the royal party could be indulged with an ingenious in-joke. Jonson capitalised not only upon the Duke's dancing but also on his acting ability. Buckingham played one of the leading parts, in itself a novelty when a gentleman was prepared to participate in the spoken action like a common player. To see his favourite displaying both familiar and unfamiliar talents would in itself be a fair guarantee of James's pleasure.

But Jonson built further on the relatively private and informal nature of the visit to write for the King in a far more intimate and personal way than ever he could have done in a masque for the court. Of all Jonson's masques for James this most clearly shows his acute grasp on the King's character and tastes, an insight which the poet had inevitably to subdue to the formal and celebratory presentation of James's majesty on state occasions. Here, within a circle which did not include ambassadors, visiting dignitaries, or censorious worthies, James could be himself.

What that self was Jonson had had plenty of opportunity to observe at close quarters over the years. Pathetically deprived in childhood and adolescence, James demanded in his maturity a paradoxical mixture of boisterous familiarity with grandiloquent adulation. His nature was a contradictory blend of the aspirational and the gross. Jonson's central notion for the masque succeeded in catching up these different strains into one triumphant whole. The result, something of a hybrid between masque and entertainment, represented the high-water mark of his masque-making career. The central idea of the show was a simple one. A party of gypsies were to invade the royal presence and read the palms of some of those present, foretelling the future and uttering spells and charms. This device allowed Jonson to play upon the age-old tension between the gypsies' remote and wonderful past with its history of magic and necromancy, and their modern local character as thieves and rogues. When the gypsies led by a disguised Buckingham penetrated the royal company, the dialogue that Jonson gave them was both personal and pointed.

The first victim of their attentions was naturally the King himself. Buckingham's pretence as the Gypsy Captain of reading the royal palm was the cue for a series of jokes that seem dangerously impudent as they lie cold on the page. They include salacious references to James's *mons veneris* and a discussion of his sexual habits, concluding with the loaded observation that he is 'not a great wencher'. Nor was James the only subject of the loose talk and gibes; another was Jonson's patron, the Earl of Pembroke and closely connected with the King. Equally daring in another way were the references to the predatory habits of Buckingham's family who had been busily engrossing what advantages they could through the young man's sudden accession to favour and prosperity. In Jonson's treatment the gypsy tribe prepares to steal all the great offices of state, symbolised by 'a Purse and a Seal' – the great Seal of England itself being at this time in the keeping of a nominee of Buckingham widely believed to be the lover of Buckingham's formidable mother.

Yet although Jonson was clearly sailing near the wind, he had judged his tack expertly. The overall effect is humorous and charming rather than insolent or dirty. It dramatises the intimacies of the King while retaining the convention of complimenting him and his family.

It had too, in the figures of the rogue-gypsies, provided Jonson with the means of importing into the rarefied world of the masque the vital 'cony-catching' tricks of the contemporary low life as enjoyed in London's citizen comedy. This offered the bonus of the kind of fun that James could unashamedly enjoy.

At all events, so far from being offended, James was intensely delighted. After its first performance on Friday 3 August 1621 at Burley the masque was revived again two nights later when the King and his party had reassembled at the Earl of Rutland's seat at Belvoir. What was quite unprecedented was that the masque also saw a third revival in the following month of September at Windsor. These closely related occasions, 3 August, 5 August and 9 September, in themselves bear witness to the King's deep pleasure. Nor was this the only evidence of royal satisfaction. Buckingham was rewarded with a burst of poetry from the old King, who had left literary pursuits behind long ago. James was moved to write at Burley some verses complimenting his host upon the entertainment, and expressing his hopes for the speedy arrival of a blessing in the form of an heir to his favourite: 'God send a smiling boy the while'. For Jonson, the gossip ran, the King's recompense would take a more substantial form than the £100 that he had already received from Buckingham – a fair sum, but only half what the musician was paid. It was said that Jonson's pension was to be more than doubled, from one hundred marks to two hundred pounds; he was also to be placed on the waiting list of those in line for the lucrative post of the Mastership of the Revels. Everything pointed to an Indian summer of royal favour for Jonson from his delighted master. The old poet had triumphed again.

CHAPTER 13

SETBACKS AND LOSSES

B UT as with so many occasions in Jonson's life the promise of royal favour was delusive. Much was promised – much was discussed. There was even talk half way through the September of 1621 that the King had offered Jonson a knighthood. This, if true, would have been a situation fraught with irony for the man who had once been imprisoned for poking fun at King James's 'thirty-pound knights', and who moreover had 'never esteemed a man for the name of a lord', attacking titles as 'the bird-lime of fools'. Jonson stayed true to his principles now. He managed to avoid the 'honour', although he was said to have 'escaped it narrowly'.

These rewards however remained all at the level of gossip. The King's largesse was not forthcoming, his munificence emotional rather than practical. The only tangible outcome of all this for Jonson was the grant to him on 5 October 1621 of the reversion of the office of the Master of the Revels by letters patent from the King. But despite the flattering reference in the document to 'our beloved servant, Benjamin Johnson, gentleman', this was an empty gesture. The post was at that time held by another gentleman who showed no signs of vacating it by conveniently dying. There was in any case another in the queue ahead of Jonson. Almost ten years previously in April of 1612 James had already granted the first reversion of the office to Sir John Astley. Two men therefore had to drop off to clear Jonson's path to this lucrative engagement, and predictably he did not succeed in outliving them to enjoy it.

Jonson was clearly casting around for new sources of money at this point. The King's pension was unreliable, often unpaid, and when it was it had proved quite inadequate to his needs. In 1621 there is evidence that he was struggling, not too well, with real financial difficulty. He had in fact borrowed the considerable sum of £36 from one John Hull, described as 'citizen and founder of London'. Not having the ready cash to pay this debt, Jonson had to take out a legal deed of assignment whereby he made over to Hull the entire amount of this half year's pension which was due the following Michaelmas. As this left three pounds still outstanding Hull was to receive this amount from the next half-yearly payment when it fell due. Jonson had effectively mortgaged his entire subsistence for the foreseeable future.

Jonson did no work for the stage during this period, and he had no masque to write between the summer of 1621 and the winter season at the end of this year. He must have been kept alive then by the bounty of friends and patrons. One of these, Lady Wroth, was a steady benefactor of Jonson, which he acknowledged not only with poetic tributes but with his services. Lady Wroth was a poet in her own right and Jonson copied out some of her sonnets for her in his clear, fair hand. In a courtly compliment he claimed that this task had improved the level of his own verse:

> I, that have been a lover, and could show it
> Though not in these,[1] in lines not wholly dumb,
> Since I exscribe your sonnets, am become
> A better lover, and much better poet . . .
>
> (*Underwood* 28).

These sonnets appeared in 1621 in a volume entitled *The Countess of Montgomery's Urania*, a romance continuing the Arcadian tradition of Lady Wroth's uncle, Sir Philip Sidney, so often commended by Jonson in verse of his own.

These developments in Jonson's life took place against the background of changes in the lives of friends. In November of 1621, 'Jack' Donne, erstwhile roisterer and libertine of the Inns of Court days, continued his spiritual pilgrimage towards grace by becoming the Dean of St Paul's Cathedral. This event caused widespread interest. As one commentator saw it:

> . . . and then we are like to have our new Dean, Dr. Donne, at Paul's; so as a pleasant [witty] companion said that if Ben Jonson might be made Dean of Westminster, that place, St. Paul's and Christ Church [Deanery of Richard Corbett the poet and Jonson's Oxford friend] should be furnished with three very pleasant poetical deans. (HS XI, 386)

1621 closed with one last excitement. On 9 December the Fortune theatre, like the great Globe before it, burned to the ground. This theatre under Henslowe's management had seen the best work of the Lord Admiral's Men and their leading actor Edward Alleyn. The company had later become the Palsgrave's Men after a 'marriage' with the Lady Elizabeth's Company. The destruction of the playhouse involved for them more than the loss of their building. With the Fortune perished the company's entire stock of costumes and their repertory of plays. It was disaster from which in the less promising temper of the times they were not to recover.

In December 1621 Jonson once again had a court masque in hand. The presentation of the Jonson masque was scheduled for the prime Twelfth Night position; on 6 January 1622 it took place amid the customary jostling for precedence of the French, Spanish and Venetian ambassadors. As the Spaniard won out on this occasion, a revival of *The Masque of Augurs* was contemplated at Shrovetide. But the King was too ill with gout to be present. Accordingly the masque was performed for the second time months later in the first week of May 1622. Whatever other ends it served, it failed of its diplomatic function. The French ambassador, receiving his invitation to attend, returned answer that 'he most humbly kissed his Majesty's hands for the honour intended him; but his stomach would not, he said, agree with cold meat' (*JAB* 126). He therefore refused to come.

King James was finding another use for his poet laureate that summer. James's interest had been taken by a poem called *Argenis*, a political and historical romance in Latin which dealt with recent events on the continent. The author was John Barclay, a Scot born in France and for both these reasons laying claim to James's attention. The poem had a great vogue early in 1622 when it became so scarce that the price rose from five shillings to fourteen. Contemporary gossip recorded that the King had ordered Jonson to translate it into English – 'but he will not be able to equal the original'(*JAB* 126). Jonson naturally did not share this view, and prepared to undertake it. His translation of *Argenis* was entered on the Stationers' Register on 2 October of the following year, 1623, indicating at least a hope if not an intention of bringing it out, but it never appeared.

The rest of this year seems to have passed quietly for Jonson, its closing weeks once again occupied by the preparation of the Christmas masque. The only disruption for him was the sudden death on 13 October 1622 of his friend Clement Edmondes, whom Jonson had encouraged at the start of his career by writing commendatory verses to his translation of Caesar. Edmondes had now fulfilled his promise by being appointed to the eminent position of Secretary of State. Sadly, however, he died without warning before he could take up his office.

1623 opened encouragingly with a performance of *The Alchemist* on 1 January. This thirteen-year-old comedy was standing up to the passage of time sufficiently well to be revived for the court by the King's players 'on New Year's Day at night'. But the new Jonson masque did not follow it as expected in its customary Twelfth Night position. *Time Vindicated to Himself and to his Honours* had been graced by the participation of the two highest in the land under the King, the Prince of Wales and the favourite of both father and son, Buckingham. But on Twelfth Night the King was not well enough to attend. Some of the court gossips whispered that the King's was a diplomatic indisposition, since the precedence dispute between the foreign ambassadors continued its wearisome course. But the King was certainly far enough from well to render this a plausible excuse.

After being postponed almost on a day-to-day basis, the masque was eventually given on Sunday 19 January 1623. Visually it was a delight. Inigo Jones had created three principal scenes; the first had a novel 'mirror effect' for court audiences, since the curtain went up to reveal a perspective of Whitehall, with the Banqueting House in view, where even as they watched, the show itself was taking place. The set subsequently gave way to two conventional masque scenes, 'the masquers in a cloud', and a woodland prospect.

Jonson's contribution (and as he would have it the 'soul' of the masque) was more contentious. What started out as a 'golden age' masque on the classical pastoral theme developed a topical relevance and a satirical slant. Jonson created a strange anti-masque of creatures called 'the Curious', through which he made indirect reference to an important issue of the day. In 1620 King James had issued a royal proclamation making it a punishable offence to speak of affairs of state. From 1621 onwards internal affairs like the economy, and foreign matters like the threat of Spanish aggression and the uneasy balance of Protestant Europe, agitated both people and Parliament alike. James was determined to restrain discussion and speculation as Parliament fastened more and more tenaciously upon freedom of speech as a vital pillar of that parliamentary prerogative which it sought.

Jonson uses his 'Curious' – creatures not fully human yet endowed with human wickedness and weakness – to discuss this question from the King's side of the debate. The 'Curious' are ignorant and evil. They talk compulsively but stupidly of matters beyond their ken. Jonson seeks to demonstrate that when such characters pry inquisitively into what they do not understand, they inevitably work against harmony and order. They can only damage what others seek to defend.

This phase of the argument is sufficiently generalised to permit of a personal, moral interpretation, if the political came too near the bone. But having used the 'Curious' to set the scene, Jonson brought on a character Chronomastix (The Scourge of the Time) whose immediate relevance could not be mistaken. This was in fact a satiric portrait of another satirist of the time, George Wither. Wither had sufficiently enraged the authorities with his satire *Abuses Stript and Whipt* to be imprisoned for it in the Marshalsea, and he was a confirmed Puritan in religion. In mounting this personal attack Jonson disregarded Wither's flattering reference in the poem to 'the deep conceits of now-flourishing Jonson' and attempted to punish Wither for presuming to comment satirically upon state affairs; he tied Wither in as an example of the vice for which he pilloried the 'Curious'. He also had a dislike of Wither as a man, attacking him as a 'self-loving braggart', no true satirist, a wretched impostor and 'mountebank of wit'. In this Jonson was only echoing the offended state. But the authorities had taken their revenge and did not want further comment upon this delicate theme. In addition Jonson had used the allegorical and impersonal framework of the masque to express feelings that were distinctly personal. Either way, so contemporaries felt, the whole business was 'become so tender an argument that it must not be touched either in jest or earnest'. Some gleefully prophesied trouble for Jonson as a result: he was thought 'like to hear of it on both sides of the head' (that is, have his ears boxed), 'for personating George Wither a poet or poetaster as he terms him' (HS X, 648).

In the event this did not occur, and the dispute was not allowed to spoil the festivities. On the contrary the revels were unusually prolonged this year. One courtier commented, 'here was nothing to write of but dancing and feasting which was more frequent now than ever I knew or remember, and continues since even till now'. The festivities did not end as they usually did according to tradition on Twelfth Night. The King had always taken enormous pleasure in watching others dance the complicated and elaborate steps of the time; now he was aware that few such Christmas revels could be his in the future.

Almost immediately after performing in Jonson's masque Prince Charles left England in pursuit of one of those matters which had so engaged the unwelcome attention of his fellow countrymen and women. On Tuesday 18 February 1623, attended only by Buckingham, Charles went to Madrid in order to negotiate a marriage between himself and the Infanta of Spain. This was a match which was regarded with the gravest misgiving by a nation with recent unhappy memories of a previous Spanish marriage, the martyr-making union of 'Bloody Mary' Tudor with Philip of Spain in 1554. Marriage was the weapon with which the Hapsburgs had conquered half of Europe – could England's precious independence be guaranteed against the might of Catholic Spain?

Ecstatic and unrestrained, therefore, was the nationwide glee when the heir to the throne returned in early October 1623 without a Spanish bride or any hope of one. Archbishop Laud described it as 'the greatest expression of joy, by all sorts of people, that ever I saw'. The religious and political obstacles had proved insuperable. In addition Buckingham's conduct of the wooing had been so unskilful that the Spaniards declared that they would rather put their Infanta down a well than entrust her to such a man. The Spanish flirtation had come to nothing. As the royal poet Jonson had to make a conventional acceptance of the union so desired by his King, and in *Underwood* 48, written in the summer of 1623 when the Prince was daily expected home with his Spanish bride, he refers politely if rather tepidly to the forthcoming jubilation 'when Charles brings home the lady.' But as a staunch Englishman and as a re-born Protestant Jonson in common with the majority of his country found the proposed match abhorrent.[2] Perhaps this accounts for an otherwise inexplicable cooling of court favour towards him in that summer. Elaborate though necessarily confidential preparations were in hand for the return of the Prince of Wales and the Infanta. There were to be masques and shows first in Southampton and then in London. From these Jonson was excluded and the direction of the whole given to Inigo Jones. He strongly resented being backwatered like this and refers with evident bitterness and hurt pride to his situation:

> . . . Though I do neither hear these news, nor tell
> Or Spain or France, or were not pricked down one
>   Of the late mystery of reception;
> Although my fame to his not under-hears
> That guides the motions, and directs the bears . . .
>   (*Underwood* 47, lines 46–50)

Jonson did not only resent being kept out of the 'late mystery of reception'; he felt slighted that Inigo Jones, whose fame was not superior to his own, was preferred, castigating him contemptuously as a mere showman like those who ran puppet shows ('motions'), and dancing bears.

Yet this long verse epistle 'answering to one that asked to be sealed of the tribe of Ben' indicates that Jonson could still attract new friends, even on his own exacting terms for friendships that are 'square, well-tagged, and permanent, / Not built with canvas, paper and false lights' (lines 64–5). He could also keep old friendships in good repair. In the same month as the Prince's return, Jonson was once more engaged, as he was intermittently throughout his life, in a legal action on behalf of a friend. On 20 October 1623 he appeared in the Court of Chancery to give evidence on behalf of Sir Walter Raleigh's widow Elizabeth. The settlement of the old hero's estate

221

had proved very troublesome, and legal proceedings against Lady Elizabeth had been instituted by a prominent London jeweller who had been concerned in the disposal of the family plate and jewels. The Chancery suit was Lady Elizabeth's response and among the friends whom she mobilised to testify for her was Jonson.

Jonson's deposition is chiefly of interest in demonstrating the extent of the friendship between him and this interesting family. He gave evidence that he had received numerous letters from Raleigh in his lifetime and could therefore with confidence identify Raleigh's autograph and bear witness to its authenticity. Nor had Jonson lost touch with the family when its principal member and his own friend had died. He told the court that he 'very well knoweth' the Lady Elizabeth, the present sense of the verb showing a continuing acquaintance over the difficult years following Raleigh's execution in 1618.

Jonson's testimony also provided some interesting personal details of the poet. He gave his age to the court as 'fifty years and upwards', a statement which tallies with his evidence in the Roe case of 1610 that he was then thirty-seven. More tantalisingly, the document described him and his place of residence as 'Benjamin Jonson of Gresham College of London, gent'. Scholars and critics of many ages have laboured to link Jonson with some established seat of learning. Of all the suggestions and hypotheses which have been advanced, a formal academic connection with this establishment provides the most likely basis. This college was the brainchild of the great Elizabethan Sir Thomas Gresham who had endowed there seven professorships for the promotion of the seven 'liberal arts' – divinity, law, physics, astronomy, geometry, rhetoric and music. Jonson's living in the college in 1623 has led to the assumption that he was in residence there as one of the lecturers. It is clear that he had not been appointed to a regular professorship. The names of the holders of these offices are on record, and his is not among them. But the use of deputies was common at the time, and he would have made an able deputy to the Professor of Rhetoric. The duties of the post were not onerous, and well within his capabilities – the lectures in rhetoric were given at 8 a.m. in English, and at 2 p.m. in Latin. And the apartments allotted to the holder of this teaching post would have provided a very attractive part of the arrangement. They were on the north side of a quiet quadrangle on the first floor, next to the Professor of Astronomy.

The suggestion that Jonson was enjoying an academic life at this time fits in well with the framework of other events and developments for him during these years. He had returned from Scotland full of serious literary plans, and as a result of honours conferred there and upon his return he had assumed a different status from that he had held previously. The Oxford degree in particular would have made possible the post; Jonson could never have been appointed without any qualification. Then again he continued to steer clear of the public stage, yet there is no evidence of much other writing. Periods of teaching and of preparing lectures would amply account for the apparent lack of literary output.

If Jonson were lecturing and teaching, then, he would need a body of material. Many critics have seen his prose *Discoveries* in this light. We need not think that this collection of extracts and comments was originally intended as a set of lecture notes. A man in the habit as Jonson was of combing books old and new for the apt and unexpected expression or thought would naturally amass such stuff in the raw state. But *Discoveries* is only superficially a commonplace book of the sort that was popular at the time. Its contents, a mixture of classical gleanings with some contemporary material, could well have been used or worked up to furnish problems of rhetoric for consideration. Another piece, the *English Grammar*, is, like the *Discoveries*, out of the line of Jonson's normal writing. He could also have brought in his translation of Horace which with the criticism of Aristotle mentioned in *Underwood* 43 (line 90) would have been very valuable basic material for a course of this nature. There is persuasive evidence of an academic bent to Jonson's work at this time, though the way in which it emerged to posterity was through a most unhappy accident.

In November 1623 Jonson suffered a great and unprecedented loss. A fire at his lodgings consumed his study, and with it both his collection of books and all the work that he had on hand at the moment. He reacted to this blow by converting his complaints into poetry, writing a rueful and humorous lament in the form of a witty counter-attack upon the 'lame lord of fire', Vulcan (*Underwood* 43). In it he called the fire-god to account for the swiftness and severity of the conflagration:

> What had I done that might call on thine ire?
> Or urge thy greedy flames thus to devour
> So many my years' labours in an hour?

What these labours were, Jonson went on to outline for the reader. He lost a translation of Horace's *Ars Poetica* into English, with a commentary on it made in the light of Aristotle's *Poetics*, from which it was believed to derive (he had read this to Drummond, or a version of it, in 1619). Burned too were an *English Grammar*; a verse account of his journey into Scotland as promised to Drummond, 'with all the adventures' he had had included; three books of the translation of Barclay's *Argenis*, which the King had commanded from Jonson the

223

year before;[3] and a prose history of Henry V which had carried the King through eight of the nine years of his reign. Apart from a fleeting reference to some 'parcels of a play' which also perished, all Jonson's lost work was of a literary and scholarly nature. Nor was it all current. In 1623 Jonson had a lifetime of work behind him. Among the likely losses are the only surviving versions of those early comedies which he had told Drummond were not in print. Also certainly destroyed were the fruits of his life-long reading, 'twice twelve years' stored-up humanity' (possibly in the form of a commonplace book), and Jonson's religious thoughts, his 'humble gleanings in divinity'. The range and eclecticism of this output is astonishing in a man of Jonson's age; at fifty-one, he had passed his half-century in a period when countless thousands did not survive their first birthday.

Of these losses, some were re-written; the work on Horace, for instance, finally appeared in the 1640 Folio. Others, however, survive only in portions, like the notes towards the *English Grammar*, or were lost in perpetuity. What is interesting is that there is a generally academic bent to the whole, and that it was the more academic of the projects which were rewritten. It has been suggested that Jonson had an immediate professional reason for rewriting his Horace, namely the need for such material as part of a course taught at Gresham. Certainly if Jonson had returned in triumph from Scotland in 1619, had taken his degree in the summer of that year, and then assumed the post and duties of a Professor of Rhetoric at Gresham College, there can have been few occupations more congenial to him and to his known interests and abilities. Whatever the nature of his residence, Jonson was living in the College in 1623; he had deserted the public stage; he had been named as one of the potential 'Olympians' of the projected Academy Royal; and he had among his friends two Gresham professors, Gunter and Osbaldston. These factors together give to his life a substantial academic bias, even without the inclusion of the teaching element.

To lose work of such quality and quantity was in the nature of a bereavement. Hardly less serious to Jonson was the loss of all his books. Here it can only be guessed what went up in the flames. Some of his books have survived from other periods of his life either because he bought them subsequently or because they had been among those which as he told Drummond he had had to sell from time to time in order to raise money. These show the extent to which he used his books, underlining what struck him as important, and annotating throughout with translation, comment and cross-reference. Against one pungent epigram of Martial, for instance, he wrote the single expressive word, 'Inigo'. He also drew on pages which he was considering; he doodled pointing hands, or stars, to add emphasis to key points. He possessed at different times, anthologies, grammars, bibles, religious works, and works of friends and contemporaries like King James, Daniel and Marston. He owned at least two editions of Aristophanes, in Geneva editions of 1607 and 1614, both featuring the Greek text with a parallel Latin translation, which would have allowed him to enjoy both versions simultaneously.

Like a true booklover Jonson also gave books as gifts – Roe, for example, received from his hands an inscribed copy of Casaubon's *Persius*, in which the author was commended as a learned satirist, and the recipient was assured that Jonson's love to him was no less than that of a parent. Equally Jonson received books as gifts; as he wrote in *Underwood* 37, 'An Epistle to a Friend',

> Sir, I am thankful, first to heaven for you;
> Next to yourself, for making your love true;
> Then to your love and gift. And all's but due.

> You have unto my store added a book,
> On which with profit I shall never look
> But must confess from whom what gift I took . . .

This friend is unnamed. But Jonson numbered among his circle many literary men, including the foremost in the kingdom. He must therefore have lost in the fire some precious tributes of respect and affection. Finally he both lent and borrowed freely so that his friends Cotton and Selden had the misfortune to have books with him at the time of the fire – Cotton lost a book on Henry V, plus 'a great bundle of original things of Henry V, unbound'.

All these woes Jonson related in his 'Execration upon Vulcan' yet in no despairing or railing tone. On the contrary the spirit of his piece is remarkably light-hearted considering the magnitude of the blow, a gallant gesture in the teeth of spiteful fate. The poet expanded his personal misfortune into a humorous literary critique, in which he discussed what literary works or individuals would merit a visitation from the 'lord of fire'. The main satiric targets are contemporary writers and forms, Nicholas Breton, for instance, whom Jonson was later to satirise in *The Staple of News*. Non-literary personages also came in for some rough handling too like the 'prophet Ball', a mad tailor who foresaw that King James would become Pope, and two notorious whores, Kate Arden and Bess Broughton. The poem in fact becomes a burlesque in which famous events, characters and even other fires are jumbled together for a mock-heroic effect.

None of the named victims of Jonson's satire reacted in print. Yet some individuals undoubtedly nourished a fierce animosity to this man who could be brutal, harsh and overbearing. His former friend

Chapman around this time was moved to write a bitter 'Invective against Mr Ben Jonson'. The close relationship of earlier days had now given way to a deep opposition. Jonson can be acquitted of provoking Chapman on this occasion. Although he displays throughout the poem his lifelong contempt for romance there is nothing in it that could seem to strike at Chapman. Yet Chapman responded on a very personal level, reverting to the hostilities of the 'War of the Theatres' more than twenty years before. He took exception to Jonson's light-hearted treatment of contemporary issues and bitterly attacked Jonson's list of his own lost works. He reproved Jonson for being domineering, and warned him not to 'fright / All us . . . with luciferous boast' of his own greatness. In the last resort Jonson was a base scandal-monger, Chapman insisted, and fully deserved the 'visitation of Vulcan'.

It is difficult to explain the hostility of this attack. The earlier strong admiration between the two men had cooled and Jonson's view of Chapman had sunk from the heights expressed in his praise of his collaborator in the *Sejanus* period. In his own copy of Chapman's translation of Homer (1616) Jonson had severely criticised in sarcastic footnotes Chapman's scholarship, his style, and his intellectual grasp. Chapman himself had laboured painfully over his Homer for twenty-six years from the publication of its first instalment until its completion in 1624. Yet this massive work never brought him the recognition that he desired and his patrons Essex, Somerset and Prince Henry had all baffled his expectations through disgrace or death. Chapman's life was an agony of hope deferred. Finally his heart sickened. Alone in the poison of envy he worked on his insult to Jonson, carefully polishing each couplet. Yet either Chapman's better nature or his fear of self-exposure prevailed. He never sent his 'Invective' abroad and Jonson never saw what his former friend had written against him. The paper was found among Chapman's effects in 1634 when death finally released the 'little hoary poet', as Dekker and Webster once described him, from his unhappy life.

In 1623 another old friend of Jonson died, William Camden. Aged seventy-three and full of years and honours, Camden had shaped many destinies, though none as illustrious as Jonson's. He had pursued his scholarly interest in antiquities and risen to become Garter King of Arms. His was the consolation that Jonson had received on the day when he saw in a vision the death of his son Benjamin. Interestingly, Jonson wrote no epitaph for the man whom he elsewhere stated had made him what he was, yet he wrote two verse contributions to accompany the 1623 First Folio of Shakespeare's plays and also a long Latin epitaph for inscription on the tomb of a young man who died unexpectedly in

December of 1623 of 'a purple fever' at only twenty-two.

Towards the end of 1623 Jonson had as before been commissioned to write the Twelfth Night masque for the court Christmas. What Jonson entitled *Neptune's Triumph for the Return of Albion* was prepared with the customary diligence. As one courtier reported:

> Here is much preparation against the masque at Twelfth Night, and many meetings at noblemen's houses in the afternoons; as, yesterday the Prince, with the rest of the retinue, were at the Lord of Bridgwater's, where they had a great banquet, and afterwards went home to supper, as the usual manner is. (*JAB* 131)

Yet in spite of all the masque was never presented. On Twelfth Night 1624 instead of *Neptune's Triumph* the court was treated to a performance of Middleton's *More Dissemblers Besides Women* by the King's Company, but in the King's absence, the Prince only being there. The King's indisposition was the reason given for the cancellation of the masque, but court gossip murmured that 'the true cause is thought to be the competition of the French and Spanish Ambassadors, which could not be accommodated in [the Royal] presence' (*JAB* 133). High-level backstage negotiations had failed to resolve this deadlock, and James could find no way to avoid an encounter between the two ambassadors which neither could tolerate. In addition the French ambassador had treated the whole thing as a slight and was threatening to return home to his country and report to his king how scurvily he had been treated.

There was however even more behind it all than this. Having once again found court favour after the coolness of the summer Jonson had indulged himself in the writing of the masque with the highly undiplomatic notion of playing on the abortive Spanish marriage. His feeling of jubilation at this occurrence had spilled over into *Neptune's Triumph for the Return of Albion*. Despite the conventional references to harmony the masque was not pacific and 'the poet' appeared in person in the anti-masque to ram home the message. All this was more than the legendary Spanish pride would swallow, or English sense of diplomacy permit. The masque was consequently withdrawn.

The court could be kept in line; not so the people. In August the public relief at the failure of the marriage negotiations and animosity to all things Spanish boiled over with a performance of Middleton's controversial and wildly successful play *A Game At Chess*. Despite its innocuous title, the play was an all-out attack upon all things Spanish through the person of the loathed ambassador Gondomar. After opening on 6 August the play ran for nine days while Londoners flocked across the river and packed the house. Among those who did so was Ben Jonson – eighteen months later in his *Staple of News* he made reference to the play in detail.

Later in the same month of August 1624 came an unusual commission for Jonson. This was the preparation of a country masque like his Entertainment at Althorp twenty-one years earlier for a royal visit to the romantic and famous Kenilworth in Warwickshire. Jonson's *Masque of Owls* was nearer to the former occasion than to a formal masque – a rural welcome to the rising sun, Prince Charles, it is a fascinating little piece of six owls 'in an ivy bush'; these weird creatures are strange tragi-comic creations and the note is one of disillusion rather than celebration. Again Jonson incorporates matters of topical relevance, satirising the 'pure native bird' of the region, the Puritanism of Coventry nearby. In the event this was thought contentious and had to be omitted. Jonson substituted a 'crop-eared scrivener' for the performance, but restored the original for printing. This *Masque of Owls* was to be one of his last unqualified successes in this vein. The year ended with a revival of one of his former triumphs; on 27 December 1624 *Volpone* was played at court.

1625 opened with what had now become the customary wrangle over the Twelfth Night masque. For this occasion Jonson had written *The Fortunate Isles and their Union*, part of which at least was a reworking of the material in the cancelled masque of the previous year, *Neptune's Triumph*. Owing to the usual difficulties over precedence, the Spanish ambassador refusing to countenance the French, the masque was postponed for three nights. As this failed to solve the deadlock, when the show was given on Sunday 9 January only the French and the Venetian ambassadors were present. To English eyes the Spanish star was on the wane, while the prominence of the French ambassador was not without portent to interpreters of the political scene, as the matrimonial game for the hand of the Prince of Wales entered its final phase.

The Fortunate Isles, successfully given with Prince Charles as the chief masquer, had another and unlooked for significance. This was the last masque that Jonson was to write for the court of King James. On 27 March 1625 the old King died in the fifty-seventh year of his life and the twenty-third of his reign. This meant the closing of the theatres as part of the public mourning with the expectation of re-opening after the king's funeral on 7 May. Instead the playhouses were to remain closed all the rest of the year by the worst outbreak of the plague since the year of James's accession, 1603.

These two appalling visitations, ushering in and ushering out the reign of the first monarch to hold sway over both England and Scotland, seemed not coincidental but epochal to his contemporaries. The first of the infected houses was shut up in April. In the week of the funeral in May, plague deaths totalled forty-five and in an echo of

228

James's own accession all shows and pageants to celebrate the entrance of the new King into the city had to be postponed. By the middle of August they had soared to the horrifying figure of nearly four and a half thousand. The distracted country could only wait for the terror to pass over.

For Jonson the implications of the succession were more serious even than the plague. The new King Charles was a keen masquer, as was the little French Queen to whom he hastened to unite himself in the weeks immediately following his father's death. Princess Henrietta Maria of France, although tiny like her husband, was elegant and cultivated, and masquing was to be a prominent feature of the court which they created together. Equally with a young fit king on the throne the monarch could now re-enter the masque in person, as its centre and ornament, in the pattern that Jonson had always treasured.

But Charles had to face the challenge of far more difficult times than ever James had met. In the changing circumstances of the country every action of the court was charged with a new significance, and the masque came to represent far more than the innocent shows of the former King's reign. At almost fifty-three Jonson was an old man now, out of touch with the fresher currents of the age, and in addition one so decisively associated with the departed regime that he was inevitably swept away with it. As the court of the new King escaped from London and wandered around the country to avoid the plague, Charles's retinue of dependants travelled with him. But for Jonson, who according to his detractors had once followed his fellow players at the tail of an old nag, it was too late to take to the road. The royal poet who had served the monarchy for so long now had to pocket up the ignominy of not being called upon for five years.

There must have been some consolation for Jonson in the continued love and support of his 'sons', the young men admitted to the 'tribe of Ben' as his friends and companions.[4] Some rallied around to repair the ravages of Vulcan; in 1624 he received a gift of a historical work of his friend and former Westminster scholar, Edmund Gunter, *The Description and Use of his Majesty's Dials in Whitehall Garden*. Others rewarded him with the fruits of their labours in prose, poetry and the drama; one anecdote records Jonson's boasting 'My son Cartwright writes all like a *Man*' (*JAB* 296). The 'sons', for their part, took enormous pride in this honour. Lucius Cary, Viscount Falkland, called himself Jonson's 'son' or 'servant' in various epistles. Another 'son' makes an endearing comparison of himself in his relation to Jonson with the fox, who only dares to approach the lion when he knows that the king of the beasts will not strike. Now, he wrote,

That which augments my courage with such store,
Is, not I like you less, but know you more.
I thought you proud, for I did surely know
Had I Ben Jonson been, I had been so.

(*JAB* 170–1)

Clearly the old lion encouraged the poetic progeny of his sons.
Herrick invoked Jonson fondly both as a person and a source of
inspiration in 'Robert Herrick – His Prayer to Ben Jonson':

When I a verse shall make
    Know I have prayed thee,
    For old religion's sake,
Saint Ben to aid me.

Make the way smooth for me,
    When I, thy Herrick,
    Honouring thee on my knee,
Offer my lyric.

Candles I'll give to thee,
    And a new altar,
    And thou, Saint Ben, shall be
Writ in my psalter.

Yet affection however dearly valued will not buy bread. Jonson's
'sons' observed his difficulties – Cary described want as 'a quotidian
trouble' to 'Father Ben'. Where was Jonson to turn? Still during
almost the whole of 1625 the plague raged, causing an eight-month
closure of the theatres. Among other old friends and colleagues of
Jonson who died in this outbreak was John Fletcher, who followed his
partner Beaumont to the grave in August of 1625. He was buried at
St Saviour's, the actors' church in Southwark, on 29 August and
Jonson's man Brome wrote an elegy for his passing:

I knew him in his strength; even then, when he
That was the master of his art, and me,
Most knowing Jonson (proud to call him son)
In friendly envy swore, he had out-done
His very self. I knew him till he died.

Ironically, according to Aubrey, Fletcher had been invited into the
country to escape the plague and stayed only to have a new suit made
for the visit – but died before the suit was ready. John Florio, another
acquaintance of Jonson's from years back, also died in the height of
this summer of 1625 of the same disease. Jonson had ranked Fletcher

with Chapman as the only capable masque-maker after himself, and had told Drummond that he loved Fletcher. Fletcher's death was a serious blow.

There were of course various academic projects with which Jonson could concern himself. A certain Caleb Morley, formerly of Balliol College Oxford and subsequently a minister, had devised a scheme for the revision of the alphabet. Its purpose was to provide 'a speedy and certain course for the attaining and retaining of languages, and other parts of good literature purposed for the general ease and benefit of the studies in either kind'. The King himself was solicited for his patronage, Morley requesting a patent granting him sole printing and publishing of his brainchild. Several senior members of Oxford University were interested in Morley's scheme 'for the more easy attaining of languages', and signed an undertaking to further and assist the project. Among these names along with his friends Cotton, Selden and others was that of Jonson. Morley's project, had it come to anything, was honorary and educational in character, not professional or paid employment. Jonson's only regular source of income was the inadequate royal pension, and even that was not, in fact, regular, but erratically paid. In these straits Jonson had no recourse but a return to the trade that he had abandoned nearly ten years before, that of playwright. During that hideous summer as the deathcarts trundled the plague victims in their thousands to the common lime-pits outside the city, Jonson worked on a new comedy for the King's Men. His satirical piece *The Staple of News* was in the repertory when at last the actors were allowed to resume playing in the last week of November 1625.

CHAPTER 14

'THE LOATHED STAGE'

THE 1626 performance of *The Staple of News* broke a ten-year absence of Jonson from the theatre. The play is an interesting mixture of old techniques with new material. Specific topical allusions indicate that he was working on the piece until shortly before its presentation. The coronation of King Charles I had taken place on 2 February 1626; this is mentioned in the Induction, which further sets the play in Shrovetide. *The Staple of News* was given at court, as a special prologue testifies. Those who saw it there may well have recognised extensive borrowings from *Neptune's Triumph*, the cancelled masque of 1624.

Jonson's later plays have been unkindly handled by the critics, who until recently failed to question Dryden's cruel dismissal of them as 'dotages'. Their composition has to be set against a background of ever-increasing distresses for Jonson, physical and mental. Writing in 1631 he later identified the time from 1626 onwards as the onset of his difficulties:

> Disease, the enemy, and his engineers,
> Want, with the rest of his concealed compeers,
> Have cast a trench about me, now, five years.
>
> (*Underwood* 71)

Although not yet disabled by illness Jonson was beginning to feel the first signs of the weakness that darkened his last days and which spelt the end of his reign as 'Father Ben', the high priest of the 'Apollo'. He was himself poignantly aware of the impairment of his faculties and in an autobiographical passage on memory in the *Discoveries* speaks of himself as old:

> Memory, of all the powers of the mind, is the most delicate and frail

... I myself could, in my youth, have repeated all that ever I had made [written]: and so continued till I was past forty. Since, it is much decayed in me.

Yet I can repeat whole books that I have read, and poems of some selected friends which I have liked to charge my memory withal. It was wont to be faithful to me, but shaken with age now, and sloth (which weakens the strongest abilities) it may perform somewhat, but cannot produce much . . . .

Whatsoever I pawned with it when I was young and a boy, it offers me readily, and without stops; but whatever I trust to it now, or have done of later years, it lays up more negligently, and often-times loses . . . (HS VIII, 579)

In addition to bodily infirmity Jonson was struggling against his lifelong enemy, 'want'. These final years have a running theme of acute financial shortage and mismanagement. A petition book of the Lord Chamberlain's office contains this dismal catalogue of proceedings for debt taken out by the following men against him:

Robert Clarke	11 January 1626	£10 5s
Nathanaell Field	10 July 1627	£16
Peter Johnson	15 January 1629	£25
Richard Millward	17 May 1630	£30
Robert Barnes	10 May 1633	£20
Thomas Farnaby	4 December 1634	£120

A financial drain like this, as demonstrated from the amounts Jonson borrowed from these actors and acquaintances, could hardly be staunched by the production of a play or two. But Jonson had no other resort. He was paying the price for living on while other members of the old Jacobean order departed with it; in 1626 his friends and patrons Edward Alleyn, Francis Bacon, and the Earl of Suffolk all died.

So too in 1627 did Lucy, Countess of Bedford, one of the most warm and enlightened of Jonson's patrons. The new year had little to offer Jonson in the way of work or emolument to set against his dwindling resources. Its only records are those of his attempts to carry on his literary life. On 18 May 1627 he noticed the passing of a child, Elizabeth Chute, aged three and a half:

> What beauty would have lovely styled,
> What manners pretty, nature mild,
> What wonder perfect, all were filed
> Upon record, in this blest child.
> And till the coming of the soul
> To fetch the flesh, we keep the roll

> (*Underwood* 35)

Jonson was also in touch during this year with literary contacts old and new. He contributed verses to Drayton's *Battle of Agincourt* in which he reflects ironically upon the nature of the relationship between them:

> It hath been questioned, Michael, if I be
> A friend at all; or if at all, to thee:
> Because who make the question have not seen
> Those ambling visits pass in verse between
> Thy muse and mine, as they expect. 'Tis true;
> You have not writ to me, nor I to you.

Nevertheless, Jonson continues, he will now make amends for his neglect of Drayton, which he proceeds to do in fifty lines of extravagant praise culminating in the triumphant couplet:

> I call the world that envies me to see
> If I can be a friend, and friend to thee.[1]

Of a more formal and conventional nature was another verse epistle of the same year, Jonson's tribute to 'my chosen friend, the learned translator of Lucan, Thomas May' on the publication of his translation of Lucan's *Pharsalia* (1627). May, a classicist and prosodist, had also translated Jonson's favourites Martial and Virgil.

In the early summer of 1627 the theatre lost another veteran playwright in Thomas Middleton. After his burial in Newington Butts on 4 July his widow petitioned the city officials for money; like so many writers of the period Middleton died in poverty. Despite a promising start Middleton had had his reversals, most seriously in 1626 when the pageant he had prepared to welcome the new King and Queen was felt to be so hopelessly bad that he was never paid in full. Nor had Middleton ever achieved the position that Jonson had in the world of letters; Jonson himself had damned him with the observation that he 'was not of the faithful, Poets', and dismissed him as 'a base fellow'.[2]

Middleton's death then did not mean for Jonson the loss of a friend, like that of Sir John Radcliffe at the end of October 1627. Radcliffe fell in action against the French, nearly thirty years after Jonson had lamented the death of his sister Margaret in 1599. Radcliffe, then the only survivor of his house, had befriended Jonson and given him books. He perished as he had lived, in pursuit of that profession which Jonson never ceased to find a true avenue to nobility.

What Middleton's death meant for Jonson was a chance to alleviate his money difficulties. Middleton had held the position of Chronologer to the City of London, a pensioned post whose holder was required 'to collect and set down all memorable acts of this city and occurrences thereof' and to be ready 'for such other employments as this Court of Aldermen shall have occasion to use him in' – the preparation of city entertainments and the like. Jonson had scorned Anthony Munday many years earlier for being a 'pageant-poet'. But now he needed whatever occupation he could get. In the following year on 2 September 1628 he was appointed to the position of City Chronologer in the place of Middleton at a remuneration of one hundred nobles a year (that is, thirty-three pounds, six shillings and eightpence). Jonson did not however accept this as the end of his financial worries – he was also, at this point, engaged in the composition of the play that was to become *The New Inn*, while he awaited his first duties in writing entertainments. Yet Jonson had reached the stage of his life where he was more often employed in writing epitaphs than celebrations. On 18 March 1628 Sir Henry Goodyere died, an intimate of John Donne and friend of Jonson from the Inns of Court circle of young wits nearly thirty years earlier. In June Jonson was engaged in writing a final tribute to Henry West, 'the brave young Lord La Warr', who although only twenty-five had died on the first of that month of a disease that 'crept like darkness through his blood' (*Underwood* 60).

More cataclysmic than these losses was the death at the end of August 1628 of the Duke of Buckingham. This mighty creature who had openly ruled the country's new ruler now that the old king had died was assassinated by a fanatic as economic and political discontents gathered to a head. As in the fraught days under Elizabeth the government had to be on its guard against rising disaffection. Protests, rumours, pamphlets and documents were circulating, in one of which Jonson, never far from trouble even at this age, was implicated. The document in question was a set of scurrilous verses addressed by the anonymous author to Buckingham's assassin Felton (HS I, 243–4). The text hails Felton's act, praises his 'valiant blood', and calls the murder 'a miracle and glory'. It was obviously written soon after the event since it urged Felton bravely to withstand the rack and the 'sharpest mischiefs' of interrogation, whereas in fact, contrary to the express wish of the outraged King, the lawyers in charge of the case had refused to countenance the use of torture, Felton being clearly quite deranged. This provocative poem openly gloried in Buckingham's death, fanning the flames of dissension from royal policy.

Jonson was one of those examined in connection with this document. He was called before the Attorney General on 26 October 1628 and asked to make a statement. Jonson had come across the verses at the house of Sir Robert Cotton at Westminster, his friend of many years' standing, where he was a frequent visitor. The Cotton circle assumed that Jonson was the author, which gives an interesting sidelight on his private views. This suspicion however lightly formed was enough to bring Jonson with his history to the attention of the authorities once again. At the enquiry Jonson utterly denied having any hand in these verses eulogising an assassin. As the official record had it, 'this examinant read them, and condemned them, and with deep protestations affirmed they were not made by him, nor did he know who made them, or had ever seen or heard them before'. His only acquaintance with the verses had been when 'coming in to Sir Robert Cotton's house as he often doth, the paper of these verses lying there upon the table after dinner', he was asked concerning them 'as if himself had been the author thereof'. Jonson denied this 'on his Christianity and his hope of salvation'.

Jonson's concern to co-operate with the Attorney General Sir Robert Heath is clear from his determination to volunteer all that he knew. When questioned as to the author he said that he had heard 'by common fame', that the author was Zouch Townley, 'a scholar and a divine' and 'student of Christchurch, Oxford'. Townley was known to Jonson, who on the Sunday following the incident at Cotton's, had heard him preach at St Margaret's Church by the Houses of Parliament in Westminster. Some friendly exchanges had passed between the two men – Townley had admired 'a dagger with a white haft which [Jonson] ordinarily wore at his girdle'. The old poet had made Townley a present of it two nights later when Townley had invited him to supper to confirm the friendship. But nothing of any 'relation to these or any other verses' had passed between them (*JAB* 140).

In the event it became clear that Jonson was innocent of any taint of sedition. He was discharged without further action. But a more serious blow was in store. At the end of 1628 Jonson suffered the paralytic stroke from which he was never fully to recover. In October he had been able to attend the Attorney General when required, and he related there his habit of visiting Sir Robert Cotton 'often'. But once 'strucken with the palsy' Jonson was henceforward bedridden, condemned to endure the frustration of a still-active mind in a recalcitrant and disordered body. Jonson had systematically abused his frame with heavy drinking and the kind of eating that converts a lanky youth into a twenty-stone man. Nature now took her revenge. From this time Jonson was no longer a man about the town he so loved, but 'walled in' his chamber, to make what he could of the remainder of his life.

It is not clear who undertook the considerable task of caring for the mammoth bulk as it wasted slowly over these last years. Jonson's long-serving man Brome was no longer with him. The apprentice had completed his indentures. Under Jonson's tutelage Brome had become a dramatist in his own right. In 1628 Brome's name appeared in the list

236

of the Queen of Bohemia's players, while early in 1629 his play *The Lovesick Maid* was licensed by the Lord Chamberlain for public performance. In the same year Brome also wrote *The Northern Lass* for the King's Men. Against this picture of busy activity in the theatre it is clear that Brome's connection with his old master had terminated.

What is known is the place of Jonson's residence, the first indication of where he was living since 1620. At his examination by the Attorney General, he is described as 'of Westminster, gent'. For the last act of his life, Jonson had removed from London to the Westminster of his youth, completing the circle begun so long before in Hartshorn Lane. Aubrey later named the house as that 'under which you pass as you go out of the churchyard into the old palace'. A diligent antiquarian tracked down the house itself from this description:

> It stood between St Margaret's church and Henry VII's chapel, and was formerly known as the Talbot. It consisted of four rooms on the ground, first and second floors, with garrets over them . . . one of the rooms on the first floor is particularly described in a deed of sale of 1650 as being 'over the passage that leading from the old Palace into the Churchyard'. The house belonged to the Dean and Chapter [of Westminster Abbey], and at the time that Jonson lived there the tenant was Sir Richard Manley. . . . It appears however to have been sub-let to a nameless old lady with whom Jonson boarded.[3]

Gossip and anecdote have supported the probability that it was a woman rather than a man who cared for Jonson in his age and decay. George Morley, when Bishop of Winchester, told Izaak Walton that he often visited Jonson 'in that time of his long retirement and sickness' at his lodgings near Westminster Abbey, where his pensions and whatever money came in were given to 'a woman that governed him, with whom he lived and died'. However, 'neither he nor she took much care for next week, and would be sure not to want wine; of which he usually took too much before he went to bed, if not oftener and sooner'. Even in his youth Jonson had dreaded age, as the epitaph on his son makes clear. Now its full miseries were come upon him and if he did drink too much, it may have been for the anodyne effects; Morley claims often to have found him 'much afflicted that he had profaned the scriptures in his plays; [he] lamented it with horror'.[4]

Jonson was not, however, entirely forgotten. On 19 January of the new year of 1629 there is an entry in the records of the Treasurer of Westminster Abbey: 'Given by Dr Price to Mr Benjamin Jonson in his sickness and want . . . £5'. This award was made to Jonson by the

Dean and Chapter of the great cathedral with the full consent of other Westminster worthies like the Master of Westminster School. The money was made available to Jonson at the end of February of that year. Price was Sub-Dean of the Abbey; the Dean, Bishop Williams, 'my Lord of Lincoln', who lent his 'good liking' to the project, has been identified as the subject of the poem of commiseration, 'An Epigram' (*Underwood* 61).

Such assistance however well meant could only be a temporary respite. The note of illness and poverty sounded at the beginning of this year is heard more insistently as time wore on. About this time too the murmuring attacks upon Jonson's reputation increased as he was no longer actively able to defend himself. He had never been entirely free of the charge of plagiarism from those unable to grasp the purpose of his re-working of the classics. Now the moths of detraction were nibbling again. Thomas May, who had had nothing but courtesy at Jonson's hands, made in a verse epistle to his friend John Ford a disparaging reference to 'that plunderer, Ben'. Happily Jonson is unlikely to have seen this particular sneer.

1629 had in any case a far worse disappointment in store for Jonson. He decided to follow up *The Staple of News* with another play for the stage. On 19 January the Master of the Revels licensed a new Jonson comedy for performance, *The New Inn*, or, *The Light Heart*. The subtitle proved to be particularly ironic in view of the play's reception – when it was put on at the Blackfriars it was hissed off the stage before the actors got as far as the epilogue. A second epilogue had been prepared for a projected court performance the following night. But in view of the play's disastrous failure in the public try-out, it had to be cancelled. Jonson was bitterly disappointed. As the title page to the subsequent edition makes clear, he laid the blame equally upon the actors and the spectators:

> The New Inn. A Comedy. As it was never acted, but most negligently played by some, the King's Servants. And more squeamishly beheld, and censured by others, the King's subjects. Now at last set at liberty to the readers . . . to be judged.

Others in contrast laid the blame cruelly and unequivocally on the playwright's failing faculties:

> Poets, who others can immortal make,
> When they grow old, their laurels them forsake,
> And seek young temples where they may grow green;
> No palsy-hands may wash in Hippocrene.
> 'Twas not tierce claret, eggs and muscadine,
> Nor goblets crowned with Greek and Spanish wine
> Could make new flames in old Ben Jonson's veins,

For his attempts proved lank and languid strains.
His New Inn, so he named his youngest play,
Proved a blind ale-house, cried down the first day:
His own dull epitaph – 'here lies Ben Jonson'
Half drunken too, he hiccuped 'Who was once one'.

(HS IX, 252)

To compound Jonson's sense of injury as he lay paralysed and isolated in his chamber, within a month his former manservant Brome scored an outstanding theatrical success. On 9 February 1629 Brome's *The Lovesick Maid* was licensed, immediately to be played to extraordinary applause by the King's Men at the Blackfriars where Jonson had just so humiliatingly failed. *The Lovesick Maid* indeed proved to be such a winner for the King's Men that their managers presented the Master of the Revels with £2 by way of gratuity, the only instance of such an unaccustomed act of benevolence.

Comparisons were in any case inevitable. Brome's success could not but be coupled with his old master's ill-fortune at the same theatre only a few weeks previously. But Jonson, lashing out wildly in his rage and disappointment, brought the whole thing to a head. From his chamber he wrote and disseminated an injudicious piece in which he reviled the contemporary audience under cover of a stern and final injunction to himself:

Come, leave the loathed stage,
And the more loathsome age:
    Where pride and impudence, in faction knit
    Usurp the chair of wit:
Indicting and arraigning every day
Something they call a play.

The poem went on to attack the popular literary taste in fuller detail, a theme not unfamiliar in Jonson. Where the 'Ode to Himself' departed from Jonson's previously expressed opinions (and also from the bounds of taste and sense) was in including a violent attack upon Brome in vicious personal terms:

No doubt some mouldy tale
Like *Pericles*, and stale
    As the shrieve's crusts, and nasty as his fish,
    Scraps out of every dish,
Thrown forth and raked into the common tub
May keep up the play club:
Brome's sweepings do as well
There, as his master's meal,
    For who the relish of these guests will fit
Needs set them but the almsbasket of wit.

(*Songs and Poems* 14)

239

Jonson contrived here not only to throw his 'man's' domestic servitude in his teeth but also to imply that Brome had picked his brains and that he, Jonson, was the real source both of Brome's inspiration and his success. Many rose to Brome's defence as the poem, circulated in manuscript, provoked a minor storm. Some commentators came out wholeheartedly on Jonson's side. Thomas Randolph wrote a reply to Jonson whose main purpose was to persuade him not to leave the stage. He accepted that 'what Brome swept' from his old master proved more acceptable to the multitude than any of Jonson's offerings, but urged him to moderate his 'great spleen'. It is, he argued, pointless to be angry

> cause moles have no eyes;
> This only in my Ben I faulty find,
> He's angry, they'll not see him that are blind.
>
> (*JAB* 144)

Randolph's conclusion commiserated with Jonson on his physical palsy, declaring that it had not affected the writer's brain.

Others felt that the truth however unpalatable had to be faced. Thomas Carew, writing to Jonson 'upon occasion of his Ode of Defiance annexed to his play of the New Inn', stated what many opinions have since confirmed:

> and yet 'tis true
> Thy comic muse from the exalted line
> Touch'd by thy *Alchemist* doth since decline
> From that her zenith, and foretells a red
> And blushing evening, when she goes to bed;
> Yet such as shall outshine the glimmering light
> With which all stars shall gild the following night.

In this mingled tone of admiration and reproof, Carew concluded by urging Jonson to avoid the expression of 'immodest rage' which seemed 'to blast thy else-immortal bays'. He had to school himself to ignore 'the detracting world and its malice', and 'trust . . . to afterdays', when his 'laboured works shall live', and time will have devoured 'the abortive offspring of [his] hasty hours' (*JAB* 147–8). But much comment was not so supportive. The anonymous author of 'the country's censure on Ben Jonson's *New Inn*' began with a cruelly trenchant direct address:

> Listen (decaying Ben) and counsel hear.
> Wits have their date, and strength of brains may wear.
> Age, steeped in sack, hath quenched thy Enthean fire;
> We pity now, whom once we did admire.

240

Jonson is ordered to surrender his 'right to the stage'. He must give up daring to write 'what others loathe to hear'. He is attacked for his 'crazy muse' and advised 'rail not at the actors; do not them abuse'; actors cannot, after all, infuse life into dullness by sheer force. Clearly Jonson's bold attack and his insistence that the fault lay with the audience had caused enormous irritation. This censurer concluded:

> Thy worth doth fail, thy arrogance increaseth,
> Pride and presumption hath dethroned thy wit.

The polemic ends with a final jibe at the 'poor crackbrain' poet, and the advice to give up writing in favour of keeping an inn himself (*JAB* 149).

But with or without the benefit of these intrusions Jonson had thought better of his action. In the subsequently published version of the poem he deleted the personal allusions. However hurt either he or Brome had been, the estrangement did not last. After the 1631 edition of the 'Ode' was published in the revised form, Jonson contributed commendatory verses to the 1632 quarto of *The Northern Lass*. The title of the piece alone breathes his desire to make amends: 'To my old faithful servant: and (by his continued virtue) my loving friend: the author of this work, Mr. Rich. Brome'.

Only one positive good came out of all this. Jonson had taken advantage of the epilogue to *The New Inn* to draw attention to his sickness and want. Hoping that his inventions had not 'miscarried', he went on:

> if they have,
> All that his faint and faltering tongue doth crave
> Is, that you not impute it to his brain.
> That's yet unhurt, although set round with pain,
> It cannot long hold out . . .
> This did he [the poet] think; and this do you forgive:
> When e'er the carcass dies, this art will live.
> And had he lived the care of King, and Queen,
> His art in something more yet had been seen . . . .

The reproach implied in the closing couplet of this section struck home. The King had been neglecting the royal poet, who had not been neglecting him – Jonson had contributed a long congratulatory epigram to 'great and good King Charles' on the anniversary of his accession on 27 March 1629 (*Underwood* 64). The King responded with the generous gift of £100 for which Jonson thanked him with a grateful epigram (*Underwood* 62). Shortly afterwards the poet laureate performed a sadder task with an 'epigram consolatory' to the young royal couple on the loss of their first-born son. The baby, baptised

Charles James, was born prematurely and lived for only a few hours. Jonson's poem is a sombre reflection on the theme of 'the Lord gave and the Lord hath taken away' from the Order for the Burial of the Dead (*Underwood* 63).

Whatever else failed for Jonson during these years he kept up his life-long habit of responding in verse to the appropriate occasion. For the death of Katherine Lady Ogle, mother of his patron the Duke of Newcastle on 18 April 1629, Jonson produced an elaborate requiem heavy with classicism and metrical variation as a display of the poet's technical virtuosity (*Ungathered Verse* 31). More highly wrought still was the elegy which he wrote on the death of the young Sir Henry Morison in the summer of 1629. This poem, 'to the immortal memory and friendship' of Morison and Jonson's 'son' Lucius Cary Viscount Falkland, was the first sustained attempt in English to imitate the Pindaric ode. Nothing more vividly illustrates the force of Jonson's chosen motto, 'tanquam explorator', than his undertaking this complex experimental feat so late in his career. Despite its intricacy this poem contains some of Jonson's most eloquent moments as he strives to persuade Cary that Morison's life, although so short, was perfect:

> It is not growing like a tree
> In bulk, doth make man better be;
> Or standing long an oak, three hundred year
> To fall a log at last, dry, bald and sere:
>   A lily of a day
>   Is fairer far in May,
> Although it fall and die that night;
> It was the plant and flower of light.
> In small proportions we just beauty see,
> And in short measure life may perfect be.
>
> Call, noble Lucius, then for wine,
> And let thy looks with gladness shine;
> Accept this garland, plant it on thy head;
> And think, nay know, thy Morison's not dead.
>   He leaped the present age,
>   Possessed with holy rage
> To see that bright eternal day,
> Of which we priests and poets say
> Such truths as we expect for happy men . . .
>   (*Underwood* 70)

There is no sign here of the failure of Jonson's faculties so harped upon by malicious spirits. And although Jonson's reputation had been blown upon by some, to others he still retained his unquestioned position at the head of English letters. In January 1629 one Joseph Webb wrote to him as his 'dear and loving friend', hailing him as 'the eldest son of our Britain's muses'. Webb's purpose was to ask Jonson's opinion of his book *Entheatus Materialis*, on the metrical principles of versification, which had been somewhat roughly handled by the contemporary critics. It is obvious from the tone of the letter that Webb expected immediate attention and warm support from Jonson, although at the current state of his own fortunes Jonson may not have felt able to supply it. His reply if he ever made one has not survived.

In these painful times Jonson's friends must have been very important to him, and although many of the older generation had now died Jonson always had the gift of making new ones. It was from 1629 onwards that Jonson was able to develop a friendship which was to be of particular significance to posterity, that of Sir Kenelm Digby his literary executor. Digby and Jonson had been acquainted at the time of the proposed Academy Royal in 1620 when both their names had been among the suggested members, but the two men were not then close. Jonson had been an established figure on the London literary scene when Digby was born in 1603 and thereafter the young man had been, in the manner of the time, brought up via Oxford University and the Grand Tour. This, with other voyages and adventures, meant that he was only intermittently in London during these years. But on 2 February 1629 Digby returned to England for an uninterrupted period of six years, most of which he spent in the capital. Jonson came to have a high regard for Digby's qualities both of mind and character:

> Though, happy muse, thou know my Digby well,
> Yet read him in these lines; he doth excel
> In honour, courtesy, and all the parts
> Court can call hers, or man could call his arts.
> He's prudent, valiant, just, and temperate . . . .
>
> (*Underwood* 78)

The 'muse' of these lines is Digby's wife, whom Jonson soon came to value enough to dignify with this appellation, and clearly the affection and respect of the brilliant, beautiful and unusual Venetia Digby was one of the chief comforts of Jonson's life at this time.

Despite the thirty-year age gap and the difference in rank, Jonson and Digby had much in common. Digby was a man of wide-ranging intellectual sympathies and, like Jonson's earlier friend Sir John Roe, extensively travelled. A proper balance between action and reflection in a man's life always appealed to Jonson and he took pride in Digby's success in action against the enemy, including the famous naval victory of Scanderoon. Further, Digby underwent the same spiritual pilgrimage as Jonson although in the reverse direction. Brought up as a Catholic, Digby was in 1629 suffering the crisis of faith that resulted in his conversion to Anglicanism in the next year. But like Jonson again he was later to revert to the religion of his father, when he reconverted to Catholicism on leaving England for France in 1635.

Jonson's friendship with Digby brought him a most valuable contact with the powerful Richard Weston, Earl of Portland and Lord High Treasurer of England. Although intensely disliked by some as a man of mean and limited spirit, Weston was a good angel to Jonson and became one of the old poet's most important patrons in his declining years. What pleased Jonson was not merely the provision of financial support but the genuine interest which this busy and highly-placed lord took in his poems. As Jonson wrote to Venetia Digby:

> Oh, what a fame 'twill be!
> What reputation to my lines and me,
> When he [Digby] shall read them at the Treasurer's board
> (The knowing Weston) and that learned lord
> Allows them! Then, what copies shall be had,
> What transcripts begged; how cried up . . .
>
> *(Underwood* 78)

Another loyal patron among the nobility remained the Earl of Pembroke. Jonson's fellow-dramatist Massinger, writing upon his own account a verse epistle to Pembroke observed:

> I know
> That Jonson much of what he hath does owe
> To you and to your family, and is never slow
> To profess it . . .
>
> *(JAB* 194–5)

Surviving patrons became the more precious as others died – 1629 also saw the passing of Susan Countess of Montgomery whose interest dated from Jonson's early days at court. Meanwhile the 'sons of Ben' had not all deserted their 'father' even though he could no longer come among them to exert his sway. The sweet-natured Cary remained faithful and generous to the old lion as the future Earl of Clarendon observed as a young man:

> He [Cary] seemed to have all his estate in trust for all worthy persons who stood in want of supplies and encouragement, as Ben Jonson . . .[5]

Similarly Thomas Randolph in his 'Gratulatory to Mr Ben Jonson for his adopting of him to be his son' written after Jonson's stroke expresses both his pride in the honour and a tender concern for his 'father's' disability:

> . . . I will boast
> No farther than my father; that's the most
> I can, or should, be proud of . . .
> . . . I entreat
> Phoebus to lend thee some of his own heat
> To cure thy palsy . . .[6]

But there was to be no improvement in Jonson's condition. His paralysis and the consequent confinement to his chamber prevented him from enjoying the great theatrical scandal of 1629. In the autumn of that year a troupe of French actors paid a visit to London, causing a sensation by giving Londoners their first chance ever to see women perform upon a public stage. The reaction was tremendous. The Puritan William Prynne wrote:

> Some French women, or monsters rather, in Michaelmas term 1629, attempted to act a French play at the playhouse in Black-friars; an impudent, shameful, unwomanish, graceless, if not more than whorish attempt, to which there was a great resort.[7]

The numbers of people thronging to view this extraordinary spectacle caused severe problems of congestion around the Blackfriars. But not for long. The English audiences were quick to express their disapproval of such filthy foreign innovations: the actresses were 'hissed, hooted and pippen-pelted from the stage'. Jonson would have loved it.

With all the difficulties of 1629 Jonson received early in 1630 welcome evidence of the continuance of royal favour. King Charles never enjoyed 'his poet' as much as his father had, but he was too discriminating a man to pass him over altogether. Doubtless encouraged by Charles' gift of money after *The New Inn* came out, Jonson made a whimsical but determined effort to jog the royal elbow once again. He composed a 'Humble Petition of Poor Ben, to the Best of Monarchs, Masters, Men, King Charles':

> That whereas your royal father,
> James the blessed, pleased the rather,
> Of his special grace to letters,
> To make all the muses debtors
> To his bounty; by extension
> Of a free poetic pension
> A large hundred marks' annuity

> To be given me in gratuity
> For done service, and to come:
> And that this so accepted sum
> Or dispensed in books, or bread
> (For with both the muse was fed) . . .
> Please your Majesty to make
> Of your grace, for goodness' sake,
> Those your father's marks, your pounds . . .
>
>   (*Underwood* 76)

Strangely, this ambling piece of doggerel struck home. Charles gave order that Jonson's pension should be raised from one hundred marks (£66.13s.4d.) to one hundred pounds, 'in consideration of the good and acceptable service done to us and to our said father'.

What would have been just as well appreciated as the raising of the pension by a third was the granting in addition of an annual cask of Canary wine to Jonson from the King's Cellar at the Palace of Whitehall. The accompanying document declared that the grant of these favours was 'especially to encourage him to proceed in those services of his wit and pen, which we have enjoined unto him, and which we expect from him'. The Treasurer's deed formally conveying these grants is dated 26 March 1630 and was signed by the King on 13 April of that year. These tokens of favour to the aged laureate were gracious and well-meant. They would have been even better had Jonson been able to rely upon obtaining them with any regularity. By Christmas of 1630 he had still not received his voucher for payment from the Exchequer and had to resort to blandishing verses to the clerk to try to hurry things along (*Underwood* 57). Matters were even more strained over the wine. The Royal Household at first refused to supply the Canary as directed and had to be versified into compliance:

> What can the cause be, when the King hath given
> His poet sack, the household will not pay?
> . . . the old bard should no Canary lack.
> 'Twere better spare a butt than spill his muse.
>   For in the genius of a poet's verse
>   The King's fame lives. Go now, deny his tierce![8]

Jonson was back then in royal favour and grateful to receive it. During the next month he was able to express his thanks with a complimentary epigram to the King on the safe arrival of a son and heir on 29 May 1630. This baby, the future Charles II, was born only a year after the Queen's first premature son had died. Because of this the pregnancy had been fraught with anxiety, but the birth was well-auspicated, with a bright star shining all day long. Jonson greeted the event with an ecstatic piece, 'And art thou born, brave babe?', which he followed with an equally joyous tribute to the Queen (*Underwood* 65 and 66). Later in the year on 16 November 1630 Jonson heralded Henrietta Maria's birthday in an elaborate ode, dwelling on the little king's love for her and their mutual joy of their child. In amply fulfilling his duties as the court poet, however, he was moving away from the wider realities of the situation. Henrietta Maria's unpopularity, and her husband's reliance upon her wrong-headed advice, were key factors in the progressive estrangement of King Charles from his people.

The arrival of the young prince was the only hopeful moment of the first half of 1630. Once again London was threatened with that regular visitant whose reappearance with the warmer weather every year menaced life and work. Plague deaths early in 1630 reached that weekly total at which all dramatic performances were banned and the theatres then had to be closed for seven months. Had not Jonson's débâcle with *The New Inn* precluded any thoughts of a new play, external events ruled it out.

Despite all his difficulties and the disarray which the plague brought with it in the London outside his chamber prison, Jonson struggled on with his 'wonted studies'. From this period comes a late letter to Cotton, Jonson's friend for so many years now:

Sir,
    as seriously as a man but faintly returning to his despaired health can, I salute you. And by these few lines request you that you would by this bearer lend me some book that would determinately satisfy me . . .
Good sir, add this to the many other courtesies you have done me that though I chance to survive now, I may hereafter die more in your debt.

The book shall be returned this night without excuse,

Your infirm
Ben now.
(HS I, 215)

The last sentence sounds like a precaution observed since the loss in Jonson's fire of 1623 of Cotton's historical books and material which happened to be with him at the time.

Yet certain of Jonson's plays remained perennially popular. On 19 November 1630 the King's Men gave a performance of *Volpone* at court in the Cockpit, the new theatre at Whitehall, three days after the Queen's birthday.[9] And as the year drew on Jonson had the satisfaction once again after a gap of six years of receiving the royal commission for the preparation of the Christmas masque – the first time for Jonson since Charles came to the throne. As 1631 dawned the court was occupied with the rehearsals for Jonson's *Love's Triumph Through Callipolis*. This was the King's Twelfth Night masque which he performed on Sunday 9 January with his lords and gentlemen assisting, as a tribute to his Queen. The novelty and success of this device bred another commission for Jonson as the Queen immediately decided to return the compliment. For the Queen therefore he wrote *Chloridia*, which the Queen and her ladies offered in their turn at Shrovetide, Tuesday 22 February. This was the first time that a queen had danced in a Jonson masque for twenty years, since Queen Anne appeared in *Love Freed from Ignorance and Folly*.

Queen Henrietta Maria was determined that *Chloridia* should not lag behind *Love's Triumph Through Callipolis*. From the beginning of February letters flew from the court announcing the preparations. It was the subject of daily rehearsals and the usual drain on the Exchequer; a warrant for £600 towards the Queen's masque on 14 February was followed on 19 February by one for a further £200. These two masques were of particular significance for Jonson. At last he had reversed his decline from court favour as a masque-maker. There had been two court masques in 1626, two in 1627, and two commissioned, though not performed, in 1628. For none of these had Jonson been employed. The court had seen nothing of his work in the masque since *Neptune's Triumph* in 1625.

But when the chance came at last Jonson was unable to capitalise upon it. Charles's court and his kingship were very different from his father's, evolving along lines which removed them from ordinary concerns and lost them their contact with the people. Where Jonson had developed for King James the comic anti-masque as a device for commenting upon and setting off the high seriousness of the masque proper, Charles was interested only in a perfectly formed and fastidiously executed ritual. The masque to him was a courtly game. Under him it became a counter-world where the difficulties and dangers of real experience were dissolved in a vision of harmony. Inevitably this development placed stress upon the 'body' or show of the masque rather than (in Jonson's word) on its 'soul'. Increasing prominence was given to the spectacular, so that where Jonson had previosly written anti-masque as well as masque (the former being one of James's chief pleasures) now, for *Love's Triumph Through Callipolis*, the anti-masque was provided by Inigo Jones.

For Jonson these developments undermined all that he had felt and believed about the masque. He had seen it as an instrument of education through which the poet could speak directly to his monarch, instructing both prince and people in ideals of virtue and good government. Charles indeed conceived of this traditional formula in reverse. The masque under him became no longer an offering of the people *to* royalty but an offering of itself *by* royalty, in its self-determined form. With his characteristic acuity Jonson perceived this shift, describing masques as 'the donatives of great princes to their peoples' in *Love's Triumph Through Callipolis* (lines 5–6). But to recognise a trend is not necessarily to be able to work within it. The Caroline masque was turning into a very different creature from its Jacobean parent and one not comfortable to Jonson's handling. *Chloridia*, the second of this related pair, was Jonson's last masque at court.

There were problems of a personal nature too. The added emphasis upon the spectacular inevitably brought Inigo Jones more to the fore, and Jonson could not tolerate the growth in importance of his former collaborator's role. To Jonson the erstwhile assistant had stepped unwelcomed into a partnership. Jones, for his part, was no longer content to play second fiddle. The smouldering disagreement between the two men flared up when Jones took exception to his name appearing after Jonson's on the title-page of *Love's Triumph Through Callipolis*, where the two men appeared as 'the Inventors, Ben Jonson, Inigo Jones'. What was a concession by Jonson was an insult to Jones.

Jonson responded to what he regarded as Jones's unwarranted presumption in a familiar way. He saw to it that Jones's name was entirely absent from the title-page of the Queen's masque, *Chloridia*, and denied any other resource he assailed Jones with a series of satirical poems. Like the attack on Brome these paper bullets of the brain were designed to hurt. There were three of them all told composed in the late spring and early summer of 1631, each of which contrived to insult Jones in a different way.

The most comprehensive is the 'Expostulation with Inigo Jones' (*Ungathered Verse* 34), where Jonson devoted one hundred and four lines to castigating his subject. He satirised in turn Jones's humble origins, his mathematical and architectural pretensions, his defective classical knowledge, and his social aspirations. Jones is stigmatised as 'tireman, mountebank and justice' (the last reference a sneer at the fact that Jones was a J.P. for Westminster). Jonson even found room for a jibe about the size of Jones's ears. Essentially, though, the poem attacks the pre-eminence of 'shows . . . mighty shows', over 'prose', 'verse', and even 'sense'. Its bitter conclusion is that 'painting and carpentry are the soul of masque' since 'this is the money-get, mechanic age'. Jonson's final thrust is at what he sees as Jones's base nature; the designer is a fraud on every level, and nothing could ever make him 'an honest man'.

The second of Jonson's satirical squibs (*Ungathered Verse* 35) centred on Jones's presumed social ambitions. Jonson hailed him as 'Inigo, Marquis Would-Be' and then proceeded to do his best to sabotage any such happy occurrence as ennoblement for the architect and designer. This piece resolved itself into an onslaught on the quality of Jones's work. Jonson harped on the triviality of Jones's productions, and styled him derisively 'the Marquis of New Ditch'. Finally Jonson wrote an epigram adapted from Martial in which he expressed surprise that Jones should think that Jonson would ever attack him or satirise his actions:

> Sir Inigo doth fear it, as I hear . . .
> That I should write upon him some sharp verse
> Able to eat into his bones and pierce
> The marrow . . .
>
> (*Ungathered Verse* 36)

Grandly Jonson dismissed this fear as mere pretension – would he, the great satirist, stoop so low? Jones, he claimed, was beneath his notice.

In this way Jonson appears to have worked his way through his resentment of Jones. But as with Jonson's earlier attack upon Brome there were many who deeply deprecated this outburst. Jonson showed himself to great disadvantage in this exchange and came off the loser. Jones's was a far stronger position at court than Jonson's and effectively Jonson's action cost him the good favour that he had only so recently won. One friend at least attempted to represent to the old boar the danger of fleshing his fangs. His 'son' James Howell wrote 'to my honoured friend and father, Mr Ben Jonson':

> Father Ben . . . I heard you censured lately at court, that you have lighted too foul upon Sir Inigo, and that you write with a porcupine's quill dipped in too much gall. Excuse me that I am so free with you; it is because I am in no common way of friendship, yours.
> (*JAB* 190)

The uncommon quality of Howell's regard is to be seen in his again bravely returning to this unwelcome topic in a longer letter:

> F.B. [Father Ben],
> The fangs of the bear, and the tusks of the wild boar, do not bite worse, and make deeper gashes sometimes; no, not the badger himself, who is said to be so tenacious of his bite that he will not give over his hold till he feel his teeth meet and the bone crack; your quill hath proved so to Mr In. J. . . . I know you have a commanding [pen] but you must not let it tyrannise in that manner. Some give out that . . . your ink was too thick with gall, else it could not have so bespattered and shaken the reputation of a royal architect . . . if

your spirit will not let you retract, yet you shall do well to repress any more copies of this satire; for to deal plainly with you, you have lost some ground at court by it; and as I hear from a good hand, the king, who hath so great a judgement in poetry (as in all other things) is not well pleased therewith. Dispense with this freedom of

Your respectful son and servitor,

J.H.

(*JAB* 190-1)

Howell's fears were prophetic. Jonson's self-indulgence in venting his ire cost him the chance of any further work at court. He was never again asked to prepare a masque for the royal family. From this time forward Jones reigned alone. Although Jonson was still occasionally commissioned by old friends who offered him the writing of country entertainments from time to time, his twenty-seven-year career as the royal masque-maker was over. He was compulsorily retired – put out to grass. Nothing could have suited his active temperament less.

CHAPTER 15

SENEX

JONSON was now without his two principal sources of income, playwriting and masque-making. 1631 had brought his troubles to a head and there were more to come. Despite the limited nature of the duties of the City Chronologer he had not fulfilled them and towards the end of the year his payment was withheld by the disgruntled City Fathers. By a decree of 10 November 1631 the Governing Body gave orders that 'Mr Chamberlain shall forbear to pay any more fee or wages unto Benjamin Jonson the City's Chronologer until he shall have presented unto this court some fruits of his labours' (*JAB* 167).

This action struck Jonson hard since the city's pension was one of only two regular sources of income that he had. Even before it took effect Jonson was in distress. In 1631 he wrote to the Lord Treasurer Weston the moving 'Epistle Mendicant'; the worst, he said, was that his muse was failing him and like the poet himself 'lies blocked up and straitened, narrowed in / Fixed to the bed and boards . . . as she had never been'. The outcome of this appeal is not known. Weston generally seems to have behaved better to Jonson than his public reputation for notorious tight-fistedness would allow.

But relief if any on this occasion was short-lived. At the very end of 1631 'in the week ushering Christmas' Jonson made another appeal for money, again as dignified as it was desperate. This was to another regular patron, the Duke of Newcastle, a genuine admirer of Jonson and one who had been in touch with him throughout the year. He had written to Newcastle on 4 February 1631 a letter which demonstrates the interest that Newcastle took in Jonson's life and work:

My noblest Lord and my patron by excellence – I have here obeyed your commands, and sent you a packet of mine own praises, which

I would not have done had I had any stock of modesty in store. But obedience is better than sacrifice, and you commanded it . . . Your Lordship's devoted Ben Jonson. (HS I, 20)

The 'packet of praises' contained three verse tributes to Jonson from his admirers among whom the Duke was anxious to be enrolled. To soften the effect of his begging letter Jonson cast it in the form of a dream fable which sheds a welcome light on his life at this time.

Recalling that he had been 'strucken with the palsy in the year 1628' Jonson informed Newcastle of a recent present. In the summer of 1631 Jonson had been sent a fox. The donor was Sir Thomas Badger who had been Master of the Royal Harriers since 1605. His acquaintance with Jonson dated back to Jonson's early days at court; Badger had performed in Jonson's *Speeches at Prince Henry's Barriers* in 1610. The unusual gift had delighted Jonson. He found in the fox both recreation and exercise, as he related to Newcastle: the 'creature by handling I endeavoured to make tame, as well for the abating of my disease, as the delight I took in speculation of his nature'.

Jonson's fox became the central character in the fable by which his old master sought to awake the benevolence of the Duke. Jonson described his dream in which he walked down to the yard where he kept the fox. (There is great poignance in this alone as Jonson had been bedridden and unable to walk for three years now.) Here he found the creature lamenting his lot 'to be condemned to the house of a poet, where nothing was to be seen but the bare walls'. Jonson, 'the paralytic master', may be contented with fire but the fox called for meat and warned Jonson that the vermin 'want' was at work in the larder. As Jonson concluded:

The interpretation both of the fable and of the dream, is that I waking do find want the worst and most working vermin in a house; and therefore my noble lord, and next the king my best patron, I am necessitated to tell it you. I am not so impudent to borrow any sum of your lordship, for I have no faculty to pay: but my needs are such, and so urging, as I do beg what your bounty can give me, in the name of good letters and the bond of an ever-grateful and acknowledging servant . . . (HS I, 214)

Jonson wrote this from his lodgings in Westminster on 20 December 1631, anticipating some gratuity at the traditional gift-time New Year's Day. The news of the withdrawal of his City Chronologer's emolument had just reached him following the official decision in November, as he told Newcastle in a bitter postscript: 'Yesterday the barbarous Court of Aldermen have withdrawn their chanderly pension'; even now he could not refrain from despising the aldermen as base tradesmen, 'chandlers'.

There were other irritations and distractions for Jonson too. During 1631 he had been attempting to get *Bartholomew Fair, The Devil Is An Ass*, and *The Staple of News* into print. This was part of a wider design to issue the three plays as part of a second Folio. But what should have been a gratification for Jonson was clouded by worries about his 'lewd printer' Beale, through whose incompetence and carelessness Jonson had to abandon the whole project. The only use made of this printing was to send out gift copies to friends and patrons of the poet. Even here this simple plan was hedged about with difficulties. At one stage he had to write to Newcastle apologising that he was unable to send his patron a full and accurate copy of his book: 'my printer and I', he wrote, 'shall afford subject enough for a tragi-comedy'. Beale had played 'the absolute knave' with him, Jonson complained, 'for with all his delays and vexations I am become almost blind'.

The other publishing event of 1631 for Jonson was the appearance in an octavo edition of *The New Inn*. He took the occasion of this publication to contribute a strongly-worded preface which showed that time had abated but not substantially diminished his sense of injury over the play's original reception; indeed he explicitly revived and attempted to substantiate 'the just indignation the author took at the vulgar censure of this play'. To do this he reverted to a practice he had not employed since 1599 when he published the quarto of *Every Man Out Of His Humour*, printing the text of the drama prefaced by a written characterisation of all the persons in it; he could get his characters across better himself than the actors had succeeded in doing. Jonson also reprinted the violent 'Ode to Himself', deleting only the offensive references to Brome with their unwarranted personal aspersions. This act in itself bears witness to the continuing strength of Jonson's hostile feelings towards his undiscerning audience. It is worth noticing that Jonson's anxiety was not only emotional but intellectual too. He equipped the text with a series of aids to the reader in the form of argument, address, and commentary. Underlying them all is the unflattering assumption that no reader will grasp the play properly by the light of his or her own understanding. Thus weighted with critical-academic apparatus *The New Inn* was released to the world to be 'judged'.

There were still those who continued to render Jonson the respect which he so desired. When Selden published the second edition of his *Titles of Honour* in 1631, he took occasion to compliment Jonson most warmly: ' . . . my beloved Ben Jonson, your curious learning and judgment may correct where I have erred, and add, where my notes and memory have left me short . . . ' Yet Jonson was never free from the sneers of the malicious. One anonymous humorist has glanced at Jonson's relations with Weston and at the Lord Treasurer's generous reception of poetry:

> Your verses were commended, as 'tis true
> That they were very good – I mean to you:
> For they returned you, Ben, I have been told,
> The seld-seen sum of forty pounds in gold.
> These verses then being rightly understood,
> His Lordship, not Ben Jonson, made them good.
>
> (HS XI, 406)

Jonson rose to this bait with a deep rage which soon breaks through the smooth surface of the couplets which seek to contain it:

> My verses were commended, thou dar'st say,
> And they were very good: yet thou think'st nay.
> For thou objectest (as thou hast been told)
> The envied return of forty pounds in gold.
> Fool, do not rate my rhymes: I've found thy vice
> Is to make cheap the lord, the lines, the price.
> But bawl thou on – I pity thee, poor cur . . .
>
> (*Ungathered Verse* 37)

The figure that Jonson presents at this time is of a man beleaguered by disease and decay, by poverty and neglect, by malice and misunderstanding. Sometimes he could take his financial difficulties lightly. He could even make humorous capital out of them, as in *Underwood* 38:

> 'Tis true I'm broke! Vows, oaths, and all I had
> Of credit lost . . .

Strictly speaking Jonson did not so much lose his credit as wear it out. Apart from the debts he contracted which are recorded in the Lord Chamberlain's office, there is an account of what sounds like a typical piece of Jonson business in *Underwood* 54; he wrote to a friend who worked at the Exchequer, 'lend me, dear Arthur, for a week five more [pounds]'. As Jonson was struggling on this hand-to-mouth basis to stay alive, some of his oldest friends died. During the course of 1631 Jonson lost Sir Robert Cotton and John Donne. Donne was Jonson's age, Cotton younger, and he could remember both men in their happiest hours. Another member of the old world of letters who died in 1631 was Michael Drayton. He and Jonson had not been close, and at almost seventy Drayton had had a good long life. But Jonson was enduring to see all the threads of the fabric of his life being severed one by one. It is interesting that Jonson noticed none of these deaths with an epitaph. He did, however, compose a long elegy on the death in pregnancy on 15 April 1631 of Lady Jane Paulet, Marchioness of Winchester (*Underwood* 83). This young woman was only 24, and was known to Jonson through her two sisters, who were both masquers in Jonson's *Chloridia* only two months earlier.

As Jonson lived on he became increasingly a legend-encrusted figure in his own lifetime, still noteworthy, still controversial, and still especially an object of fascination to the younger generation. A picture of him, drawn by a younger writer, survives from this time:

> Behind the Abbey lives a man of fame;
>   With awe and reverence we repeat his name,
> Ben Jonson; him we saw, and thought to hear
>   From him some flashes and fantastic gear.
> But he spake nothing less. His whole discourse
>   Was how mankind grew daily worse and worse,
> How God was disregarded, how men went
>   Down even to Hell, and never did repent,
> With many such sad tales; as he would teach
>   Us scholars, how thereafter we should preach.
> Great wearer of the bays, look to thy lines,
>   Lest they by chance be challenged by divines.
> Some future times will, by a gross mistake
>   Jonson a bishop, not a poet, make.

(HS I, 113)

Impoverished, bed-ridden and disenchanted Jonson was at a low ebb as 1632 approached. Meanwhile others carried on making money out of Jonson while the poet himself went short; when the King's Men staged *The Alchemist* on 1 December 1631 for Sir Henry Herbert's winter benefit the performance raised £13 for the happy recipient. At the beginning of the new year Jonson was without any court employment. He had not been commissioned to write the King's Twelfth-tide masque, nor the Queen's which was to accompany it. Court gossip canvassed the reason behind this decision:

The inventor or poet of this masque was Mr Aurelian Townshend, sometime steward to the Lord Treasurer Salisbury, Ben Jonson being for this time discarded by reason of the predominant power of his antagonist, Inigo Jones, who, this time twelvemonth, was angry with him for putting his own name before his in the title-page; which Ben Jonson has made the subject of a bitter satire or two against Inigo. (*JAB* 168)

Jones was so firmly fixed in royal favour that he could assert himself against Jonson with powerful effect, and Jonson was to find that an enemy like Jones was a luxury that he could not afford. Jones had in fact usurped Jonson's place as court masque-maker so securely that Townshend, one of Jonson's own 'sons', was commissioned merely to find words to accompany Jones's 'inventions' of *Albion's Triumph* and *Tempe Restored*. Pressed for money and denied work at court Jonson turned back for one final throw to the public stage. At the height of his creative powers Jonson had been notoriously slow in composition. Now in his age and sickness his muse peeped out only one in a hundred days. Many months of laborious effort therefore had to go into the production of *The Magnetic Lady*. During the summer of its composition, 1632, came the passing of an old adversary. Dekker died that August after many difficulties and was buried at St James Clerkenwell.

But Jonson need not necessarily have noticed Dekker's tribulations, since he had plenty of his own. Word of his new play got about before its appearance, which was hailed in a chilling aside by one court correspondent: 'Ben Jonson (who I thought had been dead) hath written a play against next term called *The Magnetic Lady*' (*JAB* 177). Towards the end of 1632 the play was ready. It was licensed to the King's Men on 12 October and performed early in the autumn season at the Blackfriars. Ill luck dogged it from its opening. First the audience never saw the play as Jonson had written it. The actors, possibly suffering a natural apprehension of the same hostile reception as that which had demolished *The New Inn*, tried to vamp up the text as they went along with the gratuitous addition of oaths and blasphemies. But contemporary regulations were firmly against such excesses of language and the actors were summoned to answer for their fault at the Court of High Commission.

There they sought to exculpate themselves by laying all the blame for the offence upon Jonson, whose previous record could only have lent substance to their charge. But as it was without foundation Jonson managed to clear himself of this difficulty. At a second hearing more than a year later on 24 October 1633 the actors were brought to accept full responsibility for the objectionable material in *The Magnetic Lady*, and the Archbishop of Canterbury, the great Laud himself, 'laid the whole fault of their play . . . upon the players'.[1] Jonson was to hear no more of this tiresome business – but it was too late to save his play. *The Magnetic Lady* had to contend with more than the actors' textual subversion. External forces were also at work to sabotage the play and Jonson now had to pay the price for striking out at those who had angered him. At the opening performance a hostile claque was in action led by his arch enemy Inigo Jones. Also present were Nathaniel Butter and Alexander Gill; Jonson had satirised Butter in *The Staple of*

News, and Gill's father in *Time Vindicated to Himself and to his Honours*. Between them these three led the audience in bursts of derisive laughter, as Gill later recorded:

> O how they friend Nat Butter 'gan to melt,
> Whenas the poorness of the plot he smelt;
> And Inigo with laughing there grew fat
> That there was nothing worth the laughing at . . .
>
> (HS XI, 347)

The King's Men struggled hard to get *The Magnetic Lady* off the ground; Gill's reference to three failed performances bears witness to their efforts and to their lack of success. This enabled Gill to attack Jonson savagely:

> . . . But to advise thee, Ben, in this strict age,
> A brick-kiln's better for thee than a stage;
> Thou better knowst a groundsel how to lay
> Than lay the plot or groundwork of a play;
> And better canst direct to cap a chimney
> Than to converse with Clio or Polyhymny.
> Fall then to work in thy old age again,
> Take up thy trug and trowel, gentle Ben;
> Let plays alone, and if thou needst must write
> And thrust thy feeble muse forth into light,
> Let Lowin cease, and Taylor fear to touch
> The loathed stage, for now thou makest it such.[2]

The destruction of Jonson's play was not Jones's only revenge upon him. He also published a verse epistle 'to my false friend Ben Jonson' denigrating Jonson's reliance on translation and finally categorising him as 'the best of poets, but the worst of men'. Jones both had and enjoyed the last laugh in his quarrel with Jonson.

In this unfortunate situation Jonson could as ever rely upon his friends. Zouch Townley sprang to Jonson's defence, scornfully dismissing Gill as a drone who has no more sting than honey. He comforted Jonson with the assurance that no-one would heed these censures and that 'time cannot kill' Jonson's worth (*JAB* 179–80). But even the loyalty of those genuinely devoted to Jonson could not entirely disguise a less-than-enthusiastic response to the play. On all sides it was seen as a falling-off from Jonson's own previous standards of excellence. As James Howell put it to him (the adverse verdict kindly wrapped up in teasing), 'you were mad when you writ your *Fox*, and madder when you writ your *Alchemist* . . . and when you writ your *Epigrams* and *The Magnetic Lady* you were not so mad . . . The madness I mean is that divine fury . . . that Ovid speaks of ' (HS XI,

416–17). The want of poetic inspiration, although a harsh verdict, is one that Jonson had already passed upon himself in the 'Epistle Mendicant' to the Lord Treasurer Weston.

But Jonson though down was never out. He struck back at 'infamous Gill' with a powerful piece of invective in which he derided the defrocked minister as savagely as Gill had attacked him, cutting him down as a 'poor wretched tyke' (*Ungathered Verse* 39). He reasserted his position as poet laureate with *Underwood* 72, an anniversary epigram for King Charles on his November birthday, and he contributed congratulatory verses to the publication of *The Northern Lass* by Richard Brome. Here he took occasion to restate his old love for Brome and to work in a vigorous sideswipe at contemporary literary practices, 'now each court hobby-horse will wince in rhyme', and 'both learned and unlearned, all write plays' (*Ungathered Verse* 38).

The early months of 1633 found Jonson in his sixtieth year with two projects in hand. The first of these, a new play, had a dual purpose, to make money and to exact revenge from the hated Inigo. The second showed that Jonson's appeals to Newcastle had aroused the Duke's active interest and not simply his benevolence. Newcastle relieved Jonson in the best way possible, by commissioning him to write a new masque, to be performed at the Duke's country seat at Welbeck in Nottinghamshire. As the occasion was a visit of the King in the course of a progress north into Scotland, Newcastle was also offering Jonson a chance to restore his fortunes in the eyes of his royal master.

As both these projects were ripening in the spring of 1633, a grievous blow fell. On May Day of that year Venetia, the wife of Jonson's friend Sir Kenelm Digby, died; as much as her husband she had endeared herself to Jonson through her remarkable character and intellect. The couple had been married for only eight years, after a satisfyingly stormy and romantic courtship. During this time Venetia had borne with exemplary grace five lovely children and her husband's extended absences. Her death was sudden and the shock of it correspondingly great. Having had Van Dyck paint her on her deathbed, Digby retreated from the world to Gresham College where for two years he lived the life of a hermit and scholar. Jonson's grief found expression in a long and deeply-felt elegy, a sequence of poems about Venetia which he sent to her husband in commiseration. Although now imperfect, the sequence 'Eupheme' originally consisted of ten linked pieces with a climactic 'elegy on my Muse, the truly honoured lady . . . who, living, gave me leave to call her so'. From the opening lines with their grim recognition of Jonson's own mortality the poet angrily vents his sense of the unfairness of things:

'Twere time that I died too, now she is dead,
   Who was my muse, and life of all I said. . . .
My wounded mind cannot sustain this stroke;
   It rages, runs, flies, stands, and would provoke
The world to ruin with it; in her fall
   I sum up mine own breaking, and wish all.

                         (*Underwood* 84, ix)

This poem passes through a finely-wrought Christian consolation and a celebration of Venetia's unusual qualities to achieve a state of resignation at its conclusion. The distinction of the writing as well as the extension of the argument over more than two hundred lines plainly indicates what this event meant to Jonson.

Other matters were treading hard on its heels, however. Jonson had determined that his new play was to give his old enemy Inigo Jones the kind of public correction that he had administered to his theatrical foes in the 'War of the Theatres' more than thirty years before. He intended to stage Jones as he had done with Marston and Dekker, satirising him through a foolish and ridiculous character Vitruvius Hoop in such a way as to make the architect an object of general scorn. From old materials incorporated into the framework of a discarded comedy Jonson put together a farce of lumpen mechanicals to lampoon the King's Surveyor.

But Jones was ahead of him. He was able to see Jonson's laboured blow coming and parry it through his contacts at court. When application was made to the Master of the Revels for the licensing of the play the extent of Jones's influence was revealed. He had made prior application to the Lord Chamberlain under whom the Master of the Revels acted, so that when the play was licensed to Queen Henrietta's Men on 7 May 1633 permission to perform it was only granted with 'Vitru. Hoop's part wholly struck out, and the motion of the tub, by command from my Lord Chamberlain; exceptions being taken against it by Inigo Jones, Surveyor of the King's Works, as a personal injury unto him' (*JAB* 176).

Jones's intervention proved to be a blessing in disguise for Jonson. The play's performance went off without any of the disagreeable scenes which had attended the production of Jonson's two previous plays. *The Tale Of A Tub*, as the new piece was sardonically entitled was staged on this occasion by the Queen Henrietta's Men at the Cockpit Theatre in Whitehall. This was a new and fashionable company run by Christopher Beeston who had been an apprentice of the great Burbage in his youth. Possibly Jonson did not trust the King's Men after two experiences in which he felt that his work had been done less than justice. But it is equally possible that

Shakespeare's old company now held Jonson to be death at the box office, having failed so notably with the last two of his plays. Beeston's company had a reputation for being avant-garde and often took risks. On this occasion though the show went off quietly enough with the controversial material excised or rewritten.

Later in the same month of May 1633 came Jonson's masque, *The King's Entertainment at Welbeck*. Charles was *en route* for Edinburgh to be crowned there and broke his journey in the Midlands. Here at the Duke of Newcastle's country seat in Nottinghamshire the King was received with great splendour, to which Jonson's show made an important contribution. Although this masque is not one of Jonson's best it had the good fortune to please the King, who had not seen any of his poet laureate's work for over two years since *Love's Triumph* and *Chloridia* early in 1631. This country welcome, built upon the idea of a mock-wedding, for once in Jonson's current writing hit the nail on the head, pleasing all and offending none.

Yet Jonson could never escape controversy. Comment and gossip continued to settle on him long after he was no longer to be seen around the theatres and taverns and his favourite haunts of London. For the one commentator who could observe that 'all men, we know, delight in Ben' (*JAB* 175), another was at hand to contradict him. One such detractor was Leonard Digges, poet, fighter and scholar, who born in the Armada year 1588 was himself now approaching his dissolution in 1635. He and Jonson had been acquainted for many years in the tightly-knit circle of literary London. Both had contributed verses to the First Folio of Shakespeare's works, where Digges had taken issue with Jonson's view that 'a good poet's made as well as born'. In these closing years of both their lives Digges made his great admiration of Shakespeare a stick with which to beat Jonson in an invidious comparison of the theatrical success of both playwrights:

> So have I seen when Caesar would appear,
> And on the stage at half-sword parley were
> Brutus and Cassius: oh, how the audience
> Were ravished, with what wonder they went thence;
> When some new day they would not brook a line
> Of tedious, though well-laboured *Catiline*.
> *Sejanus* was too irksome, they prized more
> Honest Iago, or the jealous Moor.
> And though the *Fox* and subtle *Alchemist*
> Long intermitted, could not quite be missed,
> Though those have shamed the ancients, and might raise
> Their author's merit with a crown of bays,

Yet these sometimes, even at a friend's desire
Acted, have scarce defrayed the sea-coal fire
And door-keepers; when let but Falstaff come,
Hal, Poins, the rest, you scarce shall have a room
All is so pestered . . .[3]

This theme was continued by Endymion Porter in his epigram 'upon Ben Jonson, and his zany Tom Randolph', alleging that these two cried down Shakespeare's fame in order to glorify themselves:

E'en Avon's Swan could not escape
These letter-tyrant elves;
They on his fame contrived a rape
To raise their pedant selves.
But after times with full consent
This truth will all acknowledge –
Shakespeare and Ford from heaven were sent,
But Ben and Tom from college.

(*JAB* 189)

Such was the gossip circulating about Jonson. Others took an openly vindictive attitude to the old poet, glorying in his age and deterioration. This is the voice of one anonymous critic:

Jonson, that whilom brought the guilty age
To suffer for her misdeeds on the stage,
Ruined by age now, cannot hold but play
And must be forced to throw his cards away;
For since he so ill keeps what he erst won,
Since that his reputation's lost and gone,
The age swears she'll no longer hold him play
With her attention, but without delay
Will rise, if some fresh gamester will not fit
That's furnished with a better stock of wit.

(*JAB* 187–8)

But there is no reason to believe that Jonson necessarily saw all or any of these taunts. On the whole 1633 had handled him better than the immediately preceding years had done, although it had seen like almost every year now the death of another of Jonson's old acquaintance. John Marston died in the summer of 1633 and was buried in Aldermanbury parish London on 26 June. He was followed in August by another survivor of the 'War of the Theatres', Anthony Munday, who like Marston had long retired from the stage, having endured many vicissitudes since he was lampooned as Antonio Balladino in *The Case Is Altered*. In contrast, 1633 also brought another royal birth,

262

the arrival of a second son to the Queen on 14 October. Jonson celebrated the christening of this child, the future James II, in *Underwood* 82, where he interpreted the event as a demonstration of God's love for King Charles, and His great plan for the happy future of the British people – words which succeeding developments were to load with an unintentioned irony.

New Year's Day 1634 brought Jonson a gift of the sort that he most appreciated. This was a Welsh grammar, procured for him at his request by James Howell. As Howell's letters show this had been no easy task. In 1633 he had written to Jonson 'I cannot yet light upon Mr Davies' Welsh Grammar; before Christmas I am promised one'. Jonson's desire for this book can only be attributed to his inexhaustible linguistic curiosity. Howell sent the book with a covering letter:

> Father Ben, you desired me lately to procure you Dr Davies' Welsh grammar to add to those many you have. I have lighted upon one at last, and am glad I have it in so seasonal a time that it may serve for a New Year's gift, in which quality I send it you . . . (HS I, 258–9)

Howell accompanied his gift with another thoughtful gesture, the inclusion of a thirty-four-line tribute in verse to the 'wild and wealthy' language contained in the book – 'This is the tongue the Bards sang in of old / And Druids their dark knowledge did unfold'. A satisfied Jonson recorded on the title-page his name and the motto with which he inscribed all his books, with a record of the donor and the date. Jonson's pursuit of his literary interests in view of his disabilities was remarkable; also in 1634 he contributed a verse commendation to a devotional work, the *Meditation of Man's Mortality* by Alice Sutcliffe, the wife of a courtier (*Ungathered Verse* 40).

As 1634 opened Jonson's *Tale Of A Tub* was given a court performance. Queen Henrietta's players obviously thought well enough of the piece to venture it among their severest and most sophisticated critics, the courtiers. But for reasons not known the play was disliked. In addition to this disappointment Jonson now had to accept the fact that he was decisively supplanted as a royal masque-maker. Jones had invited Sir William Davenant to write the script for *The Temple of Love* which was performed at Whitehall early in January. Davenant, who was busy advancing his own career as a dramatist by claiming among other things to be Shakespeare's illegitimate son, was also destined to follow Jonson in another important particular since he was appointed Poet Laureate after Jonson's death.

But Jonson had not entirely lost the royal favour that he had regained with *The King's Entertainment at Welbeck* the summer before. Once again the King was to pass through the Midland counties and once again the Duke of Newcastle was to play host. As the Duchess of

Newcastle later recalled:

This entertainment [at Welbeck] cost my Lord between four and five thousand pounds; which his Majesty liked so well, that a year after his return out of Scotland, he was pleased to send my Lord word that her Majesty the Queen was resolved to make a progress into the Northern parts, desiring him to prepare the like entertainment for her, as he had formerly done for him. Which my Lord did, and endeavoured for it with all possible care and industry, sparing nothing that might add splendour to that feast which both their Majesties were pleased to honour with their presence. Ben Jonson he employed in fitting such scenes and speeches as he could best devise, and sent for all the gentry of the country to come and wait on their Majesties – and in short, did all that ever he could imagine, to render it great, and worthy their royal acceptance. (HS X, 703)

Newcastle resolved to outdo his former hospitality with an even more sumptuous welcome. He plunged himself into the preparations with such generosity that where the first visit had cost him between four and five thousand pounds, the 1634 entertainment brought an outlay of more than three times as much. Jonson created for the occasion his last masque, *Love's Welcome at Bolsover*. Working for his kindly patron, Jonson was encouraged to create what he saw fit. The show that he produced was not strictly speaking new; the contention of Eros and Anteros was repeated from *A Challenge at Tilt* that Jonson had written for the Essex-Somerset wedding on New Year's Day 1614, but in a weaker form.

Another element of the masque was similarly made over from earlier work. Jonson could not resist including for their Majesties' amusement the satire on Inigo Jones which had been struck out of *The Tale Of A Tub* in May of the year before. The show opened conventionally enough, with songs of welcome to the royal couple. Then followed, as an anti-masque of the sort that Jonson used to delight the old King with, a satiric portrait of Jones as a fussy and self-important windbag. To set this before the King who had honoured and employed Jones suggests that whatever else had happened to Jonson, he had not lost his nerve. Possibly away from the hothouse atmosphere of the court and London the King and Queen were freer to enjoy this humorous portrayal than they would otherwise have been. At all events Jonson did not injure his standing with the King as he could so easily have done. The Bolsover entertainment took place on 30 July 1634. From the letter which Jonson wrote to the Duke of Newcastle to express his gratitude for the employment it is clear that the commission went a good way towards relieving Jonson's distresses. It also indicates how prompt the Duke had been to repay the needy old man, sending the money along with his personal chaplain, Payne:

My noblest lord, and my best patron,

I have done your business as your Lordship trusted me with, and the morning after I received by my beloved friend Mr Payne your Lordship's timely gratuity. I style it such: for it fell like the dew of heaven on my necessities, it came so opportunely and in season. I pray God my work have deserved it; I meant it should in the working it, and I have hope the performance will conclude it. In the meantime I tell your Lordship what I seriously think – God sends you those chargeable and magnificent honours of making feasts, to mix with your charitable succours, dropped upon me your servant; who have nothing to claim by [way] of merit, but a cheerful undertaking whatsoever your lordship's judgment thinks me able to perform. I am in the number of your humblest servants, my Lord, and the most willing; and do joy in the good friendship and fellowship of my right learned friend Mr Payne, than whom your Lordship could not have employed a more diligent and judicious man, or [one] that hath treated me with more humanity, which makes me cheerfully to insert myself into your Lordship's commands . . .

> Wholly and only
> your Lordship's
> B. Jonson.

(HSI, 212)

Newcastle expressed his thanks in the practical form of this much-needed gratuity. The King too desired to reward 'his poet'. When Charles returned to the capital late in that summer of 1634 he bore Jonson in mind despite the ever-increasing press of business with which he was faced. On 18 September 1634 the City Fathers of London, who had withheld Jonson's pension as City Chronologer since the end of 1631, met to consider an explicit directive to their governing body. The Earl of Dorset had signified to them the King's pleasure that the old poet's pension of one hundred nobles should be reinstated immediately – and it was so ordered, upon this occasion and date. What must have delighted Jonson even more was the ordered repayment of all the 'arrearages' (arrears) which had built up during the lapse of three years. The contrast between Jonson's newly improved situation and that of his old friend lately estranged, Chapman, who died in misery and poverty in the early summer of 1634, was strongly marked.

Jonson expressed his gratitude for this small renewal of court favour in the only way he knew, through poetry. For the traditional ceremony of literary presentation on New Year's Day Jonson worked up a verse gift for the King. It is a clear sign of his deterioration that the poem was not new but a recycling of old material. Jonson returned to *Pan's Anniversary*, his masque of 1620, where King James was glorified as Pan. With some shuffling James was replaced by Charles, and Queen Henrietta was recast as Pan's sister rather than his wife. The keynote of this piece (*Underwood* 79) is enthusiasm rather than accuracy, as the identification of Charles with Pan cannot be sustained throughout the length of the poem. Jonson is manifestly going through the motions of what earlier he had been able to accomplish with so much ease and grace, the making of verse epistles of an occasional nature and yet of lasting value.

In any case there was little that Jonson could hope for from the King as increasing age diminished his poetic faculties while increasing cares shook Charles's administration to its foundations. This gift-poem was the last tribute from Jonson as poet laureate to Charles. During the rest of 1635 Jonson's only literary record consists of two commendatory verses prefixed to the work of others. To Joseph Rutter, whom he affectionately described as 'my dear son and right-learned friend', Jonson wrote:

> You look, my Joseph, I should something say
> Unto the world, in praise of your first play;
> And truly, so I would, could I be heard.
> You know I never was of truth afeard . . .

With a stoical backward glance at his own theatrical days when he clung to the expression of his views but often failed to convince his audiences, Jonson went on to praise Rutter's play in warm terms – 'so soft and smooth it handles, the whole piece'. But in a sardonic conclusion Jonson deprecates the value of his own opinion; he is out of touch with the modern theatre and there is a new 'office of wit' by which works are to be judged and found wanting (*Ungathered Verse* 42).

This elegiac retrospective note also characterises Jonson's other surviving poem of 1635, his 'epigram to my jovial friend Mr Robert Dover, on his great instauration of his hunting and dancing at Cotswold'. Dover had taken it upon himself to organise a series of 'Cotswold Olympic games' from about 1612, and his published account of them in 1635 won the support of many writers. Jonson had always been interested in sporting men and he had another reason for supporting Dover's enterprise:

> But I can tell thee, Dover, how thy games
> Renew the glories of our blessed James:
> How they do keep alive his memory
> With the glad country, and posterity;
> How they advance true love and neighbourhood,
> And do both church and commonwealth the good,

In spite of hypocrites, who are the worst
Of subjects; let such envy, till they burst.

(*Ungathered Verse* 43)

Towards the end of the year between 23 October and 6 November 1636 the Royal Exchequer recorded a last payment to Jonson of £25. Such gratuities were now his only means of obtaining a basic subsistence – after *Love's Welcome at Bolsover* in the summer of 1634 he wrote no more for court or stage. It is a fair supposition that in these final years he found it almost impossible to write at all. One letter to the Duke of Newcastle, undated but clearly belonging to a time when Jonson was advanced in his distresses, shows that he could no longer turn off the stylish rhymes with which he used to solicit money but now begged without concealment:

> My noblest Lord and best patron,
> I send no borrowing epistle to provoke your lordship, for I have neither fortune to repay or security to engage, that will be taken; but I make a most humble petition to your lordship's bounty to succour my present necessities this good time of Easter, and it shall conclude all begging request hereafter, on the behalf
>
> Of your truest beadsman
> and
> most thankful servant
> B.J.

(HS I, 211–12)

It was of course an irony perfectly familiar to playwrights at this period that their plays continued to make money while they went without. Early in 1636 *Epicœne* was played twice at court on 18 February and 4 April at the Cockpit, testifying to the perennial popularity of certain of Jonson's plays. Even *Catiline* had finally vindicated its creator's faith in it more than twenty years after its composition; the 1635 quarto edition described the play with evident satisfaction as 'now acted by his Majesty's servants *with great applause*'. Jonson of course could not share these triumphs, confined as he was to his chamber through his paralysis. But grimly enough, during 1636 this was the safest place to be. In the spring of this year there was a virulent outbreak of the plague, bringing personal disaster and public demoralisation in its wake. From April 1636 to December 1637 more than thirteen thousand deaths were recorded and the theatres remained closed for the whole of that period but for three months.

But although unable to go forth Jonson did not lack company. The last glimpse of him in life comes appropriately enough in a gathering of friends, who appear to have borne with affection and good humour the infirmities of age as they manifested themselves in Jonson's behaviour. On 5 April 1535 James Howell sent this account from Westminster to his friend Sir Thomas Hawk:

Sir,
  I was invited yesternight to a solemn supper by BJ, where you were deeply remembered. There was good company, excellent cheer, choice wines and jovial welcome. One thing intervened which almost spoiled the relish of the rest, that B. began to engross all the discourse, to vapour extremely of himself, and by vilifying others, to magnify his own muse.
  T.Ca. buzzed me in the ear, that though Ben had barrelled up a great deal of knowledge, yet it seemed he had not read the *Ethics* [of Aristotle], which, among other precepts of morality, forbid self-commendation, declaring it to be an ill-favoured solecism in good manners . . . But for my part, I am content to dispense with the Roman infirmity of B. now that time hath snowed upon his *pericranium* [skull]. You know Ovid and your Horace were subject to this humour . . . as also Cicero . . . (*JAB* 194)

From this time forward the rest is silence. Jonson's last months are veiled in obscurity, although anecdotes suggest that his poverty continued to the end. Aubrey noted that 'when Ben Jonson was dying, King Charles sent him but ten pounds'. An apocryphal story later amplified this as follows:

Now men may see, how much reason Ben Jonson had, whenas lying sick in bed, very poor, and that after much importunity of courtiers, ten pounds were sent to him by the King, after the receipt of which, Ben threw them through the glass window, saying, '*this man's soul was not fit to live in an alley*'. (HS I, 183)

In June of 1637 Jonson entered his sixty-fifth year. He had had a tremendous span for one of his day and his powers of survival had seemed prodigious. As early as 1629 a savage wit of the time composed an anonymous 'letter to Ben Jonson', which began with breathtaking brutality:

Die, Jonson! Cross not our religion so
As to be thought immortal . . .
Die! Seems it not enough thy verse's date
Is endless, but thine own prolonged fate
Must equal it? For shame, engross not age,
But now thy fifth's act's ended, leave the stage . . .
(HS XI, 397–8)

Thirty years before when he lost his beloved friend Sir John Roe Jonson had contemplated his own end: 'I now / Breathe to expect my when, and make my how'. After so many years of sickness and suffering, the advent of death was hardly stealthy. One small piece of evidence shows that Jonson had anticipated its approach in a wholly characteristic way. In the debate about the publishing of Jonson's works after his death it was said that 'several of the writings and works of . . . Benjamin Jonson late deceased, were some short time before his decease presented unto and given by the said Benjamin to Sir Kenelm Digby to dispose of at his will and pleasure. To whose care and trust the said Benjamin left the publishing of and printing of them and delivered him true and perfect copies for his better and more effectual doing thereof '.[4]

At the approach of death then Jonson took final action to secure his literary legacy. A tradition current before his death records that he had already taken order for his own burial. He who had always scorned to follow the common herd in life was equally unconventional in his way of leaving it. Jonson openly declared that he could not afford the normal six feet of earth required to be buried lying down and so arranged to be interred in the upright position:

> One day, being rallied by the Dean of Westminster about being buried in the poet's corner, the poet is said to have replied (we tell the story as current in the Abbey): 'I am too poor for that, and no-one will lay out funeral charges upon me. No, sir, six feet long by two feet wide is too much for me; two feet by two feet will do for all I want'. 'You shall have it', said the Dean, and thus the conversation ended. (*JAB* 195 6)

Finally the event occurred that the town had been expecting for so long. Jonson died on 6 August 1637 and was buried three days later in Westminster Abbey. One contemporary account recorded that he was 'accompanied to his grave with all or the greatest part of the nobility and gentry then in town' (*JAB* 199). Whoever paid for Jonson's funeral charges took no order for a memorial. Jonson's grave in the north aisle of the great Abbey where he had worshipped as a boy was originally unmarked. After the burial service a visitor to the Abbey, one 'Jack Young (afterwards knighted)' in Aubrey's words, was walking by as the grave was being covered. Feeling that Jonson's resting-place should be marked with a memorial tablet 'he gave the fellow eighteen pence to cut it'. In a moment of inspired felicity, the anonymous Abbey mason carved on one of the marble slabs of the pavement the legend with which the poet has passed into eternity,

O RARE
BEN JONSON

CHAPTER 16

O RARE BEN JONSON

W HEN Jonson died on 6 August 1637 there was little to mark his passing. For one whose literary legacy was so enormous his worldly estate was pitifully small. On 22 August 1637 the administration of Jonson's goods to the value of £8 8s 10d was granted to a William Scandret, described as 'one of his creditors'. Jonson is declared to have died intestate. There was nothing else to clear up behind Jonson – no wife, children or dependants make their appearance. When King Charles in an August letter to the London Aldermen preferred another poet to Jonson's now-vacant post as City Chronologer, the last traces of Jonson's mortal existence were swept away.

Jonson's reputation was now left in the hands of posterity in which he had reposed his hopes of a full and fair assessment. Immediate responses however were of a superficial and sneering nature, like this 'epitaph upon the most learned comedian and modern poet, Benjamin Jonson, who left the church and died', by Thomas Wilford:

> Here Jonson lies, who spent his days
> In making sport, and comic plays:
> His life a play, performed the worst,
> The last act did disgrace the first;
> His part he played exceeding well
> A Catholic, until he fell
> To sects and schisms, which he did choose
> Like to a fiction of his muse . . .
>
> So ill he played the later part,
> The epilogue did break his heart.
> When death his body did surprise,
> The fatal sisters closed his eyes,

And took him to the tiring room,
Where I will leave him to his doom;
But wish that I could justly raise
Memorials of eternal praise.

(*JAB* 199–200)

This tone of low jeering was echoed by another contemporary wit, Mildmay Fane, Earl of Westmorland. He wrote this epitaph 'on the death of Ben Jonson the exceptional poet' inside the cover of his own copy of Jonson's 1616 Folio, the admiring title belying the words:

He who began from brick and lime
The Muses' hill to climb,
And whilom busied in laying stone
Thirsted to drink of Helicon,
Changing his trowel for a pen
Wrote straight the temper not of dirt but men.

Now sithence he is turned to clay and gone,
Let those [who] remain, of the occupation
He honoured once, square him a tomb [that] may say
His craft exceeded far a dauber's way.
Then write upon't, 'He could no longer tarry,
But was returned again unto the quarry'.

(HS XI, 193)

Meanwhile Sir Kenelm Digby was embarking on the daunting task of administering Jonson's literary remains. Digby's precise responsibility towards Jonson's literary estate seems to have combined the roles of literary executor and editor. The contemporary evidence declares that it was to Digby's care and trust that the papers were left for publishing and printing. There is also a manuscript statement in Digby's own hand of his desire to edit the remaining pieces of Jonson's work. Much of Jonson's output had been lost in the fire of 1623. But enough remained to make this a formidable undertaking.

In the meantime, later in 1637 Digby wrote to Dr Duppa, Dean of Christ Church, Oxford, encouraging another project. This was an idea that had arisen of gathering together the various elegies that Jonson's death had occasioned among his true friends and admirers. Duppa had 'loved [Jonson] dearly' as Digby recalled, and knew therefore that the great ghost would be more gratified with literary obsequies than with empty sacrifices at his tomb. To Digby, Jonson was 'this brave man', 'the honour of his age'. The letter closed with Digby's promise to share with the world as soon as possible 'those excellent pieces (alas that many of them are but pieces!) which he

271

hath left behind him, and that I keep religiously by me to that end' (*JAB* 201).

Other friends were active too, including the faithful Howell. He wrote to Duppa (by now Lord Bishop of Chichester) on 1 May 1638: 'It is a well-becoming and worthy work you are about, not to suffer Mr Ben Jonson to go silently to his grave, or not so suddenly' (*JAB* 202). This work crystallised early in 1638, about six months after Jonson's death when the assorted memorial tributes to the dead poet in English, Latin and Greek were gathered together and published, Duppa having set about his literary labour with more vigour than Digby. In this collection, entitled *Jonsonus Virbius* (immortal Jonson), Jonson's patron Newcastle and a host of lesser lights paid tribute to the 'Great Lord of Arts, and Father of the Age'. There are forty-six contributions in all, some of them very long and elaborate.

An engaging composite picture of Jonson emerges from this motley assortment of strenuous, sincere and low-level productions, part wild eulogy and part mythology:

> So great his art, that much which he did write
> Gave the wise wonder, and the crowd delight;
> Each sort, as well as sex, admired his wit,
> The hes, the shes, the boxes and the pit . . .
>
> (HS XI, 432)

In contrast to the loud breast-beating – 'Alas, that bard, that glorious bard is dead' – Jonson's 'son' Lucius Cary, Viscount Falkland, gave a tantalising hint of Jonson's literary plans in the final phase of his career:

> Not long before his death, our woods he meant
> To visit, and descend from Thames to Trent;
> Meet with thy elegy his pastoral. . . .
>
> (HS XI, 436)

The English pastoral alluded to here is generally taken to be the *Sad Shepherd*, a half-finished play of a style new to Jonson found among his papers after his death.

Jonson's elevation of his poetic role and material is a recurrent theme. Henry King described Jonson as one 'to whose most rich and fruitful head we owe / The purest streams of language which can flow'. Jonson appears frequently in one of his favourite roles, the poet-didact who 'taught the ruder age / To speak by grammar, and reformed the stage' (HS XI, 440–1). But amid the often hollow ballyhoo about 'Great Jonson, King of English poetry' there are some striking personal glimpses. George Fortescue recalled a critical illness he suffered when the intervention of the poet was decisive:

> I parleyed once with death, and thought to yield,
> When thou advisest me to keep the field . . .
>
> (HS XI, 445)

In addition to this formal literary monument to Jonson, comments and tributes continued to flow for the next few years. George Daniel turned in a florid sixty-four line eulogy of 'the great flame of English poets gone' (HS XI, 491). More generous and deeply felt was Zouch Townley's contribution in 1640 in which he praised Jonson's language, his classical knowledge, his skill in the construction of a scene, and his mastery of different forms. During these years it became briefly the custom to praise succeeding poets by measuring them against Jonson as the ultimate standard of literary excellence. Aspiring writers had to be assured that it was upon their shoulders that the mantle of great Jonson had fallen. This vapid convention was mocked by one poet as follows:

> As 'twere the only office of a friend
> To rhyme, and 'gainst his conscience to commend
> And swear like poets of the post [paid hacks], this . . .
> Exceeds all Jonson's works . . .
>
> (*JAB* 270)

Among those who had known him, the real Jonson continued to be remembered with affection and esteem. The Jonson addressed by the poet Herrick in his 'Bacchanalian verse' is a more substantial figure than the pompous creations of rhetorical posturing:

> Fill me a mighty bowl
> Up to the brim;
> That I may drink
> Unto my Jonson's soul.
>
> Crown it again, again,
> And thrice repeat
> That happy heat,
> To drink to thee, my Ben.
>
> Well I can quaff, I see,
> To the number five,
> Or nine; but thrive
> In frenzy ne'er like thee.
>
> (HS XI, 415)

But informal tributes, however truly felt, could not take the place of the necessary collection of Jonson's own later works as his proper memorial. At his death Jonson left a number of important pieces unpublished, since no collection of his works had been printed since the cherished Folio of 1616. Jonson's own efforts to see three of the later plays through the press had been thwarted by the slovenliness of his 'lewd printer'. Digby understandably did not feel himself equal to the formidable task of a full recension of the papers in his possession, yet as time passed he saw the need for their publication. In 1640, accordingly, he sold the Jonson papers to the stationer Walkley for £40.

Walkley took his responsibility as the publisher of these valuable literary remains seriously, laying out in addition to the original £40, another £200 on the work of bringing them through the press in a suitably dignified form. But while Walkley was working on the preparation of the long-desired second Folio of Jonson's works – Jonson himself had projected it in 1631 and failed in his endeavour – trouble ensued. Complications arose through the imperfect nature of the contemporary licensing and copyright laws which encouraged another publisher to try to cash in on the Jonson market. A legal wrangle followed,[1] to fatten the lawyers and further to delay the appearance of the book.

It appears with hindsight to be a monumental stroke of good fortune that Jonson's second Folio *Works* ever saw the light of day in 1640. Had the three years' delay after Jonson's death been any more prolonged his last papers could well have suffered the fate that overwhelmed all the rest of the old order that Jonson had loved and served. In April 1640 the King's financial desperation at last compelled him to recall the Parliament that he had staved off and governed without for so long. The so-called 'Long Parliament' that assembled on 3 November of that year sat, with intermissions, for nearly twenty years. One of its first acts was the closure and destruction of the public theatres. In the following year the last vestiges of the world that Jonson had known were swept away. In the chaos of war and revolution as it tore through England there was little time or space for literary considerations like the publishing of folios.

Yet even in these terrible times the name of Jonson repeatedly crops up in connection with King Charles, who seems to have found more affection for his laureate dead than alive. On 6 November 1638 *Volpone* was played at court. In the darkest days of the Civil War it was recorded on 27 December 1648 that 'the King is pretty merry, and spends much time in reading', alternating devotional works with the plays of Jonson and Shakespeare. As losses and disasters mounted for the Royalists, observers noted with wonder that in 1649 the King 'was no more affected with a list that was brought to Oxford of five or six thousand slain at Edgehill than to read one of Ben Jonson's tragedies'. And at Charles's final hour it was noted against him by disapproving Puritan eyes that 'this said man's soul was more fixed on Ben's verses and other romances, during the time of his imprisonment, than on those Holy Writs wherein salvation is to be sought for the soul as well as for the body' (*JAB* 292–5).

The consolation of Jonson's work in King Charles's calvary was a peculiarly appropriate posthumous use of a writer who had ever loyally tried to serve this most misguided of monarchs and men. Additionally Jonson had always loathed and fought against Puritanism, both in its personal and political implications. During the interregnum his light, along with that of the theatre and the monarchy, was out. But the Restoration of 1660 brought him back immediately into an esteem which he has never since forfeited. Pepys, the spokesman of his age, called *The Alchemist* 'a most incomparable play', saying of *Epicœne* that 'there is more wit in it than goes to ten new plays'. He summed up his enthusiasm for Jonson with 'I do love *Bartholomew Fair*', calling it 'the best comedy in the world' (*JAB* 322–30). Jonson's tragedies also regained the ground that their maker always believed that they would hold; *Catiline* was described as Jonson's 'best-loved' work by Charles Sackville Earl of Dorset in 1675. The 'royal poet', along with the royal order, had come again into his own.

In the re-establishing of Jonson's reputation the 1640 Folio played a vital part. This large and handsome work in two volumes crowned and consolidated Jonson's literary achievement, since it reproduced as the first volume the contents of the 1616 Folio, with some insignificant variations, and gave to the world in the second, Jonson's major productions since 1616: *Bartholomew Fair*, *The Devil Is An Ass*, *The Staple of News*, *The Magnetic Lady* and *A Tale Of A Tub*,[2] with all the later masques and entertainments, plus the *Underwood*, the translation of Horace's *Ars Poetica*, the *English Grammar* and the *Discoveries*. The careful assembling of all these different pieces in one volume ensured, despite some textual shortcomings, their survival for future generations.

These pieces have all been noticed in context. But the 1640 Folio also contained two productions of Jonson which are not otherwise known and which have constituted something of a puzzle for literary critics. *The Sad Shepherd* and *Mortimer His Fall* are fragments of plays found among Jonson's work after his death and included in the Folio on the grounds of complete fidelity to Jonson's total *oeuvre*. Of the two *The Sad Shepherd* is the more considerable since it consists of half of a full-length play, while of *Mortimer His Fall* there are only two scenes. Their inclusion demonstrates how carefully the printer had gathered up all that was left of Jonson's work so that his complete output would be given to the world. These books made possible the considered estimation of Jonson and his achievement in the ensuing decades. His status as one of the immortals of English literature was established beyond any doubt. To return upon Jonson the assessment that he made of his 'beloved' Shakespeare, 'he was not of an age, but for all time'.

Posterity has passed its favourable verdict on certain of Jonson's plays, and his genius as a poet is not in question. What has been consistently underestimated over the years has been the achievement of his life – or rather of his lives. The British public has been saddled with the monolithic image of Jonson as the grave classicist and stern moralist, the humourless pedant and custodian of standards of rectitude. Traces of all these are to be found in Jonson's personality and behaviour but the composite effect is both repellent and false. It fails to do justice to the journey of Jonson's life – the transitions he made from clever child, bookish rejected boy, and frustrated artisan, to theatrical, courtier, enthusiast for living and learning, eventually to become 'King of Letters' in England.

It denies, too, Jonson's capacity to maintain a multiplicity of perspectives in his conduct of events. The wretchedly thin, bitter and passionate young man of the early days in the theatre was not supplanted by the old poet, heavy with time, adventures, honours and insults who sat drinking Drummond's canary wine in 1619 but travelled with him through the years, rendering him perennially insecure, touchy and suspicious. In mature life other *personae* too entered the stage in the theatre of Jonson's life, and the polished courtier whose company delighted the most exquisite and highly-bred ladies in the land was the same man as the foul-mouthed woman-hater at home on the lowest social level among crooks and whores.

Nor has Jonson benefited from the mythologising of his life and actions along Falstaffian lines. The picture is of the jovial man's man, fat and convivial, keeping house in any tavern, quaffing and gourmandising so unselfconsciously and unrestrainedly as to be one of the prime examples of Great English Eccentrics. Herford and Simpson's Jonson is just such a 'rugged individualist', 'hearty', 'manly', and 'gregarious'. This absurd reduction of both Falstaff and Jonson wipes out the vivid picture of the 'raw-boned anatomy', 'like a charged musket', that was Jonson's own picture of himself in *Every Man Out Of His Humour*. It takes no account of Jonson's frequent moments of coldness, both emotional and intellectual, or the sense of strain that attends so much of his life and work. It glosses over his sexual philistinism and his often desperate attention-seeking in the bland image of warmth and relaxation; for taken with the known facts of his marriage and the loss of his children, the clubbability and tavern-haunting of the later years suggest a lonely and loveless man.

Any full account of Jonson must also dispense with the respectful hagiography which set in with *Jonsonus Virbius*. Jonson wished to be known and respected for his poetry and scholarship. But he had no qualms in sharing with his public the exuberant foulness of 'The Famous Voyage', or the even less flattering hurts and humiliations that he underwent. He estimated correctly that revealing the experience of these moments of self-pity and doubt would not lower him in the eyes of the 'understander'. Consider the confidence with which he draws his own griefs and frustrations into this assault on himself in his Ode upon the death of Sir Henry Morison (*Underwood* 70):

> Go now, and tell out days summed up with fears,
>   And make them years;
> Produce thy mass of miseries on the stage,
>   To swell thine age;
> Repeat of things a throng,
>   To show thou hast been long
> Not lived . . .

Even as he parades his complaints Jonson's self-awareness and his mastery of irony is such that the stanza resolves itself into a brilliant self-reproof; the poet exposes, then scourges, the whiner in him.

As this shows there is no single 'Ben Jonson' that criticism can encapsulate for posterity. His was a deeply conflicted personality, with a fierce appetative drive under the sway of a tyrannical conscience; he was a low liver and an high achiever with a characteristic pattern of surrendering to and retreating from excess. His intense egotism rendered him unduly sensitive to others, and he spent his life negotiating the paradoxes of his own disposition. In this task his writing was of the most profound significance. It was the instrument of discovery, the means of expressing and reconciling some of his tensions, and the arena of his purest triumphs of self and over self.

Jonson was always, as in his own chosen motto, an explorer. He lived his life guided by his belief in the virtue of personal experience and practical experiment, illuminated by the light of Greece and Rome in a set of permanent values at once moral and aesthetic. These values are discerned and maintained by the power of the mind, in Jonson's scheme of things; his satire is always directed at those vices which lead human beings to misuse their intelligence, rather than at those which are purely morally reprehensible. His faith in the Socratic formula that knowledge itself is virtue led him to make the basis of his life intellectual, and although this seems to have impoverished some of the affective areas of human experience for him (he never loved a woman in a full and equal relationship) he still had, when all else failed, his work. Nor did the Westminster habit of study produce nothing but arid gleanings from the work of others. In Jonson the ratiocinative powers were as keenly developed as the creative impulse, and his classicism was both a subject and an instrument of exploration, not simply an accumulation of antique knowledge.

For this Jonson had Camden to thank (as he did), Camden who first gave him the abiding concept of the importance of literary work and the dignity of the poet. This ideal proved easier for the gentle scholar to sustain in the fastness of his study than it was to be for his pupil in the brittle world of London's theatre and court life. But Camden's training, the new humanism grafted onto the classical models to form the Renaissance ideal of the poet as teacher, instructing by delight, shaped Jonson's thinking and his view of himself in a way that sustained his life and gave it purpose.

Jonson also took from Camden the acceptance of the inescapable moral responsibility which the pursuit of literature imposed upon all who undertook it. He was strongly aware of the intricate relationship that exists between intellectual, moral and social tendencies. He could not dodge what he saw as the duty of the writer to be as much keeper of the general conscience, moralist and social reformer, as dramatist, poet and critic. His determination to exercise this role and to promote his own views were often felt by his contemporaries to be offensive, vainglorious and irrelevant. It is one of the many ironies of Jonson's career that his lifelong dedication to the calm and judicious values of the classical world should have brought him into so much heated, ill-judged, muddled and malicious debate. Jonson's assumption of the vatic role opened a great gap between theory and practice into which he both fell and was pushed – but still asserting to the end the dignity of the office and his inalienable right to it.

But even the blindest of his critics could not derogate the sublime moments of his art where theory and practice become one, where he incarnated as well as preached to his contemporaries his message of sanity, grace, and simply human joy. Jonson both lived and taught the wholesome eternal principle of seasonal variation and aptness – the response due to the moment, the luxurious abandon of the dog days, the honouring of grief, the necessary slaking of human appetites for sex, food, wine and warmth, and the dignified submission to that which cannot be changed – in one of his favourite words, *decorum*.

Jonson's massive achievement in life and art has needed no defence. Few would question his eminence. But it has been severely in need of communication and expansion. Jonson's was a nature that hardened young and there remained a static quality about him. His powers grew, but his attitudes were fixed. Unquestionably too he was made of that oak which holds little kindred with those born to be

willow. The general awareness of him shares these rigid properties.
He has not enjoyed the love that has been given to other writers of
lesser growth and which he so amply repays. But anyone who cares to
read Jonson's works can become his friend. To all who do, he offers in
Underwood 47 the ultimate reward:

> So short you read my character, and theirs
> I would call mine, to which not many stairs
> Are asked to climb. First give me faith, who know
> Myself a little. I will take you so,
> As you have writ yourself. Now stand, and then –
> *Sir, you are sealed of the tribe of Ben.*

APPENDIX

THE time has come to end the hesitation and evasion over Jonson's birth date. No birth certificate or other record of the event now survives, but there are several pieces of evidence from which a conclusion emerges with reasonable certainty. These are as follows:

i)   Jonson's own reference to 'my birthday, 11 June', in *Underwood* 78, line 14, his poetic tribute to his close friend Sir Kenelm Digby.

ii) Jonson's deposition in the Rowe lawsuit of 8 May 1610, where he is referred to as 'aged thirty-seven years or thereabouts' (HS I, 228)

iii) The poem which he sent to Drummond in Scotland, which Drummond transcribed into the *Conversations* with the date of 19 January 1619; Jonson makes reference in it to his 'six and forty years' (HS I, 151)

iv) The existence of a further version of the same poem, in which Jonson has altered the age reference to 'seven and forty years' (*Underwood* 9)

v)   Jonson's deposition in the Raleigh lawsuit of 20 October 1623 in which his age is given as 'fifty years and upwards' (HS XI, 582)

None of these references is quite as simple as it may appear. There has been some confusion about the day on which Jonson was born (see (i) above). In two editions of *The Underwood*, the collection in which this poem first appeared, the line in praise of Digby's naval victory at Scanderoon reads as having taken place 'upon *his* birthday, the eleventh of June', that is, Digby's. These two editions are Benson's quarto and duodecimo volumes of 1640. Some support for this reading is afforded by an epitaph of 1665 upon Digby by one Richard

Ferrar which speaks of Digby's birth, death and naval victory, as all having occurred upon 11 June.

This is inherently improbable, to say the least. Further, Benson's edition was attacked in its own time as 'false and imperfect' (see HS IX, 95–97). The 1640 Folio reads '*my* birthday'; the Folio readings were taken from papers which went straight to the printer, Walkley, from Digby himself, to whom Jonson had left all his papers.

The reading 'my birthday' is also supported by the existence of a surviving MS version (the Harleian, British Museum). Even if we have to suppose that Digby was ignorant of the difference between his own birthday and Jonson's, or unaware of the existence of this line in a poem about himself and addressed to his wife in his name, there is evidence that Digby was not born on 11 June. A scheme to plot Digby's nativity, drawn up in his own hand, survives (Ashmole MS); it gives his birthday as 11 July (HS XI, 100).

Probably the coincidence of the two elevens caused the original confusion. But the case for 'my birthday' was persuasively argued as long ago as 1918 by W.D. Briggs (*MLN* xxxiii, 1918, 137–45). This reading has been adopted unanimously not only by Herford and Simpson, but also by Jonson's two modern scholarly editors, Ian Donaldson (1975) and George Parfitt (1975). As a final observation, it is far more Jonsonian to slip in a small personal touch, than to introduce the fact of his hero's birthday coinciding with his great victory and then make nothing of this potential 'witty conceit'. There can be little doubt that Jonson was born on 11 June.

With regard to the year of Jonson's birth, again the evidence has to be weighed. The Rowe deposition of 1610 (ii), taken with the age of 46 on 19 January 1619 (iii) means that Jonson was born between 10 May 1572 and 19 January 1573. Problems here include the looseness of the conventional formula 'or thereabouts' in (ii), and the fact that the *Conversations* survive only in transcript. There is no MS either of the original poem as Jonson sent it to Drummond, nor of Drummond's holograph copy of it into his collection of Jonson's sayings.

But we have the general agreement of scholars as to the authenticity of the original Drummond memoranda, and of the Sibbald transcript. And 19 January is a very plausible date for Drummond's receipt of such a poem, since on that date Jonson had departed from Hawthornden but had not yet left Scotland. The probability of its accuracy is further supported by the change, in the later version of the poem, to 'seven-and-forty' (iv); by the time that Jonson had walked back to London, settled in, and got down to revising work of earlier in the year, it is likely that his birthday would have passed, making him one year older; again, it is characteristically Jonson to play the pedant in small details, correcting his own age at a later revision. These considerations locate Jonson's birthdate as upon 11 June 1572.

This date is also consonant with the Raleigh deposition (v), where Jonson declared himself to be 'fifty years and upwards' in 1623. Once again this is a conventional formula, and not merely a legal one – it recalls King Lear's 'four score and upward' (IV.vii.61). It means 'over fifty', and is not to be taken literally as *only* fifty', in the way in which Herford and Simpson inexplicably take it in XI, 583, where they reverse their previous opinion in I, 1, and argue for 1573 as the year of Jonson's birth.

Two possibilities finally emerged: 11 June 1572, or 11 June 1573. If we accept the latter, we have to assume that Jonson was being strictly accurate in October of 1623, describing himself as 'fifty years and upwards', since he would then have been 50 years and 4 months. It further has to be assumed that by 'thirty-seven years or thereabouts' in 1610, Jonson or the clerk who recorded his answer meant 'almost 37', since he was then just over a month short of his thirty-seventh birthday, i.e. still 36. The Drummond poem (iii) will not fit at all, Jonson being only 45 in January of 1619; and it then has to follow that Jonson left the piece for two years, until he was 47, to revise it.

For the 1572 date, none of these difficulties emerges. While no one piece is entirely conclusive, and each remains open to discussion, the weight of the evidence in total comes down decisively in favour of 11 June 1572 as the date of Jonson's birth.

NOTES

Chapter 1:Boyhood

1   All Jonson quotations unless otherwise stated are taken from the eleven-volume edition of *Ben Jonson*, edited by C.H. Herford and Percy and Evelyn Simpson (Oxford, 1925–52), abbreviated throughout to HS.

    Jonson's 'Conversations' with William Drummond of Hawthornden are a principal source of information about him. Drummond recorded his notes on Jonson's visit to him which took place in the winter of 1618–19 — see Chapter 11 for the account of this. The original manuscript notes of Drummond's record are now lost. A transcript made by the Edinburgh antiquarian and physician Sir Robert Sibbald (1641–1722) survives in the National Library of Scotland in Edinburgh. For a detailed account of the Sibbald transcript and its subsequent publishing history see HS I, 128–31. I follow modern scholars and editors in accepting its authenticity.

    Note that the title 'Conversations' by which this record has been known since its first publication in 1711 is misleading. Drummond jotted down only Jonson's side of the exchange, omitting any questions or comments of his own. 'Conversations' is in any event too bland a word to do justice to Jonson's talk; he lectured, chatted, railed, complained, swore, read aloud both verse and prose, recited from memory his own and other writers' works, told jokes, passed on dirty stories and analysed grammar and poetical metres. Drummond called his notes 'Certain information and manners of Ben Jonson's to William Drummond', and he made them for a private memorandum only and never published them. For more information about Drummond see David Masson's *Drummond of Hawthornden* (1873) and R.H. MacDonald, *The Library of Drummond of Hawthornden* (Edinburgh, 1971).

2   Historically there existed three distinct names – patronymic Johnson, fairly common in almost any part of lowland Scotland; the Johnston adopted by any native of Perth (St John's Toun); and the Border Johnstone. It was with the last group that Jonson claimed kinship,

NOTES

though as he always called himself 'Jonson' and his contemporaries
generally called him 'Johnson' the medial 't' had dropped out before
this. I am indebted to Professor Gordon Donaldson of Edinburgh
University for this information.

3 Caroline Bingham, *James V King of the Scots* (1971), p.187.
4 C.L. Johnstone, *History of the Johnstones 1191–1909* (Edinburgh and
   Glasgow, 1909–1925).
5 Milton Waldman, *The Lady Mary* (1972), pp.195–6.
6 Thomas Dekker, *Satiromastix* IV.ii.47 and I.ii.281, and the anonymous
   Return from Parnassus II, I.ii.293.
7 This exciting discovery was made by J.M. Bamborough and reported in
   the *TLS* on 8 April 1960, p.225.
8 R.B. McKerrow (ed.), *Works of Thomas Nashe* (5 vols., 1968), I, 216.
9 'The Games of the Illusionist', *TLS*, 11 February 1977, 142–3.
10 Inexplicably Jonson's name is absent from the roll of Westminster pupils
   of his day. But his attendance there is demonstrated by his friendship
   with Camden and other Westminsters and has never been questioned.

   One continuing mystery is the identity of the 'friend' who 'put
   [Jonson] to school'. It has been suggested that this was Camden himself.
   This claim is based on the ambiguous phrasing of Drummond's note and
   on the regard and gratitude which Jonson showed him for the rest of their
   lives. If as Herford and Simpson argue Jonson did not go into the sixth
   form at the school, Camden would have been his teacher from first to
   last, since he taught up to and including the fourth form but no higher.
   Simpson discovered at Chatsworth a copy of *Cynthia's Revels* with an
   inscription to Camden in Jonson's own hand in which he describes
   Camden as 'magister olim, aeternum amicus' – 'a teacher once but now
   for ever a friend'.

   The only other contender for this honour has been the distinguished
   contemporary lawyer John Hoskyns, but the evidence is very slight.
   Aubrey recorded an anecdote which suggests that Jonson owed Hoskyns
   some debt of gratitude:

   Sergeant John Hoskyns of Herefordshire was his father. I remember his
   son (Sir Bennet Hoskyns, baronet, who was something poetical in his
   youth) told me, that when he desired to be adopted his son [Bennet
   wished to be made one of the 'tribe' of 'Father Ben' as Jonson became
   known to his younger admirers], 'No,' says he, ' 'tis honour enough for
   me to be your brother. I am your father's son, 'twas he that polished me,
   I do knowledge it.' (HS I, 179)

   On the whole this story serves to cloud rather than to illuminate the
   issue and without further documentary discoveries we are unlikely to
   recover the identity of Jonson's benefactor.
11 Foster Watson, *English Grammar Schools to 1660* (1908), p.101.
12 John Sargeaunt, *Annals of Westminster School* (1898), p.35.
13 Quotations from Jonson's poetry are taken from *Ben Jonson: Poems*, edited
   by Ian Donaldson (Oxford, 1975).
14 This supposition is based upon the construction of the Westminster

syllabus at the time that Jonson followed it. Another pointer is his later
interest in the theory of versification; at Westminster the lower forms
were confined to prose, and the study of verse was not introduced until
the upper school.

15 For a consideration of Jonson's genuine, but much later connection with
this college, see the St John's College magazine *The Eagle* xvi (1891), 237
and 389–90; xxv (1904), 302–5; and xxvi (1905), 357–8.

16 HS I, 139. 'Spolia opima' in Livy denotes the spoils taken from the
enemy general when slain by the commander of the army himself, an
interesting early indication of Jonson's lifelong habit of self-
aggrandisement.

Chapter 2: Player

1 See Mark Eccles, 'Jonson's Marriage', *Review of English Studies* xii (1936),
257–72.

2 This is not the 'Maria Johnson' erroneously identified as the daughter of
the poet in the register of St Martin's-in-the-Fields. The death, on 17
November 1593, occurs before Jonson's marriage; the name is too
common to permit of an identification, and this 'Mary' must have been
an adult since she was buried in a coffin. See HS I, 9, and XI, 575.

3 The Curtain Theatre was so called from its proximity to the 'curtain' or
outer wall of an old fortification abutting onto London wall. Its location
is commemorated today by Curtain Road, Shoreditch.

4 For a full discussion of all that is known and conjectured about Jonson's
acting career, see Fredson Thayer Bowers 'Ben Jonson the actor', *Studies
in Philology* xxxiv (1937), 392–406.

5 *Satiromastix* I.ii.354–7.

6 G.E. Bentley, *The Jacobean and Caroline Stage* (7 vols., 1941–68), VI, 122.

7 'An Execration Upon Vulcan', *Underwood* 43, I.147.

8 Thomas Middleton, *No Wit, No Help Like A Woman's* (1613).

9 The Induction to *Bartholomew Fair*, lines 78–80.

10 See Glynn Wickham, 'The Privy Council Order of 1597 for the
Destruction of all London's Theatres', *The Elizabethan Theatre*, ed David
Galloway (1969), pp. 21–44, for an interesting discussion of this.

11 Note that Herford and Simpson first state incorrectly that this episode
occurred in 1598 (HS I, 19). They later correct this view in XI, 573–4.

12 *Henslowe's Diary*, ed. R.A. Foakes and R.T. Rickert (Cambridge, 1961),
p. 96. See Bowers's 'Ben Jonson the Actor', pp. 393–4 fn., for a full
discussion of this transaction.

Chapter 3: Playwright

1 J.Q. Adams, *Shakespearean Playhouses* (Cambridge, Mass., 1917), p.64.

2 The only other play text which was published and enjoyed a comparable
popularity was John Lyly's *Campaspe* in 1584: see W.W. Greg, *A
Bibliography of the English Printed Drama to the Restoration* (4 vols., 1939–59),
I, 84.

3 Herford and Simpson date this play in 1599, or at the outset early 1600;
   see HS I, 20, 373 and 393. For the argument in favour of the early months
   of 1600, see R.A. Small, *The Stage Quarrel between Ben Jonson and the So-Called
   Poetasters* (Breslau, 1899), pp. 20–22.
4 *Apologetical Dialogue* (p.307).

Chapter 4: The 'War of the Theatres'

1 Although this play was entered anonymously on the Stationers' Register
   on 8 September 1600, critics are agreed that its author was Marston.
2 W. David Kay, 'The Shaping of Ben Jonson's Career', *Modern Philology*
   67(1970), 224–237, dates *Cynthia's Revels* in 'the autumn of 1600'. HS I, 26
   state that the performance was 'most probably in January 1601, but later
   amend this to December 1600. See too E.K. Chambers *The Elizabethan
   Stage* (Oxford, 4 vols, 1923), III, 364.
3 *Father Hubbard's Tales:The Works of Thomas Middleton*, ed. A.H. Bullen (8
   vols, 1885–6), VIII, 77.
4 *Poetaster* was produced in the early summer of 1601. Since *II Return from
   Parnassus* implies that Shakespeare answered *Poetaster*, Shakespeare's
   presumed riposte must have been composed in the latter half of 1601. The
   Shakespeare plays of about this date are *Twelfth Night, Merry Wives of
   Windsor, All's Well that Ends Well, Hamlet* and *Troilus and Cressida*. The last is
   the only one that fits the bill.

Chapter 5: New directions

1 These five years can be confidently located between Jonson's going to
   Townsend in 1602, and February 1607, when he dated his dedication to
   Volpone 'from my house in the Blackfriars'. He also told Drummond that
   he was 'in my lord D'Aubigny's house in 1604'. Mark Eccles (see note 1,
   p.285) argues for a later residence with D'Aubigny, from 1613–1618.
   This is discussed but not accepted by HS (XI, 576–7).
2 *The Magnificent Entertainment for King James*, line 336 and the *Panegyre*, 141.
3 Sir Robert was created Baron Spencer the next month, on 21 July 1603.
   The Spencer connection with the Royal Family was continued when a
   direct descendant, the Lady Diana Spencer, married the Prince of Wales
   in 1981.
4 Note that Herford and Simpson inaccurately date this entertainment
   August 1603 (I,36).
5 For Jonson's account of the proceedings, and the text of the speech, see
   HS VII, 129–130.
6 Jonson's work on Horace had an interesting history. Jonson did not
   publish it as he intended in 1605, yet he had it with him on his journey to
   Scotland in the winter of 1618–19, when he read the preface to
   Drummond. Four years later it was lost in the disastrous fire of 1623 at
   Jonson's lodgings. But he cared enough about it to rewrite it, and it
   finally appeared in the 1640 Folio, having been found among his papers
   after his death.

7 There was no public playing between March 1603 and March 1604, as the playhouses were closed first for the public mourning for Queen Elizabeth, and then because of the plague. See HS IX, 190, and Chambers III, 368 for the suggestion that the first performance of *Sejanus* in 1603 was at court, with the Globe staging in 1604 when the theatres reopened.

8 For Jonson's involvement with the Roe family see Epigrams 70, 98, 99 and 128, and HS I, 223–30.

9 H.J.C. Grierson, *The Poems of John Donne* (Oxford, 1912), I,414.

10 Joan Rees, *Samuel Daniel: A Critical and Biographical Study* (Liverpool, 1964), p.93.

11 For a fuller discussion of Harrison's contribution, see David H. Bergeron, 'Harrison, Jonson & Dekker: The Magnificent Entertainment for King James (1606)', *Journal of the Warburg and Courtauld Institutes* 31 (1968), 445–54.

12 *Dramatic Works of Thomas Dekker* (4 vols., London, 1873), I, 277.

Chapter 6: Jonson at Court

1 J.F. Bradley and J.Q. Adams, *The Jonson Allusion Book: a collection of allusions to Ben Jonson from 1597–1700* (New Haven, Oxford and London, 1922), abbreviated throughout to *JAB*.

2 For this and all the other letters relating to this episode, see HS I, 190–200.

3 See D. Matthew, *Catholicism in England 1565–1935* (1936), pp. 69, 78, 83, 84.

4 Note that Jonson made the foolish lover Matthew in *Every Man In his Humour* speak a parody of some of Daniel's lines.

Chapter 7: Royal masque-maker

1 The title-page of the Folio edition of *Volpone* states that the play was acted in the year 1605, which according to the court calendar would locate it between March 1605 and March 1606. A firmer clue to dating occurs in II.i. where Jonson refers to the discovery of a whale and porpoises in the Thames, an event which took place in January 1606 and caused great comment.

2 Jasper Mayne, in *Jonsonus Virbius* (1638), p.31.

3 *The Letters and Epigrams of Sir John Harington, together with the Prayse of Private Life*, ed. Norman Egbert McLure (New York, 1977), pp. 119–20.

4 Jonson's signature is also found in a copy of Florio's translation of Montaigne's essays. Florio, for his part, may have contributed to the commendatory verses ushering *Volpone* before the world; of the ten poems, one, signed 'I.F.', is capable of interpretation as 'John Florio'. Scholars have traced other small but suggestive links between the two men, particularly references in Jonson's work paralleling words and phrases of Florio. See R.C. Simonini Jr., 'Ben Jonson and John Florio', *Notes and Queries* 195 (1950), 512–13.

5 An ell was a cloth measure of about 1¼ yards. For further information

see Scott McMillin, 'Jonson's Early Entertainments: New Information from Hatfield House', *Renaissance Drama* NS I (1968), 153–166.

6 J.B. Nichols, *The Progresses of James I* (1828), II, 137–8.

7 Arthur Wilson, *The History of Great Britain, being the Life and Reign of King James I* (1653), p.12.

8 William Cecil, Lord Burghley and Salisbury's father, had become Lord Treasurer to Elizabeth I in 1592.

9 See G.E. Bentley's work on Shakespeare and Jonson, documenting the many literary references and allusions to Jonson between 1601 and 1610, in 'Shakespeare and the Blackfriars Theatre', *Shakespeare Survey* I (1948), 38–50.

10 A list of army captains who had been discharged in Ireland since 1603 gives the following scanty information: 'Born in England and dead in 1608: Sir John Roe'. This could possibly mean '*by* 1608' and HS conjecture (XI, 6) without apparent evidence that Roe died in 1606. This is echoed by Donaldson (p.18). But as 1608 was a particularly bad plague year, there is no good reason for disturbing the natural presumption that this statement means what it says.

11 These were the Countesses of Arundel, Derby, Huntingdon, Bedford, Essex, Montgomery; the Ladies Cranbourne, Guilford, Winter, Windsor, Clifford.

12 *Calendar of State Papers Venetian* XI, 269.

Chapter 8:Return to the stage

1 This letter is dated 18 February 1610; see *Calendar of State Papers Venetian* XI, p.426.

2 'Ode Upon Ben Jonson', *Hesperides* (1648).

3 This did not in fact appear; there was no quarto of *The Alchemist* until 1612.

4 Wroth succeeded to his father's estates in 1606 and died in 1614. Between these dates Jonson was on a familiar footing with both husband and wife, enjoying their rural hospitality and urban patronage.

5 William Winstanley, *The Lives of The Most Famous English Poets* (1687), pp.123–8.

6 Coryate was an eccentric who had travelled widely in Europe in 1608, but on his return failed to find a publisher for his account of his adventures. He appealed to many well-known people, among them Jonson, to write commendatory verses to give his work the send-off which it had failed to find. Most of the contributors, among them Jonson again, took the opportunity to make fun of him; see *Ungathered Verse*, 10, 11 and 12. As Coryate left England again in 1612, never to return, his letter must refer to the meetings of the Mermaid Club before that date.

7 For a full discussion of this see I.A. Shapiro, 'The Mermaid Club', *Modern Language Review* 45 (1950), 6–17, and a subsequent correspondence in *Modern Language Review* 46 (1951), 58–63 and 43.

8 For an interesting discussion of this idea see B.N. de Luna, *Jonson's Romish Plot: A Study of Catiline and its Historical Context* (Oxford, 1967).

Chapter 9:'The poet'

1   Interestingly enough Izaak Walton, reported by Aubrey, says that it was Camden who procured for Jonson this 'better employment' which was 'to attend or accompany [young Walter] in his travels' (HS I, 181).

2   For a suggested identification of the matter that Jonson contributed see Sir Charles Firth, 'Sir Walter Raleigh's *History of the World*', *Essays Historical and Literary* (Oxford, 1938), pp. 37–38.

3   Preface to *The White Devil*; see *JAB* 83.

4   Aubrey recounts an incident in the relationship between Sir Walter and his son: 'Sir Walter Raleigh, being invited to dinner to some great person, where his son was to go with him, said to his son, "Thou art such a quarrelsome, affronting creature that I am ashamed to have such a bear in my company". Mr Wat humbled himself to his father, and promised he would behave himself mighty mannerly. So away they went. He sat next to his father, and was very demure at least half dinner time. Then said he, "I this morning . . . went to a whore. I was very eager of her, kissed and embraced her, and went to enjoy her, but she thrust me from her, and vowed I should not: 'For your father lay with me but an hour ago'."

'Sir Walter, being so strangely surprised and put out of his countenance at so great a table, gave his son a damned blow over the face. His son, as rude as he was, would not strike his father, but strikes over the face of the gentleman that sat next to him, and said, "Box about. 'Twill come to my father anon".' Norman Lloyd Williams, *Sir Walter Raleigh*, 1962, p. 248.

5   Aubrey has a related anecdote which goes as follows: 'Mr Cambden [sic] recommended him to Sir Walter Ralegh who trusted him with the care and instruction of his eldest son Walter, a gay young spark who could not brook Ben's rigorous treatment, but perceiving one foible in his disposition made use of that to throw off the yoke of his government and this was the unlucky habit Ben had contracted through his love of jovial company, of being overtaken with liquor which Sir Walter of all vices did most abominate and has most exclaimed against. One day when Ben had taken a plentiful dose and was fallen into a sound sleep young Raleigh got a great basket and a couple of men who laid Ben in it, then with a pole carried him between their shoulders to Sir Walter, telling him their young master had sent home his tutor' (HS I, 165).

6   G.E. Bentley, *Shakespeare and Jonson, Their Reputations in the Seventeenth Century Compared* (2 vols., Chicago, 1945), I, 21–5.

7   Dedication to *The Masque of Queens*; HS VII, 281.

8   L.C. John, 'Ben Jonson's "To Sir William Cecil, on his birthday" ', *Modern Language Review* 52 (1957), 168–76.

9   'The Execration upon Vulcan', *Underwood* 43, lines 132–8.

10   Bentley argues that 'most of the allusions to the two Jonson plays are allusions praising them in the highest terms, and a number of them are written by poets of renown' (*Shakespeare and Jonson* I, 39–40).

11   First noticed by Herford and Simpson; compare *Hymenaei* 560–4 and

Ungathered Verse 18, 23–4, both after Martial. Jonson's poem was not printed in the Folio of 1616 and survived only in manuscript.
12   For its subsequent history see Chapter 5, note 6.

Chapter 10:Laureate

1   Anon, *Shakespeare's Jests, or, The Jubilee Jester*, (c.1769).
2   For the degree of social evil and human misery involved, see S.T. Bindoff, *Tudor England* (1950), pp. 290–1:

> It was the 'projectors', the speculation-mongers, who, eager to tap the funds amassed during the prosperous years before the war narrowed the investment field, conceived and floated the enterprises which the men of place and title were induced to take under their influential wings. It was the same hard-bitten crew which, once they had secured a patent, exploited it for all it was worth. Armed with its coercive or dispensatory powers they waged private war upon all who stood in their path . . . A monopoly always raised prices, some times by as much as 300 or 400 per cent.

> See too Christopher Hill, *The Century of Revolution 1603–1714* (1961), p. 38: 'In 1601 a Member of Parliament asked, when a list of monopolies was read out, "Is not bread there?" His irony exaggerated only slightly . . . [A man] washed himself with monopoly soap, his clothes in monopoly starch . . . He ate monopoly butter . . . he drank monopoly wine and spirits . . . . Mice were caught in monopoly mousetraps. Not all these patents existed at once, but all come from the first decades of the seventeenth century. In 1621 there were alleged to be 700 of them'.

3   Herford and Simpson, (IX, 14–15) discuss the date of the Folio's preparation and printing, and show that the preparation was completed by 1613 at the latest. The book includes no play later than *Catiline* (1611); *Bartholomew Fair* of 1614 was left out. There is, further, no contemporary allusion later than 1612. Jonson's labours on the Folio must account for his small output between 1612 and 1614, when he produced only three court masques during the entire period.

Chapter 11:The journey to Scotland

1   By what route is unknown. One critic thinks it 'fair to assume that from Darlington he struck westward, Carlisle-ways, so as to enter Scotland by his ancestral Annandale, and reached Edinburgh through the counties of Dumfries and Peebles' (Masson, p.89). This would have been quite out of the way; but we cannot rule out a quixotic addition to a journey that was already so whimsical.
2   Masson, p.91.
3   Masson, p. 92.
4   R.H. MacDonald, *The Library of Drummond of Hawthornden* (Edinburgh, 1971), p.23.
5   For a full record of the 'Conversations', see HS I, 137–145. It is important

to remember that Drummond made these notes only as a personal *aide-mémoire* and never published them. They were not intended as a full record of what passed between the two men. Drummond wanted to preserve Jonson's opinions, not his own.

6 Herford and Simpson (I,132) alter the MS reading 'this country' (i.e. Scotland) to 'his country' (i.e. England), adducing *The Masque of Queens* (1609) and *The Speeches at Prince Henry's Barriers* (1610), with their references to Boadicea, Merlin, the Black Prince, Richard I and Henry V, as evidence of how the subject would have been treated. This seems a perverse and unwarrantable editorial interference. Apart from the MS existence of 'this', other factors support the first meaning: Jonson's reliance as a model upon Tacitus, who as a pioneer ethnographer gave his attention to the tribes to the North of the Rhine and Danube: Jonson's declared dedication to his Scottish master's interests; and the wholly Scottish nature of the material he sought from Drummond after his return.

7 Drummond cultivated the memory of his lost love through the *persona* of the forlorn lover and the circulation of funeral sonnets and elegies. These, with an impressive foresight, he had written some time before his betrothed unexpectedly died, a rare instance of life obliging with an appropriate imitation of art.

8 This phrase is used by Jonson himself in *Every Man Out Of His Humour* (359–60), where Cordatus remarks of Buffone that 'he will sooner lose his soul than his jest'. Jonson had found the germ of the phrase in Wilson's *Art of Rhetoric*: 'Some had as leve lose their life, as not bestow their conceived jest'. Did Drummond get the phrase from Jonson himself?

Chapter 12: Father Ben

1 It is not known if Jonson had heard this news while he was in Edinburgh. It is likely that he did, and that he was pronouncing Raleigh's epitaph with his observation to Drummond that 'Sir Walter Raleigh esteemed more of fame than conscience' (HS I,138).

2 HS I, 206, and compare the first draft of this letter on p.205. The sentence in square brackets was deleted in the final version.

3 Ian Donaldson (ed), *Ben Jonson: Poems* (Oxford, 1975), p.370–1

Chapter 13: Setbacks and losses

1 That is, 'although not in lines as good as these' – a courtly compliment.

2 It has been suggested that Jonson had wedding matters of his own on his mind at this time. John Payne Collier cited from the register of St Giles Cripplegate an entry of the marriage on 27 July 1623 between 'Beniamine Johnson and Hester Hopkins'. Cripplegate is a plausible location for this, as the Royal Household bill of 1620 refers to it in connection with Jonson, and also one of his sons was baptised there. Problems remain, however, apart from Collier's notorious unreliability: 1) when did Anne die? She was certainly alive when both Jonsons were prosecuted for recusancy in

1606: 2) when did 'Hester' die, as Jonson was evidently alone in his last years? 3) why did Jonson make no mention of it? This last is not to be taken as an indication either way, as Jonson fictionalised none of his intimate personal life after the death of Benjamin in 1603.

3   As this had been entered on the Stationers' Register a month before, on 2 October 1623, Jonson had obviously brought it to a stage of readiness at which he could contemplate publication.

4   The title of 'son' was claimed by Cary, Gayton, Howell, Cartwright, Randolph, Lovelace, and Herrick. See HS XI, 94.

Chapter 14: 'The loathed stage'

1   This poem is reprinted by Donaldson as *Ungathered Verse* 30. Some critics have seen it as a satirical send-up of Drayton, too fulsome to be taken seriously. But Donaldson suggests that 'the extravagance of the poem may perhaps merely reflect Jonson's anxiety to make lavish amends to an unexpected admirer' (p.313, fn.), Drayton having praised Jonson in this volume.

2   HS I, 137. It is interesting that Middleton had borrowed at least one idea from Jonson; in the last scene of his play *The Phoenix* he has the lawyer Tangle being bled of his harsh legal terms in a clear echo of the vomiting sequence in *Poetaster* (V.iii.465–530).

3   L.E. Tanner, 'Literary links with Westminster Abbey', *Transactions of the Royal Society of Literature* (1940), xviii, pp.27–8.

4   HS I, 182. At least in this version the woman, although feckless, is well-meaning. HS (I, 184) also print a poignant if unreliable story: 'Ben: Johns: in his old age grew very poor, and having borrowed £40 of a certain woman (mistress of the Earl of Dorset), she inveigled him to come and sojourn at her house, he did so and brought with him all his books, the only household stuff he had, which she, having in possession attached [i.e., seized as security for the repayment of the debt]. The old man sent to all his friends, but could not amongst them borrow the money to redeem them, which broke his heart and so he died'.

5   *Life of Edward Hyde, Earl of Clarendon* (Oxford, 1759), I, 30 and 41. Clarendon states that when he was a law student his chief acquaintances were Jonson, Selden, Cotton, Digby, Thomas May, and others. Cary is also named as a patron of Jonson, along with Digby, by Aubrey.

6   HS XI, 390–1. Winstanley has an apocryphal account of Randolph's first meeting with Jonson:

Thomas Randolph, the wit of Cambridge, coming to London, had a great mind to see Master Jonson, who was then drinking at the Devil Tavern near Temple Bar with Master Drayton, Master Daniel, and Master Sylvester, three eminent poets of that age. He being loath to intrude into their company, and yet willing to be called, peeped in several times at the door, insomuch that Master Jonson at last took notice of him and said, 'Come in, John Bo-Peep'. Master Randolph was not so gallant in clothes as they, however he sat down amongst them. At last when the reckoning came to be paid, which was five shillings, it was agreed that he who made the best extempore verse should go scot-free, the other four to pay it all; whereupon every one of them put out their verses; at last it came to Master Randolph's turn, whose lines were these:

> I, John Bo-Peep to you four sheep,
> With each one his good fleece,
> If you are willing to pay your five shilling
> 'Tis fifteen pence apiece.

(HS XI,396)

7 J.Q. Adams, *The Dramatic Records of Sir Henry Herbert* (New Haven, Oxford and London, 1917), p.69.
8 *Underwood* 68. A tierce was a measure of liquor amounting to 42 gallons.
9 As evidence of its success in performance note that when *Every Man In His Humour* was performed by the King's Men at the Blackfriars on 18 February 1631 for Sir Henry Herbert's benefit, the second day's takings presented to the Master of the Revels totalled the impressive sum of £12 4s 0d (HS IX, 169).

Chapter 15: Senex

1 J.Q. Adams, *The Dramatic Records of Sir Henry Herbert*, p.212.
2 *JAB* 179. Lowin and Taylor were two actors of the King's Men.
3 *JAB* 188-9. Comparison between the two playwrights continued to be made, always to Jonson's disadvantage: 'In a conversation between Sir John Suckling, Sir William Davenant, Endymion Porter, Mr Hales of Eaton, and Ben Jonson, Sir John Suckling, who was a professed admirer of Shakespeare, had undertaken his defence with some warmth. Mr Hales who had sat still for some time, hearing Ben frequently reproaching him for the want of learning, and ignorance of the Ancients, told him at last, 'That if Mr Shakespeare had not read the ancients, he had likewise not stolen anything from them (a fault that the other had made no conscience of); and if he would produce any one topic finely treated by any of them, he would undertake to show something upon the same subject at least as well-written by Shakespeare'. (*JAB* 187).
4 The Chancery Bill from which these quotations are taken is reproduced by F. Marcham in 'Thomas Walkley and the Ben Jonson "Works" of 1640', *The Library* XI, 1930-31, 225-9.

Chapter 16: O rare Ben Jonson

1 Walkley had had the Jonson papers printed without entering them on the Stationers' Register, which was among other things a way of signifying ownership. Meanwhile the printer Benson had secured copies of some of the works which he then published. Walkley filed a petition with the Court of Chancery on 20 January 1640 seeking to have him restrained. See HS IX, 91-100.
2 *The New Inn* had been published in an octavo edition of 1631, and was not included in the 1640 Folio along with the other last plays.

SELECT BIBLIOGRAPHY

Books are published in London unless otherwise stated.

Life
The Man and his Work (1925), Volume I of *Ben Jonson*, edited by C.H. Herford and Percy and Evelyn Simpson (Oxford, 1925–52).
Ben Jonson of Westminster, Marchette Chute (New York, 1953).
Biographical material is also to be found in the following:
Aubrey, John, *Lives of Eminent Persons* (Oxford, 1898).
Bamborough, J.B., *Ben Jonson* (1970).
Dutton, Richard, *Ben Jonson: To The First Folio* (Cambridge, 1983).
Fuller, Thomas, *The Worthies of England* (1662).
Parfitt, George, *Ben Jonson, Public Poet and Private Man* (1976).
Smith, G. Gregory, *Ben Jonson* (1919).
Winstanley, William, *The Lives of the Most Famous English Poets* (1687).

Works
The major edition of Jonson's works is the eleven-volume edition of Herford and Simpson cited above. For individual plays the modern editions in the New Mermaids series, published by Ernest Benn Ltd, and the Regents Renaissance Drama Series, published by Edward Arnold, are clear and helpful modern-spelling texts. There are a number of good modern editions of Jonson's poetry. All references to Jonson's poems in this study are taken from *Ben Jonson: Poems*, edited by Ian Donaldson (Oxford, 1975).

Companion works
Brock, D. Heyward, *A Ben Jonson Companion* (Indiana and Sussex, 1983).
Brock, D. Heyward, and Welsh, James M., *Ben Jonson, a Quadricentennial Bibliography 1947–72*, (Metuchen, New Jersey, 1974).

Works on Jonson: Books
Barton, Anne, *Ben Jonson, Dramatist* (Cambridge, 1984).
Bentley, G.E., *Shakespeare and Jonson, their Reputations in the Seventeenth Century Compared* (2 vols, Chicago, 1945).
Bradley, J.F. and Adams, J.Q., *The Jonson Allusion Book: a Collection of Allusions to*

294

SELECT BIBLIOGRAPHY

Ben Jonson from 1597–1700 (New Haven, Oxford and London, 1922).
De Luna, B.N., *Jonson's Romish Plot: A Study of 'Catiline' and its Historical Context* (Oxford, 1967).
Duppa, Bryan (ed.), *Jonsonus Virbius: or, the Memory of Ben Johnson Revived by the Friends of the Muses* (1638).
Johnston, G.B., *Ben Jonson, Poet* (New York, 1945).
Leggatt, Alexander, *Ben Jonson, his Vision and his Art* (London and New York, 1981).
Small, R.A., *The Stage Quarrel between Ben Jonson and the So-Called Poetasters* (Breslau, 1899).

Works on Jonson: Articles

Adams, Robert, 'The Games of the Illusionist', *Times Literary Supplement*, 11 February 1977, pp. 142–3.
Bamborough, J.B. 'The Early Life of Ben Jonson', *Times Literary Supplement*, 8 April 1960, p. 225.
Bergeron, David M., 'Harrison, Jonson and Dekker: The Magnificent Entertainment for King James (1604), *Journal of the Warburg and Courtauld Institutes*, 31 (1968), 445–54.
Bowers, Fredson Thayer, 'Ben Jonson the Actor', *Studies in Philology*, XXXIV (1937), 392–406.
Eccles, Mark, 'Jonson's Marriage', *Review of English Studies* XII (1936), 257–72.
John, L.C., 'Ben Jonson's "To Sir William Cecil on his Birthday" ', *Modern Language Review* 52 (1957), 168–76.
Kay, W. David, 'The Shaping of Ben Jonson's Career', *Modern Philology* 67 (1970), 224–37.
McMillin, Scott, 'Jonson's Early Entertainments: New Information from Hatfield House', *Renaissance Drama*, NSI (1968), 153–66.
Marcham, F., 'Thomas Walkley and the Ben Jonson "Works" of 1640', *The Library* XI, 1930–31, 225–9.
Simonini, R.C., Jr, 'Ben Jonson and John Florio', *Notes and Queries* 195 (1950), 512–3.

Other texts: Books

Adams, J.Q., *The Dramatic Records of Sir Henry Herbert* (New Haven, Oxford and London, 1917).
Adams, J.Q., *Shakespearean Playhouses* (Cambridge, Mass., 1917).
Anon., *Shakespeare's Jests, or, The Jubliee Jester* (c. 1796).
Bentley, G.E., *The Jacobean and Caroline Stage* (7 vols, Oxford, 1941–68).
Bindoff, S.T., *Tudor England* (1950).
Bingham, Caroline, *James V King of the Scots* (1971).
Bowers, Fredson (ed.), *The Dramatic Works of Thomas Dekker* (4 vols. Cambridge, 1953–61).
Bullen, A.H. (ed.), *The Works of Thomas Middleton* (8 vols, 1885–6).
Chambers, E.K., *The Elizabethan Stage* (4 vols, Oxford, 1923).
Foakes, R.A., and Rickert, R.T. (eds), *Henslowe's Diary* (Cambridge, 1961).
Greg, W.W., *A Bibliography of the English Printed Drama to the Restoration* (4 vols, 1939–59).

SELECT BIBLIOGRAPHY

Grierson, H.J.C., *The Poems of John Donne* (Oxford, 1912).
Hill, Christopher, *The Century of Revolution 1603–1714* (1961).
Hyde, Edward, *The Life of Edward Hyde, Earl of Clarendon* (Oxford, 1759).
Johnstone, C.L., *History of the Johnstones 1191–1909* (Edinburgh and Glasgow, 1909–25).
Lloyd Williams, Norman, *Sir Walter Raleigh* (1962).
MacDonald, R.H., *The Library of Drummond of Hawthornden* (Edinburgh, 1971).
McKerrow, R.B. (ed.), *Works of Thomas Nashe* (5 vols, 1968).
McLure, Norman Egbert (ed.), *The Letters and Epigrams of Sir John Harington, together with The Prayse of Private Life* (New York, 1977).
Masson, David, *Drummond of Hawthornden* (1873).
Matthew, D., *Catholicism in England 1565–1935* (1936).
Nichols, J.B., *The Progresses of James I* (1828).
Rees, Joan, *Samuel Daniel: a Critical and Biographical Study* (Liverpool, 1964).
Sargeaunt, John, *Annals of Westminster School* (1898).
Scott, Sir Walter, *Provincial Antiquities of Scotland* (1819–26)
Shadwell, Thomas, *Bury Fair* (1689).
Suckling, Sir John, *Fragmenta Aurea* (1646).
Taylor, John, *The Penniless Pilgrimage* (1618).
Waldman, Milton, *The Lady Mary* (1972).
Watson, Foster, *English Grammar Schools to 1660* (1908).
Webster, John, *The White Devil* (1612).
Wilson, Arthur, *The History of Great Britain, being the Life and Reign of King James I* (1653).

Other texts: Articles
Bentley, G.E., 'Shakespeare and the Blackfriars Theatre', *Shakespeare Survey* I (1948), 38–50.
Firth, Sir Charles, 'Sir Walter Raleigh's *History of the World*', *Essays Historical and Literary* (Oxford, 1938).
Shapiro, I.A., 'The Mermaid Club', *Modern Language Review* 45 (1950), 6–17.
Tanner, L.E., 'Literary Links with Westminster Abbey', *Transactions of the Royal Society of Literature* (1940), XVIII, 27–8.
Wickham, Glynn, 'The Privy Council Order of 1597 for the Destruction of all London's Theatres', *The Elizabethan Theatre*, ed. David Galloway (1969), pp. 21–44.

INDEX

INDEX

INDEX

INDEX